The Men Who Made

SHEFFIELD WEDNESDAY
FOOTBALL CLUB

The Men Who Made

SHEFFIELD WEDNESDAY FOOTBALL CLUB

Tony Matthews

First published 2007

STADIA is an imprint of
Tempus Publishing Limited
The Mill, Brimscombe Port,
Stroud, Gloucestershire, GL5 2QG
www.tempus-publishing.com

British Library Cataloguing in Publication Data.
A catalogue record for this book is available from the British Library.

ISBN 978 0 7524 4156 6

Typesetting and origination by Tempus Publishing Limited
Printed in Great Britain

INTRODUCTION

Some of the greatest footballers in the game have played for Sheffield Wednesday and there have been some fine managers too – all of these men are featured in this easy to read 'Who's Who'.

This book will, I am sure, be appreciated by every Owls supporter and, indeed, soccer historians and statisticians.

Arguments that have raged in pubs, offices, on trains and coaches and inside a ground can now become a thing of the past when you refer to the contents of this book.

Tony Matthews
May 2007

ACKNOWLEDGEMENTS

I must say a special big thank you to Rob Sharman, Lucy Chowns and the staff at Stadia for agreeing to produce and publish this book. Also many thanks to fellow statisticians Geoff Allman, James Creasey, Mike Davage, Garth Dykes, Michael Featherstone, Maurice Golesworthy, Barry Hugman, Doug Lamming, Wade Martin, Andy Porter, Mick Renwick and Peter Wyatt… and of course, thanks again to my loving wife Margaret.

If any copyright regarding photographs has been unintentionally infringed, the copyright holder should, in the first instance, contact the publishers.

Notes on Text

The appearance and goalscoring records of Wednesday players (1880-2007) cover the Premiership, Football League, FA Cup, League Cup, Fairs Cup, UEFA Cup, Zenith Data Systems Cup, FA and London Charity Shields, play-offs, Anglo-Italian Cup, Football Alliance, InterToto Cup and Simod Cup.

Throughout this book I have referred to the club as either Wednesday or the Owls.

Several abbreviations have been used, including: AWS (Auto-Windscreen Shield), ECWC (European Cup-Winners' Cup), LDV (Leyland Daf Vans), FRT (Freight Rover Trophy), NASL (North American Soccer League), n/c (non-contract), PFA (Professional Footballers' Association), SVT (Sherpa Van Trophy) and ZDSC (Zenith Data Sytems Cup). When (L) appears in the player's career details, this indicates that he was loaned to this club while a registered player with Wednesday or another club.

Figures after the + sign in respect of a player's club record, indicates the number of substitute appearances he made. Where a single year appears in the text, this indicates, in most cases, the second half of a season: i.e. 1975 for 1974/75. However when dates appear as 1975-80, this means seasons 1975/76 to 1979/80 inclusive and not 1974/75 to 1980/81. The dates of each player's association with Wednesday (i.e. May 1946-May 1948) refer to the month and year he signed for the club and the month and year he left.

Not every player's junior, amateur and non-League clubs have been included.

It has been impossible to trace every single player's date of birth or (if applicable) the date or indeed the place or year of his death. In some instances the word deceased has been used, and also circa (indicating about this time). And in some cases no year at all has been stated in respect of a player's death. Several census registers have been referred to in respect of certain players being listed as deceased by…

Where an asterisk appears after a player's appearance and goals total, this means he is still adding to his tallies.

ADAMS, Stephen Marc
Midfield

Appearances: 18+3
Born: Plymouth, 25 September 1980

CAREER
CLUBS: Plymouth Argyle, WEDNESDAY (£50,000, March 2005-May 2007).

The recipient of both League Division Three and Two championship winning medals with Plymouth in 2002 and 2004 respectively, Steve Adams made over 175 senior appearances for the Pilgrims before joining Wednesday. Strong in the tackle, he quickly made an impact at Hillsborough with some excellent displays in midfield.

ADAMSON, Christopher
Goalkeeper

Appearances: 9+2 *
Born: Ashington, 4 November 1978

CAREER
CLUBS: West Bromwich Albion, IF Brage, Mansfield Town, Halifax Town, Plymouth Argyle, Halesowen Town, St Patrick's Athletic, Solihull Borough, WEDNESDAY (loan, January-June 2005, re-signed July 2005-May 2007).

Third in line at The Hawthorns, Chris Adamson, a clean handler of the ball who commands his area well, was recruited by manager Paul Sturrock as cover for David Lucas. He was set to leave Hillsborough after his loan spell but changed his mind at the last minute.

AGBONLAHOR, Gabriel
Forward

Appearances: 4+4
Born: Birmingham, 13 October 1986

CAREER
CLUBS: Aston Villa, Watford (L), WEDNESDAY (loan, October 2005-January 2006).

Well-built with terrific pace, Gabriel Agbonlahor, was a prolific scorer in Second XI football for Aston Villa before making his debut for the Owls against Norwich in October 2005. He later gained England Under-21 recognition after establishing himself in Villa's Premiership side.

AGOGO, Manuel (Junior)
Forward

Appearances: 0+3
Born: Accra, Ghana, 1 August 1979

CAREER
CLUBS: WEDNESDAY (October 1996-January 2000), Oldham Athletic (L), Chester City (L), Chesterfield (L), Lincoln City (L), Chicago Fire, Colorado Rapids, San Jose Earthquakes, Queens Park Rangers, Barnet, Bristol Rovers, Nottingham Forest.

Unable to make the headway, Junior Agogo made only three substitute appearances in three-and-a-half years at Hillsborough. A hard worker, he had a good spell in America before returning to give both Barnet and Bristol Rovers excellent service, scoring vital goals for the Pirates as they avoided relegation to the Third Division in 2004. Junior has gained three England semi-professional caps.

A

ALEXANDERSSON, Niclas Jens
Midfield

Appearances: 85+3 Goals: 12
Born: Halmstad, Sweden, 29 December 1971

CAREER
CLUBS: Vessigbro BK, Halmstads BK, IFK Gothenburg,
WEDNESDAY (£750,000, December 1997-July 2000),
Everton, West Ham United, IFK Gothenburg.

Tall, skilful Swedish international Niclas Alexandersson capped 15 times at under-21 and on 70 occasions at senior level (14 with the Owls) also made 12 appearances in the Olympic Games and played against England in the 2002 and 2006 World Cup finals. Sweden's Player of the Year in 1995, he netted 38 goals in 197 League games in his home country before joining the Owls, but struggled with ankle and knee problems at Everton.

ALJOFREE, Hasney
Defender

Appearances: 3
Born: Manchester, 11 July 1978

CAREER
CLUBS: Bolton Wanderers, Dundee United, Plymouth Argyle, WEDNESDAY (loan, September-October 2004).

England Youth international, strong in the air and able to occupy most defensive positions, Hasney Aljofree has a wonderful left foot and loves to have a crack at goal. He helped Plymouth win the League Division Two title in 2004. His first game for the Owls was at Wrexham, twenty-four hours after signing. His father was born in Japan with Saudi Arabian roots.

ALLAN, William
Goalkeeper

Appearances: 125
Born: Montrose, 1870
Died: Newcastle, 3 February 1948

CAREER
CLUBS: WEDNESDAY (December 1891-March 1897),
Victoria United, Millwall Athletic, Montrose, East Stirlingshire, Montrose.
OTHER: professional golfer, green keeper (bowls).

Known as 'William the Silent', Billy Allan replaced James Smith during the 1891/92 season and held his position for more than three years before handing over to Jimmy Massey. He appeared in Wednesday's first ever League game, a 1-0 win at Notts County in September 1892 and was an ever-present that season and in 1893/94. He had his boots specially made for him by a Sheffield cobbler. His brother was associated with the Owls (1895).

ALLEN, John William Alcroft
Centre forward

Appearances: 114   Goals: 85
Born: Newburn, Newcastle, 31 January 1903
Died: Burnopfield, Co. Durham, 19 November 1957

CAREER
CLUBS: Leeds United, Brentford, WEDNESDAY (£750, March 1927-June 1931), Newcastle United, Bristol Rovers, Gateshead, Ashington.
OTHER: licensee in Burnopfield.

Ex-miner Jack Allen was an aggressive, bustling centre forward with a stunning left-foot shot. After failing to make the grade with Leeds, he netted 24 goals in 54 League games for Brentford before entering the top-flight with the Owls in 1927. Top-scorer two seasons running, 1928-30, when he struck 71 goals in total, he gained a League championship winning medal in the first. It was a surprise when he left Hillsborough after losing his place to Jack Ball. In his first season with Newcastle he won the FA Cup, scoring against Arsenal from the famous 'ball over the line' cross.

His brother Ralph played for Wednesday's reserves (and for other clubs).

ANDERSON, Vivian Alexander
Full-back

Appearances: 83+13   Goals: 13
Born: Nottingham, 29 August 1956

CAREER
CLUBS: Nottingham Forest, Arsenal, Manchester United, WEDNESDAY (free, January 1991-June 1993), Barnsley (player-manager), Middlesbrough (player, assistant-manager, coach).

Viv 'Spider' Anderson appeared in more than 800 games (594 in the League) during his twenty-three years as a player. An attacking right-back, he was the first black player to win a full England cap, lining up versus Czechoslovakia in 1978. He appeared in 30 internationals all told, gained 1 Under-21 and 7 'B' caps and also represented the Football League. In the space of four years he helped Forest win the League Championship, the League Cup twice, the European Cup twice, the European Super Cup, the ASC and gain promotion from the Second Division as well as gaining a League Cup runners-up medal in 1980. He did superbly well with Wednesday, helping the Owls gain promotion to the Premiership in 1991 and reach two cup finals at Wembley in the same year, losing both to Arsenal. He became Middlesbrough's oldest League debutant, aged thirty-eight versus West Bromwich Albion in April 1995.

ANDREWS, Wayne Michael Hill
Winger

Appearances: 7+2
Born: Paddington, 25 November 1977

CAREER
CLUBS: Watford, St Albans City, Cambridge United, Peterborough United, Oldham Athletic, Colchester United, Crystal Palace, WEDNESDAY (loan, November 2006-January 2007).

Andrews started his career with Watford before having spells with St Albans City, Cambridge United, Peterborough United, Oldham Athletic, Colchester United and Crystal Palace before joining Wednesday on loan from Coventry City in November 2006.

ANTISS, Henry Augustus
Inside forward

Appearances: 12   Goals: 5
Born: Hampstead, London, 22 August 1899
Died: Isleworth, Middlesex, 9 March 1964

Viv Anderson

CAREER

CLUBS: Brentford, Millwall, Watford, Rochdale, WEDNESDAY (£1,000, July 1926-February 1927), Port Vale, Swansea Town, Crewe Alexandra, Gillingham.

A bustling inside forward with an abundance of energy, Harry Antiss was signed to replace Matt Barrass. Unfortunately he fell from favour after Dan Kirkwood arrived on the scene and subsequently joined Port Vale in exchange for Alf Strange. He scored on his debut for the Valiants, whom he helped win the Third Division (North) title in 1930. His career realised over 130 senior goals.

ANTHONY, George
Utility

Appearances: 5   Goals: 3
Born: Sheffield, 1854
Died: circa 1928

CAREER
CLUBS: WEDNESDAY (seasons 1874-1883).

George 'Nudger' Anthony occupied three different positions for Wednesday: left-back, outside right and outside left. He scored on his debut in a 2-0 FA Cup win over Providence in November 1881 and helped the Owls win the Wharncliffe Charity and Sheffield Challenge Cups in 1879 and 1883 respectively. He represented Sheffield versus Glasgow.

ANTOINE-CURIER, Mickael
Striker

Appearances: 0+1
Born: Orsay, France, 5 March 1983

CAREER
CLUBS: Nice, Paris St Germain, Nancy, Preston North End, Nottingham Forest, Mansfield Town, Brentford, Burnley, Oldham Athletic, Kidderminster

Harriers, Rochdale, WEDNESDAY (n/c November-December 2003), Notts County, Grimsby Town, SK Vard Haugesund.

Unable to settle anywhere, tall striker Antoine-Curier, a former French Under-18 international, created a new record in 2003/04 when he became the first player in Football League history to be associated with six different clubs in a peacetime season. He scored a great goal for Oldham against Wednesday and three months later switched to Hillsborough. His only outing for the Owls was as a substitute in the 0-0 home draw with Luton in November 2003.

ARANALDE, Zigor
Defender

Appearances: 1+1
Born: Ibazza, Guipuzcoa, Spain, 28 February 1973

CAREER
CLUBS: SD Eibar, Marbella, Sevilla, Albacete, CD Logrones, Walsall, WEDNESDAY (free, March-June 2005), Carlisle United

A left-sided player who struggled at times with the defensive side of his game, 'Ziggy' Aranalde made over 200 appearances for Walsall before joining the Owls for whom he made his debut in the Yorkshire derby against Huddersfield.

ARMITAGE, Harold Arthur
Right-back

Appearances: 3
Born: Sheffield, 16 August 1901
Died: Sheffield, 1973

CAREER
CLUBS: Hathersage, WEDNESDAY (free, June 1920-May 1922), Bristol Rovers, Lincoln City, Scarborough Town
OTHER: played cricket for Stapleton.

Strong, quick to assess danger and a fearless tackler, Harold Armitage had to work hard for a first team place at Hillsborough. He made 122 League appearances in four seasons with Bristol Rovers, whom he captained on several occasions.

ARMITAGE, Leonard
Forward

Appearances: 3
Born: Sheffield, 20 October 1899
Died: Wortley, Sheffield, May 1972

CAREER
CLUBS: Wadsley Bridge, WEDNESDAY (free, March 1914-June 1920), Leeds United, Wigan Borough, Stoke, Rhyl, and Port Vale.

Len Armitage was brilliant as a schoolboy and after helping Sheffield Boys win the English Schools Shield in 1914 many top managers sought his signature. In the end he joined Wednesday and after the First World War he was one of the first players to sign for newly constructed Leeds United, scoring the first League goal for the Elland Road club. Originally a centre forward, Armitage was strong, utterly fearless and had a terrific 'engine' but unfortunately failed to make much of an impact with the Owls. He helped Stoke win the Third Division (North) title in 1927 and represented the FA XI versus South Africa two years later. He made over 200 appearances for the Potters. He was the grandson of a Yorkshire cricketer.

ARMSTRONG, Harold Arthur
Outside right

Appearances: 6
Born: Southwick, County Durham, 1885
Died: Durham, 1962

CAREER
CLUBS: Southwick, WEDNESDAY (free, August 1907-May 1909).

Harry Armstrong made his debut for the Owls at Liverpool in October 1907 and gained a Midland League championship medal with the reserves in his first season. He started 1908/09 as first choice but lost out in the end to Billy Lloyd.

ARMSTRONG, Joseph Williams
Inside left

Appearances: 7
Born: Blaydon, Tyne & Wear, 10 October 1892
Died: Southwick, 14 May 1966

CAREER
CLUBS: Portsmouth, WEDNESDAY (June 1921-April 1922), Norwich City, Clapton Orient, Bournemouth.

Joe Armstrong scored 18 goals in 42 Southern League games for Pompey before transferring to Hillsborough. His weighty presence certainly demanded respect, although he was not as formidable with the Owls as he was at Fratton Park.

ARMSTRONG, Steven Craig
Midfield

Appearances: 34+6 Goals: 1
Born: South Shields, 23 May 1975

CAREER
CLUBS: Nottingham Forest, Burnley, Bristol Rovers, Gillingham, Watford, Huddersfield Town, WEDNESDAY (£100,000, February 2002-January 2005), Grimsby Town (L), Bradford City, Notts County, Cheltenham Town.

A hard-working, left-sided, midfield player, Craig Armstrong, who gained a First Division championship medal with Forest and starred for the Nationwide League Under-21 team, made 200 club appearances before joining Wednesday. Unfortunately he failed to impress the Owls' manager and after recovering from injury moved to Bradford.

ASHLEY, John Albert
Defender

Appearances: 117   Goals: 3
Born: Clowne, 13 October 1912
Died: 25 December 1992

CAREER
CLUBS: Clowne Welfare, Notts County (trial), Shirebrook, Mansfield Town, WEDNESDAY (£1,200, September 1935-August 1945).

Jack 'Jumbo' Ashley played as a full-back and centre half for Mansfield before his move to Hillsborough for what was then a record in-coming fee for the Stags (£1,100). He served the Owls very well for a decade, although the Second World War hindered his career. He gained a League (North) Cup runners-up medal with Wednesday in 1943 and scored twice in 125 appearances during the hostilities.

ATHERTON, Peter
Full-back

Appearances: 251   Goals: 9
Born: Orrell, 6 April 1970

CAREER
CLUBS: Wigan Athletic, Coventry City, WEDNESDAY (£800,000, June 1994-July 2000), Bradford City (player, caretaker-manager), Birmingham City, Halifax Town.

As a teenager, Peter Atherton represented England at schoolboy level and later added an Under-21 cap to his collection. A naturally hard tackler, strong and resolute, with the

Peter Atherton

ability to occupy a number of positions, he made 177 appearances for Wigan and 120 for Coventry before spending 6 seasons at Hillsborough, where he also starred as a holding midfield player. Not a spectacular footballer, he was nevertheless appreciated by the fans for his endeavour and tireless performances. He skippered the Owls on several occasions.

ATKINSON, Dalian Robert
Striker

Appearances: 45   Goals: 15
Born: Shrewsbury, 21 March 1968

CAREER
CLUBS: Ipswich Town, WEDNESDAY (£450,000, June 1989-August 1990), Real Sociedad, Aston Villa, Fenerbahce, Manchester City, Metz, Everton, Sheffield United, Barnsley, Al Ittihad, Taejon Citizen, Chonbuk Hyundo Motors.

Dalian Atkinson

A stocky, well-built striker, Dalian Atkinson was quick, decisive and loved to run at defenders. He scored 21 times in 69 games for Ipswich before joining the Owls for whom he averaged a goal every three games. After leaving Hillsborough (for a record fee of £1.7 million) he had mixed fortunes in Spain and at Villa Park before giving a good account of himself in Turkish football. Capped by England 'B', he won a League Cup winner's medal in 1994 and both the Asian and Saudi Cups in 1999 with Al Ittihad.

AVEYARD, Walter
Forward

Appearances: 10   Goals: 5
Born: Hemsworth, Yorkshire, 11 June 1918
Died: Blackpool, 16 July 1985

CAREER
CLUBS: WEDNESDAY (August 1938-April 1947), Birmingham City, Port Vale, Accrington Stanley.

OTHER: Army Sergeant Major, Second World War.

After playing his early football near Yorkshire coal pits, Walter Aveyard joined Wednesday at the age of twenty, but sadly the outbreak of the Second World War disrupted his career. He played in all six FA Cup games in 1945/46 but when peacetime League football returned he failed to establish himself in the side. He struggled with a thigh injury at St Andrew's but later hit 26 goals in 103 games for Port Vale, top-scoring in 1948/49 with 13.

AYRES, George Alexander
Forward

Appearances: 26   Goals: 11
Born: Islington, 5 September 1901
Died: Seaford, Essex, 17 January 1983

CAREER
CLUBS: Charlton Athletic, WEDNESDAY (free, May 1924-July 1926), Blackpool
OTHER: RAF Cranwell, cricket coach at Stamford School, played for Surrey CCC Second XI.

A good, reliable squad player with Charlton, George Ayres did very well at Hillsborough and his 11 goals included a hat-trick against Stockport in September 1924. His League career realised 20 goals in 93 games.

B

BAILEY, Gavin Joseph
Forward

Appearances: 0+1
Born: Chesterfield, 10 October 1976

CAREER
CLUBS: Derby County, WEDNESDAY (free, June 1993-May 1997), Hallam (L), Matlock Town (L),

Colwyn Bay (L), Mikkeli Palloiljate (L), Worskop Town, Sheffield Club, Hallam
OTHER: fitness leader at Esporta Health & Fitness Club (Sheffield).

Reserve forward Gavin Bailey's only senior appearance for the Owls came as an eighty-sixth-minute substitute against the Swiss side FC Basel in the InterToto Cup in June 1995.

BAILEY, Ian Charles
Left-back

Appearances: 45
Born: Middlesbrough, 20 October 1956

CAREER
CLUBS: Middlesbrough, Doncaster Rovers, Carlisle United, Bolton Wanderers, WEDNESDAY (£80,000, August 1982-May 1986), Blackpool, Bolton Wanderers; Sheffield United (physio), Rotherham United (physio).

Ian Bailey made 169 appearances for Middlesbrough before joining Wednesday. He partnered Mel Sterland in his first season at Hillsborough before suffering a leg injury against Bolton, April 1983.

BAIRD, Walter Younger
Left-back

Appearances: 1
Born: Cambuslang, Glasgow, 3 January 1913
Died: Scotland, 1989

CAREER
CLUBS: Partick Thistle, Larkhall Thistle, WEDNESDAY (£110, April 1934-May 1935), Hamilton Academical, Morton, Doncaster Rovers.

Signed as defensive cover, Wally Baird's only League game for the Owls was at home to Preston in November 1934 when Tommy Walker was injured.

BAKER, Peter Robert
Full-back

Appearances: 12
Born: Walthamstow, 24 August 1934

CAREER
CLUBS: West Ham United, Tottenham Hotspur, WEDNESDAY (free, November 1954-March 1961), Queens Park Rangers, Romford.

Peter Baker was a steady performer who, owing to the condensed form of Ron Staniforth and Norman Curtis and then Peter Johnson and Don Megson, was forced to spend most of his time at Hillsborough playing in the second team. He had to wait until 1957 before making his League debut, having failed to make the breakthrough at White Hart Lane. He was not related to the other ex-Spurs full-back of the same name.

BALL, John Thomas
Forward

Appearances: 136   Goals: 94
Born: Banks, Southport, 13 September 1907
Died: Luton, 2 February 1976

CAREER
CLUBS: Southport, Darwen, Chorley, Manchester United, WEDNESDAY (£1,300, July 1930-December 1933), Manchester United, Huddersfield Town, Luton Town, Excelsior Roubaix (player-coach), Luton Town, Vauxhall Motors (player-coach), St Albans City, Biggleswade (coach).
OTHER: worked for Motor Motors for twenty years, employed by a wholesale-manufacturing chemist, also a licensee.

Jack Ball's best years were spent at Hillsborough. Only 5ft 7ins tall, he was a brave competitor who loved a challenge. He replaced Jack Allen in the Owls' attack and hit 82 goals in his first three seasons including 14 in 10 games between October and December 1930. It came as a shock when manager Billy Walker transferred Ball back to Old Trafford in order to secure the services of Neil Dewar. He scored 11 penalties for Wednesday in 1932/33 – a record he shared with Willie Evans (Spurs) until 1971/72 when Francis Lee (Manchester City) netted 13 times from the spot. He struck 11 goals in the first 12 League games at the start of that season, including a four-timer in a 5-3 win at Wolves, and finished that campaign with 35 to his credit. He started out by scoring 58 goals in one season for Chorley and claimed 18 goals in 50 appearances in his two spells at Old Trafford. Ball played in all three Divisions of the Football League in the space of six weeks in September and October 1934. Eighteen months later, in April 1936, when Ball was pronounced unfit to take his place in Luton's attack versus Bristol Rovers, left half Joe Payne was asked to take over at centre-forward, and he celebrated by netting ten goals in a 12-0 win to set a new League scoring record. Ball, who represented Sheffield versus Glasgow, captained Banks Juniors when they won the Southport & District Junior Shield. He also enjoyed gardening, golf and bowls.

BALLAGHER, John
Inside forward

Appearances: 3
Born: Dukinfield, 21 March 1936

CAREER
CLUBS: Stalybridge Celtic, WEDNESDAY (free, February 1957-February 1961), Doncaster Rovers (exchanged for John Meredith), Gillingham
OTHER: worked for South East Gas and the British Oxygen Company.

A reserve at Hillsborough for four years, John Ballagher made his League debut at inside left in place of John Fantham in a 2-0 win at Ipswich in August 1958. He played in the next game against Stoke and his last outing was on the right wing in a 2-0 win at Leyton Orient in February 1959.

BANNISTER, Gary
Forward

Appearances: 142 + 1   Goals: 66
Born: Warrington, 22 July 1960

CAREER
CLUBS: Coventry City, Detroit Express, WEDNESDAY (£80,000, August 1981-August 1984), Queens Park Rangers, Coventry City, West Bromwich Albion, Oxford United, Nottingham Forest, Stoke City, Hong Kong Rangers, Lincoln City, Darlington (player-coach), Porthleven (player-coach).
OTHER: manager of a B&B in Cornwall.

A very positive, all-action marksman, as keen as mustard with the knack of scoring goals out of nothing, Gary Bannister had a fine career which produced 206 goals in over 600 matches. He made his debut for the Owls against Blackburn in August 1981 and before his record £200,000 transfer to QPR, was top-scorer in his three seasons at Hillsborough, claiming 22 goals each time. He formed a terrific partnership with Imre Varadi when promotion was gained from the Second Division in 1984. An England Under-21 international (capped versus Poland in 1982), he played twice at Wembley – for QPR in the 1985 League Cup final defeat by Norwich and for Darlington in the 1996 play-off final defeat by Plymouth.

BANNISTER, Keith
Defender

Appearances: 78
Born: Sheffield, 27 January 1923

CAREER
CLUBS: WEDNESDAY (free, February 1945-June 1953), Chesterfield, Macclesfield Town, WEDNESDAY (coach, scout), San Diego over-40s, Vahalla College (coach).
WARTIME GUEST APPEARANCES: York City
OTHER: RAF, Second World War, later worked as a salesman.

An accomplished defender, strong in the tackle, Keith Bannister made his League debut at left half at Bury on Christmas Day 1946. He had one other outing that term, made 15 appearances in 1948/49 and eight the following year before settling down at right-back during 1950/51. He skippered the Owls to the Second Division championship the following season before eventually giving way to Vin Kenny. He won the Cheshire Senior Cup with Macclesfield.

BARGH, George Wolfenden
Inside forward

Appearances: 5
Born: Bilsborrow, Preston, 27 May 1910
Died: Yorkshire, 13 September 1995

CAREER
CLUBS: Garstang, Preston North End, WEDNESDAY (free, September 1935-August 1936), Bury Chesterfield, Bury, Preston North End (coach). WARTIME GUEST APPEARANCES: Shelbourne, Aldershot, Blackburn Rovers, Accrington Stanley, York City, Linfield.

Coached by Alex James at Deepdale, George Bargh scored 43 goals in 141 League games for Preston before joining the Owls. Only 5ft 7ins tall, he failed to gain a regular first team place at Hillsborough. He bred dogs for a hobby.

BARKER, Richard
Forward

Appearances: 1+1
Born: Sheffield, 30 May 1975

CAREER
CLUBS: WEDNESDAY (June 1991-August 1996), Doncaster Rovers (L), Ards (L), Linfield, Brighton & Hove Albion, Macclesfield Town, Rotherham, United, Mansfield Town.

An England international at schoolboy and youth team levels, Richie Barker never got a look in with Wednesday but after leaving Hillsborough he did very well with Brighton (14 goals in 64 games) and Rotherham (17 in 155 outings, 73 as a substitute).

BARRASS, Matthew Williamson
Utility

Appearances: 49   Goals: 14
Born: Preston Colliery, North Shields, 14 February 1899
Died: Manchester, 24 June 1953

CAREER
CLUBS: Blackpool, WEDNESDAY (£1,950, March 1925-June 1926), Manchester City
OTHER: ran a fish and chip shop, was licensee of two pubs and during the Second World War, worked as a government inspector.

Matt Barrass scored 80 goals in 378 League appearances during his fourteen-year career. He gave both Blackpool and Manchester City excellent service either side his spell at Hillsborough. He played alongside Sam Powell, Harry Hill and Jimmy Trotter in the Owls' attack and scored the first of his 14 goals for

Earl Barrett

B

Wednesday in a 5-0 home win over Hull in April 1925, contributing greatly to Trotter's haul of 38 the following season when the Second Division title was won. His son, Malcolm, appeared for Bolton in the 1953 FA Cup final while his grandson played for Bury.

BARRETT, Earl Delliser
Defender

Appearances: 10+6
Born: Rochdale, 28 April 1967

CAREER
CLUBS: Manchester City, Chester City, Oldham Athletic, Aston Villa, Everton, Sheffield United, WEDNESDAY (free, February 1998-December 1999)
OTHER: later worked with young people, helping to tackle racism.

A stylish defender, able to play at right-back or centre half, Earl Barrett was already an experienced professional by the time he joined the Owls. He appeared in 486 first-class matches, gained three full England caps, represented his country at 'B' and Under-21 levels and also played for the Football League. He won the Second Division championship in 1991 with Oldham and a League Cup winners' medal three years later with Aston Villa, as well as helping Everton lift the Charity Shield in 1995. He retired in 1999 with over 500 games under his belt.

BARRETT, Graham Philip Robert
Midfield

Appearances: 5+1   Goals: 1
Born: Dublin, 6 October 1981

CAREER
CLUBS: Arsenal, Bristol Rovers, Crewe Alexandra, Colchester United, Brighton & Hove Albion, Coventry City, WEDNESDAY (loan, March-May 2005).

Left-sided midfielder Graham Barrett made two Premiership appearances for Arsenal as a teenager. Nurtured along nicely, he represented the Republic of Ireland at schoolboy and youth team levels and went on to win 24 Under-21 caps and also played in 6 full internationals. He had a season-long loan spell with Brighton and played in almost 60 games for Coventry before his loan spell with Wednesday for whom he scored on his debut against Torquay.

BARRICK, Dean
Utility

Appearances: 11   Goals: 2
Born: Hemsworth, 30 September 1969

CAREER
CLUBS: WEDNESDAY (April 1986-February 1991), Rotherham United, Cambridge United, Preston North End, Bury, Ayr United, Doncaster Rovers, Hereford United, Hucknall Town (player-manager)
OTHER: schoolteacher in Doncaster.

Unable to establish himself in Wednesday's first team, Dean Barrick did well for himself after leaving Hillsborough. A Third Division championship winner with Preston in 1996, he fractured his eye socket in two places and broke his nose playing against Chesterfield in 2000 but recovered and later helped Doncaster regain their Football League status in 2003. He fractured his leg playing for Hucknall in the 2005 FA Trophy final. His career realised over 400 appearances and almost 20 goals.

BARRON, George Ward
Outside right

Appearances: 1
Born: Wallsend-on-Tyne, April 1880
Died: Newcastle, 1961

17

CAREER

CLUBS: *Wallsend Park Villa, WEDNESDAY (£25, March 1903-March 1905).*

Reserve George Barron's only game for the Owls was at Bury in April 1903 when he deputised for Harry Davis in a 4-0 defeat.

BARRY-MURPHY, Brian
Defender

Appearances: 64+3
Born: Cork, Ireland, 27 July 1978

CAREER

CLUBS: *Cork City, Preston North End, Southend United, Hartlepool United, WEDNESDAY (free, January 2003-June 2004), Bury.*

A strong, resourceful defender, able to play as an orthodox left-back or wing-back, Brian Barry-Murphy was a near ever-present in his last season at Hillsborough. A good, honest competitor, he brought some stability to a shaky Owls' defence before his departure. A Republic of Ireland Youth international, he also gained six Under-21 caps for his country.

BARTLETT, William John
Left half

Appearances: 200   Goals: 3
Born: Noars Yard, Newcastle, 13 April 1878
Died: Belfast, 6 August 1939

CAREER

CLUBS: *Gateshead NER, WEDNESDAY (£45, April 1903-April 1910), Huddersfield Town, Linfield, Linfield Swifts (assistant trainer), Distillery (trainer), Blackburn Rovers (scout).*

A powerful and resilient defender, Billy Bartlett certainly gave a good account of himself during his seven years association with the Owls. He made his League debut (in place of Ruddlesdin) in a 2-0 win over Notts County in February 1904 and played in three more games towards the end of that championship-winning campaign. He established himself in the side the following season and was a regular in the team until his transfer to Huddersfield, playing in their first game in the Second Division against Bradford.

BART-WILLIAMS, Christopher Gerald
Midfield

Appearances: 115+41   Goals: 24
Born: Frertown, Sierra Leone, 16 June 1974

CAREER

CLUBS: *Leyton Orient, WEDNESDAY (£575,000, November 1991-July 1995), Nottingham Forest, Charlton Athletic, Ipswich Town, Leeds United, Apoel Nicosia, Marsaxlokk.*

An England Youth international with Orient, Chris Bart-Williams went on to win 1 'B' and 16 Under-21 caps and in 1998 gained a First Division championship medal with Forest. He made over 40 appearances for Orient and established himself in the Owls' line-up during the second half of 1991/92, producing some

Chris Bart-Williams

excellent performances in midfield before moving to Forest for a record fee. He reached the milestone of 500 club appearances as an Ipswich player in 2004, helping them reach the Division One play-offs before his release.

BECKETT, Albert
Right-half

Appearances: 1
Born: Sheffield, early 1867
Deceased by 1950

CAREER
CLUBS: WEDNESDAY (seasons 1885-88)
OTHER: surgical instrument fitter.

Albert Beckett's only appearance for the Owls was in the FA Cup-tie at Long Eaton Rangers in November 1887. He was the recipient of Wharncliffe Charity and Sheffield Challenge Cup winners' medals in 1886 and 1887 respectively.

BEDFORD, Lewis
Left-winger

Appearances: 11   Goals: 2
Born: Aston, Birmingham, 26 March 1899
Died: Birmingham, 29 June 1966

CAREER
CLUBS: West Bromwich Albion, Walsall, WEDNESDAY (£575, June 1925-September 1926), Walsall, Nelson, Luton Town, Walsall
OTHER: shop manager.

A midget winger, fast and tricky, Lewis Bedford made his League debut at the age of seventeen for West Bromwich Albion versus Arsenal in 1921. He found it difficult to get into the First XI at The Hawthorns but after leaving he did much better, appearing in 140 games for Walsall during his three spells at Fellows Park. With Arthur Prince out injured, he played all his games for Wednesday at the start of the 1925/26 Second Division championship-winning season, scoring on his debut in a 3-0 home win over Fulham. However, when Prince came back, Bedford was omitted and he languished in the reserves before returning to Walsall.

BEECH, George Charles
Inside forward

Appearances: 22   Goals: 5
Born: Sheffield, May 1872
Died: Sheffield, 1945

CAREER
CLUBS: Attercliffe SC, WEDNESDAY (free, August 1896-May 1904), Barnsley.

Jack Beech spent eight seasons with Wednesday, whom he joined after the team had won the FA Cup in 1896. Initially reserve to Alec Brady and Bob Ferrier, he scored on his debut from the inside left position in a 3-0 home win over Nottingham Forest in April 1897. Over the next four seasons he made only four appearances before having his best run in the First XI at the end of 1901/02, when he played in seven matches. However, he did help the Second XI win the Sheffield Association League twice, the Midland League twice and also the Sheffield Challenge Cup.

BEESON, George William
Full-back

Appearances: 75
Born: Clay Cross, Chesterfield, 31 August 1908.
Died: Wythall, Birmingham, 6 January 1999

CAREER
CLUBS: Chesterfield, WEDNESDAY (£1,250, March 1929-August 1934), Aston Villa, Walsall, Hull City
OTHER: assisted his son in a Birmingham furniture shop.

A fine figure of a man, George Beeson was a strong-tackling, hard-kicking defender who never shirked a tackle. He took time to establish himself in Wednesday's first team, finally settling at right-back early in 1932/33 as Ernie Blenkinsop's partner. Named reserve for England, he twice represented the Football League in 1933/34 before leaving Hillsborough. Beeson, who often ate two pre-match dinners to give him strength, had 71 games for Aston Villa. He died from Alzheimer's disease.

BEEVERS, Mark
Defender

Appearances: 2
Born: Barnsley, 21 November 1989

CAREER
CLUBS: WEDNESDAY

Beevers is a defender who graduated through the ranks at Hillsborough, making his senior debut *v.* Southampton in January 2007.

BELL, Derek Martin
Forward

Appearances: 5   Goals: 1
Born: Wyberton, Lincolnshire, 30 October 1956

CAREER
CLUBS: Derby County, Halifax Town, WEDNESDAY (loan, March-April 1976), Barnsley, Lincoln City, Chesterfield, Scunthorpe United, Boston United, York City (scout, youth coach, chief scout, assistant-manager), Lincoln City (staff), Wigan Athletic (staff).

Generally, Derek Bell scored regularly for all his clubs, and his senior record was impressive – 316 appearances and 94 goals – all in the lower Divisions. He played his best football with Halifax and Lincoln and was at Hillsborough

for only a short period of time, netting his only goal in a 4-2 defeat at Preston in March 1976.

BELL, Lawrence Stanley Thomas
Forward

Appearances: 54   Goals: 13
Born: Langbank, Renfrewshire, 5 May 1875
Died: Scotland, 1955

CAREER
CLUBS: Dumbarton, Third Lanark, WEDNESDAY (£50, August 1895-August 1897), Everton, Bolton Wanderers, Brentford, West Bromwich Albion, Hibernian.
OTHER: later worked in a Scottish shipyard.

The much-travelled Lawrie Bell was a constructive player who preferred the centre forward position. After doing well north of the border, he helped the Owls win the FA Cup in 1896 and gave the club excellent service for two seasons before moving to Everton. He was injured during his spell with West Bromwich Albion and returned to Scotland, ending his career with over 300 appearances to his credit. He was rewarded with Scottish League representative honours against the Irish League in 1895 and was twice named reserve to the full international side. His brother Jack played for Everton, New Brompton and Preston North End, was the first chairman of the PFA and also the first official manager at Deepdale.

BELLAS, John Edward
Right-back

Appearances: 51
Born: Bishop Auckland, County Durham, 16 September 1895
Died: Pleasley, Nottinghamshire, 23 August 1977

CAREER
CLUBS: Shildon Athletic, WEDNESDAY (£250, September 1920-June 1923), Mansfield Town, Coventry City

OTHER: worked and played cricket for Pleasley Colliery, also keen on darts, winning many local tournaments.

A strong, dependable full-back, Jack Bellas spent three years at Hillsborough, having his best run in the first team during the 1920/21 campaign when he appeared in 33 matches as partner to first Jimmy Blair and then Harry O'Neill. He helped the Owls' Second XI win the Midland League in 1923 and gained winners' medals with Mansfield in the same competition in 1924 and 1925.

BENNETT, David Anthony
Winger

Appearances: 23+8 Goals: 1
Born: Manchester, 11 July 1959

CAREER
CLUBS: Manchester City, Cardiff City, Coventry City, WEDNESDAY (£250,000, March 1989-September 1990), Swindon Town, Shrewsbury Town.

During an excellent career, Dave Bennett notched 54 goals in 332 League games for his six

David Bennett

clubs. He also represented the Football League and scored in the 1987 FA Cup final for the winners Coventry versus Spurs, having gained a runners-up medal in the same competition with Manchester City six years earlier. A fine dribbler with terrific acceleration, he played his best football at Highfield Road, netting 33 times in 208 outings for the Sky Blues. During his time at Hillsborough when he played wide on the right, he had a decent run in the side in 1989/90 when he scored his only goal for the Owls in a 4-1 ZDSC defeat at Middlesbrough.

BENNETT, William Edgar
Outside left

Appearances: 26   Goals: 18
Born: Rotherham, 6 June 1863
Died: Mexborough, 13 September 1919

CAREER
CLUBS: Rotherham Town, Mexborough, Doncaster Rovers, WEDNESDAY (free, August 1889-May 1891).

'Micky' Bennett spent two seasons with Wednesday, making senior appearances in both the Football Alliance (21) and FA Cup (5). His 12 goals helped clinch the Alliance title in 1890 and he also scored in the 6-1 FA Cup final defeat at the hands of Blackburn, having scored twice on his senior debut versus London Swifts in the first round. His brothers also played football – Walter for Sheffield United, Bristol City and England, who appeared in three FA Cup finals for the Blades, and Harry who captained Barnsley. The famous boxer 'Iron' Hague was a nephew of the Bennetts.

BENTLEY, Harold
Defender

Appearances: 53   Goals: 3
Born: Sheffield, 8 August 1891
Died: 1965

CLUBS: Heeley Friends, WEDNESDAY (£10, April 1913-May 1920), Brighton & Hove Albion, Swindon Town. OTHER: Royal Field Artillery, First World War.

A well-proportioned footballer, able to occupy both wing half positions, Harry Bentley made his League debut for the Owls in a 2-0 defeat at Oldham in April 1914 before establishing himself in the first team at right half at the start of the following campaign, replacing the injured Tom Brittleton. He made 13 appearances for the club during the First World War (3 goals) and later produced some sterling performances on the left flank for Brighton and Swindon.

BENTLEY, Willis
Defender

Appearances: 5   Goals: 1
Born: Sheffield, circa 1859
Deceased by 1925

CAREER
CLUBS: WEDNESDAY (free, August 1882-May 1889), Sheffield United
OTHER: tutor/warder at the South Yorkshire Asylum.

An amateur throughout his career and a former steel worker, Willis Bentley's debut for Wednesday was in a third round FA Cup-tie versus Nottingham Forest in January 1883 when he replaced the injured Arthur Malpas. Although he was registered with the club for seven years he was generally regarded as a reserve team player. He helped the Owls win the Wharncliffe Charity Cup in 1883.

BERESFORD, Marlon
Goalkeeper

Appearances: 4
Born: Lincoln, 2 September 1969

CAREER
CLUBS: WEDNESDAY (May 1986-August 1992), Bury, Ipswich Town, Northampton Town, Crewe Alexandra, Northampton Town, Burnley, Middlesbrough, WEDNESDAY (loan, January-February 2001), Wolverhampton Wanderers, Burnley, York City, Burnley, Bradford City, Luton Town, Barnsley, Luton Town.

Marlon Beresford failed to make a first-team appearance for the Owls in his first spell. However, as he grew older and wiser, over the next eight years (prior to his return to Hillsborough), he played in almost 350 games, the majority for Burnley. A fine shot-stopper, he was recruited (second time round) due to an injury crisis. Unfortunately he was a loser in each of his four games for Wednesday, conceding 12 goals. He was named in the PFA League One team in 2004 after helping Luton win the championship of that division.

BEST, Leon Julian Brendan
Striker

Appearances: 5+8   Goals: 2
Born: Nottingham, 19 September 1986

CAREER
CLUBS: Southampton (apprentice, September 2002; professional, September 2004), Queens Park Rangers (L, December 2004-January 2005), WEDNESDAY (loan, August 2005-September 2005 and January-May 2006), Bournemouth (L, August 2006), Yeovil Town (L, March-May 2007).

Republic of Ireland Youth international striker Leon Best, 6ft 1in tall, made three Premiership appearances for Southampton and featured in the 2005 FA Youth Cup final, beaten 3-2 on aggregate by Ipswich Town. He had a successful loan spell with QPR before joining the Owls, also on loan, at the start of the 2005/06 season, making his debut in the 0-0 draw at Stoke on the opening Saturday of the League programme. He returned to the St Mary's stadium after fracturing a bone in his foot and after a tedious wait he finally had his first game for Saints against Luton Town a fortnight before Christmas, but came back to Wednesday for a second loan spell in 2006. He later helped Yeovil reach the play-offs.

BESWETHERICK, Jonathan Barry
Defender

Appearances: 12+4
Born: Liverpool, 15 January 1978

CAREER
CLUBS: Plymouth Argyle, WEDNESDAY (free, June 2002-July 2004), Swindon Town (L), Macclesfield Town (L), Bristol Rovers, Kidderminster Harriers, Forest Green Rovers.

After making 169 senior appearances for Plymouth, whom he helped win the Division Three championship in 2002, defender Jon Beswetherick had a difficult time at Hillsborough, failing to win a regular place in the side. He was playing non-League by the time he was twenty-seven.

BETTS, William
Centre half

Appearances: 143   Goals: 4
Born: Sheffield, 26 March 1864
Died: Sheffield, 8 August 1941

CAREER
CLUBS: Heeley, WEDNESDAY (free, April 1882-October 1883), Lockwood Brothers, WEDNESDAY (player July 1885-March 1897, groundsman, assistant-trainer).

Bill Betts, somewhat on the small side, was a stern tackler and a fine header of the ball. He made his debut for the Owls during his first spell at the club, lining up at left-back in a 2-2

FA Cup draw at Nottingham Forest in January 1883. On his return in 1885 he became one of the mainstays of the side, gaining an FA Cup runners-up medal versus Blackburn in 1890. He missed only 12 of Wednesday's first 60 Football League games (1892-94) before losing his place to Tommy Crawshaw. He helped the Owls win the Football Alliance title in 1890 and both the Sheffield Challenge Cup and Wharncliffe Charity Cup finals in 1888. He was capped by England in a 4-1 win over Wales in 1889. Betts' grandson is Dennis Woodhead.

BINGLEY, John
Inside-forward

Appearances: 2
Born: Sheffield, 1854
Deceased by 1920

CAREER:
CLUBS: WEDNESDAY (July 1876-April 1882).

Jack Bingley was a reserve during his six years with Wednesday. His two senior appearances were both in the FA Cup, against Turton in January 1881 and Providence ten months later. He helped the Owls win the Sheffield Challenge Cup in 1877, 1878 and 1881 and the Wharncliffe Charity Cup in 1879. A player named Bingley was registered with Heeley in 1874; it may well have been Jack.

BINGLEY, Walter
Full-back

Appearances: 39
Born: Sheffield, 17 April 1930

CAREER
CLUBS: Bolton Wanderers, WEDNESDAY (£500, May 1955-January 1958), Swindon Town, York City, Halifax Town
OTHER: worked for Whitbread Brewery (Sheffield).

Wally Bingley was a well-built, hard-tackling, resolute full-back who made only six appearances for Bolton before joining the Owls. He worked hard during his time at Hillsborough, and had his best run in the first team between September and December 1955 when he appeared in 21 League games, mainly as partner to England's Ron Staniforth. He later made 101 League appearances for Swindon and 130 for York whom he helped reach the quarter-finals of the League Cup in 1962. A penalty expert, he only missed once from the spot during his career.

BINKS, Sydney
Centre forward

Appearances: 83   Goals: 33
Born: Whitworth, Bishop Auckland, 25 July 1899
Died: Beauchief, Sheffield, 4 February 1978

CAREER
CLUBS: Spennymoor United, Sunderland, Bishop Auckland, WEDNESDAY (exchange for Eddie Richardson, May 1922-September 1924), Huddersfield Town, Blackpool, Portsmouth, Southend United, Fulham, Heart of Midlothian, Chesterfield, WEDNESDAY (assistant-trainer, August 1932-April 1933), Rotherham United, Ashington
OTHER: a fine sprinter; later ran a Sheffield bakery for thirty years.

During his career the well-built Syd Binks appeared in 220 League games and scored 51 goals, having his best years at Hillsborough, although he did help Chesterfield win the Third Division (North) title in 1931, playing in 29 games. At his best he was alert, strong, mobile and very useful in the air. He won successive Amateur Cups with the Bishops in 1921 and 1922, scoring in both finals, and he was also capped four times by England as an amateur.

BINNEY, Charles
Forward

Appearances: 43   Goals: 6
Born: Sheffield, 24 February 1901
Died: Sheffield, 3 March 1952

CAREER
CLUBS: Leadmill St Mary's, WEDNESDAY (£10, September 1919-May 1923), Worksop Town
OTHER: cashier.

'Chas' Binney occupied four forward positions during his time with Wednesday, missing out on the left wing. Basically a reserve, he made his League debut at inside right versus Derby in 1919 and had his best spell in the first team between September and December 1920 when he scored twice in 16 consecutive outings. With an abundance of forwards at the club, he became surplus to requirements in 1923. A relative, John Billey, played for Leicester Fosse.

BIRCH, Arnold
Goalkeeper

Appearances: 29
Born: Grenoside, Sheffield, 12 July 1895
Died: Grenoside, Sheffield, 6 January 1964

CAREER
CLUBS: Grenoside, Be Quick FC, WEDNESDAY (guest, March-April 1917, signed August 1919-April 1923), Chesterfield
OTHER: worked for Newton Chambers (Sheffield) for many years, also employed as a telephonist.

Signed after playing as a guest for the Owls during the First World War (29 apps), Arnold Birch made 23 appearances for the first team in 1919/20, but after the arrival of Jack Brown his outings were restricted and he moved to Chesterfield for whom he set a record by netting five penalties in 1923/24. He had 141 outings for the Saltergate club.

BIRKS, Graham
Left-back

Appearances: 4
Born: Sheffield, 25 January 1942

CAREER
CLUBS: WEDNESDAY (May 1957-May 1964), Peterborough United, Southend United, Chester, Port Elizabeth City
OTHER: sales manager for Bass Brewery (Burton), caddy for golf professional John Mellors.

Reserve to Norman Curtis and then Don Megson at Hillsborough, Graham Birks made just four League starts for the Owls in 1962/63, the first three resulting in wins. After leaving the Owls he played in a further 247 League games, 140 for Southend.

BISCHOFF, Mikkel
Defender

Appearances: 4
Born: Denmark, 3 February 1982

CAREER
CLUBS: AB Copenhagen, Wolverhampton Wanderers (two spells), Manchester City, WEDNESDAY (loan, March-May 2006), Coventry City.

A strong, resilient 6ft 4ins Danish Youth and Under-21 international, recruited to bolster up the Owls' defence, Mikkel Bischoff's presence certainly proved vital in the battle against relegation at the end of the 2005/06 campaign. He made his debut for the club against QPR twenty-four hours after signing.

BLACKHALL, Raymond
Right-back

Appearances: 140   Goals: 1
Born: Ashington, County Durham, 19 February 1957

CAREER
CLUBS: Newcastle United, WEDNESDAY (£25,000, August 1978-July 1982), IK Tord, Mansfield Town, Carlisle United, Blyth Spartans
OTHER: worked in the steel industry before joining the police (based in Kensington).

Ray 'Bomber' Blackhall was a tough-tackling defender who made rapid progress with Newcastle before his transfer to Hillsborough after the Geordies had been relegated. He helped the Owls regain their Second Division status, making 35 League appearances in 1979/80. He missed only one game the following season before eventually losing his place to Mel Sterland. His career realised 167 League appearances.

BLAIR, Andrew
Midfield

Appearances: 75   Goals: 7
Born: Kirkcaldy, Fife, 18 December 1959

CAREER
CLUBS: Coventry City, Aston Villa, Wolverhampton Wanderers, WEDNESDAY (£60,000, August 1984-March 1986), Aston Villa, Barnsley, Northampton Town, Naxaar Lions, Kidderminster Harriers, Bedworth Town (commercial manager), Racing Club Warwick (manager)
OTHER: manager of a sportswear shop in Coventry, owner of a playschool and works on BBC WM radio.

Capped five times by Scotland at Under-21 level, Andy Blair appeared in more than 100 games for Coventry and over 60 for Aston Villa, for whom he made his debut at Wembley in the 1981 FA Charity Shield game. The following year he won a European Cup winners' medal (as a substitute) and helped Villa lift the European Super Cup. Three of his seven goals for the Owls came from the penalty spot versus Luton in a fourth round League Cup-tie in October 1984. A neat passer of the ball with a strong shot, he quit senior football in 1990 with 224 League appearances to his credit

BLAIR, James
Left-back

Appearances: 61
Born: Glenboig, Lanarkshire, 11 May 1888
Died: Sheffield, 28 February 1964

CAREER
CLUBS: Clyde, WEDNESDAY (£1,975, May 1914-August 1919), Alloa Athletic, WEDNESDAY (£250, October 1920), Cardiff City, Bournemouth, Sheppey United (player-manager), Cardiff City (coach)
WARTIME GUEST APPEARANCES: Clydebank, Glasgow Rangers
OTHER: licensee, first in Cowbridge, then in Cardiff.

Jimmy Blair was a great coup by Wednesday, who paid a record fee for his services in 1914. Twice a Scottish Cup finalist with Clyde, he was small, stylish, quick-thinking, had superb footwork and was rated one of the best full-backs in Scotland at the time of his transfer. His progress at Hillsborough was unfortunately disrupted by the First World War, this, after a succession of road accidents, had restricted his appearances to just a handful. He served in the army and gained a Scottish League championship winners' medal in 1918 with Rangers. Capped twice by Scotland as an 'Owl', having rejoined the club after a spell with Alloa, he followed his Jimmy Gill to Cardiff for £3,500 – a huge fee in those days, especially for a full-back. He made 175 appearances in 6 years at Ninian Park, gained 6 more caps and played in the 1925 FA Cup final when Cardiff lost to Sheffield United. His two sons played football – Doug for Cardiff and Jim for Blackpool, Bournemouth and Leyton Orient, the latter being capped by Scotland in 1947.

BLATSIS, Con
Defender

Appearances: 8
Born: Melbourne, Australia, 6 July 1977

CAREER
CLUBS: Clarinda, Bullen, VIS, AIS, South Melbourne, Olympiakos, Nottingham Forest, Derby County, WEDNESDAY (loan, December 2001-January 2002), Colchester United, Kokkali Spor, St Patrick's Athletic, Coventry City, FC Twente, South Melbourne.

Standing 6ft 3ins tall, Con Blatsis (the recipient of 2 full, 3 Under-23 and 4 Under-20 caps for Australia) played alongside Adrian Westwood and Des Walker as Wednesday's half-back and later helped Colchester stay in the Second Division. Via Greek ancestry, he holds an EU passport.

BLENKINSOP, Ernest
Left-back

Appearances: 425   Goals: 5
Born: Cudworth, Barnsley, 20 April 1900
Died: Sheffield, 24 April 1969

CAREER
CLUBS: Hull City, WEDNESDAY (£1,150, January 1923-March 1934), Liverpool, Cardiff City (player, player-coach), Buxton, Sheffield FC (coach), WEDNESDAY (scout, 1942-43)
WARTIME GUEST APPEARANCES: Halifax Town, Bradford Park Avenue, Bradford City
OTHER: licensee.

Ernie Blenkinsop was a superb left-back, one of best in the Football League between 1928 and 1933 when he gained 26 caps for England. This total, in fact, stood as a Wednesday record for thirty years until beaten by Ron Staniforth. He also represented the Football League eight times (1928-34). A player with a polished style, 'Blenkie' was judicious in tackling, cool and efficient in defence and was exceptional with his clearances, always trying to find a colleague rather than hoofing the ball aimlessly down field (except when in dangerous situations and under directly pressure from an opponent). The recipient of a Second Division championship winners' medal with Wednesday in 1926 (playing in 41 games), he gained a League championship winner's medal three years later and repeated that feat in 1930. Perennially young looking, after captaining the Owls and also England, as well as having a cartilage operation, he left Hillsborough for Liverpool soon after Billy Walker had taken over as manager. He made 495 League appearances in his career and was probably the best left-back Wednesday has ever had. According to legend, Hull paid £100 plus eighty pints of beer for Blenkinsop's services.

BLINKER, Reginald Waldie
Outside left

Appearances: 27+18   Goals: 3
Born: Surinam, 4 June 1969

CAREER
CLUBS: Delfia HFC, Feyenoord, Den Bosch, WEDNESDAY (£275,000, March 1996-August 1997), Celtic, Den Haag, Bolton Wanderers, RBC Roosendaal, Sparta Rotterdam, SV Deltasport.

After a settling-in period at Hillsborough, skilful Dutch international winger Reggie Blinker started 1996/97 on Wednesday's left. However, as the League programme progressed he was forced to miss several games through injury and suspension and after returning was used as a central midfielder, and towards the end of the campaign he found himself on the bench for long periods. Capped three times by Holland in 1993/94, in November 1996 he was banned by World governing body FIFA after Italian side Udinese complained that he had agreed to sign for them – two months later he became an 'Owl'. He won a League Championship medal with Celtic in 1998.

BLONDEAU, Patrick
Right-back

Appearances: 5+1
Born: Marseille, France, 27 January 1968

CAREER
CLUBS: Martigues, AS Monaco, WEDNESDAY (£1.8m, July 1997-January 1998), Girondins De Bordeaux, Olympique Marseille, Watford, Créteil.

Patrick Blondeau made almost 150 League appearances for Monaco before joining the Owls. He seemed to be just the right player to fill the problem right-back position vacated by Roland Nilsson some years earlier. Axed after only six games, having failed to produce any worthwhile form, he joined Bordeaux and appeared in the 1999 UEFA Cup final, beaten by Parma. Blondeau arrived at Hillsborough with a great reputation but left a rather disappointed man.

BODEN, Luke
Striker

Appearances: 1+1
Born: Sheffield, 26 November 1988

CAREER
CLUBS: WEDNESDAY

Striker Luke Boden made his debut for the Owls in the League Cup in 2006.

BOLDER, Robert John
Goalkeeper

Appearances: 224
Born: Dover, 2 October 1958

CAREER
CLUBS: Charlton Athletic, Dover Town, WEDNESDAY (£1,000, March 1977-August 1983), Liverpool, Sunderland, Luton Town, Charlton Athletic,

Margate, Dagenham & Redbridge, Charlton Athletic (coach, community relations officer).

While playing non-League, Bob Bolder worked as an agricultural labourer before joining Wednesday. Tall and well built, he was a Len Ashurst discovery, but it was under manager Jack Charlton that he made his League debut, taking over from Chris Turner against Rotherham halfway through 1977/78. Unfortunately he had to endure injury problems during the following campaign but after that was first choice until his transfer to Liverpool in 1983, three years after helping the Owls gain promotion to the Second Division. He failed to dislodge Bruce Grobbelaar at Anfield and had the bad luck to break an ankle in a reserve game versus Bradford City. His departure from Hillsborough led to the emergence of Martin Hodge. During his career Bolder appeared in 550 games, won a European Cup winners' medal with Liverpool in 1984 (non-playing sub) and was a runner-up with Charlton against Blackburn in the FMC final of 1987.

BOLLAND, William Thomas
Outside left

Appearances: 13   Goals: 1
Born: Darlington, December 1884
Died: 1967

CAREER
CLUBS: Washington United, WEDNESDAY (£20, May 1907-August 1909), Swindon Town, Bath City.

Reserve to George Simpson and later Frank Foxall, Tommy Bolland was a capable footballer, quick with a good temperament. He made his League debut for the Owls in a 2-1 win at Notts County in January 1908 and scored his only goal three weeks later in a 2-0 victory over Bury. A fine athlete and expert juggler, Bolland appeared in a concert in Sheffield in 1908.

BOLSOVER, Henry
Goalkeeper

Appearances: 2
Born: Sheffield, 1875
Died: Sheffield, 1939

CAREER
CLUBS: Sheffield United, Sheffield FC, WEDNESDAY (free, March-May 1900), Sheffield FC.

Harry Bolsover was recruited when the Owls' main keepers Bill Mallinson and Jimmy Massey were both injured. His two League appearances were against Burton Swifts (won 6-0) and Arsenal (won 3-1) in March 1900. He played in the FA Amateur Cup final for Sheffield in 1904.

BONVIN, Pablo Facundo
Striker

Appearances: 9+21 Goals: 5
Born: Concepcion del Uruguay, Argentina, 15 April 1981

CAREER
CLUBS: Gimnasia y Esgrima, Ferro Carril Oeste, Boca Juniors, Newcastle United, WEDNESDAY (loan, August 2001 and April-May 2002), Racing Club Buenos Aires, Newcastle United, Argentinos Juniors.

A skilful forward, Pablo Bonvon took time to settle into English League football. He eventually adapted well enough to make 30 appearances for the Owls, some as a schemer. Two of his five goals earned Wednesday a 3-1 home League win over Barnsley in late October. He failed to get a game with Newcastle. He top scored for Argentinos and the National 'B' League in 2003/04.

Andy Booth

BOOTH, Andrew David
Striker

Appearances: 143+11   Goals: 34
Born: Huddersfield, 6 December 1973

CAREER
CLUBS: Huddersfield Town, WEDNESDAY (£2.7m, July 1996-March 2001), Tottenham Hotspur (L), Huddersfield Town.

At 6ft tall and weighting 13st, striker Andy Booth has proved a handful for most defenders. A good target man, he did very well in his first spell with Huddersfield, scoring 64 goals in 155 games and gaining three England Under-21 caps. He continued to find the net for the Owls, notching 13 goals in his first season. In 2005/06, he reached the career milestones of 500 senior appearances and 150 goals.

BOSWORTH, Samuel
Outside right

Appearances: 7
Born: Basford, 1877
Died: Leicester, 1945

CAREER
CLUBS: Loughborough Town, Derby County, WEDNESDAY (£50, March 1899-October 1901), Ilkeston United.

Sam Bosworth played in seven of Wednesday's last eight League games of 1898/99, deputising for Bill Dryburgh. He had failed to make headway with Derby.

BOUGHERRA, Madjid
Defender

Appearances: 29
Born: Longvic, France, 7 October 1982

CAREER
CLUBS: FC Gueugnon, Crewe Alexandra, WEDNESDAY (May 2006), Charlton Athletic (January 2007).

An Algerian international defender, strong and mobile, Madjid Bougherra made an immediate impact when he joined the Owls from Crewe Alexandra in May 2006. He was transferred to Charlton Athletic in January 2007.

BOWLING, Ian
Goalkeeper

Appearances: 1
Born: Sheffield, 27 July 1965

CAREER
CLUBS: Gainsborough Trinity, Lincoln City, Hartlepool United, Kettering Town, Bradford City, WEDNESDAY (n/c, June-August 1995), Mansfield Town.

Giant keeper Ian Bowling's only game for the Owls was away to FC Basel in the InterToto Cup in June 1995. In March 2002 he fractured his skull playing for Kettering against Tiverton.

BOWMAN, Matthew
Striker

Appearances: 0+1
Born: Barnsley, 31 January 1990

CAREER
CLUBS: WEDNESDAY

Bowman (like Boden) made his Owls' debut *v.* Wrexham in a League Cup-tie in August 2006.

BOWNES, George Horace
Inside forward

Appearances: 2
Born: Sheffield, 1859
Deceased by 1935

CAREER
CLUBS: Pye Bank, WEDNESDAY (seasons 1882/83 and 1885/86), Clinton, Sheffield United
OTHER: building contractor in Brightside, Sheffield.

George Bowns had two spells with Wednesday, making his debut at home against Notts County in an FA Cup-tie in February 1883.

BRADBURY, Lee Michael
Striker

Appearances: 10+1 Goals: 3
Born: Cowes, Isle of Wight, 3 July 1975

CAREER
CLUBS: Portsmouth, Exeter City, Manchester City, Crystal Palace, Birmingham City, Portsmouth, WEDNESDAY (loan, December 2002-January 2003,
loan March-May 2003), Derby County, Walsall, Oxford United.
OTHER: Army.

Thrice-capped England Under-21 striker Lee Bradbury had two loan spells with the Owls and did well in his second, scoring three goals. A regular marksman despite several injury problems, he never really hit the heights expected of him. He served as a rifleman in the Prince of Wales Regiment and gained experience playing for his unit.

BRADLEY, Martin
Inside right

Appearances: 2
Born: Wolstanton, North Staffordshire, November 1886
Died: Hemsworth, December 1958

CAREER
CLUBS: Grimsby Town, Mexborough, WEDNESDAY (with 'Lol' Burkinshaw, April 1910-June 1911), Bristol Rovers.

A useful attacker with a strong shot, Martin Bradley was a regular for Grimsby before transferring to Wednesday where he never quite fitted in, making only two League appearances, his first in place of Harry Chapman in the 1-1 draw at Bury in October 1910. His brother, Jimmy, a Football League representative, played for Stoke and helped Liverpool win the League title in 1906.

BRADSHAW, Carl
Utility

Appearances: 25+19   Goals: 7
Born: Sheffield, 2 October 1968

CAREER
CLUBS: WEDNESDAY (April 1985-September 1988),

Carl Bradshaw

Barnsley (L), Manchester City, Sheffield United, Norwich City, Wigan Athletic, Scunthorpe United.

A professional for seventeen years, England Youth international Carl Bradshaw's career realised 448 senior appearances (45 goals). He found it hard to hold down a regular place in the Owls' side, having made his senior debut in a 7-0 League Cup win over Stockport in October 1986. Exchanged for Imre Varadi, he did well at Bramall Lane and Norwich and helped Wigan win the AWS in 1999.

BRADSHAW, Francis
Forward

Appearances: 94   Goals: 38
Born: Sheffield, 31 May 1884
Died: Taunton, Somerset, 1950

CAREER
CLUBS: WEDNESDAY (April 1904-July 1910), Northampton Town, Everton, Arsenal (retired, 1923), Aberdare Athletic (manager)

OTHER: worked for the Bristol Aeroplane Company; FA coach in Somerset.

Frank Bradshaw gained an FA Cup winners' medal with the Owls in 1907 and scored a hat-trick in his only game for England when Austria were beaten 11-1 a year later. He should have received a second cap (versus Ireland) but had to cry off with a knee injury which was to plague him towards the end of his career at Hillsborough. He also twice represented the Football League and won the London Challenge Cup with Arsenal in 1923. An ingenious forward, fast and dangerous with a powerful right-foot shot, he sustained several serious injuries during his career but always bounced back – a fighter to the last. He was converted into a wing half and then full-back by Arsenal for whom he appeared in 142 games. He managed Third Division (South) side Aberdare for eleven months.

BRADSHAW, Paul
Winger

Appearances: 72+2 Goals: 11
Born: Sheffield, 2 October 1953

CAREER
CLUBS: Burnley, WEDNESDAY (£19,444, September 1976-October 1978), Hallam
OTHER: assistant manager at Stocksbridge Park Steels; teacher at Silverdale School, Sheffield.

Capped by England at Schoolboy and Youth team levels, Paul Bradshaw made 13 League appearances for Burnley before transferring to Hillsborough where he quickly became a first-team regular. He scored on his debut for the Owls in a 2-2 draw at Wrexham soon after joining and held his place in the side until March 1978 when he was injured in the home game with Chester. He never regained full fitness and retired, aged twenty-five.

BRADY, Alec
Inside right

Appearances: 178   Goals: 39
Born: Cathcart, Glasgow, 2 April 1865
Died: Renton, 19 October 1913

CAREER
CLUBS: Dundee Harp, Renton, Partick Thistle, Sunderland, Burnley, Sunderland, Everton, Broxburn Shamrock, Celtic, WEDNESDAY (£50, August 1892-August 1899), Clydebank, Renton
OTHER: caulker in a Clyde shipyard.

Described as one of the most scientific of British footballers during the 1890s, the moustached Alec Brady gained FA Cup winners' medals north and south of the border: with Celtic in 1892 and Wednesday in 1896. He also helped Everton win the League title in 1891 but surprisingly, for all his efforts, he failed to win international recognition. A smart and precise passer of the ball, he was tricky and fast, although many spectators found it highly amusing to watch him in action because he took such short steps when running. He played his last competitive match for the Owls versus Stoke in April 1899, aged thirty-five. Brady was also the first player to score a League hat-trick for Everton, doing so versus Derby in January 1890.

BRANDON, Harry
Right half

Appearances: 201   Goals: 17
Born: Kilbirnie, Scotland, 1871
Died: Glasgow, 1936

CAREER
CLUBS: Paisley, St Mirren, Glasgow, Clyde, WEDNESDAY (free, December 1890-May 1898), Chesterfield Town, Silverwood (coach)
OTHER: worked at a Barnsley colliery.

Harry Brandon made his debut for the Owls in a 2-1 friendly match win over Sheffield United two days after joining the club. Of the four Brandons who served Wednesday, Harry spent the longest time at the club and although he never gained full international honours, he did represent the Football Alliance against a Football League XI at Olive Grove, Sheffield in April 1891. Although primarily a half-back, he did, on occasion, play at full-back and was a member of the Owls' FA Cup-winning side in 1896. He was a huge favourite with the supporters.

BRANDON, James
Centre forward

Appearances: 3
Born: Kilbirnie, Scotland, February 1870
Died: Glasgow, Scotland, 1934

CAREER
CLUBS: St Mirren (1889), Preston North End (1890), WEDNESDAY (free, August 1891), Bootle (August 1892-May 1893).

A reserve with the Owls, Jim Brandon played in three Football Alliance matches during his two seasons with the club.

BRANDON, Robert
Centre forward

Appearances: 20   Goals: 9
Born: Kilbirnie, Scotland, 1867
Died: Glasgow, 1944

CAREER
CLUBS: Clyde, WEDNESDAY (free, October 1890-April 1891), St Mirren.

Bob Brandon's two senior games for the Owls were in the FA Cup v. Halliwell and West Brom in the first and third rounds of the 1890/91 competition. He scored twice on his debut in a 12-0 win over Halliwell.

BRANDON, Thomas
Right-back

Appearances: 49   Goals: 2
Born: Kilbirnie, Scotland, 26 February 1869
Died: Lanarkshire, 1921

CAREER
CLUBS: St Johnstone, Port Glasgow Athletic, Renfrew Athletic, St Mirren, Blackburn Rovers, WEDNESDAY (free, September 1891-May 1893), Nelson, Blackburn Rovers, St Mirren
OTHER: worked in USA (Rhode Island), returning to Lanarkshire in 1906.

Scottish international Tom Brandon (capped once versus England in 1896) was a member of St Mirren's Renfrewshire Cup-winning team of 1888 in which his brother James also played. A buccaneering type of footballer, strong with no frills, Brandon was well built, possessed a mighty kick, used his physical strength with carefree abandon to the limit and was a huge favourite with the Owls' supporters. Prior to joining Wednesday he had appeared occasionally as a centre forward. As team captain, Brandon was credited with scoring Wednesday's first-ever League goal at Notts County in September 1892 (1-0). Tom's son William also played professional football.

BRANFOOT, Ian Grant
Right-back

Appearances: 37+4
Born: Gateshead, 26 January 1947

CAREER
CLUBS: Gateshead, WEDNESDAY (free, July 1965-December 1969), Doncaster Rovers, Lincoln City (player, assistant-manager, coach), Southampton (coach), Reading (assistant manager, coach, manager), Crystal Palace (chief scout), Southampton (manager), Fulham (manager, general manager), Swansea City (chief scout), Sunderland (academy director).

A Fourth Division championship winner under manager Graham Taylor at Lincoln in 1976, Ian Branfoot's best spell in the Owls' first team came halfway through 1967/68, when he had a run of 11 consecutive outings, wearing four different numbered shirts! After leaving Hillsborough, he appeared in 156 League games for Doncaster and 166 for Lincoln, won the FA Youth Cup and Football Combination as coach at Southampton but failed as a manager.

BRANNIGAN, Kenneth
Defender

Appearances: 1
Born: Glasgow, 8 June 1965

CAREER
CLUBS: Queen's Park, WEDNESDAY (free, June 1986-June1988), Stockport County (L), Doncaster Rovers (L), St Mirren, Kilmarnock, Falkirk, East Stirlingshire, Stranraer, Stenhousemuir, Clydebank (three spells, player, player-manager), Partick Thistle, Berwick Rangers, Stirling Albion, Airdrie United, Queen's Park
OTHER: owned taxi firms, ran a pub and also managed a food store in Scotland.

Ken Brannigan was substituted when making his only appearance for the Owls in a 6-1 League defeat at Leicester in January 1987. He failed to settle at Hillsborough and after his loan spell at Doncaster returned to Scotland, where he made over 300 appearances.

B

BRANSTON, Guy Peter Bromley
Defender

Appearances: 12+1
Born: Leicester, 9 January 1979

CAREER
CLUBS: *Leicester City, Rushden & Diamonds, Colchester United, Plymouth Argyle, Lincoln City, Rotherham United, Wycombe Wanderers, Peterborough United, WEDNESDAY (free, July, 2004-February 2005), Peterborough United (L), Oldham Athletic.*

Prior to joining the Owls, robust left-sided defender Guy Branston, as tough as teak, had amassed 169 senior appearances, having had his best spell at Rotherham (116 games). He bedded in well at Hillsborough but quickly fell from favour. His career was littered with suspensions.

BRASH, Archibald Theodore
Outside right

Appearances: 131   Goals: 23
Born: Uphall, Linlithgow, 1873
Died: Paisley, Scotland, 1938

CAREER
CLUBS: *Paisley St Mirren, WEDNESDAY (free, May 1894-July 1898), Crewe Alexandra, WEDNESDAY (April 1899-June 1900), Leicester Fosse, Aberdeen*
OTHER: *worked in the family business as a cotton-reel maker.*

Small, alert and tricky, Archie Brash starred for the Owls in their 1896 FA Cup final victory – his throw-in setting up the opening goal against Wolves after just thirty seconds. After a year away (at Crewe) he returned and helped the team win the Second Division title in 1900, scoring 6 goals in 26 League games, mainly as partner to Jack Pryce. He made his debut for the Owls with new recruits Bob Petrie, Bob

Ferrier and Tom Crawshaw, in a 3-1 defeat at Everton in September 1894.

BRATLEY, George William
Defender

Appearances: 3
Born: Wickersley, Rotherham, 17 January 1909
Died: Sheffield, April 1978

CAREER
CLUBS: *Rotherham United, WEDNESDAY (£850 plus Vic Wright, February 1933-February 1934), Rotherham United, Gainsborough Trinity, Bath City, Barrow, Swindon Town, Tunbridge Wells*
WARTIME GUEST APPEARANCES: *Brighton & Hove Albion, Crystal Palace, Halifax Town, Hull City, Leeds United, Oldham Athletic, York City.*

George Bratley deputised for Tony Leach at centre half in three League games during the second half of 1932/33, making his debut in a 2-0 defeat at West Brom when he was given a torrid time by 'W.G.' Richardson. A strong tackler, he played in both full-back positions and made over 100 appearances for Rotherham and almost 90 for Barrow before the Second World War.

BRAYSHAW, Edward
Defender

Appearances: 51   Goals: 2
Born: Kirkstall, Leeds, May 1863
Died: Wortley, Sheffield, 20 November 1908.

CAREER
CLUBS: *Walkley, WEDNESDAY (free, August 1884-April 1891), Lockwood Brothers, Sheffield Rovers, Grimsby Town*
OTHER: *licensee in Sheffield.*

'Teddy' Brayshaw, the son of a Sheffield detective, was a huge favourite with the Owls' supporters. He played his part in the club's early years, especially when the transition was made from being an amateur organisation into a professional body. A robust, well-built and resilient defender, he played for England versus Ireland at Bramall Lane in 1887 – he was so proud of his cap that he wore it in club matches for months afterwards. One of the finest defenders ever to play for the Owls, Brayshaw collected an FA Cup runners-up medal and a Football Alliance winners' medal in 1890 but a year later was forced to retire due to a serious foot injury at the age of twenty-eight. Earlier he had gained winners' medals with the Owls for triumphs in the 1887 and 1888 Sheffield Challenge Cup finals, won the 1888 Wharncliffe Charity Cup final of 1888 and had a trial for England (Blues versus Whites) in 1889/90. The last days of his life were spent in the South Yorkshire Asylum.

BREEDON, John Norman
Goalkeeper

Appearances: 47
Born: South, Hiendley, Barnsley, Yorkshire, 29 December 1907
Died: Leeds, 1990

CAREER
CLUBS: Barnsley, WEDNESDAY (£1,200, November 1930-July 1935), Manchester United, Burnley, Halifax Town (manager), Bradford Park Avenue (manager), Leeds United (scout).
WARTIME GUEST APPEARANCES: Bolton Wanderers, Manchester City, Rochdale.

Jack Breedon's chances were limited at Hillsborough owing to the form of Jack Brown. Nevertheless, when called upon he performed with confidence and style, having his best run in the League side (nineteen successive appearances) between March and October 1932. He turned down the chance to manage New Brighton in 1946, owing to his wife's reluctance to leave Leeds.

BRELSFORD, Charles Walter
Left-back

Appearances: 7
Born: Darnall, Sheffield, June 1890
Deceased by 1960

CAREER
CLUBS: Kilnhurst, Buxton, WEDNESDAY (£30, August 1911-May 1919), Sheffield United, South Shields, Castleford Town, Mansfield Town.
OTHER: army.

Reserve to Jimmy Spoors, 'Chas' Brelsford, brother of Thomas William, made only seven senior appearances for the Owls in peacetime football, his debut coming in a 5-0 home League win over Oldham in November 1912. He appeared in 88 First World War games but unfortunately failed to get into South Shields' first team. A broken leg ended his career prematurely. Three of his brothers played football – Ben for Wednesday reserves and others, Bill for Sheffield United and Tom (below).

BRELSFORD, Thomas William
Half-back

Appearances: 122   Goals: 6
Born: Attercliffe, Sheffield, 12 April 1895
Died: Sheffield, September 1946

CAREER
CLUBS: Castleford Town, WEDNESDAY (free, August 1915-April 1924), Barrow, Rotherham United, Wombwell Town.

Able to occupy all three half-back positions, Tom Brelsford succeeded Bert Eggo in the Owls' side halfway through 1920/21. He made his senior debut the previous March at Liverpool, after making 52 appearances during the First World War (2 goals). A worthy competitor, strong and mobile, he missed only four matches in 1921/22 and eventually lost his place in 1924 to

Oliver Levick. He made 184 League appearances in his career.

BRETNALL, Charles Oscar
Centre forward

Appearances: 1
Born: Chesterfield, 1889
Died: Burton-on-Trent, 1962

CAREER
CLUBS: Sheffield FC, Midland Athletic, Worksop Town, WEDNESDAY (£10, August 1919-May 1920), Rotherham County, Lincoln City, Worksop Town, Denaby United, Rotherham County.

Signed by the Owls prior to the resumption of League football after the First World War, Oscar Bretnall made only one senior appearance for the club, partnering Colin Mackay in attack in a first round FA Cup replay defeat at Darlington in January 1920. His father, Charles, played for Burton Wanderers.

BRIEN, Anthony James
Defender

Appearances: 1
Born: Dublin, 10 February 1969

CAREER
CLUBS: Leicester City, Chesterfield, Rotherham United, WEDNESDAY (n/c June-July 1995), West Bromwich Albion, Mansfield Town, Chester City, Hull City; non-League (1998-2000)
OTHER: worked for the soft drinks firm, GBL International (Chesterfield).

A Republic of Ireland youth international (capped at Leicester), Tony Brien was a strong, efficient defender whose only game for the Owls was against FC Basel in the InterToto Cup in June 1995.

BRIGHT, Mark Abraham
Striker

Appearances: 148+22   *Goals: 70*
Born: Stoke-on-Trent, 6 June 1962

CAREER
CLUBS: Port Vale, Leicester City, Crystal Palace, WEDNESDAY (£875,000, September 1992-January 1997), Millwall (L), Sion, Charlton Athletic
OTHER: soccer pundit on Sky TV.

During his eighteen-year career, Mark Bright scored over 200 goals in more than 600 matches, 114 of them in 286 outings for Palace with whom he gained a FMC winners' medal

Mark Bright

in 1991. Tall and direct, with an eye for goal, he struggled to fill the role vacated by Gary Lineker at Leicester and faced a rare degree of hostility (some of it racist) from the fans. After turning down other clubs, Bright switched to Selhurst Park where he became an instant hit, winning the Golden Boot award as the Second Division's top scorer in 1988, when Palace gained promotion to the top flight. He continued to produce the goods with the Owls, forming an excellent partnership with David Hirst. Top-scorer in his first three seasons at Hillsborough with 20, 23 and 13 goals respectively, Bright lost his place when Andy Booth and Guy Whittingham became first-choice strikers in 1996. He is married to actress and pop star, Michelle Gayle.

BRISCOE, James Patrick
Centre forward

Appearances: 5   Goals: 3
Born: Swinton-on-Deane, 14 October 1923

CAREER
CLUBS: Raith Rovers, WEDNESDAY (free, October 1944-May 1947), Gainsborough Trinity, Ramsgate, Margate, Stevenage Athletic (manager).

A reserve at Hillsborough, Jim Briscoe scored in each of his first two League games for the Owls versus Manchester City and Burnley in October 1946. At that time the club was struggling to find a regular centre forward and Briscoe was the fourth player to be used in that position that season. Although he netted again in his fourth match he failed to hold on to the no.9 shirt.

BRISCOE, Lee Stephen
Left-back

Appearances: 55+35   Goals: 1
Born: Pontefract, Yorkshire, 30 September 1975

CAREER
CLUBS: WEDNESDAY (May 1992-July 2000), Manchester City (L), Burnley, Preston North End.

An England Under-21 international (5 caps), Lee 'Brisser' Briscoe was a no-nonsense competitor who gave nothing less than 100 per cent every time he took the field. He gained a regular place in Wednesday's First XI in 1995/96 but generally was regarded as a genuine squad player. His League debut came in 1993 when, as a substitute, he helped the Owls beat Spurs 3-1 in a Premiership game at White Hart Lane. His only goal for Wednesday came in the last minute of the home encounter with Arsenal in September 1998, clinching a 1-0 win. Paolo Di Canio was sent off in this game for pushing the referee.

BRITTLETON, James Thomas
Defender

Appearances: 373   Goals: 33
Born: Winsford, Cheshire, 28 April 1879
Died: Winsford, 22 February, 1955

CAREER
CLUBS: Winsford United, Stockport County, WEDNESDAY (£300, January 1905-May 1920), Stoke, Winsford Celtic, Winsford United
OTHER: worked for ICI, later became a licensee.

Tom Brittleton started as an inside forward – signed by the Owls for a record fee of £300 – but he proved later what a versatile player he was by appearing at full-back, centre half and centre forward before settling down as a wing half, from where he performed with great endurance, determination and skill. Strong and reliable, he was a long-throw expert who could hurl the ball up to forty yards from the touchline. He starred in Wednesday's 1907 FA Cup-winning side (versus Everton), later took over as team captain and in 1912 gained the first of five full England caps. He also played twice for the Football League (1910 and 1913). Brittleton was something of a character on and off the field and in 1911 rejected the opportunity to tour South Africa with the FA, simply because he wanted to stay in England (Yorkshire) to enjoy the summer fishing. He was almost forty-one when he played his last League game for the Owls versus Oldham in May 1920 and his last senior outing for Stoke was against Blackpool in April 1925, a fortnight short of his forty-sixth birthday. He remained the oldest player ever to appear for the Potters, until October 1961 when Stan Matthews returned to the club from Blackpool aged forty-six years and nine months. Brittleton, who helped Stoke win promotion from the Second Division in 1922, made 512 League appearances during his career. He also scored 8 goals in 130 games for the Owls during the First World War. His son, John Thomas Brittleton, played for Chester and Aston Villa in the 1920s.

BROADBENT, Albert Henry

Inside, outside left

Appearances: 83   Goals: 17
Born: West Bromwich, 20 August 1934
Died: Sheffield, November 2006

CAREER
CLUBS: Dudley Town, West Bromwich Albion, Notts County, WEDNESDAY (£7,400 plus Peter Johnson, July 1955-December 1957), Rotherham United, Doncaster Rovers, Lincoln City, Doncaster Rovers, Bradford Park Avenue, Hartlepool United, Rotherham United (player, assistant trainer), Scarborough;
OTHER: Army; now lives in Hackenthorpe, Sheffield.

A very capable and enthusiastic forward who preferred the outside left berth, Albert Broadbent had an excellent career in League football, scoring almost 120 goals in over 600 appearances in 18 years. He made his debut for Notts County, aged seventeen, and played his first game for the Owls in a 5-3 home win over Plymouth in August 1955, having replaced Jackie Marriott on the left flank. He scored 12 goals in 41 League games that season, helping Wednesday win the Second Division title. A regular the following season (injuries apart), he eventually gave way to Alan Finney who switched from the right wing. After leaving Hillsborough, Broadbent did well in his two spells with Doncaster, netting 42 goals in 212 outings.

BROLLY, Thomas Henry

Defender

Appearances: 2
Born: Belfast, 1 June 1912
Died: Sutton, Surrey, 4 June 1986

CAREER
CLUBS: Linfield, Belfast Crusaders, Glenavon, Lurgan, Linfield, WEDNESDAY (£125, May 1933-July 1935), Millwall, Aldershot, Linfield, Northampton Town, Crystal Palace (trainer), Chelmsford City (trainer), Wandsworth (coach)
OTHER: worked for the GPO; Army PE instructor, Second World War.

Tom Brolly, strong, able-bodied and utterly reliable, played superbly well in Ireland but

Tom Brolly

unfortunately failed to settle at Hillsborough and made only two League appearances for the Owls, in home games against Derby and Wolves in 1933/34, before moving to Millwall. He helped the Lions reach the FA Cup semi-finals in 1937 and win the Third Division (South) championship a year later. He also gained four caps for Northern Ireland, lining up against Wales in 1937 and 1938, and England and Wales in 1939. He skippered the London club during and after the Second World War and made 260 appearances for Millwall, for whom he starred in over 100 other games. He was known as 'The Professor' when coaching.

BROMBY, Leigh David
Defender

Appearances: 117+3   Goals: 2
Born: Dewsbury, 2 June 1980

CAREER
CLUBS: WEDNESDAY (July 1998-July 2004), Mansfield Town (L), Norwich City (L), Sheffield United.

An England Schoolboy international, Leigh Bromby, a sound, competent footballer and long-throw expert, who can operate at right-back or at the heart of the defence, certainly imposed himself on opponents during his six years at Hillsborough. He played some of his best football for the Owls in 2003/04 but was then surprisingly exchanged for Blades' star Alan Quinn.

BROOMES, Marlon Charles
Defender

Appearances: 19+1
Born: Birmingham, 28 November 1977

CAREER Blackburn Rovers, Swindon Town (L), Queens Park Rangers (L), Grimsby Town (L), WEDNESDAY (free, December 2001-May 2002), Burnley, Preston North End, Stoke City.

Capped by England at Schoolboy, Youth and Under-21 levels, playing twice for the latter, Marlon Broomes, who prefers the left side of defence, produced some excellent displays during his short stay with the Owls, for whom he made his debut in a 2-1 League defeat at Gillingham in December 2001. He helped Preston reach the 2005 play-off final, when they were beaten by West Ham.

BROWN, James
Left-back

Appearances: 10
Born: Scotland, circa 1869
Deceased by 1935

CAREER
CLUBS: Dundee, WEDNESDAY (free, August 1892-April 1894).

Jim Brown spent two years with Wednesday, making his debut in place of Jack Darroch in a 6-0 home win over the FA Cup holders West Bromwich Albion in January 1893.

BROWN, John Henry
Goalkeeper

Appearances: 509
Born: Worksop, 19 March 1899
Died: Sheffield, 9 April 1962

CAREER
CLUBS: Worksop Town, WEDNESDAY (£360, February 1923-September 1937), Hartlepool United
OTHER: later a licensee; also worked for the Sheffield Drill & Twist County.

Jack Brown, who started out as a centre forward, became a goalkeeper by accident. Tall, hefty, broad-shouldered, courageous and fearsome, his usefulness was not always confined to his penalty-area – he would often race out of the box to avert danger, but without taking foolish risks. Highly efficient, sound, dependable and a safe handler of the ball, he won six caps for England and played twice for the Football League (1927-30), was an ever-present when Wednesday won the Second Division title in 1926, helped the team clinch successive First Division championships in 1929 and 1930, received an FA Cup winners' medal in 1935 and also helped win the Charity Shield. He produced some outstanding saves in the 1935 cup final against West Bromwich Albion when Ellis Rimmer scored two late goals to secure a 4-2 victory. Gaining a regular place in the side in 1924, he was the first 'keeper to make 500 appearances for the Owls and, in fact, went on to play in 465 League games for the club, being an ever-present in 1925/26 and 1928/29. He played in 97 consecutive first team games between December 1924 and February 1927 and missed only 13 League matches out of 210 between 1925 and 1930. He suffered his fair share of injuries – he was badly hurt when making his England debut in the 3-3 draw with Wales in 1927 – but he always bounced back. He lies second (behind Andy Wilson) in the club's list of top appearance-makers. Prior to joining Wednesday, Brown was superb when Worksop held Spurs to a 0-0 draw at White Hart Lane in a third round FA Cup-tie. The non-League club lost the replay 9-0.

BROWN, Robert Christopher
Midfield

Appearances: 17+4 Goals: 3
Born: Plymouth, Devon, 24 November 1953

CAREER
CLUBS: Chelsea, WEDNESDAY (free, August 1974-May 1976), Aldershot (L), Boston United, Thionville, Caen (coach), Dunkerque (coach).

Despite spending four years at Stamford Bridge, midfielder Bobby Brown failed to make Chelsea's first team. He finally made his League debut at the age of twenty, as a second-half substitute for Wednesday versus Bristol Rovers at Hillsborough in August 1974. He made 16 of his 21 senior appearances for the club in that 1974/75 relegation season when he also claimed his first goal – the winner (1-0) at Bolton in September.

BROWN, Richard Harold
Left half

Appearances: 2
Born: Sheffield, 1870
Died: Sheffield, 1940

CAREER
CLUBS: WEDNESDAY (season 1893-94).

Dick Brown's two outings for the Owls were both at home, against Newton Heath in September 1893 and Sheffield United two months later. He deputised for Scottish international Robert Glen on both occasions.

BROWN, Robert Neil
Inside forward

Appearances: 67   Goals: 9
Born: Cambuslang, Scotland, August 1870
Died: Glasgow, 1943

CAREER
CLUBS: Blantyre Celtic, Cambuslang, WEDNESDAY (free, August 1891-July 1894), Third Lanark, Bolton Wanderers, Burnley
OTHER: insurance agent.

Robert 'Sparrow' Brown played inside right in Wednesday's first-ever League game, a 1-0 win at Notts County in September 1892. A strong player with a direct approach, he scored 7 goals in 30 League and cup games during that initial campaign, including a brace on his home debut in a 5-2 win over Accrington. Later in his career Brown switched to centre half and played four games for Burnley, in that position, at the end of the 1896/97 season.

BRUCE, Alexander Stephen
Defender

Appearances: 8+1
Born: Norwich, 28 September 1984

CAREER
CLUBS: Manchester United (academy), Blackburn Rovers, Oldham Athletic, Birmingham City, Oldham Athletic, WEDNESDAY (loan, March-May 2005), Ipswich Town.

Son of Steve Bruce, the former Norwich, Gillingham and Manchester United defender, and now manager of Birmingham City, Alex Bruce had only 16 first-class games under his belt when he joined the Owls on loan in 2005. He bedded in quickly at Hillsborough and made nine appearances, helping the Owls win the play-off final versus Hartlepool.

BRUCE, Robert Frederick
Inside left

Appearances: 6
Born: Paisley, 29 January 1906
Deceased

CAREER
CLUBS: Aberdeen, Middlesbrough, WEDNESDAY (£2,500, October 1935-August 1936), Ipswich Town, Mossley (player-manager).

Scottish international inside left Bobby Bruce made all his senior appearances for the Owls over a period of four weeks in October/November 1935 when he partnered Neil Dewar in new-look forward line. Able to give a good, honest account of himself in any company, he was a

shade on the small side at 5ft 6ins but always relished a battle with much bigger and tougher opponents. Elusive when running with the ball, he was a smart, clever footballer, a neat passer but rather inconsistent. He helped the Owls win the 1935 Charity Shield and Middlesbrough the Second Division championship in 1929 when he scored 11 goals playing alongside George Camsell. His only cap was against Austria in 1933 and before moving to Ayresome Park he was the first player to score a hat-trick in a Scottish Cup-tie and still finish on the losing side – this was for Aberdeen versus Raith in 1928 (lost 4-3). He netted 45 goals in 110 games for the Dons and 71 in 253 for Middlesbrough.

BRUNT, Christopher
Midfield

*Appearances: 122+30 *   Goals: 24 **
Born: Belfast, 14 December 1984

CAREER
CLUBS: Glasgow Rangers, St Andrew's, Middlesbrough, Cardiff City, WEDNESDAY (free, March 2004).

Chris Brunt did not make a first-team appearance during his three years with Middlesbrough but he quickly made his mark at Hillsborough, scoring twice in nine games in his first season of League football. Capped by Northern Ireland at Under-21 and Under-23 levels, he's now appeared in seven full internationals, the first as a substitute against Sweden in 2004. Brunt prefers to play on the left side of midfield and he certainly gave his all in Wednesday's 2005 play-off final win over Hartlepool.

BRYANT, Steven Paul
Left-back

Appearances: 2+1
Born: Islington, 5 September 1953

CAREER

CLUBS: *Birmingham City, WEDNESDAY (loan, August-September 1976), Northampton Town, Portsmouth, Northampton Town, later played in Australia.*

Originally a winger of considerable guile, Steve Bryant was successfully converted into a left-back at St Andrew's. He appeared in 42 games for Blues and had 3 outings on loan with the Owls before joining Northampton. Switched into midfield, he made 117 appearances for the Cobblers (two spells) and later starred in 127 games for Portsmouth.

BULLEN, Lee
Defender

Appearances: 100+22 * Goals: 8 *
Born: Edinburgh, 29 March 1971

CAREER

CLUBS: *Dunfermline Athletic, Penicuik Athletic, Meadowbank Thistle, Stenhousemuir, Whitburn Stanmore CYC, Kui-Tan, Golden AA, South China AA, PAE Kalamata, Dunfermline Athletic, WEDNESDAY (free, July 2004).*

Lee Bullen joyously stepped up to collect the trophy after the Owls' 4-2 play-off final win over Hartlepool in 2005. A strong, solid defender who can also play up front in an emergency, he is good in the air and on the ground and appeared in 185 competitive games north of the border, coming on as a sub for Dunfermline in the 2004 Scottish Cup final defeat by Celtic. He also played six games for the Hong Kong national team.

BURCHILL, Mark James
Utility

Appearances: 4+1
Born: Broxburn, Scotland, 18 August 1980

CAREER

CLUBS: *Celtic Boys' Club, Celtic, Birmingham City, Ipswich Town, Portsmouth, Dundee, Wigan Athletic, WEDNESDAY (loan, December 2003-January 2004), Rotherham United, Heart of Midlothian, Dunfermline Athletic.*

Capped 6 times by Scotland at senior level and on 15 occasions by the Under-21s, former schoolboy international midfielder Mark Burchill made 64 appearances for Celtic before joining Portsmouth in 2001. He made a decent enough start to his Fratton Park career but then drifted out of contention, having to take on a series of loan spells to keep match fit. He won the Scottish League Cup with Celtic in 2000 and the First Division championship with Pompey in 2003.

BURGESS, Harry
Inside forward

Appearances: 234 Goals: 77
Born: Alderley Edge, Wilmslow, 20 August 1904
Died: Wimslow, 6 October 1957

CAREER

CLUBS: *Wimslow Albion, Alderley Edge, Stockport County, Sandbach Ramblers, WEDNESDAY (£3,500, August 1929-March 1935), Chelsea*
WARTIME GUEST APPEARANCES: *Brentford, Reading, Fulham, Southampton, Stockport County*
OTHER: *worked for the Ministry of Defence; Stockport licensee.*

An England international, capped against Ireland, Scotland, France and Belgium in 1930/31, scoring against the Irish and Belgians, Harry Burgess was a stocky, forceful inside forward, clever on the ball, who gave Wednesday six years' excellent service. He scored with clockwork regularity and was a first choice at Hillsborough until his departure. His best season was his first, 1929/30, when, as Jack Allen's partner, he scored 19 goals (includ-

Harry Burgess

Hillsborough he played in a handful of games for Rotherham before appearing in 250 senior games for Halifax whom he served for almost six years. He ended his career in 1976 with 299 League appearances under his belt.

BURKINSHAW, John Dean Lewis
Utility

Appearances: 61   Goals: 10
Born: Kilnhurst, Rotherham, 12 May 1890
Died: Wortley, Sheffield, 1947

CAREER
CLUBS: Kilnhurst Town, Grimsby Town, Rotherham County, Swindon Town, WEDNESDAY (£150, August 1913-August 1919), Rotherham Town, Bradford Park Avenue, Accrington Stanley, Denaby United, Wath Athletic, Chicago.
WARTIME GUEST APPEARANCES: Swindon Town, Barnsley.

Of footballing stock – his brothers Ralph and Lawrence also played in the 1920s – Jack Burkinshaw was seventeen when he made his League debut for Grimsby and played his last competitive game in America, aged thirty-five. A competent and versatile performer, able to occupy both wing half and inside forward positions, he appeared in all three Divisions of the Football League and also in the Southern League, his eight goals helping Swindon win the title in 1911. He scored on his home debut for the Owls versus Manchester United in September 1913 and played in 34 games in his first season at Hillsborough before slipping into the reserves. He came back strongly after the First World War, having hit 37 goals in 95 regional games during the hostilities, but his efforts weren't enough to prevent Wednesday slipping into the Second Division. He later went down with Bradford. Burkinshaw was asked to play as guest for Swindon in an exhibition match in Paris. He impressed and subsequently signed for the club.

ing one on his debut against Aston Villa) as Wednesday retained their First Division crown. He contributed 15 the following season when the Owls finished third and also found the net in the Charity Shield defeat by Arsenal (1930). Burgess, who was admired everywhere he played, scored 72 goals in 121 appearances for Stockport. He also enjoyed golf and cricket.

BURGIN, Andrew
Full-back

Appearances: 3
Born: Sheffield, 6 March 1947

CAREER
CLUBS: Hillsborough Boys Club, Sheffield Boys, WEDNESDAY (August 1962-August 1967), Rotherham United, Detroit Cougars, Rotherham United, Halifax Town, Blackburn Rovers
OTHER: health club manager, caretaker at a private school in Blackburn.

Andy Burgin made one League and two FA Cup appearances for the Owls. After leaving

BURKINSHAW, Laurence
Outside right

Appearances: 25   Goals: 7
Born: Kilnhurst, Rotherham, 2 December 1893
Died: Mexborough, 5 May 1969

CAREER
CLUBS: Kilnhurst County School, Kilnhurst Town, Mexborough Town, WEDNESDAY (£65 with Martin Bradley, April 1910-July 1914), Rotherham Town, Stalybridge Celtic, Kilnhurst Town, Birmingham, Halifax Town, Mexborough Town
WARTIME GUEST APPEARANCES: Barnsley, Rotherham Town
OTHER: employed in a Swinton steelworks.

Younger brother of John, 'Lol' Burkinshaw was a skilful, fast-raiding winger who loved to take on his full-back on the outside, having the ability to wrong-foot his opponent. He had to work hard for his place at Hillsborough, mak-

Laurence Burkinshaw

ing only 9 appearances in his first 3 seasons. He was a Second Division championship winner with Birmingham in 1921, scoring six goals and setting up plenty more for his colleagues. During his career he spent a year in prison after being found guilty, with others, of assaulting a policeman.

BURRIDGE, Ben James Herbert
Half-back

Appearances: 26
Born: Beamish, Co. Durham, 11 March 1898
Died: Oldham, 22 December 1977

CAREER
CLUBS: Oxhill Villa, Houghton Rovers, Annfield Plain, Darlington, WEDNESDAY (£1,200, June 1926-June 1930), Oldham Athletic, Macclesfield, Hyde United, Hurst (player, manager, committee member)
WARTIME GUEST APPEARANCES: Ashton National.

A player with plenty of constructive ability, Bert Burridge nevertheless struggled to hold down a regular place with Wednesday, averaging just over six appearances per season. He did, however, skipper the Owls' Central League championship winning side in 1929 as the seniors claimed the First Division title. He hit 7 goals in 92 League games for Darlington. He was a member of Macclesfield's Cheshire League and Cup double-winning team of 1932.

BURROWS, David
Left-back

Appearances: 23
Born: Dudley, 25 October 1968

CAREER
CLUBS: West Bromwich Albion, Alexandra FC (coach), Liverpool, West Ham United, Everton,

David Burrows

Coventry City, Birmingham City, WEDNESDAY (free, March 2002, caretaker-manager, October 2002, retired, May 2003).

David Burrows made his League debut for West Bromwich Albion against the Owls in April 1986 while still an apprentice. He developed fast and in 1988 Kenny Dalglish signed him for Liverpool. He went from strength to strength at Anfield, gained 3 England 'B' caps and 7 at under-21 level and was rewarded with winners' medals for triumphs in the Charity Shield (1989), Football League (1990) and FA Cup (1992), while also making over 200 appearances for the Reds. Burrows, who preferred the left-back position but could also play in central defence, spent a season with the Hammers before going back to Merseyside. He never settled at Goodison Park and after that appeared in over 100 League games for Coventry before winding down his career at St Andrew's and Hillsborough. He captained the Owls on occasions but suffered injury problems and his experience and leadership were sorely missed as the team battled against relegation. Burrows retired with almost 500 appearances under his belt.

BURROWS, Horace
Left half

Appearances: 261   Goals: 8
Born: Sutton-in-Ashfield, Notts, 11 March 1910
Died: Sutton-in-Ashfield, Notts, 22 March 1969

CAREER
CLUBS: Coventry City, Mansfield Town, WEDNESDAY (£200, May 1931-May 1942), Millwall (guest), Ollerton Colliery (player-manager)
OTHER: manager of a sports outfitter's shop in Sutton-in-Ashfield.

After making 44 appearances for Mansfield, with whom he gained a Notts FA Senior Cup winners' medal (1931), Horace Burrows joined Wednesday just as the Stags won a place in the Football League. A well-groomed, stylish and confident player, he became a regular in the Owls' first team in December 1932 and remained in the side until the outbreak of the Second World War. He gained three England caps versus Hungary, Czechoslovakia and Holland in 1934 and won FA Cup and Charity Shield winners' medals the following year. Burrows, a very creative player, had a run of 136 consecutive appearances up to March 1936. He was badly missed (through injury) in 1937 and 1938, but after regaining his fitness he performed superbly well in the last pre-Second World War campaign as the Owls just missed out on promotion from the Second Division. He made 48 first-team appearances during the hostilities when he served in Al Alamein. His son Adrian played for Mansfield, Northampton, Plymouth and Southend.

B

BURTON, Deon John
Forward

Appearances: 52+9 *   Goals: 16 *
Born: Ashford, Kent, 25 October 1976

CAREER
CLUBS: Portsmouth, Cardiff City, Derby County, Barnsley, Stoke City, Portsmouth, Walsall, Swindon Town, Brentford, Rotherham United, WEDNESDAY (free, January 2006).

Jamaican international (49 caps), Deon Burton joined the Owls to add some bite to the attack. He has now netted over 80 goals in club football, top-scoring for Brentford in 2004/05. He gained a First Division championship winners' medal with Portsmouth in 2003.

BURTON, Henry Arthur
Full-back

Appearances: 199
Born: West Bromwich, 27 April 1882
Died: Sheffield, 28 August 1923

CAREER
CLUBS: Attercliffe, WEDNESDAY (£10, August 1902-March 1909), West Bromwich Albion, Scunthorpe & Lindsay United
OTHER: played hockey for Darnell and golf at Sitwell Park.

Harry Burton was a very capable left-back, well built, who used his physique to full advantage. He won a League Championship medal with the Owls in 1904 and collected an FA Cup winners' medal three years later. Burton had the misfortune to concede a penalty and miss one at the other end as Wednesday went out of the cup to Glossop in February 1909. He played in only four more games after that, received a benefit, and eventually moved to West Bromwich Albion with George Simpson.

BURTON, Kenneth Owen
Left-back

Appearances: 58+3 Goals: 2
Born: Sheffield, 11 February 1950

CAREER
CLUBS: WEDNESDAY (July 1965-July 1973), Chesterfield (L), Peterborough United (L), Chesterfield, Halifax Town, Alfreton Town, Sheffield Club and others
OTHER: postman in Sheffield.

England Youth international Ken Burton made his League debut in November 1968 against Stoke, deputising for Don Megson. The following season he appeared in 24 games, scoring his first goal for the club in a 2-1 home defeat by Leeds. He had a further 25 outings in 1970/71 before losing his place to Dave Clements. After leaving Wednesday he hit 7 goals in 237 League games in seven years with Chesterfield.

BUTLER, Barry
Centre half

Appearances: 36   Goals: 1
Born: Stockton-on-Tees, 30 July 1934
Died: Norwich, 9 April 1966

CAREER
CLUBS: South Bank, Middlesbrough, Dundee, WEDNESDAY (£300, September 1952-July 1957), Norwich City (player-coach).

After five years at Hillsborough, where he acted as a reserve to centre half Ralph O'Donnell, Barry Butler moved to Carrow Road where he became captain and star performer, appearing in 349 senior games for the Canaries, whom he helped reach the semi-final of the FA Cup (1959) and win the League Cup (1962). He recovered from a broken leg, fractured cheekbone and wrist and a severe bout of pneumonia at Norwich, where he was regarded by many as the finest centre half in the club's history. He was sadly killed when his car collided with a bus.

BUTTERY, Edward
Defender

Appearances: 11
Born: Sheffield, 1852
Deceased by 1935

CAREER
CLUBS: WEDNESDAY (August 1876-May 1882).

Tough-tackling Ted Buttery was a regular for the Owls throughout his six-year stay at the club. He lined up at left-back in Wednesday's first-ever FA Cup-tie at Blackburn in December 1880 and, in fact, his last appearance was also against Blackburn, in the semi-final of the same competition in March 1882. He starred in four Sheffield Challenge Cup final wins (1877, 1878, 1881 and 1883) and helped Wednesday twice win the Wharncliffe Charity Cup (1879 and 1882).

BUTTERY, Thomas
Right-back

Appearances: 2
Born: Sheffield, 1855
Died: Sheffield, 1912

CAREER
CLUBS: WEDNESDAY (August 1878-August 1881), Lockwood Brothers, Preston North End.

Tom Buttery, strong and determined, played alongside his brother Ernest Edward at full-back in Wednesday's first-ever FA Cup-tie versus Blackburn in 1880 and also starred in the Owls' Wharncliffe Charity Cup-winning team of 1879 versus Heeley.

C

CALLAGHAN, John
Utility

Appearances: 4   Goals: 2
Born: Glasgow, Scotland, 1870
Died: Scotland, 1937

CAREER
CLUBS: Middlesbrough Ironopolis, Hunslet, WEDNESDAY (free, May 1895-December 1896).

Jack Callaghan occupied several positions but preferred a forward's role. He never settled with Wednesday and had his registration cancelled for disciplinary reasons after scoring twice in his last League game for the club versus West Bromwich Albion in September 1896.

CAMERON, Daniel
Full-back

Appearances: 38   Goals: 1
Born: Dundee, 9 November 1953

CAREER
CLUBS: WEDNESDAY (July 1969-April 1976), Colchester United (L), Preston North End, Dundee, PG Rangers, Hellenic
OTHER: self-employed courier; manager of a furniture delivery service; coached in South Africa.

A useful full-back, strong and competitive, Danny Campbell always worked hard at his game. He made his League debut for the Owls at West Brom in October 1973, deputising for Peter Rodrigues in a 2-0 defeat. He was given 21 outings that season and scored his only goal for the club in a 4-1 defeat at Fulham in early February. He made 122 League appearances for Preston.

C

CAMPBELL, James
Half-back

Appearances: 157 Goals: 3
Born: Newhaven, Midlothian, 12 November 1886
Died: Edinburgh, 2 May 1925.

CAREER
CLUBS: Leith Athletic, WEDNESDAY (£450 with Paterson, January 1911-May 1920), Huddersfield Town, Edinburgh St Bernard's
OTHER: Military Service – First World War.

Half-back Jimmy Campbell arrived at the club at the same time as David McLean. He developed a tremendous reputation north of the border for his elegant, graceful and inspirational performances and proved to be a terrific acquisition. He made his debut for the Owls against Bury in February 1911 and played in 110 consecutive League matches before having a break! He maintained a high standard throughout his career and was outstanding in 1912/13 when he gained his only cap for Scotland versus Wales. He was a shadow of his former self after spending four years at war.

CAMPBELL, Philip Anthony
Outside left

Appearances: 0+1
Born: Barnsley, 16 October 1961

CAREER
CLUBS: WEDNESDAY (May 1977-May 1981), Barnsley, Scarborough
OTHER: self-employed plumber.

Phil Campbell's only outing for Wednesday was as a substitute for Gordon Owen in a 2-1 home League win over Bristol City in September 1980. He had one of the shortest playing careers of any Wednesday player.

CAPEWELL, Ronald
Goalkeeper

Appearances: 30
Born: Sheffield, 26 July 1929

CAREER
CLUBS: WEDNESDAY (May 1949-July 1954), Hull City, non-League (1955-63)
OTHER: bricklayer and stonemason, later a delivery-man for Whitbread's Brewery.

Ron 'Lofty' Capewell, tall and weighty, contested the no.1 position at Hillsborough with Dave McIntosh, 26 of his 30 appearances coming in succession between September 1952 and February 1953.

CAPPER, Alfred
Winger

Appearances: 62 Goals: 4
Born: Knutsford, Cheshire, February 1891
Died: Winnington, 31 October 1955

CAREER
CLUBS: Northwich Victoria, Manchester United, Witton Albion, WEDNESDAY (£160, May 1914-August 1921), Brentford.
WARTIME GUEST APPEARANCES: Manchester City
OTHER: Army – First World War.

Alf Capper, fast and clever, was reserve to George Wall at Manchester United and made only one appearance for the Reds against Liverpool in 1912. Criticised in that game for a poor performance, he subsequently returned to non-League with Witton before switching to Wednesday. The scorer of 10 goals in 65 outings for the Owls in the First World War, he later did well with Brentford and his career realised 156 League appearances.

CARBONE, Benito
Midfield

Appearances: 96+11   Goals: 26
Born: Bagarna Calabra, Italy, 14 August 1971

CAREER
CLUBS: Calabra, Torino, Reggiana, Casertana, Ascoli, Napoli, Internationale, WEDNESDAY (£3m, October 1996-October 1999), Aston Villa, Bradford City, Derby County, Middlesbrough, Como, AC Parma, Catanzaro.

'Beni' Carbone was a talented but temperamental player. He helped Italy win the 1994 UEFA Under-21 tournament and made over 200 appearances in Serie 'A' and 'B' before moving to Hillsborough. He went on to average 1 goal every 4 games, including 6 in 27 outings in his first season (1996/97). Only 5ft 6ins tall, Carbone was never shy to battle it out with tough opponents and he certainly gave good account of himself. Very effective at running at defenders, he had great ball control and good pace over twenty to thirty yards. He left Hillsborough under a dark cloud – after refusing to play as a sub (against Southampton) he called for a cab and went off to Italy by plane. Soon afterwards he switched to Villa Park, going on to score a hat-trick in an FA Cup-tie versus Leeds, one of his strikes earning him 'Goal of the Season'. A player with a fiery temper, and at times an attitude, he was later paid £30,000 a week by Bradford.

CARGILL, David Anderson
Outside left

Appearances: 13
Born: Arbroath, 21 July 1936

CAREER
CLUBS: Burnley, WEDNESDAY (£5,000, September 1956-April 1958), Derby County, Lincoln City, Arbroath
OTHER: became a licensee.

At his best, Dave Cargill was a fast-raiding winger who spent a lot of time in the reserves at both Burnley and Wednesday before making his mark with Derby. He had Albert Broadbent ahead of him at Hillsborough and made 11 of his 13 appearances for the Owls in 1956/57.

CARR, Christopher Paul
Defender

Appearances: 0+2
Born: Newcastle, 14 December 1984

CAREER
CLUBS: Sunderland (academy), Newcastle United (academy), WEDNESDAY (free, March-December 2004), Hartlepool United, Macclesfield Town, Queen of the South.

Chris Carr started 2003/04 in Newcastle's reserve team and ended it having appeared in two League games for the Owls, while also skippering the Second XI. An assured performer who made his debut as a late substitute in a 3-2 defeat at Luton in May 2004, his contract at Hillsborough was cancelled by mutual consent.

CARR, Franz Alexander
Outside right

Appearances: 11+3
Born: Preston, 24 September 1966

CAREER
CLUBS: Blackburn Rovers, Nottingham Forest, WEDNESDAY (loan, December 1989-March 1990), West Ham United (L), Newcastle United, Sheffield United, Leicester City, Aston Villa, Reggiana, Everton, Bolton Wanderers, West Bromwich Albion, Grimsby Town, Pittsburgh Riverhounds, Runcorn
OTHER: football agent.

Franz Carr was never given a chance by Blackburn but after moving to Forest he developed as an exceptionally fine winger, winning nine England Under-21 caps, having previously played for the Youth team. He made over 150 appearances for Forest, gaining winners' medals in the FMC and League Cup finals of 1989 and 1990 respectively. Long periods in the wilderness disrupted Carr's progress after he left The City Ground and, in fact, he made less than 100 appearances in 14 years up to 1998. He made his debut for the Owls on Boxing Day 1989 at Liverpool and his last outing was at home to Manchester United three months later.

CARSON, Scott Paul
Goalkeeper

Appearances: 9
Born: Whitehaven, 3 September 1985

CAREER
CLUBS: Leeds United, Liverpool, WEDNESDAY (loan, March-May 2006), Charlton Athletic (L).

The 6ft 3ins England Youth and Under-21 international goalkeeper Scott Carson did not make the first team at Elland Road and was second choice at Anfield. He made his debut for the Owls against QPR twenty-four hours after joining the club and travelled with England to the World Cup finals in Germany in 2006.

CATLIN, Arthur Edward
Left-back

Appearances: 228
Born: Middlesbrough, 11 January 1911
Died: Sheffield, 28 November 1990

CAREER
CLUBS: South Bank, WEDNESDAY (free, April 1930-May 1945; scout, chief scout)
OTHER: licensee of four pubs in the Sheffield area; also ran a boarding house in Blackpool.

Ted Catlin

Ted Catlin succeeded Blenkinsop in Wednesday's League side, and what a terrific job he did, especially as he was asked to follow in the footsteps of one of the Owls' greatest-ever full-backs. He first tasted League action at Leicester in March 1931 and became an established member of the side in the mid-1930s when he partnered Nibloe. An FA Cup and Charity Shield winner in 1935 versus West Brom and Arsenal respectively, Catlin won five England caps in 1936/37 when deputising for Arsenal's Eddie Hapgood. He also played once for the Football League (1936). Thoughtful and composed, he was a sound kicker of the ball and rarely committed a reckless foul. Including his wartime exploits (96 outings), he made 322 appearances for the Owls, scoring 1 goal, in a 6-1 win over Notts County in a Second World War game in 1944. Badly injured in a clash with Blackpool's Jock Dodds in the first leg of the 1943 League (North) War Cup final, he retired two years later. A good cricketer, Ted once claimed nine wickets in an innings.

CAWLEY, Thomas Edward
Forward

Appearances: 86   Goals: 59
Born: Sheffield, 2 January 1860
Died: Sheffield, 28 January 1933

CAREER
CLUBS: *Sheffield Rovers, WEDNESDAY (August 1880-May 1892), Lockwood Brothers, WEDNESDAY (coach, assistant trainer, advisor to the board of directors).*

Tommy Cawley helped save Wednesday from extension in 1887. One of the men who founded rivals Sheffield Rovers, he urged his fellow rebels to give the Owls one last chance to become a professional organisation – and it worked. A terrific player during the kick-and-rush era of soccer, Cawley could use both feet, was a smart dribbler and packed a thunderous right-foot shot. An automatic choice for the Sheffield FA representative side, he was a regular in the Owls' first team until 1892. He appeared in the club's first FA Cup semi-final in 1882 (versus Blackburn) and was in the side that lost the 1890 final. That year his benefit raised £182 – a lot of money in those days. He was presented with a gold watch and chain by the club for his noble efforts as a player and organiser. Unfortunately, despite an England international trial, a full cap eluded him but he did arrange games for the famous Zulu team (a selection of players chosen to play charity matches for the families who lost loved ones during the Zulu War of 1879) which enjoyed success and popularity from 1879 to 1882. Cawley helped the Owls win the Football Alliance in 1890 (scoring 14 goals in 21 games) having earlier gained winners' medals for triumphs in the Wharncliffe Charity Cup finals of 1882, 1883, 1886 and 1888 and winners' prizes when the Sheffield Challenge Cup was won in 1887 and 1888.

During a match at Lincoln in 1888, Cawley was mistakenly sent off. The referee recognised his error and recalled Cawley to the field, but the player declined to return as a matter of principle.

After retiring as a player, Cawley remained loyal to the club for many years, acting as reserve coach. Cawley's son, Thomas, was a guest for Wednesday.

CHALMERS, Bruce
Half-back

Appearances: 29   Goals: 2
Born: Girvan, Galloway, Scotland, 1868
Died: Sheffield, 1940

CAREER
CLUBS: *Albion Rovers, Derby County, Albion Rovers, WEDNESDAY (free, August 1891-May 1893), Albion Rovers*
OTHER: *ran a garage in Girvan.*

Bruce Chalmers made 22 appearances for Derby before joining the Owls. A solid, hard-working defender who filled all three half-back positions, he spent three seasons with Wednesday, taking over at left half halfway through 1892/93. The previous season he had won both the Ayrshire and Larkhall Charity Cups with Albion Rovers. Injury ended his career. His son, Andrew, played for Dumbarton, Bradford City and Kettering in the 1920s.

CHAMBERLAIN, Mark Valentine
Outside left

Appearances: 40+48   Goals: 10
Born: Stoke-on-Trent, 19 November 1961

CAREER
CLUBS: *Port Vale, Stoke City, WEDNESDAY (£300,000, September 1985-August 1988), Portsmouth, Brighton & Hove Albion, Airdrieonians, Exeter City, Fareham Town (player-manager), Andover, Fareham (player, director of football), Fleet Town, Southampton (academy coach).*

C

An England Schoolboy international, Mark Chamberlain later won four Under-21 and eight full caps for his country, the latter against Luxembourg, Denmark, Scotland, USSR, Brazil, Uruguay, Chile and Finland, 1982-84. Fast, skilful and direct, he graduated through Port Vale's junior ranks and made his debut in August 1978. He scored 20 goals in 110 appearances for the Valiants and was named in the PFA Fourth Division side for 1981/82. After moving to Stoke, he improved ten-fold and was described as the most exciting wing prospect seen at the club since Stanley Matthews. After netting 18 goals in 125 games for the Potters he was snapped up by the Owls but failed to hold down a regular place in the side, and two thirds of his appearances for Wednesday came as a substitute. He failed to reach the heights he had achieved at Stoke and left League football in 1997 with 518 appearances and 69 goals to his name.

CHAMBERS, Adam Craig
Utility

Appearances: 9+3
Born: Sandwell, West Bromwich, 20 November 1980

CAREER
CLUBS: West Bromwich Albion, WEDNESDAY (loan, February 2004 and May-February 2005), Kidderminster Harriers.

England Youth international Adam Chambers and his brother James were the first twins to play in a League game together for West Bromwich Albion and indeed in the Premiership. A positive performer who enjoyed man-marking, he made his debut for the Owls in a 2-1 win at Rushden & Diamonds in February 2004.

CHAPMAN, Henry
Inside, outside right

Appearances: 298   Goals: 102
Born: Kiveton Park, Sheffield, 19 January 1878
Died: Hull, 29 September 1916

CAREER
CLUBS: Worksop Town, Grimsby Town, Attercliffe, WEDNESDAY (free, August 1898-April 1911), Hull City (player, secretary-manager).

At his peak, Harry Chapman was considered by many as the best inside right in the country, better even than the great Steve Bloomer who was rattling in the goals for Derby County and England. But Bloomer never let his country down and as a result Chapman failed to win the cap he deserved. A hard-working player, full of grim determination, Chapman was fast over the ground and was both imaginative and confident in everything he did. Forming a fine partnership in the Owls' attack with Harry Davis, the pair were affectionately known as the 'marionettes' and what a dynamic duo they were. At 5ft 5½ins, Chapman was both a maker and taker of chances and his efforts helped Wednesday win successive League titles in 1903 and 1904 and the FA Cup in 1907. Chapman's early death was due to tuberculosis. His brother – Herbert Chapman – managed both Huddersfield and Arsenal to League Championship and FA Cup glory in the 1920s and '30s.

CHAPMAN, Lee Roy
Striker

Appearances: 135+3   Goals: 57
Born: Lincoln, 5 December 1959

CAREER
CLUBS: Stoke City, Stafford Rangers, Plymouth Argyle, Arsenal, Sunderland, WEDNESDAY (£100,000, August 1984-June 1988), Niort, Nottingham Forest, Leeds United, Portsmouth, West Ham United,

Lee Chapman

Southend United, Ipswich Town, Leeds United, Swansea City
OTHER: later owned bars, restaurants and cafes in London and worked for Sky Sports.

A nomadic 6ft 2ins striker, Lee Chapman served 13 different clubs in 20 years, netting 264 goals in almost 700 first-class appearances, his Football League statistics being 197 goals in 552 games. Not the most graceful of players, he was nonetheless strong in all aspects of forward play, being courageous, willing, determined, brave and dangerous inside the penalty area, especially with his head (from set pieces). Capped by England at 'B' and under-21 levels, Chapman helped Forest win the 1989 League Cup and Simod Cup finals, netting twice in the latter versus Everton. He was also a member of Leeds' Second and First Division championship-winning sides of 1990 and 1992. During his four years at Hillsborough he gave the fans plenty to cheer about, netting some great goals with both head and feet. He suffered his fair share of injuries but always came up for more. He was sent off for the first time in his career in the 1987 FA Cup encounter with Derby, the subsequent suspension ending a long and satisfying run in the side. As top-scorer that season with 22 goals he won the Player of the Year

trophy. He is married to former *Men Behaving Badly* actress Lesley Ash. Lee's father, Roy, scored over 200 goals for Aston Villa, Lincoln, Mansfield, Port Vale and Chester.

CHAPMAN, William
Forward

Appearances: 4
Born: Murton, Co. Durham, 21 September 1902
Died: Murton, Co. Durham, 2 December 1967

CAREER
CLUBS: Sunderland, WEDNESDAY (free, April 1923-May 1926), Manchester United, Watford.

Bill Chapman started as a full-back in the Hetton District Churches League and became an outside right by accident when his team manager had far too many defenders to choose from! He enjoyed it and in his first season with Murton Celtic won a Seaham Amateur League championship medal. He entered League football with the Owls aged twenty-one, made his debut on the right flank in a 2-0 defeat at Oldham in April 1924, but was unable to get regular first-team action at Hillsborough, switching his allegiance to Old Trafford where he covered for Dick Spence and later former Wednesday star Rees Williams. One of three players who moved to Watford from Old Trafford, Chapman played his best football at Vicarage Road, scoring 22 goals in 210 League games. A schoolteacher by profession, he was also a wireless enthusiast and professional runner.

CHEDGZOY, Sydney
Outside right

Appearances: 4
Born: Liverpool, 17 February 1912
Died: 1983

CAREER

CLUBS: New Brighton, Burscough Rangers, Everton, Burnley, Millwall, Runcorn, Halifax Town, WEDNESDAY (free, July-October 1937), Runcorn, Swansea Town, Cardiff City, Tranmere Rovers and Aberaman.

WARTIME GUEST APPEARANCES: New Brighton.

Syd Chedgzoy was a reserve throughout his career. He failed to get into Everton's first team, made 5 appearances for Burnley, 3 for Millwall, none for Halifax and 18 for Swansea. He made his Owls' debut on the opening day of 1937/38 at Chesterfield (lost 1-0) and, in fact, was one of six players used on the right wing that campaign. His father, Sam Chedgzoy, played for Everton and England.

CLARKE, Harry Maurice
Inside left

Appearances: 1
Born: Newcastle, 29 December 1932

CAREER

CLUBS: Darlington, WEDNESDAY (free, October 1957-August 1958), Hartlepool United, South Shields
OTHER: architect.

Harry Clarke spent ten months at Hillsborough, making one appearance at inside left at home to Blackpool in October 1957 in place of Gerry Young. Prior to moving to Hillsborough he hit 20 goals in 142 League games for Darlington and later netted 43 times in 118 outings for Hartlepool, confirming he was a pretty useful player at a lower level.

CLARKE, Leon Marvin
Striker

Appearances: 3+7   Goals: 1
Born: Birmingham, 10 February 1985

CAREER

CLUBS: Kidderminster Harriers, QPR, Plymouth Argyle, WEDNESDAY (January 2007), Oldham Athletic (L, March 2007).

Striker Leon Clarke was signed from Wolves in January 2007. He had previously assisted Kidderminster Harriers, QPR and Plymouth Argyle. He later joined Oldham Athletic on loan in March 2007.

CLARKE, Matthew John
Goalkeeper

Appearances: 2+2
Born: Sheffield, 3 November 1973

CAREER

CLUBS: Rotherham United, WEDNESDAY (£325,000, July 1996-July 1999), Bradford City, Bolton Wanderers, Crystal Palace
OTHER: property developer.

A fine shot-stopper, courageous and competent, Matt Clarke (6ft 4ins tall) appeared in 141 games for Rotherham before joining the Owls as cover for Kevin Pressman. He made only two Premiership starts in his three years at Hillsborough – against Derby and Aston Villa in September 1997. After leaving Wednesday he did well with Palace, receiving the Nationwide Save of the Season award in October 2001 for a superb stop against his old club Bradford. He retired in 2004 with almost 250 appearances to his name.

CLEMENTS, David
Utility

Appearances: 87
Born: Larne, Northern Ireland, 15 September 1945

CAREER

CLUBS: Portadown, Wolverhampton Wanderers, Coventry City, WEDNESDAY (£55,000, August

1971-September 1973), Everton, Northern Ireland (manager), New York Cosmos, Denver Caribous, Colorado Rapids
OTHER: ran an Irish goods store in Georgetown, Colorado.

Well-proportioned, strong and efficient, the versatile Dave Clements made over 500 club and international appearances (391 in the Football League) during his fifteen-year career. He helped Coventry win the Second Division championship in 1967 before having two fine seasons at Hillsborough, missing only three League games in 1971/72 and four the following term. He made his debut for Everton against his old club Wolves. A Northern Ireland amateur international, he went on to represent his country's youth team before gaining three Under-23 and 48 full caps, 21 with Coventry – a club record he shared initially with Welshman Ronnie Rees, later bettered by Marcus Hedman. He skippered the Owls, Everton and his country several times.

CLOUGH, Nigel Howard
Forward

Appearances: 2
Born: Sunderland, 19 March 1966

CAREER
CLUBS: Heanor Town, Nottingham Forest, Liverpool, Manchester City, Nottingham Forest, WEDNESDAY (loan, September 1997), Burton Albion (player-manager).

An England international, capped 14 times by his country at senior level (the first versus Chile at Wembley in 1989), Nigel Clough also played in 5 Under-21 matches (1986-88), in 1 'B' international and represented the Football League. He twice won the League Cup with Forest, in 1989 when he scored twice against Luton in the final, and 1990 versus Oldham. He also helped Forest win the Simod Cup versus Everton,

1989, and the ZDSC versus Southampton, 1992. He received runners-up medals in the 1991 FA Cup final versus Spurs and the 1992 League Cup final versus Manchester United. Forest's leading scorer four seasons running (1985-89), Clough topped the charts again in 1990/91 and 1992/93 and his two spells at The City Ground brought him 131 goals in 412 senior appearances. He averaged 1 goal every 5 games for Liverpool but failed to impress with Manchester City. A centre forward who enjoyed playing a deeper role rather than an out-and-out striker, pestering defenders inside the penalty-area, his two loan outings for the Owls came in September 1997 – in the Premiership against Derby (lost 5-2) and in the League Cup at Grimsby (lost 2-0). As a manager, he took Burton Albion into the Conference as Unibond League champions in 2002 and then, in 2006, almost caused a major upset when his Burton side held Manchester United to a 0-0 draw in the third round of the FA Cup. His father was, of course, the late Brian Clough.

COBIAN, Juan Manuel
Right wing-back

Appearances: 8+2
Born: Buenos Aires, Argentina, 11 September 1975

CAREER
CLUBS: Boca Juniors, Huracan Corrientes, WEDNESDAY (£250,000, August 1998-June 1999), Barnsley, Bolton Wanderers, Charlton Athletic, Aberdeen, Swindon Town, Boston United, Deportivo Linares, Atletico Almagro.

A composed right wing-back, Juan Cobian made only 23 appearances in English and Scotland football. He played in 7 of Wednesday's first 8 Premiership games at the start of 1998/99 and looked a useful player but was inexplicably dropped and hardly figured again. He gained Under-15, Under-18 and Under-23 caps with Argentina.

C

COCKROFT, Joseph
Left half

Appearances: 97   Goals: 2
Born: Barnsley, 20 June 1911
Died: Rotherham, 12 February 1994

CAREER
CLUBS: Barnsley, Ardsley Athletic, Wombwell Town, Rotherham United, Gainsborough Trinity, West Ham United, Dartford, WEDNESDAY (£750, November 1945-November 1948), Sheffield United, Wisbech Town (player-manager);
WARTIME GUEST APPEARANCES: Chesterfield, Huddersfield Town, WEDNESDAY (December 1940-October 1945)
OTHER: licensee in Sheffield; printer.

Joe Cockroft was a consistent left-half who was an ever-present in West Ham's side for four seasons in the 1930s, being regarded as the best uncapped player in League football at that time. He made 293 appearances for the Hammers, 217 in succession between 1932 and 1937. He helped them win the League War Cup versus Blackburn at Wembley in 1940 and also had a trial for England versus The Rest. Direction of Labour in 1940 saw him return to Yorkshire where he worked at Edgar Allen's Steelworks, Sheffield. After guesting for the Owls, he transferred to Hillsborough on a permanent basis in 1945, having played in 198 Second World War games for the club (13 goals). He added almost 100 more appearances to his Wednesday tally before signing for rivals Sheffield United. A penalty expert, Cockroft never missed from the spot for the Owls but he fluffed his first two for the Blades, against Arsenal (lost 5-3) and Huddersfield (0-0). As a boy, Cockroft played in the same Barnsley Schools team as George Hunt.

CODD, Ronald William
Forward

Appearances: 2
Born: Sheffield, 3 December 1928

CAREER
CLUBS: Bolton Wanderers, WEDNESDAY (£2,500, March-April 1953), Barrow, Peterborough United, Spalding United, Burton Albion, Hyde United
OTHER: accountant; played cricket for Dronfield and Parkfield.

Ron Cobb appeared in Wednesday's troublesome centre forward position in games against Chelsea (lost 1-0) and Manchester United (0-0) at the end of 1952/53. He scored 5 goals in 31 League games for Bolton and 11 in 45 for Barrow.

COLE, William Walter
Utility

Appearances: 10   Goals: 1
Born: Sheffield, 1874
Died: circa 1947

CAREER
CLUBS: WEDNESDAY (May 1898-April 1901), Worksop Town.

Versatile Billy Cole could play on the right wing, at right-back and inside forward. He made his League debut at Bolton in September 1898 and scored his only goal for the club in a 1-1 draw at Nottingham Forest in January 1899.

COLEMAN, Anthony George
Outside left

Appearances: 27+1 Goals: 2
Born: Ellesmere Port, Cheshire, 2 May, 1945

CAREER
CLUBS: Marine, Stoke City, Ellesmere Port, Tranmere

Rovers, Preston North End, Bangor City, Doncaster Rovers, Manchester City, WEDNESDAY (£15,000, October 1969-August 1970), Blackpool, Cape Town, Durban City, Southport, Stockport County, Macclesfield Town OTHER: ran a café in Waterloo (Liverpool) and sold ice cream on Crosby beach; now works for Queensland railways in Brisbane.

Tony Coleman played for fifteen different clubs during his career. Although regarded as something of a problem boy in his day he was certainly a useful winger. He fell out with the management at Manchester City and moved to Hillsborough nine weeks into the 1969/70 campaign, making his debut for the Owls in a 1-0 defeat at Ipswich. He then had to wait until the penultimate game of the season before netting his first goal in a 2-2 draw with Manchester United. Subsequently replaced on the left wing by John Sissons, during his career Coleman scored 30 goals in 250 League games, surprisingly producing his best efforts under Joe Mercer and Malcolm Allison at Maine Road, netting 16 times in 101 outings for City with whom he won both League Championship and FA Cup winners' medals in 1968 and 1969 respectively.

COLEMAN, Simon
Defender

Appearances: 16+5 Goals: 1
Born: Worksop, 13 March 1968

CAREER
CLUBS: Mansfield Town, Middlesbrough, Manchester City, Derby County, WEDNESDAY (loan, November 1993, signed for £250,000, January 1994-October 1994), Bolton Wanderers, Wolverhampton Wanderers, Southend United, Rochdale, Ilkeston Town, Hyde United
OTHER: head of football development at Garibaldi College, Mansfield.

Simon Coleman made his League debut aged nineteen and twice helped

Simon Coleman

Mansfield win the Notts FA County Cup (1988 and 1989) while also making 119 appearances for the Stags. He had 70 outings for Middlesbrough and over 90 for Derby before joining the Owls on loan. A strong defender, good in the air, he made his debut for Wednesday in a 3-1 home Premiership win over Liverpool and scored his only goal for the club in another 3-1 victory at Tottenham the following February. He quit League football in 2002 with 474 appearances and 29 goals to his credit.

COLLIER, William
Left half

Appearances: 14
Born: Kickcaldy, 11 December 1889
Died: Dunfermline, 17 April 1954

C

CAREER

CLUBS: Raith Rovers, Kickcaldy United, Cowdenbeath, WEDNESDAY (£510, August 1924-June 1925), Kettering Town, Dartford
OTHER: licensee.

Bill Collier joined the Owls (with William Inglis) in readiness for the 1924/25 season. Recruited to bolster up the squad, he played in 10 of the first 12 League games before losing his place to Billy Powell. In 1923, both he and Inglis had earlier been rescued from the sea when the *Highland Loch* steamer, taking the Raith team on tour, ran aground after a violent storm off the coast of Spain.

COLLINS, John Lindsay
Full-back

Appearances: 11
Born: Bedwelty, Wales, 21 January 1949

CAREER
CLUBS: Tottenham Hotspur, Portsmouth, Dallas, Halifax Town, WEDNESDAY (£3,000, July-December 1976), Barnsley, Kidderminster Harriers, Baltimore
OTHER: hotelier in Ireland.

A Welsh Schoolboy international who went on to win seven Under-23 caps for his country, John Collins understudied Phil Beal, Cyril Knowles, Jimmy Collins, Joe Kinnear and Ray Evans at Tottenham, appearing in only two League games. He made over 70 appearances for Pompey, 82 for Halifax and 130 for Barnsley after leaving Hillsborough.

COLLINS, Patrick Paul
Defender

Appearances: 32+4 Goals: 1
Born: Newcastle, 4 February 1985

CAREER
CLUBS: Sunderland, WEDNESDAY (free, July 2004), Swindon Town (L), Sunderland (L, November 2005), Darlington (July 2006).

Capped by England at Youth team level, 6ft 2ins defender Pat Collins failed to make the first team at Sunderland. Although troubled with a leg injury, he did extremely well with Wednesday, entering the action as a substitute in the play-off final versus Hartlepool.

COLLINS, Wayne Anthony
Midfield

Appearances: 19+15 Goals: 6
Born: Manchester, 4 March 1969

CAREER
CLUBS: Winsford United, Crewe Alexandra, WEDNESDAY (£600,000, August 1996-January 1998), Fulham, Preston North End, Crewe Alexandra, Stockport County.

A Division Two championship winner with Fulham in 1999, right-sided midfielder Wayne Collins never really established himself in the first team following his transfer from Crewe. He started as first choice but lost his place to Graham Hyde after half a dozen matches.

CONWELL, Anthony
Full-back

Appearances: 47
Born: Bradford, 17 January, 1932

CAREER
CLUBS: Bradford Rovers, WEDNESDAY (free, December 1948-July 1955), Huddersfield Town, Derby County, Doncaster Rovers
OTHER: sold liquid fertiliser to farmers, had a milk round and worked as a bricklayer.

A strong, forceful defender with good pace, Tony Conwell worked hard at his game and did well at Hillsborough before becoming a firm favourite at Huddersfield following a transfer that also involved Jackie Marriott, Roy Shiner and Ron Staniforth. He appeared in over 100 games for both the Terriers and Derby and ended his career in 1964 having made 283 League appearances.

COOKE, Terence John
Midfield

Appearances: 35+8 Goals: 3
Born: Birmingham 5 August 1976

CAREER
CLUBS: Manchester United, Sunderland, Birmingham City, Wrexham, Manchester City, Wigan Athletic, WEDNESDAY (loan, September-November 2000 and December 2000-January 2001), Grimsby Town, Sheffield United, Grimsby Town, Bury, WEDNESDAY (free, August 2003-May 2004), Chesterfield, Barnsley, Peterborough United, Kidderminster Harriers, Oldham Athletic, Colorado Rapids.

An FA Youth Cup winner with Manchester United in 1995, when he scored in both legs of the final versus Tottenham, Terry Cooke also represented England at Youth level before going on to win four Under-21 caps. A skilful midfielder, he found it tough going at Old Trafford and after a series of loan spells moved to neighbours City. He joined the Owls on a permanent basis in 2003, after an unproductive sojourn at Grimsby. A regular during the first part of 2003/04, he was then side-lined with a knee injury, and was among thirteen players released at the end of that season.

COOPER, Alfred Duncan
Outside left

Appearances: 3
Born: Brampton, Manchester, 1895
Deceased by 1980

CAREER
CLUBS: Manchester United, Middleton, WEDNESDAY (free, August 1919-May 1920), Rotherham Town.

Alf Cooper made three League appearances for the Owls in 1919/20 after the First World War and was one of eight different players used on the left-wing during that campaign.

COOPER, Anthony
Inside right

Appearances: 1
Born: Handsworth, Sheffield, 7 April 1893
Died: Chesterfield, 12 November 1974

CAREER
CLUBS: Birmingham, Hardwick Colliery, WEDNESDAY (free, July 1919-May 1920), Barnsley.

Tony Cooper – real name Routledge – made only one League appearance for the Owls, against Notts County in September 1919 when he deputised for Harry Bentley in a 0-0 draw. He failed to make Barnsley's first team. His brother Arthur kept goal in over 100 games for Barnsley and also played for Oldham and made 24 appearances as a guest for the Owls in the First World War.

COOPER, Joseph
Forward

Appearances: 1
Born: Newbold, Chesterfield, May 1899
Died: Cleethorpes, 22 January 1959

CAREER
CLUBS: West Bromwich Albion, WEDNESDAY (trial, April 1921), Chesterfield, Notts County, Grimsby Town, Lincoln City.

Joe Cooper was attending teacher train-ing college when he was offered a trial at

Hillsborough. He jumped at the chance and was given his senior debut in the final game of 1920/21, at Bristol City, replacing Harry Hall in a 1-0 win. Unfortunately he didn't stay on and, after qualifying as a teacher, joined Chesterfield. During his career, Cooper – who was also a fine club cricketer – scored 70 goals in 272 League games, having his best spell with Grimsby (47 goals in 154 outings). He helped the Mariners win the Third Division (North) title in 1926.

COOPER, Sedley
Forward

Appearances: 19   Goals: 4
Born: Garforth, Leeds, 17 August 1911
Died: Garforth, 23 February 1981

CAREER
CLUBS: Halifax Town, WEDNESDAY (£1,050, June 1931-June 1936), Huddersfield Town, Notts County WARTIME GUEST APPEARANCES: Lincoln City, Torquay United.

Although he spent five seasons at Hillsborough, Sed Cooper never really established himself in the League side until 1933/34 when he scored 3 goals in 10 games while deputising for Ellis Rimmer on the left wing. Prior to his transfer to Wednesday, Cooper netted 20 goals in 79 League games for Halifax. He was troubled by a knee injury from 1937 onwards.

COOPER, William
Left half

Appearances: 1
Born: Sheffield, circa 1863
Deceased by 1945

CAREER
CLUBS: WEDNESDAY (seasons 1887-89).

An unknown reserve, Bill Cooper's only game for the Owls was in the first round FA Cup-tie at Belper in October 1887.

CORR, Barry
Striker

Appearances: 9+10
Born: Wicklow, Ireland, 2 April 1985

CAREER
CLUBS: Leeds United, WEDNESDAY (trial, March 2005, signed April 2005-May 2007), Swindon Town (L), Bristol City (L).

A Republic of Ireland Youth international, Barry Corr spent four years at Elland Road without making much progress. The giant 6ft 4ins striker did well when on trial at Hillsborough before signing a full contract with the Owls, making his debut against Leicester City in September 2005.

COUGHLAN, Graham
Defender

*Appearances: 52+4 *   Goals: 6**
Born: Dublin, 18 November 1974

CAREER
CLUBS: Bray Wanderers, Blackburn Rovers, Swindon Town, Livingston, Plymouth Argyle, WEDNESDAY (free, June 2005), Burnley (L, March-May 2007).

A rock at the heart of the defence at both Livingston (67 appearances) and Plymouth Argyle (193 plus 26 goals), Graham Coughlan, 6ft 2ins tall, gained a Scottish First Division championship winners' medal in 2001 and helped the Pilgrims win both Division Three and then Division Two titles in successive years (2003 and 2004). A near ever-present during his last three seasons at Home Park, Coughlan, strong at set pieces, formed a fine partnership with Paul Wooton before his transfer to Wednesday. He was chosen by his fellow professionals in the 2004 PFA Championship team and was Owls' Player of the Year in 2006.

COX, Brian Roy
Goalkeeper

Appearances: 26
Born: Sheffield, 7 May 1961

CAREER
CLUBS: WEDNESDAY (June 1977-March 1982), Huddersfield Town, Mansfield Town, Hartlepool United, Buxton
OTHER: later a driver; also worked in a betting shop and for the NHS.

Brian Cox gave his best performances at Huddersfield. He had Bob Bolder and Chris Turner challenging him for a place at Hillsborough and his longest spell in the first team came during the 1979/80 promotion-winning season when he played in fifteen consecutive games. He fell from favour at Mansfield, with whom he won the Notts FA County Cup (1989). In his career Cox appeared in 323 League games, 213 for Huddersfield.

COYLE, Robert Irvine
Midfield

Appearances: 47+3 Goals: 3
Born: Belfast, 31 January 1948

CAREER
CLUBS: Glenavon, Lomond Star, Ballyclare Comrades, Ballymena United, Glentoran, WEDNESDAY (£10,000, March 1972-October 1974), Grimsby Town, Linfield (player-manager).

Capped five times by Northern Ireland, Bobby Coyle also won the Irish Cup with Linfield in

1978, having been a defeated finalist for the previous two seasons. A fine right-sided mid-fielder, he made his League debut for the Owls at Blackpool in December 1972 and scored his first goal for the club in a 3-1 FA Cup defeat versus Chelsea in February 1973.

CRAIG, James Phillips
Utility

Appearances: 5+1
Born: Glasgow, 30 April 1943

CAREER
CLUBS: Celtic, Hellenic, WEDNESDAY (free, December 1972-May 1973)
OTHER: worked on Glasgow radio and as a journalist.

Jim Craig, of slim lines, was both shrewd and unflustered in his defensive play. A neat passer of the ball from either the full-back or midfield position, he made 231 appearances for Celtic, winning the European Cup (1967), 7 Scottish League Championships (1966-72 inclusive), 4 Scottish Cups (1967, 1969, 1971 and 1972) and 3 League Cups (1968, 1969, 1970). He was also a runner-up in the 1971 and 1972 League Cup finals. Capped by Scotland versus Wales in 1968, Jim struggled with his fitness after joining the Owls and made only six appearances, the first at Portsmouth in January 1973. A dental surgeon by profession, he gained his degree at Glasgow University.

CRAIG, Robert McAllister
Inside forward

Appearances: 95 Goals: 28
Born: Airdrie, Scotland, 8 April 1935

CAREER
CLUBS: Blantyre Celtic, Third Lanark, WEDNESDAY (£7,750, November 1959-April 1962), Blackburn

C

Bobby Craig

Rovers, Celtic, St Johnstone, Oldham Athletic, Toronto City, Johannesburg Wanderers, Third Lanark OTHER: park gardener in Toronto.

The diminutive Bobby Craig, of typical Scottish style, gained a reputation in English football with the Owls for whom he averaged more than a goal a game. He made his debut against Leeds forty-eight hours after joining and missed only 5 League matches the following season, also netting 12 goals. He was unable to settle at Blackburn, he gained a Scottish Cup runners-up medal with Celtic in 1963 but found it impossible to follow Bobby Johnstone at Oldham.

CRAIG, Thomas Brooks
Midfield

Appearances: 228+5   Goals: 39
Born: Penilee, Glasgow, 21 November 1950

CAREER
CLUBS: Aberdeen, WEDNESDAY (£100,000, May 1969-December 1974), Newcastle United, Aston Villa, Swansea City, Carlisle United (player, assistant manager), Hibernian (player, coach), Celtic (coach, chief scout), Aberdeen (assistant manager, coach), Newcastle United (coach), Hibernian (assistant manager), Scotland Under-21 (coach).

Tommy Craig was the first Scotsman to join an English club for a six-figure fee when he moved to Hillsborough. Five years later he joined Newcastle for £120,000, a Wednesday record for a departing player. A left-sided midfielder, short and stocky, he was direct, skilful, a brilliant passer of the ball, short or long, and possessed a thunderbolt shot. In his five and a half years with Wednesday he gave some brilliant performances, missing only 25 out of a possible 257 matches following his debut against Tottenham on the last day of 1968/69. Capped by Scotland versus Switzerland in 1976, he also represented his country in Schoolboy, Youth, Under-21 and Under-23 internationals (9 outings) – one of only a handful of Scots to star at five different levels. As captain, he was the recipient of a runners-up medal after Newcastle lost the 1976 League Cup final to Manchester City. He also helped Swansea win the Welsh Cup in 1981. During his career Craig, a penalty expert who also skippered his national side, appeared in 562 League games north and south of the border and scored 89 goals. His brother, John Craig, also played for Aberdeen.

CRANE, Antony Steven
Defender

Appearances: 28+33   Goals: 5
Born: Liverpool, 9 September 1982

CAREER
CLUBS: WEDNESDAY (April 1998-July 2003), Grimsby Town.

A tall, powerfully built, combative central defender, strong on the ground and in the air, Tony Crane started his professional career at Hillsborough in midfield and did extremely well, but after switching positions he had a couple of disappointing seasons, being used mainly as a substitute. He made his League debut wearing the no.9 shirt at Watford in October 2001, having scored his first goal for the Owls in a League Cup-tie at home to Crystal Palace three days earlier. His first season with Grimsby was interrupted by suspension.

CRANSON, Ian
Defender

Appearances: 34+1
Born: Easington, County Durham, 2 July 1964

CAREER
CLUBS: Ipswich Town, WEDNESDAY (£475,000, March 1988-July 1989), Stoke City (player, coach, academy director).

After making 165 appearances for Ipswich and winning five England Under-21 caps, Ian Cranson joined Wednesday at the age of twenty-three. A solid, reliable performer, he suffered with injuries during his sixteen months at Hillsborough before moving to Stoke for a then record fee of £450,000. He regained his fitness with the Potters for whom he made 280 appearances, gaining an AGT winner's medal in 1992 and a Second Division championship prize a year later. He retired with 481 club games under his belt.

CRAPPER, Christopher
Left-back

Appearances: 1
Born: Rotherham, 5 July 1884
Died: Hemsworth, 12 June 1933

CAREER
CLUBS: South Kirkby, WEDNESDAY (£125, May 1905-July 1907), Grimsby Town.

Chris Crapper spent two seasons with the Owls, making his debut in the penultimate League

game of 1905/06 against Everton when he deputised for Harry Burton in a 3-1 win. Lithe in build, he made only three appearances for Grimsby.

CRAWSHAW, Percy
Right half

Appearances: 9
Born: Attercliffe, Sheffield, 7 August 1879
Died: Sheffield, 1944

CAREER Worksop Town, WEDNESDAY (May 1899-May 1905)
OTHER: licensee in Sheffield.

Percy Crawshaw was a Wednesday reserve for five years, although towards the end of his career he struggled with injuries. Deputising for Bob Ferrier, he made his League debut at right half, alongside his brother in December 1899, in a 1-0 defeat at Chesterfield. He played his last game at Grimsby in October 1902. In addition to his brother Tom (below), another brother, George, played for the Owls in 1888/89 but did not make the first team, while his son played pre-First World War football.

CRAWSHAW, Thomas Henry
Centre half

Appearances: 466   Goals: 24
Born: Attercliffe, Sheffield, 27 December 1872
Died: Wharncliffe, Sheffield, 25 November 1960

CAREER
CLUBS: Heywood Central, WEDNESDAY (free, May 1894-June 1908), Chesterfield, Castleford Town, Glossop (secretary-manager)
OTHER: ran a newsagents shop and was a licensee in Sheffield.

A great early Wednesday hero, Tom Crawshaw starred in two FA Cup-winning teams (1896 and 1907), was a member of successive League

Championship winning sides (1903 and 1904) and helped the Owls win the Second Division title in 1900. He succeeded Billy Betts at centre half and within a year of joining Wednesday had gained the first of his 10 full England caps, also making the first of 8 appearances for the Football League (1895). In his prime he was by far the best defender (in his position) in the country. A thoroughly hard worker, superb at heading, Crawshaw was a stern but fair tackler and cleared his lines to perfection. As captain he led by example, never giving up the fight. No one fought harder or longer than he did on the field and he was quite outstanding when leading the Owls to victory in the 1907 cup final. One of the old school of centre halves, he was a great player.

CRESSWELL, Richard Paul Wesley
Striker

Appearances: 8+28 Goals: 3
Born: Bridlington, 20 September 1977

CAREER
CLUBS: York City, Mansfield Town (L), WEDNESDAY (£950,000, March 1999-September 2000), Leicester City, Preston North End, Leeds United.

An England Under-21 international (4 caps gained) Richard Cresswell scored 24 goals in 111 games for York before joining Wednesday. A smart striker, deliberate and dangerous when in front of goal, he made his debut for the Owls in a 2-1 Premiership defeat by Coventry and then came off the bench in the next six games, claiming his first goal for the club to earn victory over Liverpool in the last but one fixture of that campaign. Unfortunately he had few chances to make his mark at Hillsborough (hence his high number of substitute appearances). He failed to hit it off at Leicester but became a firm favourite at Deepdale, top-scoring for Preston in his first two seasons. He played against the Owls in the 2005 play-off final, the same year he also reached the milestone of 300 career appearances. In

May 2006, he was sent off in the second leg of the play-off semi-final against his former club Preston which Leeds won 2-0 (3-1 on aggregate) to reach the final (against Watford).

CRINSON, William James
Goalkeeper

Appearances: 4
Born: Sunderland, June 1883
Died: Sunderland, 1951

CAREER
CLUBS: Southwick, WEDNESDAY (free, May 1906-June 1908), Huddersfield Town, Brighton & Hove Albion, Sunderland Rovers, Sunderland Comrades (secretary), Brighton & Hove Albion (scout).

Billy Crinson was reserve to Jack Lyall during his time with the Owls. He made his League debut at Manchester City in January 1907 (won 1-0) but his fourth and last appearance for the club ended in a 6-1 defeat at Middlesbrough in April 1908.

CROSSLEY, Mark Geoffrey
Goalkeeper

Appearances: 18   Goals: 1
Born: Barnsley, 16 June 1967

CAREER
CLUBS: Nottingham Forest, Milwall, Middlesbrough, Stoke City, Fulham, WEDNESDAY (loan, November 2006-May 2007), Oldham Athletic (player-coach).

Goalkeeper Mark Crossley joined Wednesday on loan from Fulham in November 2006 and remained at Hillsborough until May 2007. He served with Nottingham Forest (393 games), Millwall, Middlesbrough and Stoke City before joining Fulham for £500,000 in August 2003. Capped eight times by Wales at senior level and once by the B team, he also made three Under-21 appearances for England.

CRUICKSHANK, Alexander Edwin

Outside-right

Appearances: 2
Born: Haddington, Lothian, 12 August 1900
Died: Scotland, 1972

CAREER
CLUBS: Port Glasgow, Derby County, Merthyr Town, WEDNESDAY (£200, August 1926-August 1928), Annfield Plain, Guildford City, Merthyr Town, Swindon Town.

Reserve to Rees Williams, Alex Cruickshank's two outings for the Owls were both at League level, against Birmingham and Blackburn in September 1926. Fast and lively, he scored 11 goals in a total of 75 League games for Merthyr and he also netted 5 times in 26 outings for Swindon but failed in his efforts at Derby.

CUNNINGHAM, Anthony Eugene

Forward

Appearances: 30+3 Goals: 5
Born: Kingston, Jamaica, 12 November 1957

CAREER
CLUBS: Lafferyetie, Kidderminster Harriers, Stourbridge, Lincoln City, Barnsley, WEDNESDAY(£100,000, November 1983-July 1984), Manchester City, Newcastle United, Blackpool, Bury, Bolton Wanderers, Rotherham United, Doncaster Rovers, Wycombe Wanderers, Gainsborough Trinity
OTHER: legal executive in Lincoln, later qualifying as a solicitor.

Errant traveller Tony Cunningham had a very interesting twenty-year career during which time he scored 146 goals in 591 competitive games, having his best spells with Lincoln (40 goals in 142 games), Blackpool (24 in 90) and Rotherham (29 in 87). Tall and leggy, he was a big favourite with the fans at many of his fourteen clubs. He never shirked a challenge, was a battler and, although his skills were rather limited, his overall scoring record was very good. Indeed, he made a scoring debut for Wednesday at Fulham in November 1983 (1-1) and then netted in his first home game, a 4-2 victory over his future club Newcastle. He helped Lincoln (1981), Wednesday (1984) and Rotherham (1992) gain promotion from their respective divisions.

CURRAN, Edward Terence

Forward

Appearances: 135+3 Goals: 39
Born: Hemsworth, Yorkshire, 20 March 1955

CAREER
CLUBS: Doncaster Rovers, Nottingham Forest, Bury, Derby County, Southampton, WEDNESDAY (£85,000, March 1979-August 1992), Sheffield United, Everton, Orebo, Huddersfield Town, Panionios, Hull City, Sunderland, Matlock Town, Grantham, Grimsby Town, Chesterfield, Goole Town (player-manager)
OTHER: ran a pallet business, a café and an Italian restaurant.

Journeyman Terry Curran ('T.C.') would drift in and out of a game and play moderately, but then in his next match he would perform like a world-beater. He was temperamental, likely to fly off the handle at any time, yet occasionally he produced something extra special out on the pitch. He was very disappointing at many of his sixteen clubs, his best efforts coming with the Owls for whom he played brilliantly at times. In 1979/80 he top-scored with 24 goals, helping the team climb out of the Third Division. He then netted 11 times the following season before losing his scoring touch and eventually moving to Bramall Lane. He gained a League Championship medal with Everton in 1985 and at Sunderland his manager was former Owls coach Lawrie McMenemy. In his career the controversial Curran scored 72 goals in 463 matches.

C

CURRY, Robert
Inside-right

Appearances: 1
Born: Gateshead, 2 November 1918
Died: Halstead, Essex, 23 June 2001

CAREER
CLUBS: Gateshead, WEDNESDAY (August 1937-June 1939), Gainsborough, Colchester United
WARTIME GUEST APPEARANCES: WEDNESDAY (1940/41), Bradford Park Avenue, Sheffield United, Leeds United, Mansfield Town
OTHER: builder; owned a golf course.

Reserve to George Drury and Jack Robinson during his time at Hillsborough, Bob Curry's only League outing for the Owls was against Aston Villa in September 1937 (lost 2-1). He scored 13 goals for Colchester in their first season in the Football League (1950/51).

CURTIS, William Norman
Full-back

Appearances: 324   Goals: 21
Born: Dinnington, Worksop, 10 September 1924

CAREER
CLUBS: Gainsborough Trinity, WEDNESDAY (£1,250, January 1950-August 1960), Doncaster Rovers (player-manager), Buxton
OTHER: manager of a sports shop; sales rep for Carlsberg.

Norman Curtis fought off a challenge from Vin Kenny to establish himself at left-back in Wednesday's League side. A natural successor to Kenny 'Cannonball' Curtis, quiet and studious off the field, tough, fearless and combative on it, he served the club superbly for a decade or more and helped the Owls win the Second Division championship on three occasions, 1952, 1956 and 1959, being an ever-present in the latter campaign. In 1952/53 he took over as the team's penalty-taker, scoring twice from the spot in the home League game against Derby in October and repeating that feat a month later at Portsmouth. As an emergency goalkeeper at Preston in August 1953, when he replaced the injured Dave McIntosh, he saved two penalties in a 6-0 defeat. He eventually lost his place to Don Megson.

CUSACK, David Stephen
Defender

Appearances: 106+3   Goals: 1
Born: Thurcroft, Rotherham, 6 June 1956

CAREER
CLUBS: WEDNESDAY (July 1972-September 1978), Southend United, Millwall, Doncaster Rovers (player-manager), Rotherham United (player-manager), Copenhagen Ballklub, Boston United, Doncaster Rovers, Boston United (player, caretaker-manager), Kettering Town (player-manager), Dagenham & Redbridge (player-manager), Ford United (player-coach)
OTHER: project manager with a fire proofing company.

Dave Cusack was a very capable defender who worked his way up through the ranks at Hillsborough before making his League debut in October 1975 against Millwall. He netted his only Wednesday goal in his 104th game in a 2-1 defeat at Peterborough in February 1978. After leaving the Owls, he played as a forward for Southend and occasionally for Millwall and during his career netted 31 goals in 498 League games. He broke his neck in a car crash in 1999.

CUTTS, Edward Robert
Forward

Appearances: 1
Born: Sheffield, circa 1869
Died: Sheffield 1920.

CLUBS: WEDNESDAY (July 1889-May 1892),
OTHER: Rotherham Town.

Ted Cutts' only appearance for the Owls came in the Football Alliance in 1889/90. He scored 8 goals in 24 games for Rotherham for whom his brother, Arthur, also played.

D

DAILEY, James
Centre forward

Appearances: 41   Goals: 25
Born: Airdrie, 8 September 1927
Died: Weymouth, 14 January 2002

CAREER
CLUBS: Wolverhampton Wanderers, Third Lanark, WEDNESDAY (free, October 1946-February 1949), Birmingham City, Exeter City, Workington, Rochdale, non-League (1959-62), Dorset Youth Club Under-21s (manager), Portland Town (manager), Dorchester Town (manager)
OTHER: manager of a sports shop in Weymouth; also lived in Spain.

A stocky, dynamic centre forward, strong and active, who would often dive full length in an attempt to get on the end of a low cross, Jim Dailey netted 161 goals (74 for Workington) in 346 League games for five different clubs. He gave an excellent account of himself at Hillsborough, averaging more than 1 goal every 2 games. He helped the Owls escape relegation in his first season with some crucial strikes and the following term struck a five-timer at home to Barnsley to equal Jimmy Trotter's individual club scoring record. Surprisingly, he was unable to retain his place in the side and joined Birmingham for a record fee in 1949. He was a favourite with the fans wherever he played. His grandson, also Jimmy, played for England at under-16 level in 2000.

DARLING, Malcolm
Forward

Appearances: 2+1
Born: Arbroath, 4 July 1947

CAREER
CLUBS: Blackburn Rovers, Norwich City, Rochdale, Bolton Wanderers, Chesterfield, Stockport County, WEDNESDAY (trial, August-September 1977), Hartlepool United, Morecambe, Bury, California Sunshine, Darwen, Great Harwood Town (manager)
OTHER: supervisor for people with learning difficulties.

After some enterprising displays for Blackburn (30 goals in 128 League games), Rochdale (16 in 86) and Chesterfield (33 in 104), Malcolm Darling had a trial with the Owls during which time he had three outings. His League career realised 86 goals in 361 appearances.

DARROCH, John
Defender

Appearances: 32   Goals: 3
Born: Dumbarton, 1872
Died: Dundee, 24 November 1949

CAREER
CLUBS: Dumbarton, Renton, Vale of Leven, WEDNESDAY (free, September 1891-March 1894), Dundee, Bury, Blackburn Rovers, Dundee.

Able to play in both full-back positions and at right-half, Jack Darroch was only nineteen when he joined the Owls. He made his debut in the Football Alliance and, as partner to Tom Brandon, appeared in twelve games in Wednesday's first season in the Football League (1892/93). Unable to gain a regular place in the side, he joined Dundee and later made 143 League appearances for Bury.

D

DAVIES, Brian
Forward

Appearances: 4   Goals: 1
Born: Doncaster, 21 August 1947

CAREER
CLUBS: WEDNESDAY (August 1962-September 1968),
Baltimore Bays, Boston Beacon, Doncaster Rovers
OTHER: joined the RAF, became a parachute
instructor and played Combined Services football.

Brian Davies played in only 4 games in 6 years at Hillsborough, scoring on his League debut as John Fantham's deputy in a 1-1 draw with Chelsea in May 1966.

DAVIES, George
Wing half

Appearances: 109   Goals: 2
Born: Rednal, Oswestry, 1 March, 1927

CAREER
CLUBS: Oswestry Town, WEDNESDAY (£2,050, June 1950-July 1956), Chester, Wellington Town
OTHER: baker; window cleaner.

After many years playing non-League football, George Davies entered the big time with Wednesday at the age of twenty-three and quickly made his mark with some outstanding displays in the reserves. He made his League debut against Bolton in April 1951 and played in twenty games the following season, gaining a Second Division championship medal, before taking over at left half on a regular basis in 1952/53. With Tony Kay and Tom McAnearney pressing hard for places he left Hillsborough in 1956.

DAVIS, Henry
Forward

Appearances: 184   Goals: 42
Born: Smethwick, November 1873
Died: Birmingham, 1938

CAREER
CLUBS: Small Heath Alliance, Birmingham St George's, WEDNESDAY (free, September 1892-May 1899).

Harry Davis played in Wednesday's first Football League game against Notts County in September 1892, and some sources say that he may well have got a touch to Tom Brandon's goal-bound shot that won the match 1-0. Prior to becoming an 'Owl' he had done well in the Football Alliance with Birmingham St George's. He was at his best in the mid-1890s when he helped Wednesday to FA Cup final glory over Everton in 1896. Eight months after leaving the Owls, another Harry Davis moved in.

DAVIS, Harold
Forward

Appearances: 236   Goals: 67
Born: Wombwell, Barnsley, November 1879
Died: Sheffield, 18 October 1945

CAREER
CLUBS: Barnsley, WEDNESDAY (£200, January 1900-May 1909, assistant trainer)
OTHER: licensee; served in the army during the Second World War; ran a newsagents shop in Sheffield.

Harry Davis was one of the smallest players in the First Division during the early part of the twentieth century. Yet despite his size (5ft 4ins), he was a battler through and through, full of guts and courage, and the fans nicknamed him 'Joe Pluck'. He occupied every forward position during his time with Wednesday but was best at outside right, forming a fine partnership with Harry Chapman. He scored 7 goals in 114 games when the Owls won the Second Division title in 1900 and collected a First Division championship medal four years later. Unfortunately he missed the FA Cup final in 1907 after breaking his right leg in a third round replay with Sunderland. Although he remained a registered player for two more years, he never regained full fitness and retired in 1909. As Owls' assistant-trainer, his vast experience and know-how certainly benefited several youngsters. In 1903 Davis was capped by England against Ireland, Wales and Scotland and represented the Football League.

DAVIS, John Leslie
Right-back

Appearances: 1
Born: Hackney, 31 March 1957

CAREER
CLUBS: Arsenal, Crystal Palace, Gillingham, WEDNESDAY (February 1977-September 1977), Tipples FC, London schools (coach)
OTHER: guard at a London nightclub; taxi driver.

A junior boxer, John Davies' only League game for the Owls was in the 2-0 win over Oxford in May 1977.

DAVISON, John Edward
Goalkeeper

Appearances: 424
Born: Gateshead, 2 September 1887
Died: Wortley, Sheffield, January 1971

CAREER
CLUBS: Gateshead Town, WEDNESDAY (£300, April 1908-June 1926), Mansfield Town (player-manager), Chesterfield (manager), Sheffield United (manager), Chesterfield (manager, chief scout).

Although rather on the small side for a goal-keeper (5ft 7in) Teddy Davison nevertheless served the Owls brilliantly. A placid, gentle, easy-going person, he displaced Jack Lyall and made 102 consecutive appearances up to 1913. He continued to produce the goods during and after the First World War and went on to appear in 435 games for the club (11 in the First World War). Believed to be the smallest 'keeper ever to play for England, capped versus Wales in March 1922, he also toured Australia with the FA, gained a Second Division runners-up medal in 1939 and then, as a manager, won the Third Division (North) title with Chesterfield in 1931 and led Sheffield United to the 1936 FA Cup final (beaten by Arsenal). He had terrific reflexes, was daring and acrobatic, had far greater muscular strength than was imagined and was an expert at saving penalties (17 stopped during his career). Davison served Sheffield soccer superbly well – playing for the Owls for eighteen years and managing Sheffield United for twenty. He discovered Gordon Banks for Chesterfield and signed Jimmy Hagan for the Blades.

DAVISON, Thomas Reay
Centre half

Appearances: 18
Born: West Stanley, County Durham, 3 October 1901
Died: Derby, 1 January 1971

CAREER
CLUBS: Durham City, Wolverhampton Wanderers, Derby County, WEDNESDAY (£4,850 with George Stephenson, February 1931-July 1932), Coventry City, Rhyl Athletic (player-coach), Bath City (player-coach).

Former pit worker, Tommy Davison, a durable, stout-hearted defender, powerful in the tackle, made 60 appearances for his first major club (Durham) before serving as reserve to Bill Caddick at Molineux. The sheet anchor in the Derby defence, he played 85 times for the Rams, helping them gain promotion from the

Second Division in 1926 and finish as runners-up in the top flight in 1929. After his transfer to Hillsborough (with George Stephenson) he failed to secure a regular place in the team and moved to Coventry, where he added a further 108 appearances to his tally. Davison loved greyhounds, was an accomplished crown green bowler and a fine all-round cricketer.

DE BILDE, Gilles Roger Gerard
Midfield, forward

Appearances: 59+9 Goals: 15
Born: Zellick, Belgium, 9 June 1971

CAREER
CLUBS: Zellick Sport, RSC Anderlecht, Zellick Sport, KHO Merchtem, Eendracht Aalst, RSC Anderlecht, PSV Eindhoven, WEDNESDAY (£2.8 million, July 1999-July 2001), Aston Villa (L), RSC Anderlecht, SK Lierse, Willebroek-Meerhof.

Before joining Wednesday, Gilles De Bilde had done well in both his home country and Holland, scoring 67 goals in 128 League games with 3 clubs. At the time of his arrival at Hillsborough, the Owls were struggling in the Premiership – they were eventually relegated – but despite this De Bilde did his best, top-scoring with 11 goals. A competitive player with good pace and a neat touch, he lost his way in 2000/01 and eventually returned to Anderlecht. He won over 25 caps for Belgium, starring in Euro 2000.

DEGRYSE, Marc
Striker

Appearances: 34+4 Goals: 12
Born: Roeselare, Belgium, 4 September 1965

CAREER
CLUBS: VC Ardoole, Club Brugge KV, RSC Anderlecht, WEDNESDAY (£1.5m, August 1995-January 1997),

PSV Eindhoven, KAA Ghent, Geminal Beerschof Antwerpen, Brugge KV (technical advisor).

Having represented Belgium at Youth, Olympic and Under-21 levels, Marc Degryse went on to appear in over 70 full internationals. He was an uncapped member of their 1984 European Championship squad but starred in the 1986 and 1990 World Cup finals. Brugge sold him to Anderlecht for a record fee of £1.5 million and he repaid them by scoring 50 goals in four years. He did well at Hillsborough, netting his fair share of goals, including the winner against Arsenal at Easter 1996 in front of a party of his fans who had travelled over from Belgium. He was voted Belgian Player of the Year four times.

DENT, Frederick
Forward

Appearances: 4   Goals: 1
Born: Sheffield, 24 January 1896
Died: Leeds, 11 July 1983

CAREER
CLUBS: WEDNESDAY (July 1920-March 1921), Halifax Town, Chesterfield, Mid-Rhondda United, Bristol City, Exeter City, Merthyr Town, Norwich City, Swindon Town, Luton Town
OTHER: worked in local government for many years.

The much-travelled Fred Dent was a bustling yet sprightly forward who enjoyed a long career but only ever settled at three clubs (Halifax, Exeter and Norwich). Reserve to Charles Binney, Arthur Price and Johnny McIntyre at Hillsborough, he scored on his debut for the Owls in a 3-0 League win over Fulham in November 1920 and netted 67 goals in 173 League appearances in total.

DEWAR, Neil Hamilton
Centre forward

Appearances: 96   Goals: 51
Born: Lochgilphead, Argyllshire, 11 November 1908
Died: Lochgilphead, 10 January 1982

CAREER
CLUBS: Third Lanark, Manchester United, WEDNESDAY (£3,000 deal including George Nevin and Jack Ball, December 1933-July 1937), Third Lanark
OTHER: became a well-known public speaker in Scotland.

Neil Dewar spent his youth in a Scottish fishing village, working for his father, a trawler man, on Loch Fyne and also as a hotel porter. He approached, without success, several major clubs around Glasgow before joining Third Lanark on his twenty-first birthday. He developed fast and in less than 4 seasons scored 124 goals for the Scottish club, gaining a Second Division championship medal in 1931. He also won three full caps for his country (versus England and France in 1932, and Wales in 1933) and twice represented the Scottish League. At that time he was one of the most sought-after players north of the border and it was Manchester United who eventually secured his services. A brilliant and dangerous opportunist who switched positions regularly during the course of a game, confusing defenders at will, Dewar could score goals out of nothing and bagged 14 in 36 starts for United before transferring to Hillsborough in a deal that took Jack Ball to Old Trafford. In fact, he was the first signing made by Wednesday's new manager, Billy Walker. Shortly after joining the Owls, Dewar eloped with the daughter of Councillor A.E. Thomson, a Manchester United director. The couple overlooked the residential qualification required for a registry office wedding and there were initial difficulties before the ceremony went ahead. A few weeks later, Thomson resigned his directorship in the wake of the publicity surrounding his daughter's affair.

That apart, Dewar continued to crack in the goals for Wednesday, claiming 13 in his first season. He then surprisingly lost his place to new signing Jack Palethorpe halfway through 1934/35 and as a result missed that season's FA Cup win. He bounced back in style the following term, netting 22 goals, including the Charity Shield winner versus Arsenal, and ended his association with the Owls with 10 more strikes in 1936/37.

Neil Dewar

DIALLO, Drissa
Defender

Appearances: 9+3
Born: Nouadhibou, Mauritania, 4 January 1973

CAREER
CLUBS: RC Tilluer, Sedan, AS Bevenannes, KV Mechelen, Burnley, Ipswich Town, WEDNESDAY (free, June 2005-July 2006), MK Dons.

The second defender signed by Owls' manager Paul Sturrock in the summer of 2005, Drissa Diallo, a Guinea international, 6ft 1in tall and 12st 4lbs in weight, having failed to establish himself in the Ipswich side, having earlier played in 18 games for Burnley. A strong tackler, he can also play at full-back.

DI CANIO, Paolo
Midfield, forward

Appearances: 46+2 Goals: 17
Born: Rome, Italy, 9 July 1968

CAREER
CLUBS: SC Lazio, Ternana, Juventus, Napoli,
AC Milan, Celtic, WEDNESDAY (£4.5 million, August
1997-January 1999), West Ham United, Charlton
Athletic, SC Lazio, Cisco Roma.

Prior to joining Celtic in 1996, Paolo Di Canio had scored 23 goals in 222 League games in Italy. In his only season at Parkhead he netted 16 times in 37 games as the Bhoys finished runners-up to Rangers in the Premier League and lost in the semi-final of the Scottish Cup. A hugely talented player, but very temperamental, he left Wednesday under a dark cloud following the well-documented incident where he pushed over referee Paul Alcock during the Premiership game at home against Arsenal in September 1998 and was sent off. Di Canio was subsequently charged with misconduct by the FA and was suspended for twelve matches as well as being fined. Wednesday allowed him to go home to Rome to escape the attention of the media. He was due to return to Hillsborough to play in the game against Leicester on Boxing Day but failed to turn up, stating he was suffering from stress. He never played for the Owls again and left to join West Ham. Nevertheless, during his eighteen-month stay at Hillsborough the fiery Italian certainly entertained the fans. As well as making goals, he scored some spectacular ones himself, including a brilliant solo effort against Newcastle prior to his misdemeanour against the Gunners. He continued to shine at Upton Park, scoring 51 goals in 141 out-

ings for the Hammers before having a spell with Charlton. He returned to Italian football in 2004. Surprisingly, despite his undoubted talent, Di Canio was never capped by Italy. He did, however, gain a Serie 'A' championship medal with AC Milan in 1996. Unfortunately Di Canio was again trouble in December 2005. He was branded a fascist by one of his teammates following a gesture he made at a group of his own Lazio supporters during a game against Livorno. Awarded UEFA's Fair Play Award in 1999, he won Goal of the Season in 2000.

DI PIEDI, Michele
Striker

Appearances: 10+34   Goals: 7
Born: Palermo, Italy, 4 December 1980

CAREER
CLUBS: Perugia, WEDNESDAY (free, August 2000-
May 2003), Mansfield Town, Odd Grenland, Bristol
Rovers, AS Sora, Bournemouth, Apoel Nicosia.

Giant 6ft 6ins striker Michele Di Piedi, energetic, quick and tricky for his size, endured an injury-plagued 2001/02 season at Hillsborough after making a decent start to his Wednesday career during the previous campaign when he scored 5 goals in 28 appearances. After regaining full fitness, he struggled to make the first team and was released in 2003.

DICKINSON, Walter
Full-back

Appearances: 8
Born: Sheffield, 22 December 1895
Died: Sheffield, 5 February 1968

CAREER
CLUBS: Barnsley, Southend United, Barrow, Bradford
Park Avenue, WEDNESDAY (£250, September 1922-
March 1923), Swindon Town.

Walter Dickinson spent one season at Hillsborough during which time he deputised for both Jack Bellas and George Prior, making eight appearances. He moved on once Ernie Blenkinsop and Billy Felton had bedded themselves in as full-back partners. After leaving Hillsborough, Dickinson scored 20 goals in 230 League games for Swindon. His son was killed in the Second World War.

DILLON, Francis Richard Edward
Outside right

Appearances: 9
Born: Bury, March 1913
Deceased by 2000.

CAREER
CLUBS: Manchester North End, WEDNESDAY (free, May 1938-May 1941)
WARTIME GUEST APPEARANCES: Rotherham United

Frank Dillon was signed as cover for Idris Lewis and Len Massarella. He made his first and last appearances for the club in place of the latter in the two derbies against Sheffield United in 1938/39, helping the Owls win the second match 1-0. He also played in three Second World War games for the club.

DJORDJIC, Bojan
Winger

Appearances: 4+1
Born: Belgrade, Yugoslavia, 6 February 1982

CAREER
CLUBS: Rad Beograd, Broomapojkarna (two spells), Manchester United, WEDNESDAY (loan, December 2001-January 2002), Aarhus Gymnastik Forening, Red Star Belgrade, Glasgow Rangers, Plymouth Argyle.

Lively Swedish Under-21 international (capped five times) Bojan Djordic made two appearances for Manchester United and five for the Owls before moving back to Scandinavia. His father, Branko, played for Red Star Belgrade and Yugoslavia.

DOBSON, Colin
Forward

Appearances: 188   Goals: 50
Born: Eston, Middlesbrough, 9 May 1940

CAREER
CLUBS: South Bank, WEDNESDAY (free, May 1955-August 1966), Huddersfield Town, Brighton & Hove Albion, Bristol Rovers (player-coach), Coventry City (coach), Port Vale (coach), West Riffa, Al Rayan, Aston Villa (reserve/youth team coach), Sporting Lisbon (youth coach), Gillingham (chief scout, youth coach), Coventry City (assistant youth coach), Al Arabi-Kuwait (coach), Oman (national team coach), Port Vale (coach), Coventry City (academy coach), Stoke City (chief scout).

The slightly-built Colin Dobson had to wait until September 1961 before making the first of his 188 appearances for the Owls, replacing Bobby Craig against Arsenal. A regular in the side for five seasons, he never quite fulfilled the early promise he had shown as a teenager. Capped twice by England at under-23 level versus Romania and Yugoslavia in 1963, he fell from favour after helping the Owls reach the 1966 FA Cup final. He netted 52 goals in 175 games for Huddersfield, top-scoring in his first two seasons at Leeds Road while gaining a Second Division championship winners' medal in 1970. He fractured his leg with Brighton before helping Bristol Rovers gain promotion from the Third Division. Dobson did not sign professional forms until he was twenty-one, insisting he completed his apprenticeship as a ship builder before launching his career in football.

D

DODDS, Christopher
Inside forward, centre half

Appearances: 1
Born: Gateshead, 24 March 1904
Died: Gateshead, 24 June 1990

CAREER
CLUBS: Middlesbrough, Accrington Stanley, WEDNESDAY (£790, October 1928-August 1931), Colwyn Bay United, Accrington Stanley.

Chris Dodds spent most of his early career as a reserve. Initially an inside forward, he was converted into a centre half, the position he occupied when appearing in his only League game for the Owls, in a 5-2 win at Leicester in November 1930 when he deputised for Tony Leach. He made 157 appearances for Accrington.

DONALDSON, O'Neill McKay
Striker

Appearances: 4+10 Goals: 3
Born: Birmingham, 24 November 1969

CAREER
CLUBS: Manchester United, Hinckley Town, Shrewsbury Town, Doncaster Rovers, Mansfield Town, WEDNESDAY (£50,000, January 1995-March 1998), Oxford United (L), Stoke City, Torquay United, Halesowen Town
OTHER: now helps children with special needs and juvenile offenders.

A tall, pacy striker, on the bubbly side, O'Neill Donaldson made 100 League appearances in all, having his best spells with Shrewsbury and Torquay. Ten of his fourteen outings for the Owls came as a substitute, his debut was in the Premiership at Manchester City in March 1995 and he scored his first goal in a 3-0 win over QPR six months later.

DONNELLY, Simon Thomas
Midfield

Appearances: 30+32 Goals: 8
Born: Glasgow, 1 December 1974

CAREER
CLUBS: Celtic, WEDNESDAY (free, July 1999-June 2003), Coventry City, St Johnstone, Dunfermline Athletic, Partick Thistle.

Simon Donnelly scored 43 goals in 216 games for Celtic before joining the Owls. He also won 10 full and 11 Under-21 caps for Scotland and gained winners' medals for triumphs in both the Scottish Cup (1995) and Premier League (1998). Unfortunately the attacking midfielder had a very frustrating first season at Hillsborough due to a string of niggling injuries. He regained his fitness for 2000/01 but thereafter, until his departure, had to battle to get first team action, spending a lot of time on the subs' bench. He seemed too lightweight to master the rigours of English football!

DOOLEY, Derek, MBE
Centre forward

Appearances: 63 Goals: 63
Born: Sheffield, 13 December 1929

CAREER
CLUBS: Lincoln City, WEDNESDAY (free, June 1947-July 1953, manager January 1971-December 1973), Sheffield United (commercial manager, director, managing director, chief executive, chairman).
WARTIME GUEST APPEARANCES: Dundee United
OTHER: journalist; ran the Development Fund Office at Hillsborough (October 1962-January 1971).

After top-scoring with 13 goals for Lincoln's Midland League side in 1946/47 and playing twice in the Second Division, Derek Dooley joined the Owls. He became a prolific marksman with Wednesday before tragedy struck

Derek Dooley

during a League game at Preston in February 1953. He broke his leg in a collision with opposing goalkeeper George Thompson and gangrene set in before it could be effectively treated. Sadly the limb had to be amputated to save the player's life.

At 6ft 2ins tall, Dooley wore size twelve boots and was the idol of the Spion Kop at Hillsborough after bursting onto the scene in 1951/52 with 46 goals in only 30 League games, helping the Owls win the Second Division title. He netted 16 times the following season before suffering that devastating injury at Deepdale. Dooley, who netted 180 goals at all levels for Wednesday, was awarded a benefit game in 1955 (the first under the new Hillsborough floodlights) and over £15,000 was raised. As manager of the Owls, he steered the team towards the top of the Second Division in 1973 before performances dropped and the promotion challenge fizzled out. He received a shock when, on Christmas Eve 1973, he went to the ground and was promptly sacked. Dooley signed some fine players for the club, including Dave Clements, Ken Knighton and Scottish international Willie Henderson. After

moving to Sheffield United, he has never since returned to Hillsborough to watch a game involving Wednesday – sad really for such a well-respected gentleman. Awarded the Freedom of the City of Sheffield in 1993, ten years later he received the MBE.

DOWD, Hugh Oliver
Defender

Appearances: 134+3
Born: Lurgan, Northern Ireland, 19 May 1951

CAREER
CLUBS: Newry Celtic, Glenavon, WEDNESDAY (£20,000, July 1974-August 1979), Doncaster Rovers, Sheffield FC
OTHER: employed by the Sheffield Council; later worked as a commanding officer for the Youth Offending Team.

Hugh Dowd won three caps for his country, the first with Glenavon in 1974, the others with Wednesday in 1975. He spent five years at Hillsborough before making almost 100 appearances in 4 seasons for Doncaster. A strong, well-built defender who played on the right of the Owls' back four before taking over from John Holsgrove in the centre, Dowd missed only four League games in 1976/77 – his best season with the club.

DOWLING, Michael
Forward

Appearances: 7
Born: Jarrow, 1889
Deceased by 1965

CAREER
CLUBS: Paisley St Mirren, WEDNESDAY (£40, May 1910-June 1911), Portsmouth, Jarrow, Lincoln City
OTHER: served in the Royal Navy during the First World War.

Mike Dowling made his League debut for Wednesday in a 3-1 win at Preston in September 1910. A spirited forward, described as being 'sturdy, fast and dashing', he never settled at Hillsborough and switched his allegiance to Portsmouth after one season with the Owls.

DOWNES, Steven Fleming
Forward

Appearances: 29+5 Goals: 5
Born: Leeds, 2 December 1949

CAREER
CLUBS: Wolverhampton Wanderers, Rotherham United, WEDNESDAY (£35,000, December 1969-August 1972), Chesterfield, Halifax Town, Blackburn Rovers, Scarborough, Gainsborough Trinity.
OTHER: sales rep; ran his own electrical company in Leeds.

During his League career, Steve Downes hit 45 goals in 186 games, 18 coming in 59 outings for Rotherham. A positive striker, he linked up with Jack Whitham and Alan Warboys in the Owls' attack and scored on his debut in a 2-0 win over Sunderland on Boxing Day, 1969. Injured during the game with Leicester in October 1970, he was laid low for quite some time. Returning to the side later in the season, he was never the same and eventually moved to Chesterfield.

DRABBLE, John
Half-back

Appearances: 1
Born: Sheffield, circa 1868
Died: 1929

CAREER
CLUBS: WEDNESDAY (seasons 1889-91).

A Wednesday reserve, Jack Drabble's only appearance came in the Football Alliance in 1889/90. His cousin, Frank Drabble, played for several clubs including Spurs, Nottingham Forest, Burnley, Bolton and Queens Park Rangers.

DRISCOLL, John Henry
Inside left

Appearances: 6   Goals: 2
Born: Grays, Essex, 27 July 1909
Died: Wellington, 7 October 1997

CAREER
CLUBS: Oswestry Town, Stourbridge, West Bromwich Albion, WEDNESDAY (£300, May 1937-August 1938), Wellington Town, Wrexham.

Unable to get a look in at The Hawthorns owing to the form of internationals Teddy Sandford and Walter Robbins, Jack Driscoll moved to Hillsborough where he again found it hard to get into the first team, making only six appearances, his debut coming in a 1-0 defeat at Manchester United in October 1937. His first goal earned the Owls a 1-0 win at Coventry a month later.

DRIVER, Allenby
Forward

Appearances: 12   Goals: 6
Born: Blackwell, Derbyshire, 29 September 1918
Deceased

CAREER
CLUBS: Clipstone, WEDNESDAY (free, April 1936-October 1946), Royal Artillery.
WARTIME GUEST APPEARANCES: Brentford, Millwall, Crystal Palace, Fulham, Brighton & Hove Albion, Aberdeen, Watford, Luton Town, Norwich City, Ipswich Town, Walsall, Corby Town, Frickley Colliery.
OTHER: worked for Union Carbine (Sheffield).

Allen Driver developed into an exceptionally fine marksman in the lower Divisions, scoring over 60 goals in more than 200 games for four League clubs. He had found it difficult to get regular first team action at Hillsborough when reserve to Ernie Matthews, Jack Thompson and Charlie Napier. However, when called upon he certainly proved his worth, averaging 1 goal every 2 games, netting the winner versus Chesterfield on his debut on New Year's Day 1938. He bagged 11 goals in 35 Second World War appearances for the Owls.

DRURY, George Benjamin
Forward

Appearances: 47   Goals: 11
Born: Hucknall, Notts, 22 January 1914
Died: Hucknall, Notts, June, 1972

CAREER
CLUBS: Loughborough Corinthians, West Bromwich Albion, Heanor Town, WEDNESDAY (free, September 1934-March 1938), Arsenal, Nottingham Forest, Liverpool, WEDNESDAY (January 1941-March 1942), Doncaster Rovers, Distillery, Burnley & Bury, West Bromwich Albion, Watford, Linby Colliery, Doncaster Rovers, South Normanton.
WARTIME GUEST APPEARANCES: Aberdeen.
OTHER: RAF – Second World War.

A forward of innate footballing skill, George Drury was both shrewd and gutsy. His career began with the Owls in 1934. However, he had to wait two years before making his League debut, scoring his first goal for the club a week later in a 2-2 draw at Liverpool. He made 25 appearances for the Owls in 1937/38 before moving to Arsenal. In his first season at Highbury, George played alongside the country's costliest footballer at that time, Bryn Jones, as well as the England duo of Ted Drake and Cliff Bastin. During the Second World War he twice represented the Irish Regional League against the League of Ireland, hit 6 goals in 29 games for the Owls and was top-scorer for Forest (1939/40) and Bury

(1944/45). His senior career realised 74 goals in 306 matches.

DRYBURGH, William
Outside right

Appearances: 52   Goals: 10
Born: Lochgelly, Cowdenbeath, 22 May 1876
Died: Kelty, Fife, 5 April 1951

CAREER
CLUBS: Cowdenbeath, WEDNESDAY (free, August 1897-July 1899), Millwall Athletic, WEDNESDAY (£50, May 1901-April 1902), Cowdenbeath, Tottenham Hotspur, Lochgelly United.
OTHER: miner.

Bill Dryburgh had to work hard at his game and was rewarded with 17 outings during his first spell with the Owls, scoring on his debut in a 5-2 League defeat against the 1897 double winners Aston Villa. After netting 13 goals in 88 games for Millwall, whom he helped win the Southern District Combination and finish runners-up in the Western League, he returned to Wednesday where he added a further 12 appearances to his tally before returning to Cowdenbeath.

DUNGWORTH, John William
Defender

Appearances: 49   Goals: 5
Born: Heeley, Sheffield, 1866
Died: Sheffield, 1939

CAREER
CLUBS: WEDNESDAY (March 1882-April 1892).
OTHER: works manager in Sheffield.

Jack Dungworth spent seven years with Wednesday before injury forced him to retire, aged twenty-eight. He played in 17 consecutive FA Cup games between October 1885 and the final in March 1890, when he collected a runners-up medal after the Owls had crashed 6-1 to Blackburn. A strong, reliable player, Jack also helped the Owls win the Sheffield Challenge Cup in 1887 and 1888, the Wharncliffe Charity Cup in 1886 and 1888 and the Football Alliance in 1890. Away from soccer, he was a fine middle-distance runner, one of the best in England, and won 25 medals on the track during the 1880s.

DUNLOP, William
Outside left

Appearances: 1
Born: Sheffield, March 1862
Died: 1950

CAREER
CLUBS: WEDNESDAY (May 1892-May 1893), Darwen.
OTHER: iron turner.

Bill Dunlop played in Wednesday's first ever game in the Football League, at Notts County in September 1892, his only appearance for the club.

DUNN, John Henry
Right-back

Appearances: 8
Born: Eccles, Manchester, November 1888
Died: Manchester, circa 1967

CAREER
CLUBS: Leeds City, Luton Town, WEDNESDAY (£600, August 1920-June 1921).

Jack Dunn spent one season with Luton before joining the Owls, for whom he started 1920/21 as first choice right-back – after five different players had been tried in that position the previous campaign. He eventually gave way to Jack Bellas. A knee injury ended his career.

E

EAGLES, Christopher Mark
Midfield

Appearances: 21+4 Goals: 3
Born: Hemel Hempstead, 19 November 1985

CAREER
CLUBS: Manchester United, Watford (L), WEDNESDAY (loan, July-December 2005), Watford (L), NEC Nimigen (L).

An FA Youth Cup winner with Manchester United in 2003, Chris Eagles has also played for England at Youth level. Reserve midfielder to many great stars at Old Trafford, he prefers to play on the right and represented the Football League against Italy's Serie 'B' XI in February 2006.

EARP, Martin John
Right-back

Appearances: 174 Goals: 8
Born: Sherwood, Nottinghamshire, 6 September 1872
Died: South Africa.

CAREER
CLUBS: Nottingham Forest, Everton, Nottingham Forest, Corinthians, WEDNESDAY (free, August 1893-May 1900), Stockport County.
OTHER: emigrated to South Africa and joined the police force.

Amateur full-back Jack Earp did not depend on football for a living. Nevertheless, he was a man of deep conviction and strong principle and would never play on Christmas Day. He loved the hurly-burly of the game and as a long-serving player and committee man, made 50 appearances in 2 spells with Forest whom he helped win the Football Alliance in 1892. After

10 outings for Everton he joined the Owls and in 1896 collected an FA Cup winners' medal. Immensely popular with his colleagues and supporters alike, he skippered the Owls in that final against Wolves. Two years later he starred for the Football League against the Irish League – his only representative honour.

His brother Fred also played for Nottingham Forest (1878-85).

EATON, Walter
Right-back

Appearances: 1
Born: Sheffield, August 1881
Died: circa 1958

CAREER
CLUBS: WEDNESDAY (1904/05).
OTHER: worked as a halloware stamper.

An Owls' reserve-team player, Wally Eaton's only appearance for the first team was against Derby County in April 1905 when he deputised for Willie Layton.

EDMUNDSON, James
Centre forward

Appearances: 14   Goals: 2
Born: Carleton, Yorkshire, 1890
Died: Leeds, 1964

CAREER
CLUBS: Leyland, Leeds City, WEDNESDAY (£1,000, October 1919-May 1920), Swansea Town, Exeter City.
WARTIME GUEST APPEARANCES: Preston North End.

One of the many players who left Leeds City when that club went bust in 1919, 'Joe' Edmundson was a useful centre forward, strong and mobile, who had scored 16 goals in 31 games during his time at Elland Road, including 10 in 20 First World War fixtures. He

never reached the heights expected of him at Hillsborough and, after leaving the Owls, netted 33 times in 60 League games for Swansea.

EDWARDS, Leonard Owen
Half-back

Appearances: 2
Born: Wrexham, 30 May 1930

CAREER
CLUBS: Wrexham, Llay Welfare, WEDNESDAY (£115, January 1951-March 1954), Brighton & Hove Albion, Crewe Alexandra.

A reserve with Wednesday and Brighton, Len Edwards had his best spell in the game with Crewe, for whom he made 40 League appearances. A strong tackler, he deputised in the Owls' defence for George Davies in successive away games at West Ham (won 6-0) and Doncaster (1-1) in December 1951.

EGGO, Robert Mollison
Defender

Appearances: 23
Born: Brechin, 22 November 1895
Died: Sheffield, 23 May 1977

CAREER
CLUBS: Brechin City, Heart of Midlothian, Dunfermline Athletic, WEDNESDAY (free, August 1919-May 1921), Reading.
OTHER: licensee; also worked in a hospital kitchen.

Bert Eggo lost his place in Wednesday's League side through pleurisy after some very useful and positive displays in the right half position during the first half of 1920/21, having made his debut for the club at Burnley the previous February. Scrupulously fair, he was a model of consistency at Reading, for whom he made 312 appearances, and gained a Third Division

(South) championship medal in 1926 before announcing his retirement after a testimonial match versus Tottenham Hotspur in 1928. At that point he returned to Scotland and worked as a porter at Dundee hospital.

EKOKU, Efanwangu Goziem
Striker

Appearances: 62+9 Goals: 21
Born: Manchester, 8 June 1967

CAREER
CLUBS: Sutton United, Charlton Athletic, Bournemouth, Norwich City, Wimbledon, Grasshopper-Club Zurich, WEDNESDAY (free, October 2000-September 2002), Luton Town, Rushden & Diamonds, Brentford, Dublin City.
OTHER: worked as a soccer pundit on TV; insurance salesman.

Efan Ekoku scored 25 goals for Bournemouth, 17 for Norwich, 44 for Wimbledon and 22 for the Grasshopper club before manager Paul Jewell signed him for the Owls to boost a flagging attack. In his first season at Hillsborough his endeavour, commitment, pace and strength proved highly effective and quickly earned a place in the hearts of the fans – especially after he scored both goals in a League Cup win over Sheffield United. His form was not quite so good the following term as injuries continued to plague him.

ELLIS, Keith Duncan
Centre forward

Appearances: 118 Goals: 60
Born: Sheffield, 6 November 1935

CAREER
CLUBS: Edgar Allen's, WEDNESDAY (April 1953-March 1963), Scunthorpe United, Cardiff City, Lincoln City.

OTHER: worked in the licensing trade and looked after hospitality boxes for a brewery at Elland Road (Leeds United FC), at the Sheffield Steelers Ice Hockey club and Wakefield Wildcats Rugby League Club.

Keith Ellis made his League debut for the Owls at home to Preston in March 1955. Restricted to just 24 first-team games in his first 5 seasons as a professional at Hillsborough, Ellis burst on the scene in 1959/60 when he netted 14 goals in 26 outings. He followed up with 19 in 37 starts in the Owls' Second Division 1960/61 promotion campaign, including a hat-trick in a 7-2 FA Cup win at Old Trafford. He then scored 11 times in 27 outings in 1961/62, one of his strikes being Wednesday's first ever goal in Europe versus Olympique Lyonnais in the Inter-Cities Fairs Cup in the September, but after that he found it hard to hold down a place in the side and when David Layne arrived Ellis switched his allegiance to Scunthorpe. Nicknamed 'The Big Yank', he helped Cardiff win the Welsh Cup in 1965.

ELLIS, Samuel
Defender

Appearances: 179+3 Goals: 1
Born: Ashton-under-Lyne, 12 September 1946

CAREER
CLUBS: WEDNESDAY (July 1964-March 1972), Mansfield Town, Lincoln City, Watford (player-coach), Blackpool (manager), Bury (manager), Manchester City (assistant manager), Lincoln City (assistant coach, manager), Burnley (assistant manager), Leeds United (assistant manager).

Sam Ellis is one of the few players to make his FA Cup debut in a final at Wembley, doing so in 1966, at the age of eighteen, for the Owls against Everton in place of the injured Vic Mobley. At that point he had made only 10 League appearances, the first in a 3-0 home win over Blackpool six weeks earlier. He established himself in the side the following season (missing only one League game) but in 1967/68 lost out when Mobley returned. Ellis, a strong, determined and forthright competitor, always full of confidence, went on to appear in over 180 senior games for the Owls and won three England Under-23 caps before transferring to Mansfield, signed by ex-Hillsborough manager Danny Williams. He played in 64 games for the Stags, helping them win the Notts FA County Cup in 1972. He then appeared in 173 games for Lincoln, skippering both the Imps and Watford when they won the Fourth Division title under Graham Taylor's management. Retiring as a player with almost 450 appearances under his belt, Ellis was subsequently guided along by Taylor and Alan Brown in the field of management, working perilously hard, and in 1985 he took Blackpool to promotion from the Fourth Division – his only major achievement as a boss. Ellis, who gained thirteen GCEs at Audenshaw Grammar School, was all set to start a banking career before Wednesday stepped in and turned him into a footballer.

EUSTACE, Peter
Midfield

Appearances: 268+12   Goals: 26
Born: Stocksbridge, Yorkshire, 31 July 1944

CAREER
CLUBS: WEDNESDAY (August 1959-December 1969), West Ham United, Rotherham United, WEDNESDAY (loan, August 1972, signed for £13,900, November 1972), Worksop Town (two spells), Peterborough United, Sunderland (coach), WEDNESDAY (assistant manager, coach, July 1984, manager, October 1988-February 1989), Leyton Orient (assistant manager, manager).
OTHER: ran a pub in Yorkshire.

A brilliant, creative player, Peter Eustace reached his peak in the mid-1960s and was a

Peter Eustace

star performer when the Owls reached the 1966 FA Cup final. A superb passer of the ball, cool and precise in his overall play, he made the team tick and was described by his manager, Danny Williams, as the best player he ever had. Soon afterwards Eustace was sold to West Ham for £90,000, replacing England's World Cup-winning star Martin Peters who was set to join Tottenham. However, Eustace, who actually played his first game for the Hammers against Wednesday in January 1970 (won 3-2) didn't quite fit the bill and after a loan spell at Millmoor he was brought back to Hillsborough by Derek Dooley for a reduced fee. In his second spell with Wednesday he was used as a sweeper and once took over in goal. But when the Owls' decline got worse he left for Peterborough and later became coach at Sunderland before returning as assistant to manager Howard Wilkinson at Hillsborough, taking the hot seat himself in 1988. As manager of Orient he sold Chris Bart-Williams to the Owls. In 1994 Eustace was replaced at Brisbane Road by joint managers John Sitton and ex-Wednesday goalkeeper Chris Turner.

E

EVANS, Paul
Goalkeeper

Appearances: 7
Born: Newcastle, South Africa, 28 December 1973

CAREER
CLUBS: *Wits University, Leeds United, Crystal Palace, Bradford City, Supersport United, Mamelodi Sundowns, Wits University, Jomo Cosmos, WEDNESDAY (trial, March-April 2002), Huddersfield Town, WEDNESDAY (free, August 2002-October 2003), Crewe Alexandra, Rushden & Diamonds, Bath City.*

Paul Evans, 6ft 4ins tall, failed to get into the First XI at Elland Road. After a twelve-week trial he was recruited by Wednesday as cover for Kevin Pressman and appeared in seven games before slipping into the reserves. He injured his shoulder after moving to Rushden & Diamonds. A South African international, Evans won 2 full, 4 Under-20 and 3 Under-23 caps.

EVANS, Richard, Glyn
Wide midfield

Appearances: 9+2   Goals: 1
Born: Cardiff, 19 June 1983

CAREER
CLUBS: *Arsenal, Everton, Coventry City, Cardiff City, Birmingham City, Moor Green, WEDNESDAY (free, March 2003-January 2006), Swansea City, Colchester United.*

A lively winger with a good attitude, Richard Evans quickly made his mark with the Owls, scoring in his fourth outing, a 7-2 League win at Burnley in April 2003. He suffered a cruciate ligament injury five months later and took quite some time to regain full fitness, missing virtually all of the 2003/04 campaign. He has represented Wales at under-21 level.

EYRE, Claude Ronald
Centre forward

Appearances: 1
Born: Hucknall, Notts, 6 November 1901
Died: Bournemouth, 18 August 1969

CAREER
CLUBS: *WEDNESDAY (trial, September-October 1923, signed January 1925), Bournemouth, Christchurch.*
OTHER: *an auxiliary fireman for the West Hampshire Water Board, also worked for the Southern Electricity Board.*

Ron Eyre's only League outing for the Owls came in the 2-1 home defeat by Oldham in March 1924 when he deputised for Sid Binks. After leaving Wednesday he became a legend at Bournemouth for whom he netted 205 goals in 325 games in 8 years. He also played bowls.

EYRE, Isaac John
Forward

Appearances: 1
Born: Heeley, Sheffield, March 1875
Died: Gainsborough, 1947

CAREER
CLUBS: *Sheffield FC, WEDNESDAY (free, August 1903-April 1904).*

A reserve with the Owls, Jack Eyre became the fifth player to appear in the centre forward position in successive League games when he made his debut for Wednesday in a 1-0 home win over Stoke in March 1904. He was released at the end of the season. His son, Edmund Eyre, played for Rotherham Town, Birmingham, Aston Villa and Middlesbrough before the First World War.

F

FALLON, William Joseph
Outside left

Appearances: 50   Goals: 13
Born: Larne, Republic of Ireland, 14 January 1912
Died: Nottingham, March, 1989

CAREER
CLUBS: Dublin Dolphin, Notts County, WEDNESDAY (£3,000 plus Jack Roy, March 1938-December 1939). WARTIME GUEST APPEARANCES: Shamrock Rovers, Shelbourne, Dundalk, Notts County, Exeter City, Peterborough United.

Bill Fallon, a Republic of Ireland international (nine caps won, 1935-39) had an interesting career that spanned twenty years during which time he appeared in over 300 matches, 135 in the League for Notts County and 100 during the Second World War, when he assisted three Irish clubs. He spent one full season at Hillsborough, netting 11 goals in 40 games in the last pre-Second World War campaign after taking over from Ellis Rimmer. Quick and clever, with an eye for goal, he was a big hit with the fans and one of his best displays for Wednesday was against Norwich in November 1938 when he teased and tormented the Canaries' defence in a 7-0 win. He was thirty-nine when he retired. His younger brother, Peter, played for Exeter and QPR in the 1940s.

FANTHAM, John
Inside left

Appearances: 426+9 Goals: 167
Born: Sheffield, 6 February 1939

CAREER
CLUBS: WEDNESDAY (£10, amateur, April 1954; professional, October 1956), Rotherham United (£5,000, October 1969), Macclesfield Town (May 1971-72), Hallam (coach, assistant manager). OTHER: owner of a machine tool business.

One of the great marksmen in Wednesday's history and the holder of the club's post Second World War aggregate scoring record, John Fantham simply had the knack of being in the right place (inside the penalty area) at the right time, and he seemed to find the net with consummate ease. Some of his goals were tap-ins, some deflections, a few headers and several beauties. For just a £10 signing-on fee – Wednesday beat Wolves for Fantham's services – he turned out to be a wonderful acquisition, giving Sheffield Wednesday football club tremendous service for a total of fifteen years (thirteen as a professional). He made his League debut in February 1958 at home to Tottenham, secured a first-team place the following season (after Albert Quixall had left for Manchester United), claimed his first goal in a 3-1 win at Brighton in October 1958 and remained a regular in the side (injuries apart) until 1969. He represented the Football League on three occasions (1960/61), played for the FA, and collected one Under-23 cap versus Italy in 1960 and one full cap versus Luxembourg a year later. In 1968, he grabbed his 150th goal for the Owls which, at the time, took him to the top of the club's post-war scoring list, ahead of Redfern Froggatt. He helped Wednesday win the Second Division in 1959 (scoring 12 goals) and played in the 1966 FA Cup final defeat by Everton. After leaving Hillsborough he bagged 8 goals in 53 League games for Rotherham. As a youngster Fantham also played cricket for Sheffield and Yorkshire Schools and if he hadn't chosen football as a career, he would have certainly reached county standard in an all-white kit. He is now a very fine golfer. Fantham played in the same Sheffield Boys' team as David Layne and Gordon Banks and his father, John Thomas, also played League football.

F

FAULKNER, David Peter
Defender

Appearances: 0+1
Born: Sheffield, 8 October 19875

CAREER
CLUBS: WEDNESDAY (September 1991-August 1996), Cape Cod Crusaders (L), Darlington, Waterford, Gainsborough Trinity, Hallam, Alfreton, Gresley Rovers, Sheffield FC.
OTHER: teacher in Hucknall, Notts.

Reserve defender David Faulkner came on as substitute for David German for his only senior outing for the Owls against FC Basel in the InterToto Cup in June 1995.

FEE, Gregory Paul
Defender

Appearances: 20+11   Goals: 1
Born: Halifax, 24 June 1964

CAREER
CLUBS: Bradford City, Kettering Town, Boston United, WEDNESDAY (£20,000, August 1987-March 1991), Preston North End (L), Northampton Town (L), Preston North End (L), Leyton Orient (L), Mansfield Town, Chesterfield (L), played for eight non-League clubs (1992-2002).
OTHER: teacher; worked for BP; now runs petrol stations in Yorkshire.

Greg Fee made 118 League appearances in 10 years with 7 major clubs. He covered for Lawrie Madden most of the time at Hillsborough, having his best spell in the First XI at the end of 1988/89, playing in eight successive League games. In 1993, he appeared in the semi-final of the AGT for Chesterfield against Stockport and three days later (after being recalled by Mansfield) played for the Stags v. Chesterfield in a League game at Edgeley Park. He helped Mansfield gain promotion from the Fourth Division in 1992.

FEELY, Peter John
Forward

Appearances: 21+3 Goals: 2
Born: Westminster, London, 3 January 1950

CAREER
CLUBS: Tottenham Hotspur, Enfield, Chelsea, Bournemouth, Fulham, Gillingham, WEDNESDAY (£8,000, February 1976-May 1979), Stockport County (L), Slough Town, also played in Norway and Hong Kong.
OTHER: quantity surveyor in the Far East.

As a teenager, Peter Feely represented England in Amateur and Youth internationals. He scored on his League debut for Chelsea versus Coventry in April 1971 but failed to win a place in the first team at Stamford Bridge, or at Bournemouth and Fulham. He netted 22 goals for Gillingham before joining the Owls. After a bright start when he partnered Mike Prendergast in attack, he struggled with his form and fitness. He is now a millionaire.

FELTON, William
Right-back

Appearances: 164
Born: Heworth, Gateshead, 1 August, 1900
Died: Manchester, 22 April 1977

CAREER
CLUBS: Jarrow, Grimsby Town, WEDNESDAY (£1,450, January 1923-March 1929), Manchester City, Tottenham Hotspur, Altrincham.

A former miner, strong and muscular, quick in recovery with a splendid kick, Billy Felton occupied both full-back positions but preferred the right. He joined the Owls in unusual circumstances on New Year's Day 1923. He was on his way to Accrington with his Grimsby teammates when a Wednesday official called him off the train and signed him – just in time to play against Southampton that same after-noon. Shortly afterwards Ernie Blenkinsop was recruited and they became the Owls' regular full-back pairing over the next couple of seasons. Capped by England against France in March 1925, Felton helped Wednesday win the Second Division the following season. After losing his place in the side, he was reserve to Tommy Walker and Blenkinsop before moving to Manchester City for whom he made 83 appearances. He followed up with another 78 outings for Spurs whom he skippered to promotion from the Second Division in 1933. Felton made over 350 club appearances in a fine career. He was also a very keen golfer.

FENWICK, Arthur George
Forward

Appearances: 1
Born: Sheffield, 1867
Died: 1928

CAREER
CLUBS: WEDNESDAY (1890/91).

Arthur Fenwick played in one Football Alliance game in his only season with the Owls.

FERGUSON, George Edward
Half-back, forward

Appearances: 5
Born: Ecclesfield, Sheffield, 1865
Died: 1925

CAREER
CLUBS: Lockwood Brothers, WEDNESDAY (August 1890-August 1892), Bolton Wanderers.

George Ferguson played five times (in different positions) for the Owls in the 1890/91 Football Alliance campaign. He scored 3 goals in 16 League games for Bolton.

FERGUSON, Robert
Goalkeeper

Appearances: 5
Born: Ardrossan, Ayrshire, 1 March 1945

CAREER
CLUBS: Kilmarnock, West Ham United, WEDNESDAY (loan, February-March 1974), Leicester City, Adelaide City, Adelaide Rugby Club (trainer).
OTHER: ran a scuba diving club in Adelaide, also sold carpets and tiles and later ran snack bars; he still lives in Australia.

Bobby Ferguson started off like a world-beater and in 1967, when he joined West Ham, the fee involved (£65,000) was the biggest ever paid between two British clubs for a goalkeeper. In fact, the Hammers had to wait before Ferguson put pen to paper because his club, Kilmarnock, had reached the semi-final stage of the European Cup. He left Rugby Park after 'Killie' had been defeated over two legs by Leeds. He produced many superb displays between the posts but unfortunately spent the last seven years of his career at Upton Park in the reserves and jumped at the chance of assisting the Owls. Inconsistency was a problem at times, although during his career he won seven Scottish caps (1965-67), played twice for the Scottish League and also starred in one Under-23 international. He made 276 appearances for West Ham and helped Kilmarnock win the Scottish League title in 1965. Ferguson also enjoys a round of golf and had a handicap of 8 at one stage. His best friend was tragically killed by a shark when scuba diving out of Bobby's complex.

FERGUSON, Ronald Charles
Forward

Appearances: 10+1 Goals: 1
Born: Accrington, 9 February 1957

F

CAREER

CLUBS: WEDNESDAY (July 1973-February 1976), Scunthorpe United (L), Darlington, Racing Jet Brussels, La Louviere.

OTHER: ran a printing company in Gainsborough.

After doing reasonably well at Hillsborough – albeit in a struggling side – Ron Ferguson went on to score 18 goals in 114 League games for Darlington. His only strike for the Owls came on his debut, in a 3-0 win at home over York City in November 1974.

FERRIER, Robert
Utility

Appearances: 329   Goals: 18
Born: Dumbarton, July 1874
Died: Motherwell, 11 December 1947

CAREER

CLUBS: Dumbarton, WEDNESDAY (May 1894-June 1906), WEDNESDAY (scout, 1920-39).

OTHER: boilermaker at Denny's shipyard.

When he joined Wednesday, Bob Ferrier was playing as an inside forward and almost instantly struck up a fine understanding with his winger Archie Brash. The pair was regarded in the mid-1890s as one of the best partnerships in the country. He scored 6 goals in 26 games in his first season but an injury prevented him from taking his place in the following year's FA Cup final. In 1898 he was switched to right half and after that became a class act, going on to appear in almost 330 senior games for the Owls, collecting a Second Division championship winners' medal in 1900 and following up with two more winners' medals for successive League title triumphs in 1903 and 1904. After losing his place to Herrod Ruddlesdin, Ferrier played a few games in the reserves before returning Scotland. His son, also named Bob, scored over 200 goals in 625 appearances for Motherwell. Some years later his grandson became an established sports writer.

FINNEY, Alan
Winger

Appearances: 504   Goals: 88
Born: Langwith, Yorkshire, 31 October 1933

CAREER

CLUBS: WEDNESDAY (April 1949-January 1966) Doncaster Rovers, Alfreton Town, Doncaster Dentists FC.

OTHER: worked at Armthorpe Colliery before becoming a bookmaker.

A League debutant, aged seventeen, versus Chelsea in February 1951, Alan Finney scored his first goal in a 6-0 home win over Everton on the last day of that 1950/51 season and the fol-

Alan Finney

lowing year helped Wednesday win the Second Division title, playing in 26 games on the right flank with Jackie Sewell his partner. He and Sewell were superb together and later it was the Finney-Albert Quixall partnership that kept the Owls' fans on a high. Finney, a fast, decisive player, with a powerful shot, who at times held on to the ball perhaps a shade too long, collected his second Football League Second Division winners' medal in 1956 and added a third to his tally in 1959, by which time he had switched to the left wing with John Fantham as his inside partner. Capped by England versus Scotland at 'B' and Under-23 levels in 1956 and 1957 respectively, he was always popular at Hillsborough. Alan served with the Royal Signals Unit, with Quixall, during his National Service.

FISH, Thomas
Left half

Appearances: 7
Born: Birtley, County Durham, June 1877
Died: 1935

CAREER
CLUBS: Birtley, WEDNESDAY (£10, May 1899-April 1903).

A reserve with the Owls for four seasons, Tom Fish deputised at left half for Herrod Ruddleshin in 6 of his 7 appearances, making his debut in a 3-1 win over Everton in March 1901.

FLEMING, John Ian Hares
Forward

Appearances: 17   Goals: 2
Born: Maybole, Strathclyde, 15 January 1953

CAREER
CLUBS: Kilmarnock, Aberdeen, WEDNESDAY (£48,000, February 1979-February 1980), Dundee,

Brechin City, FH Hafnajorforder (manager), Forfar Athletic (assistant manager), Arbroath (assistant manager), Aberdeen (scout, coach).
OTHER: works for an electrical company.

Ian Fleming scored 23 goals in 116 appearances for Aberdeen before spending a year at Hillsborough. Injury ruled him out on the Dons' 1977 Scottish League Cup final win but he played in the 1978 Cup final defeat by Rangers. A positive player, who occupied three central forward positions at Pittodrie, he was injured on his debut for the Owls at Southend in February 1979. He never really settled in Yorkshire.

FLETCHER, Brough
Utility

Appearances: 2
Born: Mealsgate, Cumberland, 9 March 1893
Died: Bristol, 12 March 1972

CAREER
CLUBS: Barnsley, WEDNESDAY (£600, February-December 1926), Barnsley (player, coach, manager), Bristol Rovers (manager), Walsall (manager).

A distinguished footballer, small and robust, Brough Fletcher was a prolific marksman during his first spell with Barnsley. Unfortunately he failed to settle down at Hillsborough and returned to Oakwell within ten months, after appearing in two Second Division matches for the Owls versus Hull and Stoke in April 1926, deputising for Harry Hill. As a manager, he guided Barnsley to the Third Division (North) title in 1934. He was later responsible for selling the Eastville Stadium (Bristol Rovers' ground) to a greyhound company. He was dismissed as Rovers' boss in 1949 after an FA inquiry into the club's involvement with the same greyhound company. Fletcher spent twenty-four years with Barnsley and hit 73 goals in 312 League games as a player.

F

FLETCHER, Douglas
Forward

Appearances: 4
Born: Sheffield, 17 September 1930

CAREER
CLUBS: WEDNESDAY (January 1948-May 1951), Bury, Scunthorpe United, Darlington, Halifax Town, non-League (1960-64).
OTHER: worked in Traffic Maintenance Department, Stocksbridge.

A reserve at Hillsborough, Doug Fletcher made his League debut at home to Leicester in April 1949 when he took over at centre forward from Clarrie Jordan. After leaving Wednesday he scored 60 goals in 184 League games for his 3 other clubs.

FLETCHER, Henry
Left half

Appearances: 1
Born: Sheffield, circa 1858
Died: circa 1921

CAREER
CLUBS: WEDNESDAY (1880/81).

Harry Fletcher's only game for the Owls was against Turton in an FA Cup-tie in January 1881.

FOLLY, Yoann
Midfield

Appearances: 34+10 *
Born: Togo, 6 June 1985

CAREER
CLUBS: St Etienne, Southampton, Nottingham Forest (L), Preston North End (L), WEDNESDAY (loan, January-May 2006; signed July 2006).

French Youth and Under-21 international midfielder Yoann Folly made 12 appearances in the Premiership for Southampton. A refined, dexterous player with neat skills, he has fine anticipation and did very well during his loan spell with Wednesday.

FORD, David
Outside left

Appearances: 130+5   Goals: 37
Born: Sheffield, 2 March 1945

CAREER
CLUBS: WEDNESDAY (April 1961-December 1969), Newcastle United, Sheffield United, Halifax Town.
OTHER: ran his own central heating and plumbing business in Sheffield and looked after the executive suite at Hillsborough.

David Ford, fast and direct with an eye for goal, figured prominently in Wednesday's 1966 FA Cup run. Prior to that he had worked hard to secure a first-team place and in that season (1965/66) scored 14 goals in 24 games, following up with 15 in 44 in the next campaign. Thereafter he was never quite the same player, especially after his fiancée was killed in a car crash while he suffered serious knee and scalp injuries. It took quite some time for the scars to heal. In fact, he never really got over that tragedy. Although he continued to give the club excellent service, averaging a goal every four games, he switched his allegiance to Newcastle in 1969, with winger Jackie Sinclair moving to Hillsborough. David, who was the first substitute used by Wednesday in a League game, replacing Don Megson in a 3-1 win over Sunderland in October 1965, was capped twice by England at under-23 level versus Wales and Scotland in 1966/67. He also helped rivals Sheffield United win promotion to the First Division in 1971.

FOX, Oscar
Forward

Appearances: 47   Goals: 4
Born: Sheffield, 1 January 1921
Died: Sheffield, 15 January 1990

CAREER
CLUBS: Wadsley Amateurs, WEDNESDAY (October 1943-June 1950), Mansfield Town (player, assistant manager), Liverpool (scout).
OTHER: worked for an engineering firm.

A pugnacious footballer, Oscar Fox was a regular in Wednesday's League side during the first half of 1948/49 having previously been reserve to Jackie Marriott and others. He made 37 appearances for the Owls during the Second World War and after leaving, played in more than 250 games for Mansfield, helping the Stags finish runners-up in the Third Division (North) in 1951. Fox's father, also Oscar, was a pre-First World War footballer with Castleford Town and Bradford City.

FOX, Peter David
Goalkeeper

Appearances: 52
Born: Scunthorpe, 5 July 1957

CAREER
CLUBS: WEDNESDAY (apprentice, July 1972; professional, June 1975), West Ham United (L, November 1977), Barnsley (L, December 1977), Team Hawaii/NASL (L, January-March 1978), Stoke City (£15,000, March 1978), Linfield (L, September-October 1992), Exeter City (free, July 1993; player/manager, July 1995-January 1999), later employed as a regional scout and goalkeeping coach at Rochdale (from 2001) and coach at 2007 play-off final winners Blackpool.
OTHER: reporter for the Press Association.

Peter Fox remained very consistent and reliable throughout his career. Never the flashy type, he

Peter Fox

ing the second half of 1975/76 (28 outings) before moving to Stoke once Chris Turner had established himself between the posts. Fox made 477 appearances for Stoke – a record for a goalkeeper – while helping the Potters win the AGT in 1992 and the Second Division title twelve months later.

FOX, William
Forward

Appearances: 4
Born: Scotland, circa 1871
Died: Scotland, circa 1940

CAREER
CLUBS: WEDNESDAY (trial, December 1894-April 1895), Carfin Club, Albion Rovers.

On trial with Wednesday for five months, Bill Fox made the first of his four League appearances in a 0-0 draw at Small Heath and his last in a 6-0 defeat by FA Cup finalists West Bromwich Albion.

F

FOXALL, Frank
Forward

Appearances: 44   Goals: 9
Born: Sheffield, June, 1883
Died: 1965

CAREER
CLUBS: Doncaster Rovers, Gainsborough Trinity, WEDNESDAY (April 1907-July 1910), Birmingham, Shrewsbury Town.

Frank Foxall did well with Wednesday but after losing his place to George Robertson, he quickly moved to Birmingham. A smart footballer with an eye for goal, he made his debut for the Owls in the derby defeat at Sheffield United in April 1907 and struck his first goal in his next game at Blackburn (won 2-0). He won the Chard Cup with Roundel in 1900, netted 38 times in 125 League games for Gainsborough and during his career hit 52 goals in 203 League outings.

FRANCIS, Trevor John
Forward

Appearances: 38+49   Goals: 9
Born: Plymouth, Devon, 19 April 1954

CAREER
CLUBS: Birmingham City, Detroit Express, Nottingham Forest, Detroit Express, Manchester City, Sampdoria, Atalanta, Glasgow Rangers, Queens Park Rangers (player, player-manager), WEDNESDAY (n/c February 1990, manager June 1991-May 1995), Birmingham City (manager), Crystal Palace (manager).
OTHER: soccer pundit on Sky Sports.

Trevor Francis was Britain's first £1 million footballer, signed by Nottingham Forest in 1979. He scored 15 goals in his first 16 League games for Birmingham, including 4 against Bolton Wanderers when only sixteen. Blessed with electrifying pace, intricate ball skills, a powerful

Trevor Francis

right-foot shot and amazing self-confidence, he helped Blues win promotion to the First Division in 1972 and struck 133 goals in 329 outings for the second city club. He then netted the winning goal for Forest in the 1979 European Cup final win over Malmö and a year later gained a Super Cup winners' medal, a League Cup runners-up medal but missed a second European Cup final through injury. Francis spent five seasons in Italy, gaining a Cup winners' medal with Sampdoria in 1985. He added a Scottish League Cup winners' medal to his collection in 1988 with Rangers and three years later, following his transfer to Hillsborough, he starred in Wednesday's Second Division promotion winning side and received a runners-up medal in the League Cup as a non-playing substitute against Manchester United. Then in 1993 (as manager) he gained both FA Cup and League Cup runners-up prizes. In 2001, as Birmingham boss, he lost to Liverpool on penalties in the final of the same competition at Cardiff. During his five-year tenure at St Andrew's he took Blues to the First Division play-offs three seasons running, losing each time. He was replaced by Steve Bruce as Blues manager – the man he took over from at Crystal Palace!

Capped 52 times by England and on five occasions at Under-21 level, Francis hit 225 goals in 752 appearances during his career. In his four years in charge at Hillsborough, the Owls finished third (promoted) in 1991, took third place again to reach the Premiership the following season and were seventh in both 1993 and 1994. They were runners-up in both the FA Cup and League Cup finals of 1993.

FROGGATT, Frank
Defender

Appearances: 96   Goals: 1
Born: Sheffield, 21 March 1898
Died: Sheffield, 6 March 1944

CAREER
CLUBS: Denaby United, WEDNESDAY (£650, October 1921-November 1927), Notts County, Chesterfield, Scarborough, Manchester North End, WEDNESDAY (scout, 1942-44).
OTHER: worked at Fox's Steelworks (Stocksbridge).

A tough, weighty defender whose sturdiness set him in good stead for constant battles with rugged opponents, Frank Froggatt was understudy for some considerable time to George Wilson before finally engaging himself in the centre half position on a permanent basis in the mid-1920s. An ever-present and captain of the side when the Second Division championship was won in 1925/26, he eventually gave way to Fred Keane, and after leaving the Owls appeared in 115 League games for Notts County. His son was Redfern Froggatt.

FROGGATT, Redfern
Forward

Appearances: 458   Goals: 148
Born: Sheffield, 23 August 1924
Died: Sheffield, 26 December 2003

CAREER
CLUBS: WEDNESDAY (July 1942-May 1962), Stalybridge Celtic.
OTHER: salesman for an oil company; worked for local hospital radio.

Redfern Froggatt, a finely built inside forward, was an Owl for almost twenty years. The motivating force behind the Wednesday attack, he was constructive, committed, possessed a fine array of skills, was a superb passer of the ball and scored and made many goals. A Second Division championship winner in 1952, 1956 and 1959, he also played for England on 4 occasions versus Wales, Belgium, Scotland and USA in 1952/53 (2 goals), won a 'B' cap versus Switzerland in 1950, played once for the Football League (1953) and scored 3 times in 3 outings for Sheffield versus Glasgow (1949-55). He also netted 18 times in 80 Second World War appearances for the Owls and, in all, made almost 550 appearances for the First XI. A hero with the fans, he emulated his father by skippering the side to the Second Division title (1959). Preferring the inside left position, he also played on the left wing and, in fact, many thought he produced his best football as a winger. Despite the signing of Jackie Sewell and the emergence of Albert Quixall, Redfern remained a key member of the squad and it was a sad day when he left Hillsborough. His son Paul was a Wednesday youth player.

FRYE, John Marr
Inside right

Appearances: 1
Born: Ardrossan, Ayrshire, 27 July 1933
Died: Androssan, 7 March 2005

CAREER
CLUBS: Hibernian, St Mirren, WEDNESDAY (£3,500, January-October 1961), Tranmere Rovers, Queen of the South, Hamilton Academical, Stranraer.
OTHER: oil-tanker driver.

F

John Frye's only senior appearance for the Owls was in a 2-0 defeat by Burnley in a sixth round FA Cup replay in March 1961. A member of the Hamilton side that crashed to a record 11-1 defeat against Hibs in 1965, his career realised 221 appearances. His father Derek played for Queen of the South and Stranraer.

G

GALE, Thomas
Defender

Appearances: 13
Born: Washington, County Durham, 4 November 1920
Died: Bath, 29 January 1975

CAREER
CLUBS: Gateshead, WEDNESDAY (£10, August 1944-August 1947), York City, non-League (1949-58).

Powerfully built, Tom Gale made his first appearance for the Owls against Notts County in September 1944. His FA Cup and League debuts followed in 1946 and 1947 against York City and Leicester respectively and besides his 13 senior outings for the Owls, he also played in 38 Second World War matches. He later made 80 appearances in 2 seasons for York.

GALLACHER, Kevin William
Forward

Appearances: 0+4
Born: Clydebank, 23 November 1966

CAREER
CLUBS: Duntocher Boys Club, Dundee United, Coventry City, Blackburn Rovers, Newcastle United, Preston North End, WEDNESDAY (free, March 2002-August 2002), Huddersfield Town.

Scottish international Kevin Gallacher scored 136 goals in 527 appearances before joining the Owls on a free transfer in 2002. Vastly experienced with 53 full, 2 'B', 7 Under-21 and several Youth and Schoolboy caps under his belt, he unfortunately made little impact in his short stay at Hillsborough.

GALLACHER, Paul James
Goalkeeper

Appearances: 8
Born: Glasgow, 16 August 1979

CAREER
CLUBS: Lochee United, Dundee United, Airdrieonians, Norwich City, Gillingham, WEDNESDAY (loan, March-May 2005), Stoke City.

Scottish international goalkeeper Paul Gallacher, capped 7 times at Under-21 level and on 8 occasions by the senior side, made 138 appearances for Dundee United but found himself third choice at Carrow Road. He joined the Owls as the promotion race hotted up in 2005 and produced some excellent performances as deputy for David Lucas

GALVIN, Anthony
Midfield

Appearances: 26+18   Goals: 2
Born: Huddersfield, 12 July 1956

CAREER
CLUBS: Goole Town, Tottenham Hotspur, WEDNESDAY (£140,000, August 1987-August 1989), Swindon Town (player, assistant manager), Newcastle United (assistant manager), Royston Town (manager).
OTHER: lecturer in leisure and tourism in Hertford and London.

Honoured by England as a schoolboy, Tony Galvin gained 29 full caps for the Republic of Ireland (the last 9 with the Owls). He also made 273 appearances for Spurs (31 goals), gaining 2 FA Cup winner's medals (1981 and 1982) and a UEFA Cup-winning prize in 1984, while in between times he was a League Cup runner-up. He spent half his time at Hillsborough on the subs' bench and although his experience shone through at times, his career was winding down when he joined Swindon, whom he helped reach the First Division via the play-offs in his first season, although the Robins were ultimately relegated following financial irregularities within the club. He gained a Bachelor of Arts degree in Russian Studies at Hull University. His brother, Chris, played for Leeds, Hull and Stockport in the 1970s.

GANNON, Edward
Wing half

Appearances: 219   Goals: 4
Born: Dublin, 3 January 1921
Died: Dublin, 31 July 1989

CAREER
CLUBS: Distillery, Shelbourne, Notts County, WEDNESDAY (£15,000, March 1949-August 1955), Shelbourne (player-manager), Bolton Athletic (manager).
OTHER: worked for The Irish Power Company.

A strong, powerful attacking wing half, Eddie Gannon was outstanding when the Owls gained promotion from the Second Division in 1950 and again in 1952 but reached his peak in 1953/54 when Wednesday reached the FA Cup semi-finals. Rewarded with 14 caps by the Republic of Ireland (the last 11 gained with Wednesday). Two of his four League goals for the Owls were scored against Manchester United and Arsenal.

GEARY, Derek Peter
Wing-back

Appearances: 116+11
Born: Dublin, 19 June 1980

CAREER
CLUBS: Cherry Orchard, WEDNESDAY (£10,000, November 1997-July 2004), Stockport County, Sheffield United.

Del Geary gave the Owls excellent service before becoming one of thirteen out-of-contract players who left the club in 2004. Hard-working and effective, he was very popular with the Hillsborough fans who were certainly disappointed when he departed. He made his League debut as a substitute at Gillingham in September 2000 and gained a regular place in the side twelve months later.

GEMMELL, Duncan
Forward

Appearances: 28   Goals: 10
Born: Glasgow, 1870
Died: Glasgow, 1948

CAREER
CLUBS: Elderslee Rangers Swifts, WEDNESDAY (March 1891-June 1892), Woolwich Arsenal.
OTHER: railway porter in Glasgow.

Duncan Gemmell was a competitive forward who made his debut for Wednesday in the Football Alliance, later having three FA Cup outings against Bolton, Small Heath and West Bromwich Albion in 1891/92. He made eight appearances for the Gunners.

G

GERMAN, David
Right-back

Appearances: 1
Born: Sheffield, 16 October 1973

CAREER
CLUBS: WEDNESDAY (schoolboy, April 1989-June 1990), Halifax Town, WEDNESDAY (n/c June 1995), Macclesfield Town, Ashton United, Leigh RMI, Stalybridge Celtic, Ashton United.
OTHER: fireman.

Released by Wednesday as a youngster, David German was re-signed on a non-contract basis to play against FC Basel in the InterToto Cup in June 1995. He appeared for the Great Britain Firemen's team in 2005.

GIBSON, Arthur Leonard
Utility

Appearances: 3
Born: Sheffield, May 1870
Died: Dumfries, 1943

CAREER
CLUBS: WEDNESDAY (1890/91).

Squad member Arthur Gibson played in three Football Alliance games for the Owls in 1890/91.

GIBSON, Thomas Richard Donald
Right half

Appearances: 84   Goals: 3
Born: Manchester, 12 May 1929

CAREER
CLUBS: Manchester United, WEDNESDAY (£8,000, June 1955-June 1960), Leyton Orient, Buxton (player-manager).
OTHER: ran a confectionary shop in Burnage for many years.

Don Gibson was introduced to League football by his father-in-law, Matt Busby, in 1950. He appeared in 114 games for United, gaining a First Division championship medal in 1952. He added two Second Division winners' medals to his collection with the Owls (1956 and 1959) before losing his place to Tony Kay. But when Kay was injured, Gibson returned and gave many more fine performances before joining Orient.

GILBERT, Eric Peter
Left-back

Appearances: 22+1 *
Born: Newcastle, 31 July 1983

CAREER
CLUBS: Birmingham City, Plymouth Argyle, Leicester City, WEDNESDAY (loan, November-December 2005, signed January 2006), Doncaster Rovers (L, January-February 2007).

A Welsh Under-21 international, capped 12 times (the first versus Latvia, 2005), Gilbert failed to make Birmingham's First XI but did well with Plymouth before joining Leicester. He had played under manager Paul Sturrock at Home Park and had no hesitation in teaming up with his ex-boss at Hillsborough. An attacking left-back, Peter can deliver an excellent cross .

GILL, Arnold Oscar
Half-back

Appearances: 2
Born: Sheffield, 1866
Deceased by 1935

CAREER
CLUBS: WEDNESDAY (seasons 1889-91).

A reserve with the Owls, Arnold Gill appeared in two games in the Football Alliance (1889/90). His son was James Gill.

GILL, James
Forward

Appearances: 43   Goals: 10
Born: Sheffield, 9 November 1894
Died: Sheffield, December 1964

CAREER
CLUBS: WEDNESDAY (June 1913-June 1920), Cardiff City, Blackpool, Derby County, Crystal Palace, Scarborough.

A player with exceptional ability and goalscoring acumen, Jim Gill had a splendid career. An England schoolboy international, he appeared in all five forward positions and besides his senior record for the Owls, he netted 3 goals in 6 First World War games. With Wednesday beset by financial problems, they sold Jimmy to Cardiff and he netted twice in City's first ever League game versus Stockport, going on to claim 83 goals in almost 200 appearances, helping the Welsh club gain promotion from the Second Division in 1921 and also played in the 1925 FA Cup final defeat by Sheffield United. A year later he helped Derby gain promotion to the top flight.

GILLIES, Alexander
Centre forward

Appearances: 2
Born: Cowdenbeath, 1874
Died: Lochgelly, 1921

CAREER
CLUBS: Bolton Wanderers, Ardwick, Lochgelly United, Heart of Midlothian, WEDNESDAY (£100, February-August 1897), Leicester Fosse, Dumbarton, Lochgelly United, Dumbarton, Lochgelly United.

Signed after an injury to Harry Davis, Alex Gillies spent five months with the Owls, his two League outings coming against Burnley and Wolves in March 1897.

GLEN, Robert
Defender

Appearances:
Born: Renton, 16 January 1875
Died: Glasgow, 1949

CAREER
CLUBS: Renton, WEDNESDAY (free, August 1893-April 1895), Renton, Glasgow Rangers, Hibernian.

A Scottish international, capped against Wales in 1895 and 1896 and Ireland in 1900, Bobby Glen also twice represented the Scottish League. He captained Renton when they lost the 1895 Scottish Cup final but made amends by gaining a winners' medal with Hibs in the same competition in 1900. An unassuming character with a strong tackle, he played only once for the Owls, in a 5-1 League defeat at Blackburn. Sadly, his young daughter died in 1907.

GLENNON, Joseph Edward
Forward

Appearances: 133   Goals: 42
Born: Whitwick, 17 October 1889
Died: Ashby-de-la-Zouch, 26 June 1926

CAREER
CLUBS: Grimsby Town, Denaby United, WEDNESDAY (£60, August 1910-July 1919), Rotherham County, Rotherham Town.
OTHER: licensee.

'Teddy' Glennon started out as a half-back before becoming a quality goalscorer for Wednesday for whom he made his debut at Oldham on Christmas Eve, 1910. He scored the first of his 42 goals versus Tottenham a week later and after leaving Hillsborough he did well with Rotherham. Also a useful cricketer, he played twice for Leicestershire in 1921.

G

GOODFELLOW, Derwick Ormond
Goalkeeper

Appearances: 77
Born: Shilbottle, Northumberland, 26 June 1914
Died: Alnwick, 9 December 2001

CAREER
CLUBS: Gateshead, WEDNESDAY (free, May 1936-
June 1947), Middlesbrough, Exeter City.
WARTIME GUEST APPEARANCES: Exeter City
OTHER: social club steward; pub licensee.

Derwick Goodfellow's career realised 135 League appearances. Very tall, he was a neat and tidy player who contested with Roy Smith for the right to take over from Jack Brown at Hillsborough. Goodfellow succeeded and (injuries apart) was first choice from August 1937 to January 1939. He had 22 outings for the club during the Second World War.

GOOING, William Henry
Centre forward

Appearances: 3   Goals: 1
Born: Penistone, 1874
Died: Derbyshire, 1944

CAREER
CLUBS: WEDNESDAY (September 1895-August 1897),
Chesterfield, Woolwich Arsenal, Northampton
Town.

Signed as cover for Lawrie Bell and Harry Davis, Bill Gooing scored on his debut for the Owls in a 1-1 draw at Small Heath in February 1896. He netted 48 goals in 106 games for Arsenal, helping the Gunners gain promotion to the First Division in 1904.

GOSLING, William Walter
Full-back

Appearances: 5
Born: Durham, 1878
Deceased by 1965

CAREER
CLUBS: WEDNESDAY (February 1901-April 1902).

Reserve to Willie Layton and Ambrose Langley, tough-tackling Bill Gosling made his Owls debut at Liverpool three weeks after joining. He was later suspended by the club for 'serious misconduct' after being found guilty of drunk and disorderly behaviour.

GOWDY, William Alexander
Wing half

Appearances: 2
Born: Belfast, 1905
Died: USA, 1987

CAREER
CLUBS: Crusaders, Cliftonville, Ards, Hull City,
WEDNESDAY (£350, December 1931-March 1933),
Gateshead, Linfield, Hibernian, Goole Town,
Altrincham, Aldershot.
WARTIME GUEST APPEARANCES: Hull City.
OTHER: emigrated to California; owner of a ranch
in Santa Monica.

A Northern Ireland international, capped six times (1932-36), Bill Gowdy also represented the Irish League on three occasions. A writer of the time described him as being, 'a bundle of restless activity. Preferred the ball on the ground and endeavoured to keep it there; daring in method and inclined to rove.' Gowdy, who had his best spell with Hull (73 appearances), made his League debut for the Owls in place of Alf Strange against Portsmouth in April 1932.

GRAHAM, David
Forward

Appearances: 21+9 Goals: 3
Born: Edinburgh, 6 October 1978

CAREER
CLUBS: Dunfermline Athletic, Inverness, Caledonian
Thistle, Torquay United, Wigan Athletic, WEDNESDAY
(August 2005), Huddersfield Town, Bradford City
(L), Torquay United (L).

Capped eight times by Scotland at under-21
level, David Graham's best spell north of the
border was with Dunfermline (5 goals in 45
appearances). He did well with Torquay (49
goals) and was voted the Gulls' Player of the
Season in 2003/04. After helping Wigan reach
the Premiership, he joined the Owls but unfortunately never quite mastered Championship
football and was loaned out to Huddersfield
in 2006.

GRANT, David
Full-back

Appearances: 147+3   Goals: 5
Born: Sheffield, 2 June 1960

CAREER
CLUBS: WEDNESDAY (July 1976-February 1978),
Oxford United, Chesterfield, Crystal Palace, Cardiff
City, Rochdale, Macclesfield Town, Boston United.

Developed under manager Jack Charlton at
Hillsborough, David Grant was a very capable
and efficient full-back, strong with no frills
attached, who gained a regular place in the
Owls' first team in 1977/78 and two seasons
later missed only two games when promotion
was gained to the Second Division. He lost his
place to Charlie Williamson and after leaving
the club made a further 153 League appearances, 97 for Rochdale.

GRAY, George William
Right-back

Appearances: 33
Born: Sheffield, 27 February 1896
Died: Norwich, 5 May 1962

CAREER Grimsby Town, Norwich City, WEDNESDAY
(£1,300 plus Joe Armstrong, November 1921-May
1923).
OTHER: Army – First World War; licensee; crane
driver.

A player with plenty of resource, George Gray
was a strong kicker and often sent his clearances fifty to sixty yards downfield. A first-team
regular with the Owls from December 1921 to
November 1922, he gave way to Jack Bellas
and when Ernie Blenkinsop and Billy Felton
became full-back partners, he was released. He
appeared in Norwich's first game in the Football
League against Plymouth (August 1920).

GRAYSON, Simon Nicholas
Defender

Appearances: 5
Born: Ripon, 16 December 1969

CAREER
CLUBS: Leeds United, Leicester City, Aston Villa,
Blackburn Rovers, WEDNESDAY (loan, August-
September 2000), Stockport County, Notts County,
Bradford City, Blackpool (player-coach, manager).

Simon Grayson was already an experienced
defender with almost 340 appearances under
his belt when he joined the Owls. He played in
the first five League games of 2000/01, the first
against Wolves. Twice voted Player of the Year at
Leicester, he played in four play-off finals (won
two, lost two), suffered relegation, spent two
seasons in the Premiership, helped Leicester
win the League Cup in 1997 and Blackpool
the LDV Vans Trophy in 2004. A year later he

reached the milestone of 500 club appearances. His brother Paul played cricket for Essex and Lancashire.

GREEN, Adam
Midfield

Appearances: 3
Born: Hillingdon, 12 January 1984

CAREER
CLUBS: Fulham, WEDNESDAY (loan, January-February 2005), Bournemouth.

A calm, accomplished and stylish footballer, Adam Green filled in well on the left-hand side of Wednesday's midfield, making his debut at MK Dons in January 2005.

GREEN, Albert Willis
Outside left

Appearances: 6   Goals: 1
Born: Sheffield, October 1916
Died: circa 1990

CAREER
CLUBS: Dore FC, WEDNESDAY (£20, August 1936-August 1938), Barnsley, Gainsborough Trinity.

Reserve to Ellis Rimmer, Bert Green scored in his second outing for the Owls at Birmingham, having made his debut at home to Leeds a week earlier (November 1936).

GREEN, Ryan Michael
Right-back

Appearances: 4
Born: Cardiff, 20 October 1980

CAREER
CLUBS: Wolverhampton Wanderers, Torquay United,

Millwall, Cardiff City, WEDNESDAY (free, November 2002-July 2003), Hereford United, Bristol Rovers.

Honoured by Wales as a Youth player, Ryan Green later won 16 Under-21 and 2 full caps. A compact full-back who enjoys driving forward, he failed to establish himself at Molineux, Millwall or Cardiff and made only four appearances for the Owls. He helped Bristol Rovers to win the 2007 play-off final.

GREENSMITH, Ronald
Outside left

Appearances: 6   Goals: 1
Born: Sheffield, 22 January 1933

CAREER
CLUBS: WEDNESDAY (January 1954-January 1958), York City, Scarborough, Bridlington Town, Selby Town.
OTHER: worked for a soft drinks company and on the railways.

Ron Greensmith's 6 games for the Owls came in 4 years. He scored his only goal in a 2-1 win versus Hastings in a third round FA Cup-tie in January 1955. He had 43 outings for York.

GREENWOOD, Ross Michael
Full-back

Appearances: 1+3
Born: York, 1 November 1985

CAREER
CLUBS: WEDNESDAY (April 2002-July 2005), Stockport County.

Ross Greenwood made an impressive debut for the Owls in a League Cup-tie versus Coventry in September 2004 but unfortunately he wasn't part of the club's future plans and was subsequently released.

GREGG, Robert Edmond
Forward

Appearances: 39   Goals: 7
Born: Ferryhill, County Durham, 4 February 1904
Died: Hounslow, May 1991

CAREER
CLUBS: Durham City, Ferryhill Athletic, Darlington,
WEDNESDAY (£730, May 1928-January 1931),
Birmingham, Chelsea, Boston United, Sligo Rovers.

Two years after gaining a First Division championship medal with the Owls (1929), tricky forward Bob Gregg was a runner-up with Birmingham after they were defeated in the FA Cup final by West Brom. He did well at Hillsborough but his days were numbered when Harry Burgess arrived. He struggled a lot with injuries and during his career appeared in more games for the reserves than he did at senior level.

GREGORY, Anthony Gerard
Midfield

Appearances: 16+5 Goals: 1
Born: Doncaster, 21 March 1968

CAREER
CLUBS: WEDNESDAY (April 1984-August 1990),
Halifax Town, Buxton, Emley, Eden Grove Pinkney
(player-manager).
OTHER: coached young people; chiropodist.

Capped by England at schoolboy and youth team levels, Tony Gregory spent six years at Hillsborough without ever really threatening to establish himself in the senior side. He made his League debut at Manchester City in August 1985 and scored his only goal in a 2-0 win over Chelsea a year later.

GREGORY, Robert
Forward

Appearances: 17   Goals: 14
Born: Sheffield, August 1853
Died: Sheffield, October 1910

CAREER
CLUBS: Hallam, WEDNESDAY (August 1873-April
1884).

Bob Gregory was a forthright competitor for the Owls in the club's first 17 FA Cup matches, played between December 1880 and December 1883. He scored a hat-trick in the initial tie against Blackburn Rovers (won 4-0) and hit a five-timer in a 12-0 win over Spilsby in November 1882. He played for the North (versus the South) in an England international trial in 1881.

GREGSON, Colin
Midfield

Appearances: 2+1
Born: Newcastle, 19 January 1958

CAREER
CLUBS: West Bromwich Albion, WEDNESDAY (free,
July 1977-May 1979), Berwick Rangers, Adelaide.
OTHER: employed by Newcastle Council.

An FA Youth Cup winner with West Brom in 1976, Colin Gregson failed to make the first team at The Hawthorns. He appeared in three matches for the Owls, making his debut in a 2-2 League Cup draw at Blackpool in August 1977.

GRIFFIN, William
Inside forward

Appearances: 37   Goals: 21
Born: Bircotes, Worksop, 24 September 1940

G

Billy Griffin

CAREER

CLUBS: WEDNESDAY (1955), Hillsborough Boys Club, WEDNESDAY (September 1957-Decmeber 1962), Bury, Workington, Rotherham United, Cambridge City, Frickley.
OTHER: worked in a glass factory, for the Milk Marketing Board and as a shoe maker.

Despite a wonderful scoring record with the Owls, Billy Griffin was never a regular in the side. He had his best bout of scoring in 1960/61, netting 8 times in 12 League games. He made his debut versus Cardiff in November 1958 and after leaving Hillsborough he upped his League record to 39 goals to 187 games.

GROSVENOR, Arthur Thomas
Utility

Appearances: 23   Goals: 1
Born: Netherton, Dudley, 22 November 1908
Died: Dudley, 31 October 1972

CAREER
CLUBS: Stourbridge, West Bromwich Albion, Wolverhampton Wanderers, Birmingham,

WEDNESDAY (£3,650, February 1936-May 1937), Bolton Wanderers, Dudley Town.
OTHER: sheet metal worker in Smethwick; also kept racing pigeons and grew prize-winning tomatoes.

An England international, capped in 1933 versus Ireland, France and Wales, Tom Grosvenor also represented the Football League. Tall and lanky, he scored 18 goals in 115 games for Birmingham before joining the Owls. Likened in some respects to Charlie Buchan, he was a brilliant ball player and a creator of chances rather than a marksman himself. Unfortunately two broken legs hampered his career. His only strike for Wednesday came on his debut at Derby in February 1936 (lost 2-1).

His two brothers, Percy and Cliff, both played for Leicester, while Percy also assisted West Bromwich Albion.

GRUMMITT, Peter Malcolm
Goalkeeper

Appearances: 130
Born: Bourne, Lincolnshire, 19 August 1942

CAREER
CLUBS: Bourne Town, Birmingham City, Notts County, Nottingham Forest, WEDNESDAY (£35,000, January 1970-January 1974), Brighton & Hove Albion (L), Dover, Worthing Town, Lewes (manager).
OTHER: ran a tobacconist/confectionary shop in Brighton; landscape gardener.

A Football League representative player and winner of three England Under-23 caps, Peter Grummitt appeared in 357 games for Forest before joining the Owls. He took over from Peter Springett after he produced some superb displays. However, injury cost him dear and he eventually moved to Brighton, helping the Seagulls gain promotion from the Third Division in 1977. His career realised 570 League appearances.

HALL, Alex Richmond
Half-back

Appearances: 36   Goals: 5
Born: Kirkcaldy, Fife, 1865
Died: Dunfermline, 1938

CAREER Raith Rovers, WEDNESDAY (£25, May 1891-August 1893), Raith Rovers, Heart of Midlothian, Dundee, Tottenham Hotspur, Aberdour.

A combative wing half, 'Sandy' Hall made his mark in Scottish football before spending two seasons with the Owls for whom he occupied all three half-back positions. Later in his career he gave good service to Tottenham, for whom he once kept goal versus Thames Ironworks in 1898. He was suspended by Spurs in January 1899 for 'neglect of training rules'.

HALL, Henry
Forward

Appearances: 31   Goals: 1
Born: Newark, Nottinghamshire, November 1893
Deceased by 1965

CAREER
CLUBS: Gainsborough Trinity, Newark, Long Eaton St Helens, Sheffield United, Worksop Town, Long Eaton, Ilkeston Town, WEDNESDAY (£300, December 1920-February 1922), Lincoln City, Gainsborough Trinity, Newark Town, Long Eaton St Helens, Grantham Town, Ransome & Marles.

Harry Hall scored his only goal for the Owls in his seventh game against Blackpool in February 1921. He played in five League matches for the Blades before the First World War but failed to make Lincoln's first team.

HAMILTON, Henry Gilhespy
Forward

Appearances: 7
Born: South Shields, August 1887
Died: South Shields, June 1938

CAREER
CLUBS: Craghead United, WEDNESDAY (£10, December 1908-April 1910), Huddersfield Town, Southampton, Belfast Celtic, South Shields.

After scoring plenty of goals in second team football, Henry Hamilton was perhaps out of his depth in the first team when deputising for Andy Wilson and Frank Rollinson. In March 1912 he was suspended, with his Huddersfield teammate Andrew Gibson, for a serious breach of club discipline. Both players received *sine die* suspensions and they left Leeds Road within a week.

HAMSHAW, Matthew Thomas
Outside right

Appearances: 45+43   Goals: 6
Born: Rotherham, 1 January 1982

CAREER
CLUBS: WEDNESDAY (April 1998-January 1999-June 2003), Stockport County, Mansfield Town.

A pacy, direct winger who gained England caps at Schoolboy and Youth levels, Matt Hamshaw had two useful seasons with the Owls before suffering cruciate knee ligament damage *v.* Nottingham Forest in December 2002. He regained his fitness but was never the same player again.

HANFORD, Harold
Defender

Appearances: 94   Goals: 1
Born: Blaengwynfi, Wales, 9 October 1907
Died: Melbourne, Australia, 26 November 1996

Harold Hanford

HARDY, Robin
Wing half

Appearances: 33   Goals: 1
Born: Worksop, 18 January 1941

CAREER
CLUBS: WEDNESDAY (April 1956-February 1965), Rotherham United, Cambridge United, Gainsborough Trinity.
OTHER: worked for an engineering company.

Rob Hardy was a hard working wing half who had his best spell in the side at the end of 1961/62 and the start of the following season. After leaving Hillsborough he made 42 League appearances for Rotherham and played for Cambridge in their first season of League football.

HARGREAVES, Leonard
Outside left

Appearances: 2   Goals: 1
Born: Kimblesworth near Durham, 1906
Deceased by 1980

CAREER
CLUBS: Doncaster Rovers, Sunderland, WEDNESDAY (£2,700, May 1929-May 1931), Shelbourne (L), York City, Workington, Doncaster Rovers, Luton Town, Peterborough & Fletton United.
OTHER: locomotive fitter.

After identical League records with his first two clubs, Len Hargreaves was reserve to Ellis Rimmer at Hillsborough. He scored in his second outing versus Manchester United.

HARKES, John Andrew
Utility

Appearances: 95+23   Goals: 11
Born: Kearny, New Jersey, USA, 8 March 1967

CAREER
CLUBS: Swansea Town, WEDNESDAY (£3,600 plus Peter Leyland, February 1936-May 1946), Northampton Town (trainer), Exeter City (trainer)
WARTIME GUEST APPEARANCES: Swansea Town, Swindon Town, Aberaman.
OTHER: Second World War police reserve; ran private physiotherapy practice; emigrated to Australia where he worked at a power station.

Harry Hanford was a strong, reliable no-nonsense defender, cool but clever, a real stopper, who appeared in 200 League games for Swansea before joining the Owls. He skippered the Swans whom he helped to reach the Welsh Cup final in 1932 and win two Welsh League titles. He settled down quickly at Hillsborough, adjusting from Second to First Division football with consummate ease. He missed only 3 out of 50 games in the last pre-Second World War season. A Welsh international, capped seven times, Hanford's career with the Owls was cut short by injury.

John Harkes

CAREER

CLUBS: *Missouri Athletic club, US Soccer Federation, WEDNESDAY (trial, January 1990), Blackburn Rovers, Celtic, WEDNESDAY (loan September 1990, signed for £100,000, December 1990-August 1993), Derby County, US Soccer Federation, West Ham United, Washington DC United, Nottingham Forest, New England Revolution, Columbus Crew, Washington DC United (director of youth development).*

John Harkes won 90 caps for USA, acting as captain several times, including the 1996 World Cup finals. A versatile midfielder (or right-back) he could use both feet, possessed explosive shooting ability and seemed to fit in comfortably with all his clubs. A League Cup winner with the Owls in 1991, he was certainly a consistent performer during his three years at Hillsborough.

HARKNESS, Stephen
Defender

Appearances: 30+2 Goals: 1
Born: Carlisle, 27 August 1971

CAREER
CLUBS: *Carlisle United, Liverpool, Huddersfield Town, Southend United, Benfica, Blackburn Rovers, WEDNESDAY (£200,000, September 2000-May 2002), Chester City.*

An England Youth international, Steve Harkness made 141 appearances for Liverpool. He never settled in Portugal and struggled to get his game together at Blackburn but bedded efficiently into the Owls' line-up at left-back from where he produced some enthusiastic and determined performances in his first season before injury forced him to miss the whole of 2001/02.

HARPER, Alan
Utility

Appearances: 35+4
Born: Liverpool, 1 November 1960

Alan Harper

103

CAREER

CLUBS: Liverpool, Everton, WEDNESDAY (£275,000, July 1988-December 1989), Manchester City, Everton, Luton Town, Burnley, Cardiff City.

An England Youth international, Alan Harper won two League titles (1985 and 1987), gained a League Cup runners-up medal in 1984 and starred in two FA Charity Shield games (1986 and 1987) as an Everton player. Very adaptable, able to play in a variety of positions, he had an excellent career and amassed 437 appearances (340 in the Football League). His first and last appearances for the Owls were ironically against his future club Luton.

HARPER, Edward Cashfield
Centre forward

Appearances: 22   Goals: 16
Born: Sheerness, Kent, 22 August 1901
Died: Blackburn: 22 July 1959

CAREER

CLUBS: Whitstable Town, Sheppey United, Blackburn Rovers, WEDNESDAY (£4,400, November 1927-March 1929), Tottenham Hotspur, Preston North End, Blackburn Rovers (player, coach).
OTHER: worked for English Electric.

Prolific marksman Ted Harper – a former shipwright – scored 260 goals for his 4 major clubs. He netted 122 in 177 games in 2 spells with Blackburn and won an England cap versus Scotland in 1926. A clumsy looking footballer whose ball control was practically zero, he was, nevertheless, lethal inside the penalty area and simply had the knack of hitting the target as regular as clockwork. Signed for a club record fee in 1927, his stay at Hillsborough lasted barely fifteen months, yet in that time he notched 16 goals, including a hat-trick on his debut against Derby. He found the net 63 times in 67 games for Spurs and actually broke the individual scoring

records at Blackburn, Tottenham and Preston. He twice scored five goals in a game – for Blackburn at Newcastle in 1925 and for Spurs against Reading in 1930.

HARRISON, Walter
Outside right

Appearances: 2   Goals: 3
Born: Rhyl, 1860
Died: 1925

CAREER

CLUBS: WEDNESDAY (1882/83), Heeley.

Wally Harrison's two appearances for the Owls were against Nottingham Forest in FA Cup encounters in January 1883. He scored in both games, including two in a 3-2 replay win.

HARRON, Joseph
Outside left

Appearances: 64   Goals: 6
Born: Langley Park, 14 March 1900
Died: 19 February 1961

CAREER

CLUBS: Hull City, Northampton Town, York City, WEDNESDAY (£300, March 1923-November 1924), York City, Kettering Town, York City, Scarborough, Barnsley, Dartford (player, manager).

During the 1920s Joe Harron moved in and out of the Football League on a regular basis. He had his best season with the Owls in 1923/24 when he made 38 League appearances on the left wing with Charlie Petrie as his inside partner. A clever ball player, he scored on his home debut in a 2-0 Second Division win over South Shields in March 1923.

HART, Paul Anthony
Defender

Appearances: 59   Goals: 3
Born: Golborne, Manchester, 4 May 1953

CAREER
CLUBS: Preston North End, Whalley Grange, Stockport County, Blackpool, Leeds United, Nottingham Forest, WEDNESDAY (free, June 1985-December 1986), Birmingham City, Notts County, Chesterfield (player-manager), Grantham Town, Nottingham Forest (youth coach), Leeds United (director of youth coaching), WEDNESDAY (coach, 1994/95, caretaker-manager, September 1996), Nottingham Forest (coach, Youth Academy director, manager), Barnsley (manager), Leeds United (Youth Academy coach), Rushden & Diamonds (manager).

A solid, uncompromising stopper, Paul Hart was recognised as one of the hard men of English football during the 1970s and '80s. He made 87 League appearances for Stockport, 143 for Blackpool, 191 for Leeds and 87 for Forest before joining the Owls. His first

Paul Hart

game for the club was at home to Chelsea in August 1985 when he partnered Mick Lyons in defence, his last at Manchester City on Boxing Day 1986. After moving to St Andrew's he suffered a broken leg on his debut against Plymouth. He failed to achieve success as manager. His brother Nigel played for Wigan Athletic, Leicester, Blackburn, Crewe and Bury. His father was Johnny Hart (ex-Manchester City player and manager).

HARVEY, Edward Lee
Outside left

Appearances: 12
Born: Sheffield, 1893
Died: 1965

CAREER
CLUBS: Heeley, WEDNESDAY (August 1919-September 1921), Bristol Rovers.

One of eleven players to appear in the left wing for the Owls during the first two seasons following the First World War, reserve Ted Harvey made his League debut in a 0-0 draw at Old Trafford in September 1919.

HARVEY, James Colin
Midfield

Appearances: 48   Goals: 2
Born: Liverpool, 16 November 1944

CAREER
CLUBS: Everton, WEDNESDAY (£66,666, September 1974-May 1976), Everton (coach, manager, assistant manager), Burnley (assistant manager).

Colin Harvey made 387 appearances for Everton – the first in the European Cup versus Inter Milan in 1963 – and he shares with Brian Labone the record for the most European appearances for the Merseysiders (19). He was an FA Cup winner in 1966 (versus Wednesday) and loser in 1968, gaining a League championship medal in 1970. Nicknamed 'The White Pele', he possessed exquisite ball control, was an accurate passer and was capped by England against Malta in 1971. He also played in five Under-23 internationals. Linking up with Tommy Craig in midfield for the Owls, he starred in a 1-0 win at Bolton on his debut.

HARVEY, William Henry Tompkins
Outside right

Appearances: 20   Goals: 1
Born: Freemantle, Hampshire, 12 April 1896
Died: South Africa, July 1970

CAREER
CLUBS: WEDNESDAY (amateur, October 1919-July 1921), Birmingham, Southend United, Birmingham (assistant secretary, manager), Chesterfield (manager), Gillingham (manager).
WARTIME GUEST APPEARANCES: Yorkshire Amateurs, Pembroke, Bradford City.
OTHER: 2nd Battalion West Riding Regiment.

Bill Harvey always posed a threat to defenders. Capped by England as an amateur, he toured South Africa with the FA in 1920, after making his League debut for the Owls in a 4-2 defeat at Manchester City in October 1919. He had two decent spells in the First XI before moving to Birmingham, whom he later served as secretary and manager. He guided Chesterfield to the Third Division (North) title in 1936 and played cricket for Warwickshire and Border Province, South Africa.

HASLAM, Steven Robert
Utility

Appearances: 139+32   Goals: 2
Born: Sheffield, 6 September 1979

CAREER
CLUBS: WEDNESDAY (August 1995-May 2004), Huddersfield Town, Burton Albion, Halifax Town, Northampton Town, Halifax Town.

Capped by England at Schoolboy and Youth levels, Steve Haslam made a name for himself in Wednesday's League side in 1999/2000. He quickly made his mark and over the next four years occupied several positions, preferring a holding role in midfield. A hernia injury disrupted his final season at Hillsborough.

HATFIELD, Samuel Ernest
Full-back

Appearances: 1
Born: Bradford, 16 January 1905
Died: Romford, 1984

CAREER
CLUBS: Wombwell Athletic, WEDNESDAY (£100, November 1927-April 1930), Wolverhampton Wanderers, Southend United.

After failing to establish himself at Hillsborough and Molineux, Ernie Hatfield made over 50 appearances in 2 seasons with Southend. His only outing for the Owls came in the 6-0 home win over West Ham in April 1929 when he deputised for Ernie Blenkinsop (on England duty). Hatfield was a cabinet maker by trade.

HAZEL, Desmond St Lloyd
Forward

Appearances: 6+2
Born: Bradford, 15 July 1967

CAREER
CLUBS: WEDNESDAY (July 1983-July 1988), Grimsby Town (L), Rotherham United, Chesterfield, Guiseley, Joodalup, Guiseley, Halifax Town (coach).

A useful right-sided player, he never quite hit it off with the Owls, but after leaving Hillsborough Des Hazel developed into a quality performer who scored 40 goals in 291 games for Rotherham, helping the Millers win the Fourth Division title in 1989.

HAZELWOOD, John
Forward

Appearances: 2   Goals: 1
Born: Sheffield, 1865
Deceased by 1945

CAREER
CLUBS: WEDNESDAY (1889/90).

Reserve Jack Hazelwood made his two appearances for the Owls in the Football Alliance.

HEALD, Paul Andrew
Goalkeeper

Appearances: 6
Born: Wath-on-Dearne, 20 September 1968

CAREER
CLUBS: Barnsley, Sheffield United, Leyton Orient, Coventry City, FF Malmö, Leeds United, Swindon Town, Wimbledon (player, player-coach), WEDNESDAY (loan, January-February 2002).

Paul Heald was precisely the right height and build for the duties of a goalkeeper and he did very well, especially with Orient for whom he appeared in 219 games. He was signed by the Owls when Pressman was injured.

HEARD, Timothy Patrick
Utility

Appearances: 30+3 Goals: 3
Born: Hull, 17 March 1960

CAREER
CLUBS: Everton, Aston Villa, WEDNESDAY (£50,000, January 1983), Newcastle United, Middlesbrough, Hull City, Rotherham United, Cardiff City, Hull City, Hall Road Rangers, Brunei.
OTHER: involved in overseas property management.

England Youth international Pat Heard failed to make the grade at Everton, although he did win an FA Youth Cup winners' medal in 1977. A useful stand-in at Villa Park during their 1980/81 League championship-winning season, he gained a European Cup winners' medal the following year as a non-playing substitute. He made his debut for the Owls *v.* Middlesbrough in January 1983 and scored his first goal for the club *v.* Newcastle. He made over 300 appearances at club level.

HECKINGBOTTOM, Paul
Utility

Appearances: 41+1 Goals: 4
Born: Barnsley, 17 July 1977

CAREER
CLUBS: Manchester United, Sunderland, Scarborough, Hartlepool United, Darlington, Norwich City, Bradford City, WEDNESDAY (July, 2004-January 2006), Barnsley.

A utility player able to occupy several positions, Paul Heckingbottom failed to get a game at Old Trafford, made 135 appearances for Darlington and contributed vital goals in his first season at Hillsborough, as Wednesday won promotion after beating Hartlepool in the play-off final.

Whilst on loan, he helped Barnsley win the 2006 League One play-off final (against Swansea City).

H

HEDLEY, Graeme
Midfield

Appearances: 6   Goals: 1
Born: Easington, County Durham, 1 March 1957

CAREER
CLUBS: Middlesbrough, WEDNESDAY (loan, February-March 1978), Darlington, York City, Hartlepool United, Horden Colliery Welfare, Whitby Town.

Graeme Hedley made 107 League appearances for 5 clubs in 10 years. His only goal for the Owls in his six-match spell came from the penalty spot to earn a 1-1 draw at Lincoln.

HEESON, George Alfred
Inside left

Appearances: 1
Born: Soothill Nether, York, 1866
Died: 1924

CAREER
CLUBS: WEDNESDAY (1884/85).

Reserve Alf Heeson made his only appearance in an FA Cup win at Long Eaton Rangers.

HEMMINGFIELD, William Edmund
Utility

Appearances: 47   Goals: 13
Born: Wortley, Sheffield, August 1875
Died: Cleethorpes, 11 June 1953

CAREER
CLUBS: Mexborough Town, WEDNESDAY (free, August 1898-June 1899), Grimsby Town, WEDNESDAY (£75, August 1903-May 1907), Grimsby Town (trainer), WEDNESDAY (coach, June 1928-May 1931).

A valuable and versatile footballer, Bill Hemmingfield* was originally a centre forward before switching to defence, where he developed a bone-shaking tackle. Possessing a strong right-foot shot, he netted his fair share of goals for the Owls, including one on his debut versus Nottingham Forest in September 1898. Earlier, he netted 10 times in 101 outings for Grimsby, gaining a Second Division championship medal in 1901. His son, Robert played for Grimsby in 1927/28.
* Some reference books spell his name as Hemingfield.

HENDERSON, William
Outside right

Appearances: 50+6 Goals: 5
Born: Caldercruix, Airdrie, 24 January 1944

CAREER
CLUBS: Edinburgh Athletic, Glasgow Rangers, Durban City, WEDNESDAY (£750, July 1972-April 1974), Miami Toros (L), Hong Kong Rangers, Carolina Hill, Sliema Wanderers, Airdrieonians, Hong Kong (national team coach).
OTHER: went on to run bars in Spain and Scotland.

A youthful prodigy who was in Rangers' side aged seventeen, Willie Henderson was capped a year later and became a regular in the First XI at Ibrox Park before he was twenty. He may have been both myopic and diminutive but anyone who saw him in action knew he was a giant of a player. An outside right, full of tricks and blistering pace, he scored 62 goals in 426 matches for the 'Gers, whom he helped win 2 League titles, 4 Scottish Cups and 2 League Cups, as well as collecting a handful of runners-up medals in various competitions. He won 29 caps between October 1962 and April 1971 after starring for his country at Schoolboy level. He also played in two Under-23 internationals and represented the Scottish League. A loser in the 1967 European Cup-winners' Cup final versus Bayern Munich, five years later he helped Rangers reach the final of the same competition, but did not play in the match itself against Dynamo Moscow. Henderson, who wore contact lenses, seemed to possess an in-built radar system as his crosses more often than not found their way to grateful teammates. A fun-loving character off the pitch and at times a genius on it, he was signed by Derek Dooley for the Owls and for two seasons thrilled the fans with some terrific perform-ances – it was a pity he never got to display his skills in the First Division. In 1975, Henderson had the pleasure of skippering the Hong Kong national team.

HENDON, Ian Michael
Defender

Appearances: 53   Goals: 2
Born: Ilford, 5 December 1971

CAREER
CLUBS: Tottenham Hotspur, Portsmouth (loan, January 1992), Leyton Orient, Barnsley, Leyton Orient, Birmingham City, Notts County, Northampton Town, WEDNESDAY (£40,000, October 2000-January 2003), Barnet (L), Peterborough United, Barnet (player-coach, assistant manager).

Ian Hendon gained 3 Schoolboy, 19 Youth and seven Under-21 caps for England and amassed over 500 club appearances – 164 for Orient – during a fine career. He helped Notts County win the Third Division title in 1988 and in 2005 was a member of Barnet's Conference champi-onship-winning team. Tall and versatile, a hard tackler, he preferred the left-back position and found a niche for himself at Hillsborough. One of four players arrested at the club's 2002 Christmas party in Leeds, he departed soon afterwards.

HENRY, Gerald Robert
Forward

Appearances: 40   Goals: 7
Born: Hemsworth, Barnsley, 5 October 1920
Died: Dewsbury, 1 September 1979

CAREER
CLUBS: Leeds United, Bradford Park Avenue, WEDNESDAY (£8,000, February 1950-December 1951), Halifax Town (player, player-manager).
WARTIME GUEST APPEARANCES: Halifax Town, Doncaster Rovers, Huddersfield Town, Manchester City.

The well-built Gerry Henry scored 94 of his 99 goals for Leeds during the Second World War. After moving to Bradford he continued to find the net before slowing up at Hillsborough. He took over from Clarrie Jordan in the Owls front line and netted his first two goals for the club in a 5-2 win over his former team, Leeds, in March 1950. He played at right half in 1950/51.

HENSHALL, Horace Vincent
Forward

Appearances: 17   Goals: 1
Born: Hednesford, 14 June 1889
Died: Nottingham, 7 December 1951

CAREER
CLUBS: Crewe Alexandra, Aston Villa, Notts County, WEDNESDAY (player, reserve-team coach, June 1922-June 1923), Chesterfield, Lincoln City (secretary-manager), Notts County (secretary-manager)
WARTIME GUEST APPEARANCES: Barnsley, West Ham United.
OTHER: licensee.

Horace Henshall played for England as a junior against Scotland in 1908 and for the Birmingham FA versus Scotland Juniors a year later. A hard-running, enthusiastic forward with a powerful right-foot shot, his only goal for the Owls came in a 4-1 home win over Stockport in February 1923 when he occupied the left-wing position. Prior to his exploits at Hillsborough, he did reasonably well at Villa Park and netted 27 goals in 164 League appearances for Notts County. A very popular figure at Meadow Lane, he returned there as manager in 1927 and guided the Magpies to the Third Division (South) title in 1931. With the Royal Navy Air Service in the First World War, he enjoyed photography.

HENSON, Philip Michael
Midfield

Appearances: 72+8 Goals: 9
Born: Manchester, 30 March 1953

CAREER
CLUBS: Manchester City, Swansea City, WEDNESDAY (£44,000, February 1975-July 1971), Sparta Rotterdam, Stockport County, Rotherham United (player, assistant manager, manager, general manager).

Phil Henson's career realised 249 League appearances (29 goals). He had his best spell with his last club, Rotherham, for whom

Philip Henson

he played in almost 100 matches. He made his debut for the Owls against Blackpool in February 1975 and had a run of 33 consecutive outings in the side before suffering injury problems. He spent over six years at Hillsborough.

HERBERT, David Ronald
Forward

Appearances: 13+6 Goals: 4
Born: Sheffield, 23 January 1956

CAREER
CLUBS: WEDNESDAY (July 1971-July 1976), Chesterfield, Buxton, Northern Woodseats, Rawlinson Youth Club.

Dave Herbert's career was cut short by injury. He had done extraordinarily well with the Owls after making his League debut against West Bromwich Albion in March 1975, scoring his first goal in his second game outing, earning a point in a 3-3 draw versus Brighton.

HIBBERT, Henry Crookes
Defender

Appearances: 2
Born: Dore, Sheffield, 1887
Died: Sheffield, circa 1966

CAREER
CLUBS: WEDNESDAY (July 1907-May 1908), Stockport County, Lincoln City, Rotherham County, Sheffield United.
WARTIME GUEST APPEARANCES: Chesterfield Town

Despite a long career, Harry Hibbert made only 7 League appearances in total – 4 of these were for Lincoln, whom he captained in the Midland League. His two outings for the Owls were both in the centre half position against Blackburn and Birmingham in April 1908.

HICKTON, John
Centre forward

Appearances: 55+1 Goals: 21
Born: Brimingham, Chesterfield, 24 September 1944

CAREER
CLUBS: WEDNESDAY (April 1960-September 1966), Middlesbrough, Hull City, Fort Lauderdale Strikers, Staveley Works.
OTHER: ran a Redcar off licence/newsagent shop.

John Hickton scored eight goals in an FA youth game before making his League debut for the Owls at right-back in March 1964 (against Aston Villa). But when manager Alan Brown was having problems up front, he was pushed forward and responded magnificently, netting 10 goals in 1964/65 before being demoted in February 1966, missing the FA Cup final as a result. He scored 185 goals in 482 games for Middlesbrough, helping them win the Second Division title in 1974 under manager Jack Charlton. Unfortunately Hickton broke his right leg on his debut for Fort Lauderdale and took a while to regain his fitness.

HILL, Brian
Left half

Appearances: 121+1   Goals: 1
Born: Sheffield, 6 October 1937
Died: Sheffield, 5 April 1968

CAREER
CLUBS: WEDNESDAY (April 1955-June 1967), Club Brugge.

There was nothing flashy about Brian Hill's displays for Wednesday. A competent, clean-kicking left half, he served the club very well for a decade before moving to Belgium. He made the first of his 122 appearances for the Owls against Blackpool in March 1957 and scored his only goal in a 2-1 defeat at Everton in September 1959. He was only thirty when he died.

HILL, Harold
Inside forward

Appearances: 99   Goals: 40
Born: Blackwell, Derbyshire, 24 September 1899
Died: Blackwell, 14 February 1969

CAREER
CLUBS: Notts County, WEDNESDAY (£1,700, October 1924-June 1929), Scarborough, Chesterfield (player-coach), Mansfield Town, Sutton Town, Bolsover Colliery.
OTHER: miner at B Winning Colliery.

Described as the 'Tom Thumb' of the Owls' side in the 1920s, Harry Hill made up for his lack of inches with some enterprising displays from both inside forward positions. His tenacious style made the most reliable and experienced defenders hop around and his scoring record for Wednesday was excellent. He came into his own in 1925/26 when partnering Arthur Prince on the left and his contribution of 12 goals went a long way in helping the Owls win the Second Division title – he had gained a winners' medal in the same section with Notts County three years earlier. The form of Jimmy Seed, Jimmy Trotter and Jack Allen eventually led to Hill's departure from Hillsborough. He won the Midland League title with Scarborough in 1930. His grandson, Hedley Hill, served briefly as commercial manager of Mansfield Town in 1994/95.

HILL, Haydn Harold Clifford
Goalkeeper

Appearances: 4
Born: Cresswell, Derbyshire, 4 July 1913
Died: Weymouth, 3 November 1992

CLUBS: Worksop Town, Chesterfield, Sheffield United, WEDNESDAY (December 1934-January 1935), Clowne Welfare, Corinthians, Yorkshire City, Bournemouth, Weymouth.
OTHER: maths teacher.

Haydn Hill, capped fives times by England at amateur level and also represented Great Britain in the 1936 Olympic Games, was signed as cover for Jack Brown and made his First Division debut for Wednesday in a 4-0 win over Tottenham in April 1935. His last outing ended in a 4-3 defeat at Everton eight months later.

HILLER, Carl
Outside right

Appearances: 1
Born: Sheffield, September 1866
Deceased by 1939

CAREER
CLUBS: Heeley, WEDNESDAY (seasons 1883-89).

Carl Hiller, brother of Walpole (below), made his only appearance for Wednesday in a 3-1 FA Cup second round defeat at Staveley in December 1883. He helped the Owls win the Sheffield Challenge Cup and Wharncliffe Charity Cup in 1888.

HILLER, Walpole
Forward

Appearances: 8   Goals: 2
Born: Sheffield, October 1867
Died: Sheffield, May 1928

CAREER
CLUBS: Heeley, WEDNESDAY (August 1882-April 1889).

Wally Hiller made the first of his eight appearances for Wednesday in a 2-1 FA Cup defeat by Nottingham Forest in January 1885. His first goal for the club was the winner (1-0) in a fourth-round tie against the Crusaders in December 1887. He also excelled in cricket, swimming and cycling and was a solicitor by profession.

HILLS, John David
Utility

Appearances: 43+3
Born: Blackpool, 21 April 1978

CAREER
CLUBS: Blackpool, Everton, Swansea City, Blackpool, Gillingham, WEDNESDAY (free, June 2005-May 2007).

Left-sided defender, and occasional midfielder, John Hills gives nothing less than 100 per cent. He made three Premiership appearances for Everton and played in 193 games for Blackpool, whom he helped win the LDV Vans Trophy in 2002.

HINCH, James Andrew
Forward

Appearances: 0+1
Born: Sheffield, 8 November 1947

CAREER
CLUBS: Bradford Park Avenue, Bangor City, Bethesda, Portmadoc, Tranmere Rovers, Plymouth Argyle, Hereford United, York City, Southport, Los Angeles Skyhawks, WEDNESDAY (trial, October-December 1977), Barnsley, California Surf Frecheville Community Association, California Surf (assistant coach), San Diego Sockers (assistant coach).
OTHER: ran a soccer camp in the USA before forming his own company, Chelsea Mortgage.

Jim Hinch scored 61 goals in 248 League games before joining the Owls. Obviously well past his best, his only senior outing for Wednesday was as a second-half substitute at Cambridge United in December 1977. He did well in the States.

HINCHCLIFFE, Alan Arthur
Goalkeeper

Appearances: 2
Born: Staveley, Chesterfield, 8 December 1936

CAREER
CLUBS: WEDNESDAY (March 1952-July 1959), Chesterfield, non-League (1960-70)
OTHER: project manager.

Reserve to Dave McIntosh, Alan Hinchcliffe's two League games in November 1956, both ended in defeats against Bolton at home and Leeds away.

HINCHCLIFFE, Alfred G.
Left half

Appearances: 1
Born: Wadsley Bridge, Sheffield, 26 August 1897
Died: circa 1972

CAREER
CLUBS: WEDNESDAY (trial, August 1919-August 1920).

Alf Hinchcliffe's only League game for the Owls was at left-half at home to Everton in January 1920 (won 1-0).

HINCHCLIFFE, Andrew
Defender

Appearances: 96+1 Goals: 7
Born: Manchester, 5 February 1969

CAREER
CLUBS: Manchester City, Everton, WEDNESDAY (£2.75 million, January 1998-March 2002).
OTHER: moved into coaching.

After making over 450 appearances for his 3 clubs and winning 7 caps for England, plus 1 at Under-21 and 3 at Youth levels, Andy Hinchcliffe was forced to retire with an Achilles injury, aged thirty-three. Also capable of playing on the left side of midfield, he gained both FA Cup and Charity Shield winners' medals with Everton in 1995 before his £2.8 million transfer to Hillsborough. A polished performer, with a keen and enthusiastic approach, he was superb in 1998/99 when the Owls had a watertight defence. After that he had to battle against injuries but when fit always gave 100 per cent. He made his debut for Wednesday *v.* Wimbledon in March 1998.

HIRST, David Eric
Striker

Appearances: 309+49 Goals: 128
Born: Cudworth, Yorkshire, 7 December 1967

CAREER
CLUBS: Barnsley, WEDNESDAY (£300,000, August 1986-October 1997), Southampton, Brunsmeer Athletic.

David Hirst

H

OTHER: match day host at Hillsborough; also assists local radio.

A player who sustained his fair share of injuries during his career, David Hirst, nevertheless, is listed among the best strikers in Owls' history. Honoured by England at 4 different levels, he gained 3 Youth, 7 Under-21, 3 'B' and 3 full caps. He scored nine goals for Barnsley before establishing himself as a firm favourite with the Hillsborough fans. An all-round player who loved to run with the ball, he was fast, decisive, and strong in the air and certainly knew where the net was. He made his debut for the Owls as a substitute at Charlton on the opening day of 1986/87 and netted his first goal forty-eight hours later in a 2-2 home draw with Everton. A League Cup winner in 1991, he spent over thirteen years with Wednesday before joining Southampton for £2 million.

HODDER, William
Outside left

Appearances: 15   Goals: 1
Born: Stroud, July 1867
Died: Nottingham, March 1897

CAREER
CLUBS: Notts Rangers, Notts County, Nottingham Forest, Kidderminster Olympic, WEDNESDAY (free, November 1889), Lincoln City.

Bill Hodder played the majority of his games for Wednesday in the Football Alliance, having appeared for Notts County in the first season of League football. His only goal for the Owls came against Derby in a second round FA Cup win in January 1891 when he partnered Harry Woolhouse on the left wing.

HODGE, Martin
Goalkeeper

Appearances: 249
Born: Southport, 4 February 1959

CAREER
CLUBS: Plymouth Argyle, Everton, Preston North End (L), Oldham Athletic (L), Gillingham (L), Preston North End (L), WEDNESDAY (£50,000, July 1983-August 1988), Leicester City, Hartlepool United, Rochdale, Plymouth Argyle (player-coach, youth team manager), WEDNESDAY (coach, reserve team manager, July 1996-October 2002), Rochdale (coach), Leeds United (coach).

After gaining experience with Plymouth and appearing in 25 First Division games for Everton, Martin Hodge made a huge impact at Hillsborough. Standing well over 6ft tall and weighing 14st 2lbs, he was an ever-present in his first four seasons, helped the Owls gain promotion to the top flight in 1984 and, in fact, missed only 11 League games out of 208 during his 5 years at the club. In February 1987, he made his 214th consecutive appearance and as a result overtook Mark Hooper's club record that had stood for 55 years. He captained the Owls in 1986 and was placed on stand-by for

Martin Hodge

the England World Cup final squad in Mexico. He moved to Leicester after losing his place to Kevin Pressman. Hodge, who was utterly reliable and very consistent, made 616 appearances (520 in the Football League) during a wonderful career.

HODKISS, Thomas
Right-back

Appearances: 2
Born: Sheffield, 1904
Deceased

CAREER
CLUBS: WEDNESDAY (November 1923-June 1930), Reading.

Reserve to Billy Felton and then Tommy Walker at Hillsborough, Tom Hodgkiss made just 2 League appearances for the Owls in 6 years. His debut was at home to Burnley in March 1928 and a week later he played at Bury. He had 50 outings for Reading.

HODGSON, David James
Forward

Appearances: 7+5   Goals: 2
Born: Gateshead, 1 November 1960

CAREER
CLUBS: Ipswich Town, Bolton Wanderers, WEDNESDAY (trial, 1976), Middlesbrough, Liverpool, Sunderland, Norwich City, Middlesbrough, Jerez Club de Portivo, WEDNESDAY (free, July 1988-March 1989), Metz, Swansea City, Mazda Hiroshima, Darlington (coach, manager).
OTHER: football agent.

Capped seven times by England at under-21 level and the recipient of a First Division championship medal with Liverpool in 1983, David Hodgson had an excellent career that spanned

sixteen years. After scoring 20 goals in 140 games for Middlesbrough, he moved to Anfield and maintained his form on Merseyside, adding a further 49 appearances (10 goals) to his tally before playing in 60 games for Sunderland. His form dipped slightly after that and, following a spell with Norwich and an unhappy sojourn in Spain, he played in only 12 competitive games for Wednesday, making his Owls' debut as a substitute versus Southampton in October 1988. He failed to achieve any success as a manager.

HOLBEM, Walter
Defender

Appearances: 89
Born: Sheffield, November 1884
Died: Ascot, 18 June 1930

CAREER
CLUBS: Heeley Friends, WEDNESDAY (September 1906-September 1911), Everton, St Mirren, Preston North End, Southport Central.
OTHER: bookmaker.

After spending practically two years playing centre half in Wednesday's second team, Wally Holbem became a regular in the League side in 1908/09 when he partnered both Willie Layton and Harry Burton at full-back. He moved on following the emergence of fellow full-backs Jimmy Spoors and Ted Worrall. While working at Ascot racecourse, a bolt of lightening struck his umbrella and knocked him unconscious. He died in hospital.

HOLLIDAY, Edwin
Outside left

Appearances: 62   Goals: 14
Born: Royston, Barnsley, 7 June 1939

H

CAREER

CLUBS: Middlesbrough, WEDNESDAY (£25,000, March 1962-June 1965), Middlesbrough, Hereford United, Workington, Peterborough United.

A strong and thrustful outside left with a variety of tricks and a powerful shot in both feet, Eddie Holliday won 5 Under-23 and 3 full caps for England and also played 3 times for the Football League side. A key member of 'Boro's marvellous attack of the late 1950s, that included Brian Clough and Alan Peacock, he caused havoc down the opposition right at times – if he'd been with a more fashionable club he would have surely gained many more honours for his country. He took over from Colin Dobson on Wednesday's left and had a run of 34 consecutive outings before being sidelined through injury. He came back strongly in 1963/64 and after returning to his former club he took his tally of senior appearances with 'Boro to 169. A broken leg in November 1970 effectively ended Eddie's career. His nephew, Colin Grainger, played for Sheffield United, Sunderland and England.

HOLMES, Darren Peter
Midfield

Appearances: 1
Born: Sheffield, 30 January 1975

CAREER
CLUBS: WEDNESDAY (April 1991-August 1996), Bangor City (L), Cape Cod Crusaders (L), Scunthorpe United, Boston United, Notts County, Lincoln City, non-League (1996-2003).
OTHER: employed by LCV Commercial Vans (Middlewood).

Darren Holmes' only first-class game for the Owls was against FC Basel in the InterToto Cup in Switzerland in June 1995. He failed to make the grade in top-line football but did reasonably well in non-League circles.

HOLMES, George William
Right-back

Appearances: 21
Born: Goldenhill, Staffs, September, 1896
Deceased by 1975

CAREER
CLUBS: Ton Pentre, Port Vale, Army, Merthyr Town, WEDNESDAY (£435, June 1921-September 1922), Wrexham.

George Holmes lost a big chunk of his career to the First World War. Released by Port Vale before competitive football resumed in 1919, he made only 72 League appearances, for Merthyr, the Owls and Wrexham, before retiring. He contested the right-back position with George Gray at Hillsborough.

HOLSGROVE, John William
Defender

Appearances: 114+1   Goals: 5
Born: Southwark, London, 27 September 1945

John Holsgrove

CAREER

CLUBS: *Arsenal, Tottenham Hotspur, Crystal Palace, Wolverhampton Wanderers, WEDNESDAY (£50,000, June 1971), Stockport County, Stalybridge Celtic. OTHER: financial advisor with Lombard North Central, Surrey.*

England Youth international John Holsgrove was released by both Arsenal and Spurs and made only 18 League appearances for Palace before joining Wolves. He helped the Molineux club win promotion to the First Division in 1967 and made 202 appearances in 6 seasons prior to his transfer to Wednesday. Known as 'Big John' he brought some experience to the Owls' defence and took over as team captain for a while. His first goal for the club earned a point from a 2-2 draw against Luton in December 1971. He was given a free transfer following relegation in 1975. A very able guitarist, he was a great friend of pop star Lulu. His son, Paul, played for Aldershot, Luton and had loan spells with Wimbledon, West Brom and Stoke among others.

HOLT, Grant
Forward

Appearances: 15+15   Goals: 4
Born: Carlisle, 12 April 1981

CAREER

CLUBS: *Workington, Halifax Town, Barrow, Workington, Sengkang Marine, Barrow, WEDNESDAY (£7,500, March 2003-January 2004), Rochdale, Nottingham Forest.*

A big target man, Grant Holt failed to gain a regular place in Wednesday's line-up, spending half his time on the bench during his ten months at Hillsborough. His first goal for the Owls earned a point from a 1-1 draw at Brighton in April 2003. He was Rochdale's Player of the Year in 2005.

HOOPER, Mark
Outside right

Appearances: 425   Goals: 135
Born: Darlington, 14 July 1901
Died: Sheffield, 9 March 1974

CAREER

CLUBS: *Darlington, WEDNESDAY (£1,950, January 1927-April 1939), Rotherham United (later coach). OTHER: army; later ran a tobacconist shop near Hillsborough.*

Widely recognised as one of the finest uncapped outside rights in League football during the late twenties and early thirties, Mark Hooper was only 5ft 6ins tall, weighed barely 10st and wore size four boots. Initially told that he was too small to make the grade as a professional footballer (he kept goal at the time), he put his nose in the air and went on to prove all his critics wrong by switching to an outfield player and appearing in over 400 games for Wednesday, whom he served for twelve years. Before moving to Hillsborough, he helped Darlington win the Third Division

Mark Hooper

(North) title in 1925 and the following year played a blinder for the Feethams club in a 5-1 win over Wednesday in a League game. This performance undoubtedly led to him joining the Owls and in his first full season he set a new record for a winger by scoring 22 goals. Despite this tally being bettered later by his opposite number, Ellis Rimmer, Hooper was never inferior to the England international. Indeed, he and Rimmer were said to be one of the best pair of extreme wingers in the game at this time and they celebrated by helping the Owls lift the FA Cup in 1935, Hooper scoring the second goal and Rimmer the last two in a 4-2 win over West Bromwich Albion. Hooper then gained a Charity Shield winners' prize later that year and he also scored 3 goals in 7 representative matches for the Sheffield FA. Hooper was the nephew of Charlie Roberts, the Manchester United centre half.

Bobby Hope

HOPE, Robert
Midfield

Appearances: 43+3 Goals: 9
Born: Bridge of Allan, Stirlingshire, 28 September, 1943

CAREER
CLUBS: Sunderland, West Bromwich Albion, Birmingham City, Philadelphia Atoms, Dallas Tornados, WEDNESDAY (free, September 1976-August 1978), Dallas Tornados (L), Bromsgrove Rovers (player-coach, manager), Burton Albion (manager), Wolverhampton Wanderers (part-time scout), Bromsgrove Rovers (manager), West Bromwich Albion (youth recruitment officer, chief scout).
OTHER: owned post offices in Handsworth Wood (Birmingham) and Boldmere (Sutton Coldfield); owned three sandwich bars; now runs a shop in Walsall.

Moving to The Hawthorns a month after playing for his country in a schoolboy interna-

tional, Bobby Hope was an amateur when he made his League debut for West Brom versus Arsenal in April 1960. He went on to score 42 goals in 403 appearances for the Baggies, helping them win the League Cup (1966) and FA Cup (1968), while also playing in two losing League Cup finals (1967 and 1970). Capped once by Scotland's Under-23 side and twice by the seniors, he was a diminutive midfielder with the ability to deliver a terrific long pass. He was well past his best when he joined the Owls, for whom he scored on his debut versus Chesterfield. He had a good first season at Hillsborough, linking up in centre-field with Jeff Johnson. During his career (all levels) 'Hopey' appeared in 549 matches and scored 60 goals.

HORNE, Barry
Midfield

Appearances: 7
Born: St Asaph, Denbighshire, 18 May 1962

CAREER

CLUBS: *Rhyl, Wrexham, Portsmouth, Southampton, Everton, Birmingham City, Huddersfield Town, WEDNESDAY (free, March-August 2000), Kidderminster Harriers, Walsall, Belper Town.*
OTHER: *chairman of the PFA; attended teacher training college; worked as football pundit for BBC Radio Wales, BBC Radio 5 Live and Sky.*

An experienced Welsh international with 59 full caps under his belt, Barry Horne joined the Owls aged thirty-seven. In his heyday he was the anchorman in midfield for each of his clubs, scoring 23 goals in 168 games for Wrexham, 7 in 79 for Portsmouth, 13 in 151 for Southampton, 3 in 151 for Everton, none in 39 for Birmingham and 1 in 73 for Huddersfield. He made his debut for Wednesday against Wimbledon in April 2000 and after leaving Hillsborough made 34 appearances for Kidderminster (one goal) and 3 for Walsall, moving into non-League with 764 club and international games behind him (48 goals). He won the Welsh Cup with Wrexham in 1986 and the FA Cup and Charity Shield with Everton in 1995. Horne gained his BSc in 1983 and added a master's degree in engineering the following year.

HORNSBY, Brian Geoffrey
Midfield

Appearances: 120+4   Goals: 30
Born: Great Shelford, Cambridgeshire, 10 September 1954

CAREER
CLUBS: *Peterborough United, Leicester City, Bristol City, Arsenal, Shrewsbury Town, WEDNESDAY (£40,000, March 197-November 1981), Chester (L), Edmonton Drillers (L), Carlisle United, Chesterfield, IK Brage, Spalding United, Holbeach United (player-manager).*
OTHER: *owner of a shed, summerhouse and conservatory business.*

An England Schoolboy and Youth international midfielder, Brian Hornsby won the FA Youth Cup with Arsenal in 1971. With so much talent at Highbury, he moved down the ladder to Shrewsbury in 1976 before switching to Wednesday for whom he made his debut at Lincoln. Hard working with great stamina, he held his position in the team until promotion was won in 1980 but after that was never really in contention. Hornsby made a total of 221 League appearances (48 goals).

HORROBIN, Thomas
Full-back

Appearances: 3.
Born: Askern, Doncaster, 8 August 1943

CAREER
CLUBS: *WEDNESDAY (August 1958-May 1963), Frickley Colliery.*
OTHER: *worked at Armthorpe Colliery and at a Doncaster timber yard.*

Reserve Tom Horrobin had to wait until September 1962 before making his League debut (in place of the injured Peter Johnson) in a 1-0 win at home to Manchester United in front of 40,000 fans.

HOUNSFIELD, Reginald Ernest
Outside right

Appearances: 2
Born: Hackentorpe, Derby, 14 August 1882
Died: Derby 1951

CAREER
CLUBS: *Sheffield FC, WEDNESDAY (free, March 1902-October 1903), Derby County.*

Regarded as one of the fastest players in his position in the early part of the twentieth century, Reg Hounsfield spent eighteen months with Wednesday, making his League debut in place of Harry Davis at Notts County in October 1902 and having his second game twenty-four hours later versus Liverpool.

HOWELLS, Peter
Wing forward

Appearances: 3   Goals: 1
Born: Middlesbrough, 23 September 1932
Died: Middlesbrough, 16 January 1993

CAREER
CLUBS: WEDNESDAY (April 1951-November 1956), Hartlepool United.

Reserve to Dennis Woodhead, Peter Howells made his League debut versus Manchester City in November 1954 and scored his only goal for the Owls in a 3-3 draw at West Ham in April 1956.

HOYLAND, George A.
Forward

Appearances: 3   Goals: 1
Born: Sheffield, 1880
Deceased by 1955

CAREER
CLUBS: Sheffield FC, WEDNESDAY (free, November 1903-May 1905).

Reserve George Hoyland made his League debut against Manchester City in March 1904 and scored his only goal nine months later at Notts County (2-2).

HUDSON, John
Defender

Appearances: 16
Born: Sheffield, 11 October 1860
Died: Worksop, 21 November 1941

CAREER
CLUBS: Sheffield FC, WEDNESDAY (free, April 1880-August 1889), Walkley, Heeley, Lockwood Brothers, Blackburn Olympic, Sheffield United.
OTHER: hotelier.

Jack Hudson occupied all three half-back positions and played in the 1882 FA Cup semi-final defeat by Blackburn, the club he made his first-class debut against in a second round tie two years earlier. He helped Wednesday win the Sheffield Challenge Cup in 1881, 1883, 1887 and 1888 and the Wharncliffe Charity Cup in 1882, 1883 and 1888. His daughter married ex-Owls star Jimmy Spoors.

HUKIN, Arthur
Forward

Appearances: 6   Goals: 3
Born: Sheffield, 22 October 1937
Died: Bedford, 21 November 1983

CAREER
CLUBS: WEDNESDAY (April 1951-April 1957), Bury, non-League (1957-66).

Arthur Hukin never made it in the Football League but was a prolific marksman in non-League football. He scored twice on his Owls' debut in a 4-3 defeat at Leicester in November 1954 when deputised for Redfern Froggatt. Also a fine sprinter, he sadly died of cancer.

HULL, Gary
Full-back

Appearances: 6+2
Born: Sheffield, 21 June 1956

CAREER
CLUBS: WEDNESDAY (July 1971-July 1977), non-League to 1983
OTHER: builder.

Mainly reserve to Peter Rodrigues and Bernard Shaw, Gary Hull's eight outings came in the 1975/76 Third Division season. He made his debut in a 3-1 home win over Aldershot in February.

HULL, John Smellie
Right half

Appearances: 1
Born: Motherwell, 22 April 1913
Died: Scotland, 1977

CAREER
CLUBS: WEDNESDAY (November 1935-April 1937)

Signed as cover for Wilf Sharp, Jack Hull's only game for the Owls was against Portsmouth in February 1936 (lost 1-0).

HUMPHREYS, Richard John
Midfield

Appearances: 43+39   Goals: 9
Born: Sheffield, 30 November 1977

CAREER
CLUBS: WEDNESDAY (April 1994-February 2001), Scunthorpe United (L), Cardiff City (L), Cambridge United, Hartlepool United.

Capped twice by England Youth and three times at Under-21 level, Richie Humphreys gives his all every time he takes the field. He had his best spell with the Owls in 1996/97 (29 League appearances) but when Peter Shreeves became manager, he left for Cambridge. He played for Hartlepool versus Wednesday in the 2005 play-off final. His book *From Tears to Cheers* was published in 2003.

HUNT, Douglas Arthur
Centre forward

Appearances: 47   Goals: 31
Born: Shipton Bellinger, Hampshire, 19 May 1914
Died: Yeovil, 30 May 1989

CAREER
CLUBS: Winchester City, Southampton, Northfleet, Tottenham Hotspur, Barnsley, WEDNESDAY (£3,875, March 1938-April 1946), Leyton Orient (player, assistant manager), Gloucester City (manager), Yeovil Town (trainer-coach), Tonbridge (manager), Yeovil (trainer).
WARTIME GUEST APPEARANCES: Aldershot, Brentford, Fulham, Spurs, West Ham United.

Doug Hunt took over from Ted Drake as leader of Winchester's attack. The Owls had tried six players at centre forward in 1937/38 before signing Hunt. He netted 6 times in his first 12 games at the end of that season, following up with 25 in 1938/39, including a double hat-trick in a 7-0 home win over Norwich – the only player to achieve this feat for Wednesday – and a treble in his next game versus Luton. He also notched 7 goals in 19 Second World War games and helped Brentford win the London War Cup in 1942. He was Yeovil's trainer for twenty-eight years (1958-86).

HUNT, George Samuel
Centre forward

Appearances: 35   Goals: 9
Born: Barnsley, 22 February 1910
Died: Bolton, 19 September 1996

CAREER
CLUBS: Barnsley, Sheffield United, Burslem Port Vale, Chesterfield, Tottenham Hotspur, Arsenal, Bolton Wanderers, WEDNESDAY (£3,000, November 1946-May 1948), Bolton Wanderers (coach, trainer).
WARTIME GUEST APPEARANCES: Liverpool, Luton Town, Rochdale
OTHER: manager of a Bolton carwash.

H

Known as 'The Chesterfield Tough', George Hunt was turned away by Arsenal boss Herbert Chapman when playing for Chesterfield. Eight years later he replaced Ted Drake in the Gunners' attack, having by then scored 134 goals in 199 League games. He helped Spurs win promotion to the First Division in 1933, gained three England caps that same year versus Scotland, Italy and Switzerland and won a League championship medal with Arsenal in 1938 and the League (North) Cup with Bolton in 1945. He was thirty-six when he joined Wednesday and unfortunately he did not have a happy debut as the Owls lost 4-0 at Newcastle. In a fine career, Hunt, physically strong and fearless, scored 169 goals in 294 League games with 5 clubs. He died from Alzheimer's.

HUNTER, Andrew Stanley
Outside right

Appearances: 14   Goals: 3
Born: Belfast, 1882
Died: Belfast, circa 1966

CAREER
CLUBS: Distillery, Glentoran, Belfast Celtic, WEDNESDAY (£205, March 1909-August 1910), Glentoran.

An Irish international (eight caps won) Andy Hunter was a smart, compact winger who made over 200 appearances in his homeland before joining the Owls. He made his debut in a 4-0 League defeat at Manchester City and netted his first goal in a 2-1 win at Liverpool three weeks later. He won the Antrim County Shield, Charity Cup and Irish Cup with Glentoran.

HUNTER, John
Defender

Appearances: 3
Born: Crookes, Sheffield, September 1852
Died: Blackburn, 10 April 1903

CAREER
CLUBS: WEDNESDAY (September 1880-April 1882), Blackburn Olympic, Blackburn Rovers, Heeley, Blackburn Rovers (assistant trainer, groundsman). OTHER: licensee.

Powerful and clean kicking, Jack Hunter – a former athlete – was one of the finest defenders of his time. He appeared in Wednesday's first three FA Cup games versus Blackburn, Turton and Darwen in 1880/81. After his international trial (North versus South) he gained seven full caps (1882-87) and as a Blackburn Olympic player, won an FA Cup winners' medal in 1883. He died of consumption.

HUTTON, Robert
Forward

Appearances: 5   Goals: 1
Born: Eccleshall, Sheffield, 1880
Deceased by 1960

CAREER
CLUBS: WEDNESDAY (August 1898-April 1900), Worksop Town, WEDNESDAY (May 1901-May 1902), Chesterfield, Worksop Town. OTHER: joiner.

A reliable reserve, Bob Hutton made his League debut versus Stoke in March 1899 when he partnered Harry Davis on the right wing.

HYDE, Graham
Midfield
Appearances: 164+54 Goals: 16
Born: Doncaster, 19 November 1970

CAREER

CLUBS: WEDNESDAY (April 1987-February 1999), Birmingham City, Chesterfield, Peterborough United, Bristol Rovers, Hereford United, Worcester City.

Graham Hyde had a few injury problems during the latter stages of his Owls' career but, when fit, he was an aggressive ball-winner and smart passer. He had his best seasons in the mid-1990s, when he was a regular in the side, and made his League debut away to Manchester City in September 1991, partnering Danny Wilson and Carlton Palmer in the engine room.

I

IBBOTSON, Wilfred
Forward

Appearances: 1
Born: Sheffield, 1 October 1926

CAREER
CLUBS: WEDNESDAY (November 1942-August 1948), Mansfield Town, Goole Town.
OTHER: draughtsman.

Wilf Ibbotson was a semi-professional throughout his career. His only League appearance for the Owls was against Coventry in November 1947, when he deputised for Redfern Froggatt. He also played in nine Second World War matches for Wednesday.

INGESSON, Klas
Utility

Appearances: 15+6 Goals: 2
Born: Odeshog, Sweden, 20 August 1968

CAREER
CLUBS: IFK Gothenburg, KV Mechelen, PSV Eindhoven, WEDNESDAY (£800,000, September 1994-November 1995), Bari, Bologna, Olympique Marseille, Lecce, Elfsborg, Odeshog (player-manager).

A Swedish international, capped almost 60 times, Klas Ingesson was never able to adapt to the English game. Looking overweight, he was used as a sweeper and in midfield by manager David Pleat, and made his Premiership debut versus Nottingham Forest in September 1994. His first goal came on Boxing Day that same year in a 4-1 win at Everton. He made over 400 club appearances in total.

INGLIS, William White
Right-back

Appearances: 31
Born: Kirkcaldy, 2 March 1897
Died: Sale, 20 January 1968

CAREER
CLUBS: Kirkcaldy United, Raith Rovers, WEDNESDAY (£100, June 1924-May 1925), Manchester United, Northampton Town, Manchester United (assistant trainer).

Three times Bill Inglis was named as a reserve by Scotland but he never won a full cap – his only representative honour was to play for the Home Scots against the Anglo Scots in 1922. Nimble with a finely-tuned tackle, he was an excellent positional player who made his Owls' debut at Derby in September 1924 when he partnered Billy Felton. After impressing in three games against Manchester United that season he was signed by the Reds. He captained the Second XI at Old Trafford for many years and as assistant trainer was the father figure to many of the up-and-coming Busby Babes. He served United for a total of thirty-two years.

I

INGRAM, William
Forward

Appearances: 48   Goals: 22
Born: Sheffield, 11 December 1866
Died: Shiregreen, Sheffield, 19 March 1949

CAREER
CLUBS: Lockwood Brothers, Heeley, WEDNESDAY (free, November 1886-May 1892).

A gutsy, energetic and sometimes brilliant forward, Bill Ingram helped the Owls win the Football Alliance in 1890. He appeared in 16 consecutive FA Cup games between 1887 and 1891, scoring 8 goals, including a hat-trick against Nottingham Forest in a fifth-round tie in January 1888. He also helped Wednesday win the Sheffield Challenge Cup and Wharncliffe Charity Cup in 1888.

IRVINE, Archibald
Midfield

Appearances: 31+4 Goals: 1
Born: Coatbridge, Scotland, 25 June 1946

CAREER
CLUBS: Airdrieonians, WEDNESDAY (£15,000, September 1968-December 1969), Doncaster Rovers, Scunthorpe United, Spa Social.
OTHER: driver; laid concrete floors.

Competitive and creative, Archie Irvine never shirked a tackle. He made his debut for the Owls versus QPR in October 1968 and scored his only goal for the club in a 3-0 win at Wolves two months later. He played in 228 League games for Shrewsbury.

J

JACKSON, Jerimiah
Outside right

Appearances: 1
Born: Burnley, circa 1873
Died: Cleethorpes, 22 July 1927

CAREER
CLUBS: Burnley (player, trainer), Lincoln City (trainer), WEDNESDAY (trainer, August 1920-May 1924), Reading (trainer).

The club's trainer, Jerry Jackson, was called up by Wednesday in an emergency, chosen to play on the right-wing at Port Vale in August 1923 when Rees Williams was absent. He left the field, exhausted, after thirty-five minutes. Believed to be forty-six at the time, he is the oldest player ever to appear for the Owls' Senior XI.

JACKSON, Norman Edward
Defender

Appearances: 31
Born: Bradford, 6 July 1925

CAREER
CLUBS: WEDNESDAY (October 1948-June 1954), Bristol City, Oldham Athletic.
OTHER: licensee; director of a Sheffield safety equipment company; also a fine club cricketer.

Norman Jackson was twenty-nine when he made his debut for the Owls versus Bury in April 1950. He helped Wednesday and Bristol City win the Second and Third Division (South) titles in 1951/52 and 1954/55 respectively. He made fewer than 50 senior appearances during his career.

JACOBS, Wayne Graham
Full-back

Appearances: 9+1
Born: Sheffield, 3 February 1969

CAREER
CLUBS: WEDNESDAY (July 1985-March 1988), Hull City, Rotherham United, Bradford City, Halifax Town (player, asssistant manager).

Wayne Jacobs, who struggled to get to grips with his game at Hillsborough, made the first of his ten appearances for the Owls versus Oxford United in August 1987. He later had almost 350 games for Bradford City, whom he helped reach the Premiership in 1999.

JALAL, Shwan
Goalkeeper

Appearances: 0
Born: Baghdad, Iraq, 14 August 1983

CAREER
CLUBS: Tottenham Hotspur, Woking, WEDNESDAY (loan, November-December 2006), Woking.

Jalal was on loan from Woking during November and December 2006.

JAMESON, Joseph B.
Defender

Appearances: 7
Born: Durham, 1885
Deceased by 1964

CAREER
CLUBS: Wallsend Park Villa, WEDNESDAY (August 1905-May 1909), Castleford.

A Wednesday reserve, Joe Jameson made his League debut against Sheffield United in April 1907, when players were rested ahead of the FA Cup final.

JAMIESON, James
Left half

Appearances: 135   Goals: 3
Born: Cambuslang, Glasgow, 3 November 1871
Died: Scotland, circa 1945

CAREER Everton, WEDNESDAY (June 1893-May 1899).

Not a first-team regular at Everton, Jim Jamieson served Wednesday extremely well, but had the ill-luck – Charlie Petrie being preferred due to the conditions – to miss the 1896 FA Cup final win over Wolves. He lost his place to Herrod Ruddleshin in 1898.

JARVIS, Richard Thomas
Goalkeeper

Appearances: 6
Born: Whitwick, Leicestershire, 1880
Died: Leicester, 1924

CAREER
CLUBS: WEDNESDAY (June 1903-August 1905), Hastings, St Leonard's, Luton Town.

Dick Jarvis, 6ft 2ins tall, deputised for Jack Lyall in each of his six outings for the Owls, the first and last against Notts County in April 1904 and April 1905.

JEEVES, John
Right-back

Appearances: 1
Born: Sheffield, May 1862
Deceased by 1933

J

CAREER

CLUBS: WEDNESDAY (January 1883-May 1884).

Jack Jeeves was studying medicine when registered with Wednesday. His only appearance was against Staveley in a first round FA Cup-tie in December 1883 when he deputised for Harry Wilkinson.

JEFFERSON, Derek
Defender

Appearances: 6
Born: Morpeth, 5 September 1948

CAREER

CLUBS: Ipswich Town, Wolverhampton Wanderers, WEDNESDAY (loan, October 1976), Hereford United (player-coach), Boston, Washington Diplomats, Hereford United (player-coach), Birmingham City (coach).
OTHER: ran childrens' courses in the Bristol St Paul's area; coached at the Christian Centre of Sport, Ipswich; salesman for the pharmaceutical company Glaxo.

Derek Jefferson was a vastly experienced professional, having made 175 appearances for Ipswich and 52 for Wolves, when he joined Wednesday during an injury crisis. He helped Ipswich gain promotion to the First Division in 1968.

JEMSON, Nigel Bradley
Forward

Appearances: 34+34   Goals: 11
Born: Hutton, Preston, 10 October 1969

CAREER

CLUBS: Preston North End, Nottingham Forest, Bolton Wanderers, Preston North End, WEDNESDAY (£800,000, September 1991-September 1994), Grimsby Town (L), Notts County, Watford, Rotherham United,

Nigel Jemson

Oxford United, Bury, Portuguese football, Ayr United, Oxford United, Shrewsbury Town, Lincoln City, Bristol Rovers, Ballymena, Ilkeston Town.

Journeyman Nigel Jemson scored over 120 goals in more than 450 games during his career. Capped once by England at under-21 level, he was a hard working and skilful forward who held the ball up well. He netted Nottingham Forest's winner in the 1990 League Cup final win over Oldham and six years later was an AWS winner with Rotherham. He partnered David Hirst in the Owls' attack and made 20 League appearances in his first season at Hillsborough.

JOHNSON, David Alan
Forward

Appearances: 5+1
Born: Dinnington, Sheffield, 29 October 1970

CAREER

CLUBS: Rotherham United Juniors, WEDNESDAY (free, July 1986-August 1993), Hartlepool United ((L), signed later), Lincoln City, Chesterfield, Altrincham, Worksop Town.

OTHER: worked in his father's butcher shop and gained a degree in Sports/Events Management.

Tall and powerful, David Johnson – nicknamed 'Magic' after the American basketball player – found it tough to get first team football with the Owls owing to the presence of David Hirst and Mark Bright. His 6 games for the Owls came in 4 months (January-April 1992).

JOHNSON, David Anthony
Forward

Appearances: 7   Goals: 2
Born: Kingston, Jamaica, 15 August 1976

CAREER
CLUBS: Manchester United, Bury, Ipswich Town, Nottingham Forest, WEDNESDAY (loan, February-March 2002), Burnley, Sheffield United.

Honoured by England at schoolboy and 'B' team levels, David Johnson later gained four caps for Jamaica. Released after winning the FA Youth Cup with Manchester United in 1995, he made his mark with Bury, helping the Shakers win the Second Division title in 1997. He did very well with Ipswich and also with Nottingham Forest. Fast and direct, he broke his leg playing for Forest against Sheffield United in 2003 – this set him back. He made his debut for Wednesday against Preston in February 2002 and scored his first Owls' goal in a 2-0 win at Bradford City in his sixth outing.

JOHNSON, George Albert
Forward

Appearances: 1   Goals: 1
Born: Ashington, 20 July 1905
Died: Reading, 26 May 1985

CAREER
CLUBS: Ashington, WEDNESDAY (£500, May 1929-November 1932), Reading, Watford, Krooger FC (coach), Gauda (coach), Chelsea (scout), Oxford City (coach, groundsman).

A reserve at Hillsborough, George Johnson's only League game for the Owls was at Blackpool in April 1931 when he deputised for Jack Ball, scoring in a 4-0 win. He netted a hat-trick on his debut for Reading, for whom he made 179 appearances. He coached in Holland.

JOHNSON, Jeffrey David
Midfield

Appearances: 206+5   Goals: 9
Born: Cardiff, 26 November 1953

CAREER
CLUBS: Manchester City, Swansea City, Crystal Palace, WEDNESDAY (free, June 1976), Newport County, Gillingham, Port Vale, Barrow.
OTHER: taxi driver.

A Welsh Schoolboy, Youth and Under-23 international, Jeff Johnson was a resilient midfielder who made over 500 appearances – 444 in the Football League. He served the Owls very well for five seasons, helping them gain promotion from the Third Division in 1979/80 when he was voted the Supporters' Player of the Year. A broken leg ended his career.

JOHNSON, Jermaine
Midfield

Appearances: 31+5 Goals: 5
Born: Jamaica, 25 June 1980

CAREER
CLUBS: Oldham Athletic, Bolton Wanderers, Yeovil, Bradford City, WEDNESDAY (January 2007).

Midfielder Jermaine Johnson signed from Bradford City in January 2007, he had earlier assisted Oldham Athletic, Bolton Wanderers and Yeovil.

JOHNSON, Kevin Peter
Midfield

Appearances: 0+1
Born: Doncaster, 29 August 1952

CAREER
CLUBS: WEDNESDAY (August 1966), Southend United, Gillingham, Workington, Hartlepool United, Huddersfield Town, Halifax Town, Hartlepool United, Gateshead.

The older he got, the better Kevin Johnson performed. He struggled with his first four clubs but came good at Hartlepool. He proved what a fine player he was, especially in the lower divisions, and went on to amass 320 League appearances and 46 goals. Playing wide left, his only appearance for Wednesday – in six years – was as a second-half substitute for Paul Taylor in a 3-0 defeat at QPR in August 1971.

JOHNSON, Peter
Full-back

Appearances: 207   Goals: 6
Born: Rotherham, 31 July 1931

CAREER
CLUBS: Rotherham United, WEDNESDAY (£6,000 plus Albert Broadbent, December 1957-July 1965), Peterborough United.
OTHER: later employed at the Templeborough steelworks.

After scoring 23 goals – some as a centre for-ward – in 153 League games for Rotherham, 'Charlie' Peter Johnson moved to Hillsborough where eventually he took over at right-back

from Ron Staniforth. Nicknamed 'Charlie', he was a resourceful player, strong and mobile, who helped the Owls to win the Second Division title in 1958/59 – albeit playing in only seven League games – and finish runners-up in the top flight in 1960/61, when was an ever-present. He lost his place to Brian Hill.

JOHNSON, Thomas
Forward

Appearances: 9   Goals: 3
Born: Newcastle, 15 January 1971

CAREER
CLUBS: Notts County, Derby County, Aston Villa, Celtic, Everton, WEDNESDAY (loan, September-December 2001), Kilmarnock, Gillingham, Sheffield United, Scunthorpe United.

Tommy Johnson scored 57 goals in 149 games for Notts County and 41 in 129 outings for Derby but lost his way at Villa Park – despite winning the League Cup in 1996 – and suffered a serious injury at Celtic which sidelined him for six months. He regained fitness at Everton and, after returning to Parkhead, helped the Bhoys win the Scottish League Cup in 2000, adding Premier League and Scottish Cup winners' medals to his collection the following year. He never settled at Hillsborough, although he did score 1 goal every 3 games for the Owls – his first earning a point at Wimbledon. He gained seven England Under-21 caps.

JOHNSTON, Allan
Forward

Appearances: 12   Goals: 2
Born: Glasgow, 14 December 1973

CAREER
CLUBS: Glasgow Rangers Juniors, Heart of Midlothian, Stade Rennais, Sunderland,

Birmingham City, Bolton Wanderers, Glasgow Rangers, Middlesbrough, WEDNESDAY (loan, December 2002-March 2003), Kilmarnock.

A Scottish international, gaining 2 'B', 3 Under-21 and 17 full caps, Allan Johnston has had a nomadic career, winning only one domestic medal in 1999 with Sunderland as Division One champions. When on form he was certainly a fine player, but niggling injuries and loss of form interrupted his game. He had his best spells with Hearts and Sunderland and his two goals for the Owls came in home League wins over Nottingham Forest and Reading.

JOICEY, Brian
Striker

Appearances: 160+6   Goals: 53
Born: Winlanton, County Durham, 19 December, 1945

CAREER
CLUBS: Ashington, Blyth Spartans, Tow Law Town, North Shields (August 1965), Coventry City, WEDNESDAY (£55,000, August 1971-May 1976), Barnsley, Frickley Colliery, Matlock Town.
OTHER: sales manager for Peter Brookes Honda (Sheffield).

Brian Joicey's arrival at Hillsborough injected some extra life into the team. He became a big favourite with the fans and scored plenty of goals in his first three seasons, including hat-tricks in a 3-1 League win over Leyton Orient in April 1972 and a 3-2 FA Cup replay victory over Crystal Palace in February 1973. Strong in all aspects for forward play, Brian battled against injury in 1974/75 but managed to claim his fiftieth goal for the club to earn a point at Oxford. He netted over 70 goals for North Shields – 45 in 1968/69 when he struck home the winner in the FA Amateur Cup final. He netted four times when playing for the FA XI against the UAU at Hillsborough.

JONES, Bradley
Goalkeeper

Appearances: 15
Born: Armidale, Australia, 19 March 1982

CAREER
CLUBS: Middlesbrough, Stockport County (L), Blackpool (L), WEDNESDAY (loan, August-November 2006).

A Youth, Under-23 and full international, Jones signed for 'Boro in 1997 and turned professional two years later. He has also played on loan with Stockport County and Blackpool (two spells), helping the latter club win the LDV Vans Trophy in 2004.

JONES, Kenwyne Joel
Striker

Appearances: 7   Goals: 7
Born: Trinidad, 5 October 1984

CAREER
CLUBS: Vibe CT 105 W Connection, Glasgow Rangers, West Ham United, Southampton, WEDNESDAY (loan, December 2004-January 2005), Stoke City, Southampton.

Trinidad and Tobagonian international at Under-17, Under-20 and senior levels (he played against England in the 2006 World Cup finals), Kenwyne Jones averaged a goal a game while on loan to the Owls. Ironically, on his return to Hillsborough in August 2005, he scored Saints' winner against Wednesday.

JONES, Ryan Anthony
Midfield

Appearances: 43+6 Goals: 7
Born: Sheffield, 23 July 1973

J

CAREER

CLUBS: WEDNESDAY (July 1989-May 1997), Scunthorpe United (L), Worksop Town, Glapwell, Colley WMC, Maltby MW, Parkgate, Staveley.
OTHER: manager of a car-hire company.

Injury ruined Ryan Jones's career – this after he had represented Wales in 1 full, 1 'B' and 4 Under-21 internationals. Strong and athletic, with a smart left foot, he failed to hold down a place in Wednesday's first team after a difficult 1994/95. He made his League debut against Coventry in March 1993.

JONES, Thomas John
Forward

Appearances: 29   Goals: 6
Born: Tonypandy, Glamorgan, 11 August 1908
Died: West Bromwich, 29 August 1971

CAREER

CLUBS: Mid-Rhondda, Dundee, Tranmere Rovers, WEDNESDAY (£1,500, June 1929-June 1934), Manchester United, Watford, Guildford City, Tranmere Rovers (trainer-coach), Workington (trainer-coach), Birmingham City (assistant trainer), West Bromwich Albion (physio).
WARTIME GUEST APPEARANCES: Arsenal.

Unfortunately the form of first Ellis Rimmer and then Mark Hooper kept Tommy Jones out of the Wednesday side. Nevertheless he still made a name for himself in the game, scoring 62 goals in 260 League games. Strongly-built and able to play on the left wing or inside, he made his debut for the Owls on the left wing in a 3-1 win at Liverpool in April 1930. Two of his six goals were scored in a 6-1 win over West Ham in March 1932. He was capped by Wales against Northern Ireland in 1932 and then France a year later.

JONK, Wim
Midfield

Appearances: 80+1 Goals: 5
Born: Volendam, Holland, 12 October 1966

CAREER

CLUBS: RKAV Volendam, FC Volendam, Ajax Amsterdam, Inter Milan, PSV Eindhoven, WEDNESDAY (£2.5 million, August 1998-July 2001).

Playmaker Wim Jonk was an influential figure in the team, his pin-point passes and general cohesion proving to be of great importance to the Owls as they battled to cope with the strain of First Division football. The Dutch international – who won 49 caps – arrived at Hillsborough having played with Ruud Gullit, Marco Van Basten and Dennis Bergkamp. He scored 79 goals in 368 League games, was the recipient of both Dutch League and Cup winners' medals and won the UEFA Cup with both Ajax (1992) and Inter Milan (1994).

JONSSON, Sigurdur
Midfield

Appearances: 64+9 Goals: 6
Born: Akranes, Iceland, 27 September 1966

CAREER

CLUBS: IA Akranes, WEDNESDAY (£25,000, February 1985-July 1989), Barnsley (L), Arsenal, IA Akranes, Orebo, Dundee United, IA Akranes, FH Hafnarfjarder (player, retired 1992, assistant coach), Vikingur (manager).

Icelandic international Siggi Jonsson (21 caps gained) was an efficient, hard-working midfielder but never a regular in the Owls' first team, spreading his 73 appearances over 4 seasons. He made his debut for the Owls in place of Andy Blair in a 3-1 defeat at Leicester in March 1985 and scored his first goal for the club at Oxford five months later (1-0).

Sigurdur Jonsson

JORDAN, Clarence
Centre forward

Appearances: 94   Goals: 36
Born: South Kirby, 20 June 1922
Died: Doncaster, 24 February 1992

CAREER
CLUBS: Doncaster Rovers, South Kirby Colliery, WEDNESDAY (£3,000 plus Arnold Lowes, February 1948-June 1955).
WARTIME GUEST APPEARANCES: Aldershot, Leeds United, Birmingham City.
OTHER: steward in South Kirby; licensee in Norton.

Ex-miner Clarrie Jordan scored 47 goals in 60 League games for Doncaster – 44 in 1946/47 when Rovers won the Third Division (North) title with a record 72 points. Feeding off Eddie Quigley and Redfern Froggatt at Hillsborough, he found it difficult at a higher level, although injuries didn't help his cause. He had his best season with the Owls in 1948/49 (14 goals) and the following year hit a four-timer against Hull as Wednesday gained promotion from the Second Division. Injury affected his game after that, and he made only 18 appearances in five years before retiring due to an arthritic knee.

Before he died in 1992 Clarrie had both legs amputated due to diabetes.

JORDAN, John William
Forward

Appearances: 11   Goals: 2
Born: Romford, 8 November 1921

CAREER
CLUBS: West Ham United, Tottenham Hotspur, Juventus, Birmingham City, WEDNESDAY (£7,500, September 1950-June 1951), Tonbridge, Bedford Town.
OTHER: Army; manager of a menswear shop.

After scoring 13 goals in 27 games for Spurs, England Amateur international reserve Johnny Jordan became one of the first English professionals to go abroad after the Second World War. He spent seven months with Juventus before returning to play for Birmingham. He made his debut for the Owls in a 4-3 win at Huddersfield in September 1950 and scored the first of his two goals in a 2-1 win at West Brom three months later. He left the club once Jackie Sewell had settled in the inside right position. He was the cousin of Clarrie Jordan.

KAY, Anthony Herbert
Wing half

Appearances: 203   Goals: 10
Born: Sheffield, 13 May 1937

CAREER
CLUBS: WEDNESDAY (June 1952-December 1962), Everton.
OTHER: bookmaker; bar manager in Spain; worked in a London sports centre.

K

Tony Kay

Tony Kay's fiery play matched his flame-coloured hair. A rugged, tough-tackling, terrier-like wing half who loved to drive forward, he helped Wednesday win the Second Division in 1959 and four years later was a member of Everton's First Division-winning side. He was also capped by England versus Switzerland in 1963, having earlier represented his country in seven Under-23 matches as well as playing three games for the Football League (1959-61). Unfortunately Kay's career came to sensational end in 1965. Following an article in a Sunday newspaper, published in 1964, he, along with teammates David Layne and Peter Swan (and others), were sent to prison and banned from playing professional football after being found guilty of involvement in a betting coup to fix the result of a League game between Wednesday and Ipswich. Kay's last competitive game was for Everton against Wolves in April 1964 – having played his first for the Owls against Bolton as a seventeen year old in April 1955. His ban was lifted in 1972 and he later worked on a film about the infamous match-fixing years.

KAYE, Albert
Centre forward

Appearances: 44   Goals: 13
Born: Staveley, 1875
Died: Staveley, September 1935

CAREER
CLUBS: WEDNESDAY (May 1897-August 1899), Chatham, West Ham United, Stockport County.

Blessed with aggression and commitment, Albert Kaye did well in non-League football before showing his worth with the Owls. He made his debut at Bury in September 1897, scoring his first two goals a week later in a 4-2 win over Liverpool. He moved on when Jack Pryce took over at centre forward. He played in West Ham's first-ever Southern League game in 1900.

KEAN, Frederick William
Half-back

Appearances: 247   Goals: 8
Born: Sheffield, 3 April 1899
Died: Sheffield, 28 October 1973

CAREER
CLUBS: Sheffield FC, Hallam, WEDNESDAY (free, July 1920-September 1928), Bolton Wanderers, Luton Town, Sutton Town (player-coach).
WARTIME GUEST APPEARANCES: Portsmouth.
OTHER: licensee.

Fred Kean began as an inside forward and succeeded Frank Froggatt as captain at Hillsborough, helping Wednesday to win the Second Division in 1926. Noticeable on the field for his upright, guardsman-like build, he was a very competent footballer, aggressive, good with his head and both feet and was a very positive and firm tackler. Capped nine times by England between 1923 and 1929, he played for the Football League on four occasions, appeared in several

K

Sheffield versus Glasgow inter-city matches and gained an FA Cup winners' medal with Bolton (1929). During an excellent career, he made over 450 senior appearances. Kean was also a very capable cricketer.

KELL, George James
Full-back

Appearances: 6
Born: Gateshead, 13 July 1896
Died: Sheffield, April 1985

CAREER
CLUBS: WEDNESDAY (May 1920-June 1922), Brentford, Hartlepool United, Gainsborough Trinity.

Able to occupy both full-back positions, George Kell deputised for Harry O'Neill during his time with Wednesday, making his debut in a 1-1 draw at Blackpool in February 1921. He played in 76 League games for Brentford and 71 for Hartlepool.

KENNEDY, John
Forward

Appearances: 3
Born: Edinburgh, Scotland, 1873
Died: Scotland 1940

CAREER
CLUBS: Queen's Park Juniors, WEDNESDAY (free, August 1890-May 1892), Hibernian, Stoke, Glossop.

Jack Kennedy's three appearances for the Owls were all the Football Alliance in 1890/91. He never quite fitted but improved considerably on his return to Scotland, helping Hibs reach the 1896 Scottish Cup final before winning his first cap against Wales. He made over 100 appearances for Hibs and scored 12 goals in 70 games for Stoke.

KENNY, Vincent
Full-back

Appearances: 152
Born: Sheffield, 29 December 1924
Died: 24 February 2006

CAREER
CLUBS: WEDNESDAY (April 1944-July 1955), Carlisle United.
OTHER: salesman for Sunblest Bread.

A dependable and tough-tackling full-back, Vince Kenny could play equally well on both flanks. He established himself in the Owls' first team in 1949, forming an excellent partnership with Harry Swift when promotion was gained to the top flight. Two years later he had Keith Bannister as his partner when the Owls won the Second Division championship in their first year competing for the title. Sometimes called 'Mick', Kenny was the first Owls player to get sent off after the Second World War, being dismissed following a tussle with Jimmy Hagan in a third round FA Cup replay at Sheffield United in January 1954. The ten men of Wednesday still won 3-1. After eleven years' association with the Owls, Kenny moved to Carlisle, for whom he made over 100 appearances.

KENT, Michael John
Midfield

Appearances: 5+1
Born: Rotherham, 2 January 1951

CAREER
CLUBS: Rotherham United, Wath Wanderers, Wolverhampton Wanderers, Gillingham, Highland Power, WEDNESDAY (free, September 1973-May 1974), Johannesburg Rangers, Barnsley, Norwich City, Worksop Town.
OTHER: salesman; licensee; nightclub manager; chauffeur; was once married to the daughter of comedian Charlie Williams.

Mick Kent made 2 substitute appearances for Wolves and 11 starts for Gillingham before having a season at Hillsborough where he never quite made the grade. He broke his leg twice – on his debut for Johannesburg and again on his return to England when training with the Owls.

KEY, Lance William
Goalkeeper

Appearances: 0+1
Born: Kettering, 13 May 1968

CAREER
CLUBS: WEDNESDAY (April 1990-July 1996), York City (L), Portadown, Oldham Athletic, Portsmouth, Oxford United, Lincoln City, Hartlepool United, Rochdale, Dundee United, Tranmere Rovers, Linfield, Sheffield United, Rochdale, Northwich Victoria, Altrincham, Kingstonian, Histon (player-coach). OTHER: chauffeur.

In six years at Hillsborough, Lance Key's only first-team game was as substitute in the away FA Cup-tie with Gillingham in January 1995 after Kevin Pressman had been sent off. He was capped by England at semi-professional level versus Belgium in 2003. Brother Richard played for Cambridge United.

KILSHAW, Edward Ainsworth
Outside right

Appearances: 19   Goals: 1
Born: Prescot, 25 December 1919

CAREER
CLUBS: Bury, WEDNESDAY (£20,000, November 1948-May 1951), Prescot & Huyton Boys (coach); WARTIME GUEST APPEARANCES: Manchester United. OTHER: head of science at Huyton Secondary Modern School; schoolteacher in St Columba.

Eddie Kilshaw made well over 100 appearances for Bury before joining the Owls – he was signed to replace Oscar Fox. The club's first £20,000 footballer, all of his 19 games were in succession, the first being away to Luton in December 1948. An injury allowed Fox to return to the side. Eddie flew Sunderland bombers during the Second World War and on one occasion, as a co-pilot, his plane crashed over Italy, killing three of the crew.

KING, Jeffrey
Midfield

Appearances: 65+3 Goals: 7
Born: Fauldhouse, Edinburgh, 9 November 1953

CAREER
CLUBS: Albion Rovers, Derby County, Notts County, Portsmouth, Walsall, WEDNESDAY (August 1979-January 1982), Hibernian, Sheffield United, Chesterfield, Stafford Rangers, Altrincham, Burton Albion, Kettering Town, Torquay United, Jubilee Sports, Wadsley Bridge. OTHER: painter and decorator.

Jeff King amassed over 200 appearances in his career – 167 in the Football League. He did well in Scotland but took time to settle into the English game, finally establishing himself with Walsall in 1977. He made his debut for Wednesday in a 0-0 draw with Hull in August 1979 and performed doggedly for a season and a half, helping the Owls climb out of the Third Division in 1980 before they fell back down under Jack Charlton. He helped the Blades win the Fourth Division title in 1982.

KING, Philip Geoffrey
Full-back

Appearances: 154+5   Goals: 2
Born: Bristol, 28 December 1967

Philip King

CAREER

CLUBS: Exeter City, Torquay United, Swindon Town, WEDNESDAY (£400,000, November 1989-August 1994), Notts County (L), Aston Villa, West Bromwich Albion, Swindon Town (player, player-coach), Blackpool, Chester City, Brighton & Hove Albion, Kidderminster Harriers, Bath City, Clifton FC, Dolphin FC, Cinderford Town.
OTHER: pub manager in Swindon.

Capped by England 'B' versus Switzerland in 1991, the same year he gained a League Cup winners' medal with the Owls, competent left-back Phil King was an excellent crosser of the ball whose general play was always of a high quality. At Hillsborough he became a successful partner to Roland Nilsson and later Viv Anderson. He scored his first goal for the Owls in the local derby with Sheffield United in March 1992 (lost 3-1). During his career King played in over 400 games.

KINGHORN, Henry McGill
Goalkeeper

Appearances: 25
Born: Midlothian, Scotland, February 1881
Died: Montrose, 16 April 1955

CAREER

CLUBS: Alloa, Leith Athletic, WEDNESDAY (£290, January 1909-May 1911), Bournemouth Athletic (player, trainer).
OTHER: served in the army during the First World War.

Signed as cover for Jack Lyall, Harry Kinghorn made his debut for the Owls in a 4-1 League defeat at Preston in February 1909. He had his best run in the first team between March and October 1910. He was forty-eight when asked to play in a League game for Bournemouth against Brentford in 1929 – the oldest player ever to appear for the Cherries. His son William played for Queen's Park and Liverpool.

KINMAN
Inside left

Appearances: 1
Born: Sheffield, 1864
Died: 1927

CAREER

CLUBS: WEDNESDAY (1887/88).
A reserve with Wednesday, possibly named George, Kinman's only appearance for the club was against Belper in an FA Cup-tie in October 1887.

KIPPAX, Dennis Hobson
Outside right

Appearances: 1
Born: Sheffield, 7 August 1926
Died: Sheffield, 18 May 1970

CAREER

CLUBS: WEDNESDAY (March 1946-August 1948), Goole Town.
OTHER: served in the navy; played cricket in Stocksbridge.

K

Dennis Kippax's only game for the Owls was at Millwall in September 1946, when he became the fourth player to be used in the outside right position that season.

KIRBY, Eric
Wing half

Appearances: 1
Born: Sheffield, 12 October 1926

CAREER
CLUBS: WEDNESDAY (August 1948-August 1952), York City.
OTHER: worked for Armstrong Patents (York) and Osborn Mushet Tools (Sheffield).

Eric Kirby played in one League game for each of his two clubs, making his Owls' debut against Huddersfield in February 1951 when he deputised for Eddie Gannon. He played in the RAF Cup final of 1949 while serving with bomber command.

KIRBY, George
Centre forward

Appearances: 3
Born: Liverpool, 20 December 1933
Died: Yorkshire, 24 March 2000

CAREER
CLUBS: Everton, WEDNESDAY (£8,000, March 1959-January 1960), Plymouth Argyle, Southampton, Coventry City, Swansea Town, Walsall, New York Generals, Brentford, Worcester City (player-manager), Halifax Town (manager), Watford (manager), IA Akranes (manager), Halifax Town (manager), Khaitan (coach), Mercua Buana, Queens Park Rangers (scout.)
OTHER: insurance broker.

A tall, bustling, robust centre forward, strong and fearless, George Kirby gave defenders

plenty to think about during his nomadic career. He entered League football in 1956 – seven years after joining Everton – making his debut against Sheffield Utd. After averaging 1 goal in every 3 games for the Merseysiders, he joined the Owls as cover for Roy Shiner but had to wait six months before getting his first outing, against Bolton. Unfortunately he never settled at Hillsborough and left soon afterwards. He retired in 1969 with 119 goals in 309 League games. He scored a hat-trick in four minutes for Southampton versus Middlesbrough in 1962. Kirby won three Icelandic League titles as manager of IA Akranes. He died of cancer.

KIRKMAN, Samuel
Outside right

Appearances: 201   Goals: 40
Born: Bury, July 1889
Died: Blackburn, 2 November 1960

CAREER
CLUBS: Carlisle United, WEDNESDAY (£75, May 1909-June 1920), Southport Central (guest), Mid-Rhondda, Bury, Wombwell Town.
OTHER: manager of a garage in Sheffield.

A huge favourite at Hillsborough, Sam Kirkman replaced Harry Davis at outside right early in 1909/10 and remained first choice, injuries apart, until League football was suspended in 1915. Fast, direct and skilful, he had an eye for an opening and netted some spectacular and, indeed, crucial goals during his time with the Owls, and if the hostilities hadn't started when they did, Kirkman may well have represented England. He scored 4 goals in 12 First World War games for Wednesday when free from his army duties as a despatch rider.

KIRKWOOD, Daniel
Inside right

Appearances: 19   Goals: 1
Born: Dalserf, Scotland, 24 December 1900
Died: Stonehouse, Lanarks, 20 October 1977

CAREER
CLUBS: Airdrieonians, Glasgow Rangers, St Johnstone, WEDNESDAY (£1,500, November 1926-June 1928), Brighton & Hove Albion, Luton Town, Swindon Town.
OTHER: coalminer; also won the Scottish County bowls title.

After failing to make headway with Rangers and St Johnstone, Dan Kirkwood joined Wednesday, quickly making his debut against Aston Villa. Performing well for six months, he scored in a 3-0 home win over Cardiff before losing his place to Jack Allen. His brother Andy also played for Rangers.

KITE, Percy Alexander
Goalkeeper

Appearances: 1
Born: Warrington, July 1892
Died: Lymm, 18 February 1960

CAREER
CLUBS: Warrington, Manchester United, WEDNESDAY (amateur, April 1920-May 1921), Lancashire Tool Company, Mossley.

Percy Kite's only appearance for the Owls was at home to Oldham on the last day of the 1919/20 League programme. Signed twenty-four hours before kick-off, he deputised for Teddy Davison in a 1-0 victory.

Ian Knight

KNIGHT, Ian John
Defender

Appearances: 27
Born: Hartlepool, 26 October 1966

CAREER
CLUBS: Barnsley, WEDNESDAY (free, July 1985-January 1990), Scunthorpe United (L), Grimsby Town, Carlisle United, Boston United, Grantham, Grimsby Town (community officer), Wednesday (community officer), Grimsby Town (director of youth development).

An England Under-21 international (2 caps), Ian Knight never really established himself with any club. A solid defender, he made his debut for Wednesday against Aston Villa in April 1986, playing alongside Paul Hart and Lawrie Madden in a 2-0 victory.

KNIGHT, Leon Leroy
Midfield

Appearances: 16+11   Goals: 3
Born: Hackney, 16 September 1982

K

CAREER

CLUBS: Chelsea, Queens Park Rangers, Huddersfield Town, WEDNESDAY (loan, July 2002-April 2003), Brighton & Hove Albion, Swansea City, Barnsley.

At 5ft 4ins tall and under 10st in weight, Leon Knight spent a rather disappointing season on loan at Hillsborough. After demonstrating his scoring technique at Huddersfield, it was hoped he would continue to find the net for the Owls. It didn't happen and he netted only three times and spent quite some time on the subs' bench before returning to Chelsea. He scored a penalty winner for Brighton in the Division Two play-off final versus Bristol City in 2004 and was selected in the PFA's Division Two team that same season. His goals then helped keep the Seagulls in the Championship in 2005. A year later – after his £125,000 transfer – he helped Swansea reach the League One play-off final against Barnsley, having scored twice in the second leg of the semi-final against Brentford. Knight represented England at Youth level as a teenager.

KNIGHTON, Kenneth
Wing half

Appearances: 79+5 Goals: 4
Born: Mexborough, 20 February 1944

CAREER

CLUBS: Mexborough Rovers, Wath Wanderers, Wolverhampton Wanderers, Oldham Athletic, Preston North End, Blackburn Rovers, Hull City, WEDNESDAY (£57,777, August 1973-January 1976, coaching staff), Sunderland (chief coach, manager), Leyton Orient (manager), Dagenham (manager), Trowbridge Town (manager), Portishead (manager).
OTHER: worked for Plessey Telecommunications and Mercury Communications; director of marketing for Data Sharp based in Truro.

A tall, blond Yorkshireman who excelled in both defence and attack, Ken Knighton was a hard man on the field who made over 400 appearances during his career. He toured New Zealand with the FA in 1969 but never won a medal at club level. He was outstanding for the Owls in 1973/74 and his eighty-sixth minute winner against Bolton on the last day of the League programme saved the club from relegation.

KOVACEVIC, Darko
Striker

Appearances: 9+8 Goals: 4
Born: Belgrade, Yugoslavia, 18 November 1973

CAREER

CLUBS: Radnicki Kovin, Protetyer Zrenjanin, Red Star Belgrade, WEDNESDAY (£2.5 million with Dejan Stefanovic, December 1995-June 1996), Real Sociedad, Juventus, Lazio, Real Sociedad.

Tall, slim striker Darko Kovacevic didn't get too many chances to show his worth at Hillsborough and the fans were bitterly disappointed when he left the club for Spain. He won League and Cup medals with Red Star and by 2006 had scored over 200 career goals while also winning more than 50 caps for Serbia and Montenegro. His brother was tragically killed in 2002.

KUQI, Shefki
Forward

Appearances: 62+6 Goals: 19
Born: Voqitern, Kosovo, 10 November 1976

CAREER

CLUBS: Mikkelin Palloiliat (three spells), Kapa, HJK Helsinki, FC Jokerit, Wolverhampton Wanderers, Stockport County, WEDNESDAY (£700,000, January 2002), Ipswich Town (loan, signed later), Blackburn Rovers, Crystal Palace.

A Finnish international with over 40 caps to his credit – 11 with Wednesday – Shefki Kuqi is a strong, forceful forward who holds the ball up well and makes chances for his colleagues as well as scoring his fair share of goals himself. His first game for the Owls was against Crewe in January 2002 and in October 2006 he scored for Crystal Palace against Wednesday at Hillsborough.

L

LAMB, John William
Half-back

Appearances: 5
Born: Worksop, 1893
Died: Derby, 1949

CAREER
CLUBS: WEDNESDAY (April 1912-May 1920), Luton Town, Matlock Town.
WARTIME GUEST APPEARANCES: Brentford, Notts County, St Bernard's.

A reserve with the Owls, Jack Lamb made his debut in September 1913 against Oldham Athletic, deputising for Bob McSkimming. He added a further 24 appearances to his tally during the First World War.

LAMB, Walter Charles
Full-back

Appearances: 2
Born: Tarleton, Southport, 8 August 1897
Died: Huddersfield, 1973

CAREER
CLUBS: Liverpool, Fleetwood, WEDNESDAY (free, August 1921-August 1922), Swansea Town, Southend United, Rhyl, Abergele.

Reserve Walter Lamb made his League debut for the Owls in a 1-0 win at Derby in August 1921.

LANG, James Jeremiah
Utility

Appearances: 5
Born: Glasgow, March 1851
Died: Glasgow: 1912

CAREER
CLUBS: Glasgow Eastern, Clydesdale, Third Lanark, WEDNESDAY (free, October 1876-August 1877), Third Lanark, WEDNESDAY (free, May 1879-April 1882).

The versatile Jimmy Lang – reputed to be the first Scotsman to cross the border and play in England – occupied seven different positions with the Owls, helping them win the Sheffield Challenge Cup in 1877, 1878 and 1881 and the Wharncliffe Charity Cup in 1882. His five appearances were all in the FA Cup – the first was against Blackburn Rovers in December 1880 (won 4-0). He lost an eye in a Clydebank shipyard accident but that was kept a secret by Wednesday so that opponents would not take advantage of his blind side. A hardy bundle of energy, he was a first-class dribbler, had good speed and was capable of unleashing a stunning right-foot shot. He represented Glasgow against Sheffield in the annual challenge match, gained three caps for Scotland (1876-78) and was twice a Scottish Cup finalist, with Clydesdale in 1874 and Third Lanark in 1878. One of Wednesday's first professionals, Lang's wages was paid by Walter Fearnehough, who employed him at his works in Sheffield.

L

LANGLEY, Ambrose
Right-back

Appearances: 318   Goals: 14
Born: Horncastle, Lincolnshire, 10 March 1870
Died: Sheffield, 29 January 1937

CAREER
CLUBS: Boston Town, Grimsby Town, Middlesbrough Ironopolis, Everton, WEDNESDAY (free, May 1893, office/scouting duties from 1903), Hull City (player-manager), WEDNESDAY (assistant secretary, June 1913-November 1919), Huddersfield Town (manager).

Ambrose Langley won a fine reputation for consistency with Wednesday, whom he served as a player for ten years. Very agile for a six-footer, Langley was vulnerable at times when facing a fleet-footed winger but his positional sense enabled him to prevail more times than he suffered humiliation. A totally committed footballer, he could be quite reckless in the tackle and was occasionally in trouble with referees. He represented the Football League versus The Scottish League (1898), won the FA Cup (1896), the Second Division championship as captain (1900) and the League title (1903). He also played in eight games when the League crown was retained in 1904. A bad injury suffered at Sunderland (October 1903) effectively ended his playing career with the Owls. After retiring he became a successful manager and laid the foundations for the great Huddersfield side of the mid-1920s, having successfully guided the Terriers into the top flight as runners-up and to the FA Cup final – beaten 1-0 by Aston Villa – in 1920. Earlier in his career, he twice won the North League championship with Ironopolis (1892 and 1893).

LAW, Alexander
Centre forward

Appearances: 9   Goals: 4
Born: Bathgate, 28 April 1910
Died: Chester, 1954

CAREER
CLUBS: Bo'ness, WEDNESDAY (free, June 1932-June 1935), Brighton & Hove Albion, Chester.

Signed as cover for Jack Ball, Alex Law made his League debut as leader of the Owls' attack in a 3-1 win at Liverpool in December 1933. He then had to play second fiddle to Neil Dewar, although he did score plenty of goals for the Second XI. He netted twice in his last outing in a 4-0 win over Tottenham in April 1935.

LAWSON, William
Outside left

Appearances: 11+1
Born: Dundee, 28 November 1947

CAREER
CLUBS: Brechin City, WEDNESDAY (£5,000, October 1969-February 1971), St Mirren, East Fife, Dundee Downfield.

Bill Lawson made his debut for the Owls in a 4-2 defeat at Burnley in October 1969. In fact 9 of his 12 appearances came in 1969/70, when he deputised mainly for Tony Coleman.

LAYNE, David Richard
Centre forward

Appearances: 81   Goals: 58
Born: Sheffield, 29 July 1939

CAREER
CLUBS: Chesterfield, Sheffield United (juniors), English Steel, Rotherham United, Swindon Town,

Bradford City, WEDNESDAY (£22,500, February 1962, contract cancelled January 1965), Thorpe Arch Open Prison, WEDNESDAY (free, July 1972-March 1973), Hereford United (L), Matlock Town.
OTHER: licensee..

David 'Bronco' Layne played in the same Sheffield Boys' team as John Fantham and England goalkeeper Gordon Banks. After establishing himself as a prolific marksman in the lower divisions, he joined the Owls and did superbly well in his first two seasons at Hillsborough, netting 53 goals in 78 outings. By far the best centre forward since Derek Dooley, Layne unfortunately got tied up in the match-fixing scandal that also involved Tony Kay and as a result was banned from the game. After serving a prison sentence, the ban was lifted and he returned to Hillsborough but failed to gain a place in the First XI. During his career Layne scored 128 goals in 155 League games.

LAYTON, William
Full-back

Appearances: 362   Goals: 4
Born: Lower Gornal, Dudley, 3 August 1875
Died: Australia, 7 April 1944

CAREER
CLUBS: Chesterfield, WEDNESDAY (trial, October 1895; signed November 1895-May 1910), St Lawrence.
OTHER: emigrated to Australia, 1912.

Born in the Black Country and missed by both West Bromwich Albion and Wolves, Billy Layton was as tough as steel, a formidable defender who served the Owls for over twelve years. Working down the pit as a youngster while registered with Chesterfield, he gave up his night shift to play in a Wednesday trial. He came through with flying colours, said farewell to Chesterfield and signed as a professional for the Owls. He made his League debut in place of Ambrose Langley at Everton in January 1898, claimed a

regular place in the side the following season and when the Second Division championship was won in 1900 he was quite outstanding, likewise when the Owls clinched successive First Division titles in 1903 and 1904 and lifted the FA Cup in 1907. Strong in all aspects of defensive play, he possessed a solid tackle and a very powerful kick. He represented the Football League against the Irish League in 1901 but missed out on a full England cap. Layton played for the same Blackwell Colliery side as Sheffield United's 24st goalkeeper Billy Foulke. His brother Arthur played for Sheffield United, Rotherham, Aston Villa, Middlesbrough, Cardiff and Stockport (1905-1923).

LEACH, Thomas James
Half-back

Appearances: 261
Born: Sheffield, 23 September 1903
Died: Owston Ferry, Doncaster, 30 January 1968

CAREER
CLUBS: Blackburn Wesleyans, Wath Athletic, Rotherham County, Liverpool, WEDNESDAY (£150, October 1925-June 1934), Newcastle United, Stockport County, Carlisle United, Lincoln City.
OTHER: builder.

Considered by many as one of the finest centre halves of his time – his lithe physique being a distinct asset – 'Tony' Leach started his career as a forward. He was then switched to wing half before successfully taking over the pivotal position from Fred Kean in 1928. Twice capped by England against Ireland (won 5-1) and Wales (won 4-0) in 1930, he also represented the Football League (1931) and helped Wednesday win successive League titles (1929 and 1930). Three years after leaving Hillsborough he gained a Third Division (North) winners' medal with Stockport. Unfortunately he was involved in a minor scandal towards the end of his career, receiving a four-week ban and a £20 fine for accepting 'incentives' from a Stockport director during the run-up to the championship triumph in 1937. At the time Leach was a Lincoln player and his old club, Stockport, wanted the Imps to lose to Carlisle to boost their chances of winning the League title.

LEDGER, H.
Goalkeeper

Appearances: 13
Born: Sheffield, 1858
Deceased by 1928

CAREER
CLUBS: WEDNESDAY (amateur, May 1880-May 1883).

Ledger made all his appearances in the FA Cup. Tall and well built, he made his debut in a 2-0 win at Turton in January 1881. He was eventually replaced by George Ulyett. His brother Richard kept goal for Rotherham in 1893/94.

LEE, George
Outside right

Appearances: 6   Goals: 1
Born: Stockton-on-Tees, 1876
Died: Rotherham, 28 March 1906

CAREER
CLUBS: Darlington, Stockton, Rotherham Town, Whitworth, WEDNESDAY (free, May 1899-April 1901), Amberley.

A reserve with the Owls, George Lee made his debut in a 2-1 home win over Bolton in September 1899 and scored his only goal for the club in a 5-0 win over Burton Swifts a month later. His last game was in the FA Cup defeat by Sheffield United in February 1900.

LEE, Graeme Barry
Defender

Appearances: 68+4 Goals: 6
Born: Middlesbrough, 31 May 1978

CAREER Hartlepool United, WEDNESDAY (free, July 2003-January 2006), Doncaster Rovers.

Graeme Lee, 6ft 2ins tall, followed manager Chris Turner to Hillsborough after making 252 appearances for Hartlepool. A very effective defender who can tackle and distribute the ball as well as anyone, he missed the second half of the 2003/04 season after suffering stress fractures to both legs and was injured again the following term.

LEKAJ, Rocky
Midfield

Appearances: 0+2
Born: Kosovo, 1987

CAREER
CLUBS: SF Grei, WEDNESDAY (July 2006).

Born in Kosovo but a Norwegian national, Lekaj joined the Owls with his brother Leon from SF Grei (Norway) in July 2006. A midfielder, he made his debut against QPR in March 2007.

LEMAN, Dennis
Midfield

Appearances: 102+14 Goals: 10
Born: Newcastle, 1 December 1954

CAREER
CLUBS: Manchester City, WEDNESDAY (£8,500, December 1976-August 1982), Wrexham (L), Scunthorpe United, Burton Albion, Cardiff City.
OTHER: chief deputy administrator for the PFA.

England Schoolboy international Dennis Leman hardly got a look-in with Manchester City but after joining the Owls developed into a very efficient, hard-working midfielder who teamed up well with Bobby Hope. He scored on his debut in a 3-1 League win over Tranmere in December 1976 and made ten appearances when promotion was gained from the Third Division in 1980.

LESCOTT, Aaron Anthony
Midfield

Appearances: 24+19
Born: Birmingham, 2 December 1978

CAREER
CLUBS: Aston Villa, Lincoln City, WEDNESDAY (£100,000, October 2000), Stockport County, Bristol Rovers.

A tenacious midfielder with a big heart, Aaron Lescott failed to make the breakthrough with Aston Villa, having just one substitute outing. He proved to be a useful acquisition by Owls' boss Paul Jewell and after a smart debut against West Bromwich Albion he did well in his first season, when he also played as an emergency forward. He made over 80 appearances for Stockport before joining Bristol Rovers. His brother Joleon plays for Everton.

LESTER, Frederick Charles
Left-back

Appearances: 21
Born: Chatham, 20 February 1911
Died: Chatham, 28 June 1974

CAREER
CLUBS: Chatham, Gillingham, WEDNESDAY (£1,150 with Cyril Walker, October 1937-May 1939), Gravesend.
WARTIME GUEST APPEARANCES: Shorts Sports.

Reserve to Ted Catlin, Fred Lester made his debut for Wednesday in a 1-0 defeat at Manchester United in October 1937. He had a run of fifteen consecutive games as Albert Ashley's partner halfway through the 1938/39 campaign. He made 21 appearances for the Owls during the Second World War.

LEVICK, Oliver
Left half

Appearances: 21
Born: Rotherham, September 1899
Died: Sheffield, March 1965

CAREER
CLUBS: WEDNESDAY (July 1919-May 1926), Stockport County, York City, Boston Town.

A very capable reserve, Olly Levick made only 21 first-team appearances in 7 years – the first in January 1921 against Port Vale when he deputised for Arthur Price. Thirteen of his outings came in 1923/24. His brother, Frank, played for Wednesday's Second XI (1905/06) and also for Rotherham and Sheffield United.

LEWIS, Idris
Winger

Appearances: 23   Goals: 8
Born: Trelaw, 26 August 1915
Died: Swansea, March 1996

CAREER
CLUBS: Swansea Town, WEDNESDAY (£50 with Dicky Rhodes, August 1938-March 1939), Swansea Town, Bristol Rovers, Newport County.
WARTIME GUEST APPEARANCES: Coventry City, Cardiff City.
OTHER: Army – First World War.

Idris Lewis made 136 League appearances either side of the Second World War – 78 in

2 spells with Swansea. He spent a little over seven months at Hillsborough when he occupied both flanks. He made his debut against Bury in August 1938 and scored his first goal in a 2-0 win over Tranmere a fortnight later. He left after Ernie Toseland had taken over the right-wing position.

LINDSAY, John McArthur
Centre forward

Appearances: 1   Goals: 1
Born: Cambuslang, 11 December 1921
Died: Carlisle, 9 February 2006

CAREER
CLUBS: Greenock Morton, WEDNESDAY (free, September 1944-October 1946), Bury, Carlisle United, Southport, Wigan Athletic (non-League), Carlisle United, Liverpool (scout), Blackburn Rovers (scout).
OTHER: security manager for Spaceadam rocket testing site; engineer for Courtaulds and Pirelli.

Reserve Jack Lindsay scored on his debut for the Owls against Barnsley in September 1946, having earlier netted 25 goals in 46 Second World War games for the club, including a hat-trick in a 7-0 win over Halifax. Three of the four goals he netted for Southport in a 5-1 win over Scunthorpe in February 1952 came in the space of three minutes.

LINIGHAN, Brian
Right-back

Appearances: 3
Born: Hartlepool, 2 November 1973

CAREER
CLUBS: WEDNESDAY (April 1990-July 1997), Bury, non-League (2000-04).
OTHER: maintenance electrician.

In ten years of football, Brian Linighan appeared in only eight senior matches, making his League debut for the Owls versus Wimbledon in January 1994. His three games for the Owls were in different competitions. His father, Brian, and two of his brothers also played professionally; one of them, Andy, scored a dramatic last-gasp extra-time winner for Arsenal against Wednesday in the 1993 FA Cup final. A third brother, Brian's twin John, was on Wednesday's books in 1993/94.

LLOYD, William
Forward

Appearances: 85   Goals: 6
Born: South Hylton, 1884
Deceased by 1975

CAREER
CLUBS: Jarrow, WEDNESDAY (free, August 1906-May 1913), Rotherham County, WEDNESDAY (assistant-trainer, labourer, December 1920-May 1925), Bradford City (reserves).
OTHER: served with the 1st Battalion of the York & Lancs Regiment during the First World War.

After a breaking-in period Billy Lloyd gained a regular place in Wednesday's League side at outside right in 1908/09 but after that he had to battle long and hard to get a senior game, despite his undoubted talent. He made his debut against Bury in December 1906 and scored the first of his six goals in his twelfth outing – the winner against Bristol City (2-1) in October 1908. He moved on after Sammy Kirkman had established himself on the right wing.

LOCHERTY, Joseph
Utility

Appearances: 12
Born: Dundee, 5 September 1925

CAREER

CLUBS: *Lochee Harp, WEDNESDAY (£200, September 1947-August 1950), Colchester United, Scarborough, Dundee United.*

OTHER: *worked in insurance and at a service station.*

Joe Locherty played in Wednesday's Second XI for fifteen months before making his League debut against Bradford in December 1948, when he deputised for Doug Witcomb at right half. He was with Colchester as they embarked on their first season in the Football League.

LODGE, Robert William
Outside right

Appearances: 3   Goals: 2
Born: *Retford, 1 July 1941*

CAREER

CLUBS: *WEDNESDAY (March 1959-May 1961), Doncaster Rovers, Buxton Sheffield FC.*
OTHER: *worked in a post office and for Ventura Ltd.*

Derek Wilkinson and Billy Griffin were ahead of Bob Lodge for the outside right position at Hillsborough. However, when called into action, he certainly made his mark, scoring twice on his League debut in a 5-4 win over Blackburn in December 1960.

LOFTHOUSE, James
Outside left

Appearances: 98   Goals: 13
Born: *St Helens, 24 March 1894*
Died: *Windsor, August, 1954*

CAREER

CLUBS: *Stalybridge Celtic, Reading, WEDNESDAY (£650, August 1920-March 1923), Rotherham County, Bristol Rovers, Queens Park Rangers, Aldershot.*
WARTIME GUEST APPEARANCES: *Manchester United.*

OTHER: *Army; social club steward, worked and played for the GPO (Reading).*

A regular for two seasons, the pint-sized Jim Lofthouse was a steady performer, quick over short distances, with the ability to beat his full-back with skill rather than pace and deliver corner-kicks with precision. His first three games for Wednesday all ended in 0-0 draws and he starred in 76 consecutive League outings before his run came to an end following the arrival of Horace Henshall. Lofthouse scored 63 goals in 306 League games.

LOGAN, John William
Wing half

Appearances: 6
Born: *Easington, Co. Durham, 16 August 1912*
Died: *Barnsley, October, 1980*

CAREER

CLUBS: *Charlton Athletic, Darlington, Barnsley; WEDNESDAY (£2,000, December 1946-April 1951, reserve-team manager, trainer).*
WARTIME GUEST APPEARANCES: *Hartlepool United, Huddersfield Town, Bradford City, Bradford Park Avenue, Everton, Darlington.*
OTHER: *foundry worker; Athersley Social & Athersley Hotel team (coach).*

Jack Logan was thirty-four when he joined the Owls in 1947, having already made over 160 League appearances, making a big impression at Darlington. An experienced squad member, he made his debut for Wednesday against Luton in December 1946, deputising for Joe Cockroft.

LOWDELL, Arthur Edward
Utility

Appearances: 116   Goals: 6
Born: *Edmonton, 7 November 1897*
Died: *Canvey Island, 29 July, 1979*

L

CAREER

CLUBS: Ton Pentre, WEDNESDAY (£1,150, January 1922-August 1927), Tottenham Hotspur.
OTHER: Army.

After serving in France during the First World War, 'Darkie' Lowdell started on the right wing for Wednesday before successfully switching to right half. He helped the team gain promotion to the First Division in 1926 while also coming close to international honours following an England trail. He developed into a strong, resourceful defender and made 90 appearances for Spurs before a thigh injury ended his career.

LOWE, H.G.
Inside left

Appearances: 2
Born: Sheffield, 1870
Deceased by 1945

CAREER
CLUBS: WEDNESDAY (seasons 1893-96).

An unknown reserve with the Owls, Lowe's two League outings were against Stoke and Nottingham Forest in December 1894, when he deputised for Alec Brady.

LOWES, Arnold Richardson
Forward

Appearances: 44   Goals: 10
Born: Sunderland, 27 February 1919
Died: 1994

CAREER
CLUBS: Washington Chemicals, WEDNESDAY (October 1937-February 1948), Doncaster Rovers.
OTHER: Army – Second World War.

Arnold Lowes deputised for Doug Hunt when scoring on his League debut against Tranmere at Hillsborough in September 1938 (won 2-0). He played in six first-class games that season before his career was interrupted by the Second World War. During the hostilities he served overseas and played in 20 Regional games for the Owls. On the resumption of League football in 1946, Lowes became a key member of Wednesday's side, scoring 3 times in 22 games in that first post-war campaign. He made over 75 appearances for Doncaster.

LOWEY, John Anthony
Midfield

Appearances: 43+7 Goals: 6
Born: Manchester, 7 March 1958

CAREER
CLUBS: Manchester United, Chicago Sting, Blackburn Rovers, Port Vale, California Sunshine, WEDNESDAY (free, October 1978-November 1980), Blackburn Rovers, Wigan Athletic, Chesterfield, York City, Preston North End, Chester City, Brisbane Lions, Mount Gravatt.
OTHER: now runs two businesses in Australia.

John Lowey did not play first-team football with any of his first three clubs. He gained experience in the NASL before making his League debut for Wednesday in October 1978 versus Oxford in the Third Division. He made 36 appearances that season but then struggled to get into the First XI, although he did play in 13 League games in the promotion-winning campaign of 1979/80. He had over 150 games for Blackburn.

LUCAS, David Anthony
Goalkeeper

Appearances: 80 *
Born: Preston, 23 November 1977

CAREER

CLUBS: *Preston North End, Darlington, Scunthorpe United, WEDNESDAY (loan, October-November 2003 and December 2003-February 2004, signed for £100,000, June 2004).*

Former England Under-18 and Under-20 international David Lucas made 150 appearances for Preston before joining the Owls on a full-time basis, following two loan spells at Hillsborough. Well-built and a safe handler, despite a slight injury worry, Lucas starred for the Owls in their play-off final victory over Hartlepool in May 2005.

LUKE, Charles Edwin
Forward

Appearances: 43   Goals: 8
Born: Esh Winning, Co. Durham, 16 March 1909
Died: Whitstable, 16 October 1983

CAREER

CLUBS: *Portsmouth, Tow Law Town, Darlington, Esh Winning, Bishop Auckland, Huddersfield Town, WEDNESDAY (£4,000, January 1936-February 1938), Blackburn Rovers, Chesterfield, Whitstable.*
OTHER: *miner.*

Charlie Luke, a former Durham miner who could play on both wings and as an inside forward, netted 61 goals in 39 games for Bishop Auckland in 1930/31 and followed up with 40 goals in 130 League games for Huddersfield. At 5ft 3ins tall and barely 10st, he was one of the smallest players ever to have played for Wednesday and was impressive when they avoided relegation in 1936, but he couldn't prevent demotion a year later.

LUNN, Frederick Levi
Centre forward

Appearances: 12   Goals: 4
Born: Marsden, Huddersfield, 8 November 1895
Died: Huddersfield, February 1972

CAREER

CLUBS: *Huddersfield Town, WEDNESDAY (£100, August 1921-May 1922), Bristol Rovers, Southend United, Nuneaton Town.*
OTHER: *Army.*

Signed as cover for former teammate Sam Taylor and Archie Ratcliffe, Fred Lunn did a good job when called upon to lead the Owls' attack. He was goalless in his first 5 matches but then netted 4 times in his next 5. He had his best spell with Bristol Rovers.

LUNT, Kenneth
Midfield

Appearances: 33   Goals: 7**
Born: Runcorn, Cheshire, 20 November 1979

CAREER

CLUBS: *Crewe Alexandra, WEDNESDAY (May 2006).*

Kenny Lunt was signed with Madjid Bougherra from Crewe Alexandra in May 2006. An England Schoolboy and Youth international, he joined the 'Alex' initially in 1995, turned professional in 1997 and scored 37 goals in 418 appearances during his time at Gresty Road.

LYALL, John
Goalkeeper

Appearances: 296
Born: Dundee, 16 April 1881
Died: Detroit, USA, 17 February 1944

CAREER

CLUBS: Jarrow, WEDNESDAY (£100 plus Bill Gosling, February 1901-September 1900), Manchester City, Dundee, Ayr United, Jarrow.

WARTIME GUEST APPEARANCES: WEDNESDAY (September 1916-February 1917).

OTHER: Army; later emigrated to Canada.

In 1902, while residing in Jarrow, Jack Lyall was selected to play for England. He declared he had been born north of the border and in 1905 was capped by Scotland against England. Standing 6ft 2ins tall, he had a splendid reach and was superb at dealing with high shots. He cleared his lines with hefty punts downfield, often requiring minimum space in which to do so. A firm favourite with the fans, he got his chance in the first team after Frank Stubbs had had a nightmare against Notts County. Making his debut against Bolton in September 1901 (won 5-1), he remained a permanent fixture in the side for eight years, helping the Owls win successive League titles in 1902 and 1903 and the FA Cup in 1907, having played in two losing semi-finals prior to that. Eventually replaced by Teddy Davison, he returned as a guest during the First World War, playing 19 games.

LYONS, Michael Joseph
Defender

Appearances: 164   Goals: 14

Born: Croxteth, Liverpool, 8 December 1951

CAREER

CLUBS: Everton, WEDNESDAY (£80,000, August 1982-November 1985), Grimsby Town (player-coach), Everton (coach), Wigan Athletic (coach), Huddersfield Town (coach), Brunei (coach, three spells), Canberra Cosmos (manager), Southampton (director of football, Perth Academy).

Mick Lyons made 460 appearances for Everton before joining the Owls. A solid performer who would run through a brick wall for his team, he

gained a League Cup runners-up medal in 1977 and played in two losing FA Cup semi-finals. During his three years at Hillsborough he skippered the Owls, helping them climb out of the Second Division as runners-up to Chelsea on goal difference in 1984. Generally adding composure and resolve to the side, Lyons represented England in 1 'B' and 5 Under-23 internationals and his career realised 653 first-class appearances. The world's richest man, the Sultan of Brunei, appointed him as national coach for Brunei.

M

MACKENZIE, Matthew Laurence
Utility

Appearances: 6

Born: Glasgow, 7 July 1924

CAREER

CLUBS: Clydebank Celtic, WEDNESDAY (£25, March 1946-July 1949), Grimsby Town, Gainsborough Trinity, Scarborough.

OTHER: baker.

Matt Mackenzie had plenty of pace, was strong in both feet but never really made his mark in top-class football. His first appearance for Wednesday was at home to Bolton in the Football League (North) in April 1946, the first of two Second World War outings. His son, Malcolm, is a well-known golfer.

MACKENZIE, Stephen
Midfield

Appearances: 5+10 Goals: 2

Born: Romford, Essex, November 1961

CAREER

CLUBS: Crystal Palace, Manchester City, West Bromwich Albion, Charlton Athletic, WEDNESDAY

(£100,000, February 1991), Shrewsbury Town, Willenhall Town, Bromsgrove Rovers, Stafford Rangers, Atherstone United (player-coach, assistant manager, manager), Pelsall Villa (player-manager), Gresley Rovers (player-coach), West Bromwich Albion (School of Excellence coach).
OTHER: commentator for the Press Association.

Steve Mackenzie scored a stunning goal for Manchester City in their 1981 FA Cup final replay defeat by Spurs – this after leaving Selhurst Park for a then record fee, for a teenager, of £250,000 without ever having played in a first-class match for Crystal Palace. Signed by Ron Atkinson for West Bromwich Albion, he did exceptionally well at The Hawthorns, netting 25 times in 184 games. He made his debut for the Owls against Notts County in March 1991 and netted his first goal for the club at Plymouth (1-1) later in the month. Capped by England 15 times as a Youth, Mackenzie also played in 2 'B' and 4 Under-21 internationals. He was twice an FA Youth Cup winner, first with Palace (1977) and then Manchester City (1978). He suffered a pelvic injury in 1981 when on the brink of full international honours.

MACKEY, Thomas Scott
Defender

Appearances: 4
Born: Cassop, Co. Durham, 22 October 1908
Died: Silsoe, Bedfordshire, 27 July 1969

CAREER
CLUBS: Hartlepool United, WEDNESDAY (£3,000 plus Dorman Bell, December 1929-May 1932), Luton Town (player, coach).
OTHER: licensee.

Tom Mackey started his senior career with Hartlepool in 1927. A decade later he had 225 games under his belt – 217 in the Football League, of which 183 were with Luton. Initially reserve to Tony Leach, he made his Owls'

debut at centre half at home to Birmingham in April 1929.

MacLEAN, Steven
Striker

Appearances: 65+24 *   Goals: 35 *
Born: Edinburgh, 23 August 1982

CAREER
CLUBS: Glasgow Rangers, Partick Thistle, Scunthorpe United, WEDNESDAY (July 2004).

Capped four times by Scotland at under-21 level, Steve MacLean spent five years as a reserve team player in his home country before netting 25 goals (including 3 hat-tricks) in 52 games for Scunthorpe. Sidelined with a broken foot, suffered against Doncaster in March 2005, he recovered in time to figure as a substitute in the play-off final win over Hartlepool. He then had the misfortune to break a leg in a pre-season game against Manchester City and missed the first half of 2005/06, but he bounced back in style the following year.

MADDEN, Lawrence David
Defender

Appearances: 251+15   Goals: 5
Born: Hackney, 28 September 1955

CAREER
CLUBS: Arsenal, Manchester University, Mansfield Town, Glasgow Celtic, Boston United, Tottenham Hotspur, Charlton Athletic, Millwall, WEDNESDAY (free, August 1983-August 1991), Leicester City (L), Derby County, Wolverhampton Wanderers, Darlington, Chesterfield, Emly Town.
OTHER: worked for Sky Sports and Sheffield Star.

During his twenty-year career, Lawrie Madden amassed 583 appearances (494 in the Football League), having by far his best spell at

M

Hillsborough. Talented and constructive, reliable, confident, assuring and aggressive when required, he was already an experienced campaigner when he joined the Owls, having played over 125 times for Charlton and 50 for Millwall. He made his debut for Wednesday at Swansea in August 1983 and helped the team win promotion from the Second Division in his first season when he partnered Mick Lyons at the back. He won the League Cup in 1991 and reached the 1995 Third Division play-offs with Chesterfield, for whom he played his last game aged thirty-nine years and 349 days versus Oxford in August 1995 – the second eldest player ever to appear for that club.

MADDIX, Daniel Shawn
Defender

Appearances: 62+4 Goals: 3
Born: Ashford, 11 October 1967

CAREER
CLUBS: Tottenham Hotspur, Southend United, Queens Park Rangers, WEDNESDAY (trial, June-July

Daniel Maddix

2001, signed free August 2001-March 2003), Barnet (player, joint caretaker-manager).

A Jamaican international (2 caps), Danny Maddix made almost 350 appearances for QPR before joining Wednesday for the start of the 2001/02 season. Playing in a struggling team, he never really got going at Hillsborough despite his commitment. He took over the captaincy of the side before moving to Barnet, whom he helped regain Football League status in 2005.

MAGILTON, James
Midfield

Appearances: 17+13 Goals: 1
Born: Belfast, 6 May 1969

CAREER
CLUBS: Liverpool, Oxford United, Southampton, WEDNESDAY (£1.6 million, September 1997-January 1999), Ipswich Town (player, manager).

Having failed to get a single first-team game with Liverpool, Jim Magilton made 174 appearances for Oxford and 156 for Southampton before joining the Owls for £1.6 million. Unfortunately he never settled at Hillsborough and after 30 outings in 16 months he moved to Ipswich. Positive in his style, with a good temperament and fine passing technique, he represented his country (Northern Ireland) at both Schoolboy and Youth levels before gaining 1 Under-23, 2 Under-21 and 52 full caps. He skippered the Tractor Boys in 2005 and also reached the milestone of 700 appearances at club and international level.

MALLINSON, William H.
Goalkeeper

Appearances: 6
Born: Leicester, circa 1873
Died: Deceased by 1944

CAREER

CLUBS: Mexborough, WEDNESDAY (free, April 1897-May 1900), Royston.

Reserve to Jimmy Massey, Bill Mallinson made a winning start with Wednesday, who beat Everton 2-1 at home on his debut day in February 1898. One of his other five first-team outings was in the FA Cup against Sheffield United in 1900 (lost 2-0).

MALLOCH, Gavin Cooper
Left half

Appearances: 89
Born: Glasgow, 18 July 1905
Died: Glasgow, 10 December 1974

CAREER

CLUBS: Benburb, Derby County, WEDNESDAY (£1,400, December 1931-August 1936), Millwall, Barrow, Greenock Morton.
OTHER: worked in engineering.

Carefully nurtured in Derby's Second XI, Gavin Malloch became the Rams' regular left half in 1929 and made almost 100 appearances for the club before following Jackie Whitehouse, Teddy Davison and George Stephenson to Hillsborough. He made his debut for the Owls at Liverpool on Christmas Day 1931 and was first choice until the end of 1932/33, when he gave way to Harry Burrows. Malloch also excelled as a dancer and a contemporary report tells how he astonished the Danes on a Derby tour with 'weird but graceful gyrations'.

MALLOCH, John Napier
Inside, outside left

Appearances: 154   Goals: 11
Born: East Craigie, Dundee, 3 November 1879
Died: Moorthorpe, December 1935

CAREER

CLUBS: Dundee, Brighton United, WEDNESDAY (£50, April 1900-May 1909), Barnsley (loan, signed later), South Kirkby Colliery.

Jock Malloch had two spells with the Owls. He failed to make the first team in his first but, after gaining Southern League experience with Brighton, he returned a more accomplished player and went on to appear in over 150 games for the club before leaving in 1907. A strong, powerful forward, he had plenty of tricks up his sleeve and caused problems for even the most dedicated opponents. He made his Wednesday debut on the left wing in a 2-2 draw at Manchester City in September 1900 and struck his first goal for the club six weeks later in a 2-2 draw at Blackburn. He missed only one game when the League Championship was won in 1903 and was absent nine times when it was retained the following season. The Mallochs may have been related.

MALPAS, Arthur
Defender

Appearances: 15
Born: Sheffield, 1859
Deceased by 1933

CAREER

CLUBS: Attercliffe, WEDNESDAY (August 1879-April 1884).

Arthur Malpas spent five seasons with Wednesday, during which time he helped the team win the Sheffield Challenge Cup in 1881 and 1883 and the Wharncliffe Charity Cup in 1882 and 1883. A strong, resilient defender he played in Wednesday's first-ever FA Cup-tie against Blackburn Rovers in December 1880 and appeared in the semi-final against the same opponents in March 1882. His career ended prematurely through injury. He also played cricket for Mexborough CC and Carlton CC (Edinburgh).

MARRIOTT, John Leonard
Winger

Appearances: 159   Goals: 19
Born: Scunthorpe, 1 April 1928

CAREER
CLUBS: Scunthorpe United, WEDNESDAY (£2,500*, February 1947-July 1955), Huddersfield Town, Scunthorpe United.
OTHER: worked at Firth Vickers Stainless Steel; salesman for an oil company.

Jackie Marriott's best years with Wednesday were between 1949 and 1955 when he helped the side twice gain promotion from the Second Division (1950 and 1952). Highly effective on his day, he was able to play on both wings, was quick over twenty to thirty yards, possessed a strong shot and could withstand the heftiest of challenges. With competition keen, he held his position well and, although his scoring efforts weren't too good, he did net some crucial goals while also laying on plenty of chances for his colleagues. He was with Scunthorpe when they gained Football League status in 1950 and in his second spell with the Iron he netted 30 goals in 228 games.
* The transfer involved three other players: Roy Shiner, Ron Staniforth and Tony Conwell.

MARRISON, Thomas
Inside forward

Appearances: 5   Goals: 1
Born: Rotherham, 1 January 1885
Died: Sheffield, 26 August 1926

CAREER
CLUBS: WEDNESDAY (February, 1902-May 1905), Rotherham Town, Nottingham Forest (November 1906), Oldham Athletic, Bristol City.
OTHER: moulder.

Tom Marrison, an England Schoolboy international, never really made his mark with

Wednesday, for whom his only goal came on his League debut against Stoke in March 1903 (won 1-0).

MARSDEN, Christopher
Midfield

Appearances: 18
Born: Sheffield, 3 January 1969

CAREER
CLUBS: Sheffield United, Huddersfield Town, Coventry City, Wolverhampton Wanderers, Notts County, Birmingham City, Southampton, Buskan Icons, WEDNESDAY (£125,000, July 2004, retired, March 2005).

Appointed team captain on his arrival at Hillsborough, the experienced Chris Marsden had amassed 500 appearances for his 7 English clubs before moving to Korea, where he played under ex-Wednesday player and manager Ian Porterfield. He was certainly well past his best when he became an Owl and played in only 18 games before a hamstring injury ended his career.

MARSDEN, William
Utility

Appearances: 221   Goals: 9
Born: Silksworth, Co. Durham, 10 November 1901
Died: Sheffield, 20 September 1983

CAREER
CLUBS: Sunderland, WEDNESDAY (£450, May 1924-October 1931), Gateshead (coach), Be Quick (coach), Hermes DWS (coach), Dutch FA (coach), WEDNESDAY (part-time coach, August 1942-April 1944), Doncaster Rovers (part-time manager), Doncaster Rovers (part-time manager), Worksop Town (coach).
OTHER: licensee.

Bill Marsden understudied Charlie Buchan at Sunderland and joined the Owls as an inside forward but was quickly switched to half-back, where he became a star performer. Predominantly right-footed, he trained long and hard and after a while was able to use his left foot equally well. He was an ever-present when the Owls won the Second Division in 1926 and a key member of the team that won the First Division title in 1929 and 1930. A shrewd tackler and excellent passer of the ball, he was always looking to prompt his attack. It was a blow when he was forced to quit at the age of twenty-eight due to a spinal injury and broken neck suffered in a collision with his teammate Roy Goodall, of Huddersfield, when playing in his third international for England, against Germany, in Berlin, May 1930. He battled without success to regain full fitness but in the end had to accept defeat. Marsden, who also represented the Football League, received £750 in compensation.

MARSON, Frederick
Forward

Appearances: 10
Born: Moxley, Bilston, 8 January 1900
Died: Lichfield, December 1976

CAREER
CLUBS: Wolverhampton Wanderers, WEDNESDAY (£100, September 1926-August 1928), Swansea Town, Darlaston, Wellington Town, Shrewsbury Town.

An average player throughout his career, Fred Marson made only 32 League appearances in total for his 3 major clubs. His debut for Wednesday was on the left wing in a 6-2 League defeat at Arsenal in October 1926, when he deputised for Jack Wilkinson.

MARTIN, John Grieve
Full-back

Appearances: 66
Born: Dundee, 20 August 1935

CAREER
CLUBS: Dundee North End, WEDNESDAY (£490, February 1954-June 1962), Rochdale, Alfreton.
OTHER: employed in the steel industry (Stocksbridge).

A reliable player who took over at right-back from Tony Conwell for the last 13 League games of the 1954/55 season, Jack Martin spent eight years at Hillsborough and was never realistically a regular in the side. He moved on after Peter Johnson had established himself as partner to Don Megson.

MARWOOD, Brian
Forward

Appearances: 157+4   Goals: 35
Born: Seaham Harbour, Co. Durham, 5 February 1960

CAREER
CLUBS: Hull City, WEDNESDAY (£115,000, August 1984-March 1988), Arsenal, Sheffield United, Middlesbrough, Swindon Town, Barnet.
OTHER: chief executive with the PFA; pundit on Sky Sports.

An England international, capped against Saudi Arabia in November 1988, Brian Marwood was an incisive player and quick to seize a scoring opportunity. At the time of his departure to Hillsborough he was Hull's longest-serving player. He gave the Owls fine service for three and a half years, appearing in over 160 games, missing only 1 League fixture in 1984/85 and 5 the following term. A League championship winner with Arsenal in 1989, he made almost 400 appearances at club level

Brian Marwood

during his eighteen-year career. Marwood turned down the chance to play cricket for Northants' Second XI as a teenager.

MASSARELLA, Leonard
Outside right

Appearances: 34   Goals: 10
Born: Doncaster, 14 February 1917
Died: Doncaster, 16 January 1999

CAREER
CLUBS: Doncaster Rovers, Denaby United, WEDNESDAY (free, December 1937-May 1945), Doncaster Rovers.

Unfortunately the outbreak of the Second World War ruined Len Massarella's playing career. He did well at Hillsborough after taking over on the right wing in January 1938 to become the seventh player used in the position that season. He scored on his debut in a 1-1 draw at Swansea and netted four more goals to help the Owls avoid relegation to the Third Division (North). He battled with Idris Lewis, Frank Dillon and Ernie Toseland for a place in the team in 1938/39 and netted 16 goals in 51 Second World War matches for Wednesday.

MASSEY, James
Goalkeeper

Appearances: 174
Born: Wolverhampton, October 1869
Died: Denaby, 1935

CAREER
CLUBS: Wolverhampton Wanderers, Denaby United, Doncaster Rovers, WEDNESDAY (free, August 1893-May 1901), Denaby United.

Jim Massey made his League debut for Wednesday in a 1-0 home win over Aston Villa in November 1894. Unfortunately, owing to inconsistency, he had to fight to get a game in the First XI after that, but come 1896 he was regarded as first choice and went on to serve the club for another five years, amassing over 170 appearances. An FA Cup winner in 1896, he missed only five games when the Second Division was won in 1900.

MATTHEWS, Ernest
Centre forward

Appearances: 16   Goals: 7
Born: Chester-le-Street, 8 November 1912
Deceased

CAREER
CLUBS: Bury, WEDNESDAY (£3,750, September 1937-May 1938), Colchester United, Ashington, Mansfield Town.

Scorer of 46 goals in 73 League games for Bury, Ernie Matthews arrived at Hillsborough when the Owls were struggling up front. He bedded in quickly, netted his first goal in his second game versus Spurs and continued to do well until new signing Doug Hunt replaced him as leader of the attack. Matthews was also a professional sprint champion.

Ernest Matthews

MATTHEWSON, Thomas James
Outside right

Appearances: 1
Born: Gateshead, 9 May 1903
Died: Sheffield, 19 May 1966

CAREER
CLUBS: WEDNESDAY (September 1921-August 1923), North Shields.
OTHER: manager of Daniel Doncaster Works.

Grandfather of Trevor (below), Tom Matthewson was a Wednesday reserve for two seasons, making his only League appearance against Coventry in December 1921. He was outstanding as captain of South Shields, for whom he scored 44 goals in 219 games. His son, Reg, played for Sheffield United among others. His wife was the laundry lady at Hillsborough for twenty-five years and she was followed by Tom's daughter who washed and ironed the kit for forty-three years.

MATTHEWSON, Trevor
Defender

Appearances: 5
Born: Sheffield, 12 February 1963

CAREER
CLUBS: WEDNESDAY (June 1979-October 1983), Newport County, Stockport County, Lincoln City, Birmingham City, Preston North End, Bury, Witton Albion, Hereford United, non-League (1998-2001). OTHER: now runs a shop near Hillsborough.

Very competitive and always involved in the action, Trevor Matthewson had a useful career which realised over 460 appearances of which only 5 were made with Wednesday. He made his debut for the Owls against West Ham in May 1981 and had his last outing against Southend in an FA Cup replay in January 1983. A Vauxhall Conference championship winner with Lincoln in 1988, he won the Leyland DAF Cup with Birmingham in 1991 – one of 203 games for Blues.

MAXWELL, James Morton
Outside right

Appearances: 27   Goals: 6
Born: New Cummock, Scotland, 1888
Died: 1916

CAREER
CLUBS: Kilmarnock, WEDNESDAY (£500, March 1907-May 1908), Woolwich Arsenal, Hurlford & Galston, Carlisle United, Lanemark, Kilmarnock.

Jimmy Maxwell was only 5ft 5ins tall, fast and mobile, and never afraid to get involved with the burly opponents who marked him. He never really settled in England and after leaving Wednesday played in only two League games for Arsenal. Signed from Kilmarnock for a record fee of £500 three weeks before the 1907 FA Cup final, he made his Owls' debut against the Gunners and scored his first goal in a 2-1 defeat at Bramall Lane in his second outing. He missed out on a final place, Harry Chapman moving from inside right to the wing to accommodate Frank Bradshaw. His son Bud played junior football north and south of the border.

MAY, Lawrence Charles
Defender

Appearances: 37+1 Goals: 1
Born: Sutton Coldfield, 26 December 1958

CAREER
CLUBS: Leicester City, New England Tea Men, Barnsley, WEDNESDAY (£200,000, February 1987-September 1988), Brighton & Hove Albion (player, youth coach), Ringmer (coach), Portsmouth (coach), Crawley Council (football development officer), Surrey FA (coaching development manager).

Lawrence May

When he first set foot inside Hillsborough, Larry May had already played in over 300 League games for his two previous clubs. He spent eighteen months with Wednesday before bolstering up Brighton's leaky defence. Strong and mobile, he made his debut for the Owls against Watford in February 1987 in place of Lawrie Madden. When Madden returned, May moved to the right side of the defence. Twice a Second Division promotion winner with Leicester (1980 and 1983), a knee injury ended his career.

MAYRLEB, Christian
Forward

Appearances: 0+3
Born: Wels, Austria, 8 June 1972

CAREER
CLUBS: Admira Wacker, FC Tirol, WEDNESDAY (loan, January-June 1998), Austria Vienna, FC Superfund.

The pacy Christian Mayrleb played in three Premiership games, all as a substitute; his first was against Wimbledon soon after signing. The Austrian international netted over 125 goals in 440 games in his home country.

McANEARNEY, James
Inside forward

Appearances: 40   Goals: 10
Born: Dundee, 20 March 1935

CAREER
CLUBS: Dundee St Stephen's, WEDNESDAY (April 1950-January 1960), Plymouth Argyle, Watford, Bradford City (player-coach, caretaker-manager), Rotherham United (coach, manager), WEDNESDAY (reserve team manager, May 1974, caretaker-manager, September 1975-January 1976), Leeds United (coach, chief scout), Frickley Colliery (part-time

manager), Scarborough (manager), Hallam FC (committee).

OTHER: worked in industry and as an after-dinner speaker.

During his career, slightly-built Jim McAnearney scored 68 goals in more than 300 League games. However, unlike his brother, Thomas McAnearney (below, who was signed as an amateur at the same time), he never really established himself as a first-team regular at Hillsborough, owing to the dearth of inside forward talent. He had his best season in 1958/59 – making 11 appearances – before moving to Plymouth (George Kirby switching to Hillsborough). He was employed by Tommy Docherty as coach at Rotherham but, after the 'Doc' left, he had to sell players in order for the club to survive – one of these was future England centre half Dave Watson, who was sold to Sunderland for £100,000. He later returned to Wednesday as coach to Steve Burtenshaw, having a brief spell in charge of the team in 1975, prior to the arrival of Len Ashurst. Another brother, John, also played football.

McANEARNEY, Thomas
Wing half

Appearances: 382   Goals: 22
Born: Dundee, 6 January 1933

CAREER
CLUBS: Dundee St Stephens, WEDNESDAY (April 1950-November 1965), Peterborough United, Aldershot (player, manager) WEDNESDAY (assistant manager, October 1968-May 1970), Bury (manager), Aldershot (manager), Chelsea (coach).
OTHER: postman.

A tall, thoughtful and perceptive wing half, Tom McAnearney served Wednesday superbly for more than fifteen years (as amateur and professional), during which time he appeared in more than 380 senior games, helping the Owls twice win the Second Division title (1956 and 1959).

He made his League debut in 1952 against Liverpool at Hillsborough and played his last game for the club against the other Merseyside club, Everton, in March 1965. A penalty expert, hardly ever missing from the spot, he was part of a terrific half-back line that included Peter Swan and Tony Kay. Elected team captain in the early 1960s, he later returned to Hillsborough and, as a manager, helped Aldershot win promotion to the Third Division in 1973. He now lives in Sheffield.

McARDLE, Rory Alexander
Defender

Appearances: 0+2*
Born: Sheffield, 1 May 1987

CAREER
CLUBS: WEDNESDAY (apprentice, June 2003; professional, July 2005), Rochdale (L).

A Northern Ireland Youth and Under-21 international, Rory McArdle spent most of 2005/06 and 2006/07 on loan to Rochdale. He signed professional forms for the Owls in July 2005.

McALLISTER, Sean Brian
Midfield

Appearances: 2+7
Born: Bolton, 15 August 1987

CAREER
CLUBS: Bolton Wanderers, WEDNESDAY (July 2003).

A tenacious, hard-working and lively midfielder, McAllister made his senior debut for the Owls towards the end of the 2005/06 season after some impressive displays for the Second XI.

McCAFFERTY, Michael
Centre half

Appearances: 1
Born: Belfast, 1875
Deceased by 1960

CAREER
CLUBS: Celtic, WEDNESDAY (free, October 1898-April 1899).

Mick McCafferty spent seven months with the Owls, making his only appearance against Burnley in April 1899 when he deputised for Tom Crawshaw in a 1-0 win.

McCALL, Stephen Harold
Utility

Appearances: 24+12   Goals: 2
Born: Carlisle, 15 October 1960

CAREER
CLUBS: Ipswich Town, WEDNESDAY (£250,000, June 1987-March 1992), Carlisle United (L), Plymouth Argyle (player, assistant manager, manager), Torquay United (player, coach), Ipswich Town (coach).

Stephen McCall

During his long career, Steve McCall appeared in almost 600 games – 319 for Ipswich, whom he helped win the UEFA Cup in 1981 – and also gained 3 Youth, 1 'B' and 6 Under-21 caps for England. Strong in all aspects of midfield play, he was also solid in the left-back position. He spent almost five years at Hillsborough but, owing to injury and the form of other players vying for the same positions, he made only 36 appearances.

McCALLIOG, James
Midfield

Appearances: 174   Goals: 27
Born: Glasgow, 23 September 1946

CAREER
CLUBS: Leeds United, Chelsea, WEDNESDAY (£37,500, October 1965-August 1969), Wolverhampton Wanderers, Manchester United, Southampton, Chicago Sting, Lynn Oslo (player-coach), Lincoln City (player-coach), Runcorn (player-manager), Blackburn Rovers (football in the community officer), Halifax Town (coach, caretaker-manager, manager), Leyton Orient (scout).
OTHER: licensee in Wetherby; hotelier in Harrogate.

Jim McCalliog was one of the most expensive teenagers in football when he joined the Owls from Chelsea for £37,500, having earlier made his League debut for the Londoners at the age of eighteen.

Developing into a top-class midfielder who represented Scotland in 5 full and 2 Under-23 internationals, having starred at both Schoolboy and Youth levels, he made his Owls' debut against Aston Villa shortly after joining the club. He gained an FA Cup runners-up prize at the end of that season and a decade later celebrated with a winners' prize after Southampton beat his former club, Manchester United, 1-0 in the final. He played for Wolves in their 1972 UEFA Cup final defeat by Spurs and three years later helped Manchester United win the Second Division title. During his nomadic career McCalliog – who was a fine passer of the ball – accumulated more than 550 club appearances. When he joined Wednesday, his mother and father, three brothers and his sister all moved into the same house near Hillsborough. One of his brothers, Fred, was also on Wednesday's books for a short while

McCAMBRIDGE, James
Forward

Appearances: 2
Born: Larne, Ireland, 24 September 1905
Died: Larne, 15 May 1990

CAREER
CLUBS: Ballymena, Everton, Cardiff City, Ballymena, Bristol Rovers, Exeter City, WEDNESDAY (£250, September 1936-January 1937), Hartlepools United, Cheltenham Town.

An Irish international, capped four times (1930-32), Jim McCambridge was an aggressive, all-action forward, an opportunist whose marksmanship was exceptional. His career brought him 131 goals in 275 games, including a haul of 50 in 95 starts for Cardiff. A joiner by trade, he appeared in every outfield position but played only twice for the Owls – against Arsenal and Charlton, both in London in October 1936, when he deputised for Neil Dewar.

McCARTER, James Joseph
Outside left

Appearances: 6
Born: Glasgow, 19 March 1923
Died: Weymouth, 22 August 2002

CAREER
CLUBS: Vale of Clyde, WEDNESDAY (£75, April 1944-August 1948), Mansfield Town, Weymouth, Dorchester Town.
OTHER: shoe repairer; postman.

A direct winger who loved to cut inside his full-back, Jim McCarter was totally left-footed and therefore his style was cramped when facing an experienced defender. He made his League debut for the Owls against Millwall in September 1946 when he deputised for Charlie Tomlinson – having had four games during the Second World War.

McCARTHY, Jonathan David
Outside right

Appearances: 4
Born: Middlesbrough, 18 August 1970

CAREER
CLUBS: Hartlepool United, Shepshed Charterhouse, York City, Port Vale, Birmingham City, WEDNESDAY (loan, March-April 2002), Port Vale, Doncaster Rovers, York City, Carlisle United, Hucknall Town, Northwich Victoria.
OTHER: science teacher in Cheshire.

Capped twice by Northern Ireland at under-21 level and on 18 occasions by the senior side, Jon McCarthy had a wonderful career. A direct, purposeful and enterprising right-winger, he loved to hug the touchline and his pace usually took him past his marker. Unfortunately, he broke his right leg three times in quick succession in 2000 and never regained full fitness. A League Cup runner-up with Birmingham in 2001, he was a record signing by Blues from Port Vale. The first of his four League outings for Wednesday was against Coventry in March 2002.

M

McCONACHIE, Robert
Outside left

Appearances: 18   Goals: 4
Born: Scotland, 1872
Deceased by 1950

CAREER
CLUBS: WEDNESDAY (March 1891-April 1893).

Reserve to Fred Spiksley, Bob McConachie's only League appearance was against Stoke in April 1893. His 17 other games came in the Football Alliance.

McCONNELL, James English
Defender

Appearances: 50
Born: Larne, Ireland, 1885
Died: Belfast, 21 June 1928

CAREER
CLUBS: Cliftonville, Glentoran, Sunderland, WEDNESDAY (£285, May 1908-April 1910), Chelsea, South Shields, Linfield, Chelsea.

An Irish international, capped 12 times between 1904 and 1910 (his last five as a Wednesday player), English McConnell was a polished and stylish centre half and very much attack-minded. He underwent a cartilage operation in 1911, after which he struggled to regain full fitness despite playing for two other clubs. Prior to joining the Owls, he made 45 appearances for Sunderland. Signed after eight different players had been used in the pivotal position, McConnell made his debut for Wednesday on the opening day of 1908/09 versus Preston and, injuries apart, remained first choice until leaving for Chelsea – Bob McSkimming taking over.

McCULLOCH, Andrew
Forward

Appearances: 146+3   Goals: 49
Born: Northampton, 3 January 1950

CAREER
CLUBS: Fleet Town, Tottenham Hotspur, Walton & Hersham, Queens Park Rangers, Cardiff City, Oxford United, Brentford, WEDNESDAY (£60,000, June 1979-June 1983), Crystal Palace, Aldershot, Esher United (manager).
OTHER: ran his own furniture cleaning business.

Andy McCulloch scored 155 goals in 474 League and Cup games – 140 coming in 424 outings in the Football League. Tall, strong and mobile, he was an unorthodox forward who suffered his fair share of injuries but always came back for more. He hit top form with Brentford and did superbly well at Hillsborough, helping Wednesday bounce back into the Second Division in 1980 when he, Ian Mellor and Terry Curran conjured up 46 goals between them. McCulloch was capped once by Scotland at Under-23 level. His father, Adam, was also a professional footballer.

McEVOY, Donald William
Centre half

Appearances: 112   Goals: 1
Born: Golcar, Huddersfield, 3 December 1928

CAREER
CLUBS: Huddersfield Town, WEDNESDAY (£20,000, December 1954-January 1959), Lincoln City, Barrow (player-manager), Halifax Town (manager), Southport (manager), Barrow (manager).
OTHER: licensee.

Don McEvoy started as a centre forward but was quickly switched to centre half. He made 155 appearances for Huddersfield, whom he helped gain promotion from the Second

Division in 1953 when part of a terrific defence that remained unchanged for over a year (55 games). A strong, positive tackler, he made his debut for Wednesday against Wolves in December 1954 and went down with the team that season, skippering them a year later when promotion was achieved at the first attempt.

McGOVERN, Jon-Paul
Midfield

Appearances: 57+4 Goals: 8
Born: Glasgow, Scotland, 3 October 1980

CAREER
CLUBS: Heart of Midlothian, Celtic, Sheffield United, Livingston, WEDNESDAY (free, June 2004-July 2006), MK Dons (player exchange deal).

Jon-Paul McGovern had the pleasure of scoring the 150th goal at the Millennium Stadium to give the Owls the lead in the Second Division play-off final versus Hartlepool in 2005. A right-sided midfielder with good pace, he is strong on the ball, has a great attitude and his work rate is exceptional. He made his debut for Wednesday at home to Colchester in August 2004 (lost 3-0).

McGREGOR, James
Centre forward

Appearances: 6   Goals: 2
Born: Dumfries, 1890
Deceased by 1970

CAREER
CLUBS: Albion Rovers, WEDNESDAY (free, May 1913-August 1914), Portsmouth.
OTHER: served in the army during the First World War.

A Wednesday reserve, spotted in a trial, Jim McGregor made his League debut against

Tottenham just before Christmas 1913 and scored his first goal in the 1-1 draw with Bolton nine days later.

McILVENNY, Patrick
Centre forward

Appearances: 1
Born: Belfast, 18 November 1900
Died: Hinckley, 25 February 1955

CAREER
CLUBS: Belfast Distillery, Cardiff City, WEDNESDAY (£1,150 plus George Beadles, November 1925-March 1926), Shelbourne, Northampton Town, Boston United, Hinckley Town, Linfield.

Irish international Pat McIlvenny, capped once against Wales shortly before joining the Owls, deputised for Jimmy Trotter when making his only appearance for the club in a 1-0 defeat at Blackpool in December 1925.

McINTOSH, David
Goalkeeper

Appearances: 308
Born: Girvan, Scotland, 4 May 1925
Died: Sheffield, July 1995

CAREER
CLUBS: WEDNESDAY (October 1947-January 1958), Doncaster Rovers.
OTHER: Fleet Air Arm – Second World War; delivery driver for a beer company.

Dave McIntosh was third choice behind Roy Smith and Albert Morton but, owing to injuries to the aforementioned duo, he was called up for first team duty against Fulham in April 1948 and never looked back. Daring and courageous, he was an ever-present in 1948/49 and missed only three games when the Second Division championship was won in 1950. Two years later he

David McIntosh

played in every game again as the Owls captured the Second Division title once more. A series of niggling injuries – he broke his arm twice in one year – restricted him at times, but he always came back and it wasn't until 1957 that he was finally replaced at Hillsborough. The last competitive game of his career was for Doncaster against Wednesday in the Sheffield County Cup of 1959.

McINTOSH, Thomas
Forward

Appearances: 9   Goals: 1
Born: Scotland, 1871
Deceased by 1950

CAREER
CLUBS: WEDNESDAY (seasons 1892-94).

Tom McIntosh occupied four different positions for the Owls in two seasons with the club. He scored on his League debut in a 5-1 defeat by Aston Villa in January 1893.

McINTYRE, John McGregor
Forward

Appearances: 70   Goals: 36
Born: Glasgow, 4 January 1895
Died: Blackpool, February 1974

CAREER
CLUBS: Partick Thistle, Fulham, WEDNESDAY (£1,750, March 1900-January 1922), Blackburn Rovers, Blackpool, Chorley, Derby Co-op Welfare. OTHER: licensee.

McIntyre left Fulham after disobeying a curfew. He became a regular marksman with Wednesday and later with Blackburn. He scored 4 goals in 5 minutes for the latter club against Everton in September 1922 – a feat equalled later by West Brom's 'W.G.' Richardson versus West Ham in 1931. Between 1919 and 1929, McIntyre, who also played outside left and centre forward, was converted into a left half by Blackburn, for whom he netted 38 goals in 194 games.

McIVER, Frederick
Midfield

Appearances: 39+3
Born: Birtley, 14 February 1952

CAREER
CLUBS: Sunderland, Racing Jet Brussels, WEDNESDAY (£11,680, July 1974-May 1976), Gateshead. OTHER: milkman; ran a newsagent shop and post office.

Fred McIver had two decent seasons with Wednesday during which time he wore eight different numbered shirts while appearing in 42 games. He made his debut at Oldham in August 1974 when he partnered Tommy Craig in midfield.

McJARROW, Hugh
Centre forward

Appearances: 47   Goals: 21
Born: New Harthill, Motherwell, 29 January 1928
Died: Brigstock, Northants, 25 July 1987

CAREER
CLUBS: Chesterfield, WEDNESDAY (£4,500, March 1950-February 1952), Luton Town, Plymouth Argyle, Peterborough United, Matlock Town, Clay Cross & Danesmoor MW, Chesterfield Tube Works.

A Bevin Boy during the Second World War, Hugh McJarrow scored 45 times in 124 League games. He netted almost 1 every 2 outings for the Owls, for whom he made his debut at QPR in March 1950, just as the Second Division promotion race was hotting up. He notched five crucial goals at the end of that season as Wednesday finished runners-up to clinch a place in the top flight. He was converted into a wing half by Plymouth.

McKAY, Colin Campbell
Utility

Appearances: 14   Goals: 3
Born: Portobello, Lothian, 24 August 1896
Died: Edinburgh, 1978

CAREER
CLUBS: Raith Rovers, Cowdenbeath, Heart of Midlothian, WEDNESDAY (free, December 1919-May 1920), Huddersfield Town, Bradford City, Aberavon.
OTHER: Army – First World War.

Colin Mackay spent five seasons in Scottish League football before joining Wednesday for whom he made his debut in a 3-1 defeat at Arsenal shortly before Christmas 1919. A sprightly player, the first of his three goals earned victory over Bradford City on the Boxing Day.

McKEEVER, Mark Anthony
Midfield

Appearances: 2+5
Born: Derry, Ireland, 16 November 1978

CAREER
CLUBS: Norwich City, Peterborough United, WEDNESDAY (£375,000, April 1997-May 2001), Bristol Rovers (L), Reading (L), Bristol Rovers, Weston-Super-Mare.

Capped by Northern Ireland at Youth international level, Mark McKeever later added four Republic of Ireland Under-21 caps to his tally. Quick and tricky, he was unable to establish himself in Wednesday's First XI and slipped out of League football at the age of twenty-four after making just 65 appearances in 8 years.

McKEOWN, Isaac Lindsay
Midfield

Appearances: 7+5
Born: Belfast, 11 July 1957

CAREER
CLUBS: Manchester United, WEDNESDAY (free, July 1976-May 1979), Linfield.
OTHER: salesman for an electrical company.

Having failed to make the first team at Old Trafford, Lindsay McKeown was unable to assert himself during his three years with the Owls, spending most of his time in the reserves. He deputised for Bobby Hope when making his debut against Darlington in the FA Cup in December 1976.

McLAREN, John James Roy
Goalkeeper

Appearances: 34
Born: Auchterarder, Tayside, 12 February, 1930

M

CAREER

CLUBS: St Johnstone, Bury, WEDNESDAY (£4,200, October 1958-May 1965), Grimsby Town (coach), Huddersfield Town (coach), Aston Villa (assistant manager), Ipswich Town (scout), Southampton (scout), Northcote City (coach), Heidelberg United (coach), Altona Gate (coach), Moorabbin City (coach).
OTHER: later ran his own business.

First choice between the posts for Bury, Roy McLaren took over from the injured Ron Springett in the Owls' goal after amateur Mike Pinner had played in a couple of games in March 1959. He did well, helping the team clinch the Second Division title that season. After that he played second fiddle to Springett while accumulating over 150 Second XI appearances. He was coach with Villa when they won the League Cup, First Division championship, European Cup and Super Cup (1974-84). His brother Dave kept goal for Leicester, Plymouth, Southampton and Wolves.

McLAREN, Paul Andrew
Midfield

Appearances: 92+14   Goals: 9
Born: High Wycombe, 17 November 1976

CAREER Luton Town, WEDNESDAY (free, June 2001-August 2004), Rotherham United.

A tall, well-built central midfielder, Paul McLaren, when free from injury, was a very competitive performer who made over 200 appearances for Luton and more than 100 for Wednesday over a period of ten years. He made his debut for the Owls versus Burnley on the opening day of the 2001/02 League season, and was one of thirteen players released by the club in the summer of 2004.

McLEAN, David Prophet
Centre forward

Appearances: 147   Goals: 100
Born: Forfar, Scotland, 13 December 1887
Died: Forfar, 21 December 1967

CAREER

CLUBS: Forfar West End, Forfar Celtic, Forfar Athletic, Forfar Celtic, Forfar Athletic, Ayr, Preston North End, WEDNESDAY (£1,000, February 1911-May 1913), Forfar Athletic (L), WEDNESDAY (£250, December 1914-December 1915), Bradford Park Avenue, Dundee, Forfar Athletic, Dykehead, East Fife (secretary-manager), Bristol Rovers (manager).
WARTIME GUEST APPEARANCES: Glasgow Rangers, Third Lanark, Dykehead.
OTHER: Army – First World War.

Davie McLean arrived at the club at the same time as fellow Scot Jimmy Campbell and was the first Owls' player to demand a four-figure fee (£1,000). Solidly built, he had netted 24 goals in 49 games for Preston and when he moved from Deepdale he became the tenth player to be used at centre forward by Wednesday that season (1910/11). He scored in his second outing for the Owls and the following term set a new club record by claiming 38 goals in 40 appearances. Unfortunately, at the end of the 1912/13 season, amidst much public debate, McLean left the club after a disagreement over wages – one director followed suit. He returned after eighteen months, added several more goals to his tally and later gained a Scottish Cup runners-up medal with Dundee (1925). McLean, who possessed a terrific shot in both feet, had a distinctively stiff gait and was capped by Scotland versus England in 1912. He notched 510 goals during his career. His brother, George, played for Forfar Athletic and Bradford Park Avenue – netting 139 goals in 265 games for the latter club.

McMAHON, Lewis
Midfield

Appearances: 25+6 Goals: 2
Born: Doncaster, 2 May 1985

CAREER
CLUBS: Nottingham Forest, Edenthorpe Cougars, WEDNESDAY (May 2001-June 2005), Notts County.

Entering competitive football before he was twenty, Lewis McMahon showed a calmness and maturity beyond his years. He made his senior debut in the LDV Vans semi-final win over Scunthorpe in January 2004 and was a key member of the side during the early stages of the following campaign before a leg injury meant a lengthy lay-off.

McMORDIE, Alexander
Midfield

Appearances: 9   Goals: 6
Born: Belfast, 12 August 1946

CAREER
CLUBS: Dundela, Manchester United, Dundela, Glentoran, Middlesbrough, WEDNESDAY (loan, October-December 1974), York City, Hartlepool United.
OTHER: worked for a builder's merchants; ran a food and alcohol store in Middlesbrough.

'Eric' McMordie gained one Under-21 and 21 full caps for Northern Ireland (1968-73). A big pal of the late George Best, he failed to make the grade at Old Trafford, despite two attempts. He went on, however, to score 25 goals in 273 games for Middlesbrough, helping Jack Charlton's team win the Second Division title in 1974. A very talented footballer, he was signed by Jack as a loan player and netted on his debut for the Owls against Hull City in October 1974. He retired with over 400 appearances to his name.

McSKIMMING, Robert
Defender

Appearances: 194
Born: Hamilton, 1888
Died: Dunedin, New Zealand, December 1952

CAREER
CLUBS: Albion Rovers, WEDNESDAY (£165, March 1910-March 1920), Wishaw Thistle, Motherwell, Albion Rovers, Ayr United, Hilenberg, Auchin Sharry Juveniles, Denny Hibs.

Able to play in both full-back positions and as centre half, Bob McSkimming took over from Walter Holbeam at left-back in Wednesday's League side during the latter stages of 1909/10. A powerful competitor with square, solid shoulders, he was a regular in the side until 1915. Serving in the army, he appeared in two First World War games for the Owls before returning to Scotland. His cousin, also Robert, played for Stoke and Burslem Port Vale.

McWATT, Herbert
Goalkeeper

Appearances: 2
Born: Sheffield, 1877
Deceased by 1950

CAREER
CLUBS: WEDNESDAY (seasons 1889-92).

Reserve to Jack Smith during Wednesday's three Football Alliance seasons, Bert McWatt* made just two appearances in the First XI. *Some reference books have this player listed as H. Mowatt.

M

McWHINNIE, William G.
Outside right

Appearances: 9
Born: Wiltshire, July 1872
Died: USA, 1936

CAREER
CLUBS: *Reading, Ayr United, Third Lanark, WEDNESDAY (£75, May 1900-August 1905), Hibernian, Staten Island (USA).*

Bill McWhinnie was reserve to Harry Davis, whom he replaced when making his debut against Manchester City on the opening day of the 1900/01 League season. He struggled with injury for three years.

MEGSON, Donald Harry
Full-back

Appearances: 442   Goals: 7
Born: Sale, 12 June 1936

CAREER
CLUBS: *Mossley, WEDNESDAY (amateur, October 1952, signed for £50, June 1953-March 1970), Bristol Rovers (player-coach, manager), Portland Timbers (coach), Bournemouth (manager), Norwich City (scout), Blackpool (scout), Stockport County (scout), Stoke City (scout), West Bromwich Albion (scout), Nottingham Forest (scout).*

Don Megson had plenty of pace and passion. He was a strong, confident tackler and, above all, a dedicated club man who gave Wednesday eleven years' excellent service. He arrived at Hillsborough as a sixteen-year-old outside left and occupied every outfield position before settling down at left-back – he was placed there initially by manager Harry Catterick. He made his League debut against Burnley in November 1959 – when he partnered Peter Johnson – and quickly established himself as a regular, becoming a huge favourite with the fans. He suc-

Don Megson

ceeded Tom McAnearney as captain and took the Owls to the 1966 FA Cup final, where they were beaten by Everton. He represented the Football League against the Italian League in 1960 and his last game for the club was against Scunthorpe in the fourth round of the FA Cup in January 1970. He guided Bristol Rovers to victory in the Watney Cup final of 1972 and two years later gained promotion with the same club from the Third Division. Megson was appointed manager by a new four-man consortium in charge of Bournemouth in 1983. He later scouted for all the clubs subsequently managed by his son, Gary (below).

MEGSON, Gary John
Midfield

Appearances: 283+3 apps   Goals: 83
Born: Manchester, 2 May 1959

scored his first goal for the club in a 3-0 win at Luton a fortnight later. In 1983/84 he was an ever-present when promotion was gained to the First Division. Megson played in three losing FA Cup semi-finals (1980, 1983 and 1986) and as a manager he twice took West Bromwich Albion into the Premiership.

MELIA, James
Right-back

Appearances: 7
Born: Darlington, 2 April 1874
Died: Darlington, February 1905

CAREER
CLUBS: Stockton, WEDNESDAY (free, July 1895-May 1898), Tottenham Hotspur, Preston North End.

After two years as a Wednesday reserve, Jim Melia made his League debut in place of the injured Jack Earp at Everton in September 1896. He did much better with Spurs, appearing in almost 100 games. He represented the Southern League against the Southern Amateurs in a War Fund match in February 1900. Taken ill in January 1905, he died a month later.

MELLOR, Ian
Wing forward

Appearances: 61+18   Goals: 11
Born: Manchester, 19 February 1950

CAREER
CLUBS: Manchester City, Norwich City, Brighton & Hove Albion, Chester City, WEDNESDAY (£50,000, June 1979-June 1982), Bradford City, Tung Sing Hong Kong, Worksop Town, Matlock Town, Gainsborough Trinity, Burton Albion.
OTHER: worked for sports manufacturers Puma and Gola; appointed executive with the PFA in 1993, handling commercial deals.

Gary Megson

CAREER
CLUBS: Plymouth Argyle, Everton, WEDNESDAY (£108,500, August 1981-August 1984), Nottingham Forest, Newcastle United, WEDNESDAY (loan, December 1985, signed January 1986-January 1989), Manchester City, Norwich City (player, assistant manager), Lincoln City, Bradford City (assistant manager, coach), Shrewsbury Town, Norwich City (manager), Blackpool (manager), Stockport County (manager), Stoke City (manager), West Bromwich Albion (manager), Nottingham Forest (manager).

A tall, hard-working, aggressive midfielder, Gary Megson made 588 appearances and scored 51 goals in 20 years as a player. He had his best spells with Wednesday – particularly his first when he was absent on just 3 occasions out of a possible 99 matches – and his worst (no games) with Nottingham Forest, whom he later managed. He made his debut for the Owls versus Blackburn in August 1981 (won 1-0) and

M

A former postman, Ian Mellor scored 66 goals in 337 League appearances while playing for 6 major clubs. A tall, loose-limbed, ball-playing winger, he had to work hard at his game at Manchester City and Norwich before having more than 125 outings with Brighton. He netted on his debut for Wednesday in a 3-0 win at Barnsley on the opening day of the 1979/80 Third Division promotion-winning season – during which he notched 11 goals, some of them earning vital points.

MELLOR, William
Right half

Appearances: 1
Born: Manchester, August 1870
Died: Sheffield, 1932

CAREER
CLUBS: Sheffield United, WEDNESDAY (£50, June 1893-May 1895), Loughborough Town.

Bill Mellor's only League appearance for Wednesday was at right half in place of Harry Brandon in a 1-0 win at Burnley in March 1894.

MELLORS, Richard Dugdale
Goalkeeper

Appearances: 14
Born: Mansfield, 17 March 1902
Died: Sydney, Australia, October 1960

CAREER
CLUBS: Chesterfield, Mansfield Town, WEDNESDAY (£10, December 1925-August 1931), Reading, Bournemouth Athletic, Queen of the South, Bournemouth (trainer).
WARTIME GUEST APPEARANCES: Lincoln City.
OTHER: Army – Second World War; emigrated to Australia.

Dick Mellors – 6ft 3ins tall – understudied Jack Brown for six years at Hillsborough. He made only 14 appearances in that time, the first at Huddersfield in February 1927 when the Owls lost 4-3. He helped Reading gain the runners-up spot in the Third Division (South) in 1932.

MEREDITH, John Frederick
Outside left

Appearances: 1
Born: Dunsville, Doncaster, 23 September, 1940

CAREER
CLUBS: Doncaster Rovers, WEDNESDAY (£7,000 plus Jack Ballagher, February 1961-July 1962), Chesterfield, Gillingham, Bournemouth.
OTHER: worked in insurance.

When Derek Wilkinson was ruled out of Wednesday's League game against the FA Cup-holders Wolves in March 1961, Jack Meredith was called into the forward line for his only senior appearance for the club – Alan Finney switching wings to accommodate him. After leaving Hillsborough he made 81 appearances for Chesterfield, 228 for Gillingham and 51 for Bournemouth. One who got away?

MILLAR, Harry
Centre forward

Appearances: 34   Goals: 16
Born: Paisley, June 1874
Died: Scotland, 1930

CAREER
CLUBS: Abercorn, Paisley St Mirren, Preston North End, Bury, Reading, WEDNESDAY (£100, June 1899-August 1901), Queens Park Rangers.

Thin and upright, Harry Millar never fitted in at Preston but netted 38 goals in 109 League games for Bury, starring in the Shakers' first-ever game in the competition versus Manchester City in September 1894. He gained a Second Division championship-winning medal that season. After a disappointing time with Reading, he netted twice on his debut for Wednesday in a 5-1 home win over Chesterfield in September 1899 and ended that season with 14 goals as the Second Division title was won. He was suspended in 1900 for failing to attend a training session.

MILLER, James
Right half

Appearances: 31
Born: Glasgow, 1890
Died: Glasgow circa 1950

CAREER
CLUBS: Maryhill, WEDNESDAY (£20 with Bill Weir, May 1909-June 1914) Airdrieonians.

Jock Miller, a Scottish Junior international, was a forceful wing half, and reserve to Tom Brittleton, who made his League debut for the Owls at Middlesbrough in January 1913. He made 23 appearances the following season before Harry Bentley took over.

MILLER, John
Centre forward

Appearances: 13   Goals: 7
Born: Dumbarton, 1868
Died: Glasgow, 1933

CAREER
CLUBS: Dumbarton, Liverpool, WEDNESDAY (£50, August 1893-April 1894), Airdrieonians.
OTHER: steeplejack.

John Miller was a Scottish League Championship winner in 1891 with Dumbarton – when they shared the title with Rangers. He also top-scored in Lancashire and FA Cup football for Liverpool in his only season at Anfield. An aggressive centre forward, short and stout, he then struck both goals on his debut for Wednesday in a 2-2 draw with Sunderland in September 1893. He returned to Scotland at the end of the season, where he became a steeplejack, repairing tall chimneys. His brother Jack and two sons, Arthur and Tom, all played football.

MILLER, Walter
Forward

Appearances: 3
Born: Newcastle, February 1882
Died: Dundee, 1928

CAREER
CLUBS: Third Lanark, WEDNESDAY (free, May 1907-October 1908), West Ham United, Blackpool, Lincoln City, Merthyr Town, Dundee.

A write-up in 1913 described Wally Miller as: 'A born centre, unselfish, a dead shot and has the knack of keeping his men well together.' Prior to that he had done well with Third Lanark, but struggled with the Owls, for whom he made his debut in a 4-1 League defeat at Manchester United in March 1908, and also with West Ham and Blackpool. He finished as leading scorer for Lincoln with 20 goals when they won the inaugural Central League championship in 1912. Unfortunately, towards the end of his association with the Imps, Miller ran into trouble with the management, for neglect of training and general misconduct, and was suspended on at least two occasions.

MILLERSHIP, Walter
Utility

Appearances: 238   Goals: 33
Born: Warsop Vale, Notts, 8 June 1910
Died: Brimington, Chesterfield, 1978

M

CAREER
CLUBS: *Bradford Park Avenue, WEDNESDAY (£2,600, March 1930-August 1945), Denaby United.*
OTHER: *licensee; miner.*

Walt Millership – who was often referred to as Wednesday's 'Battleship' – was a terrific defender, durable, honest, and totally committed. He joined the club as an inside forward but was quickly switched to the centre half position, where he became a household name after gaining a regular place in the side. A former miner, he made his debut for the Owls in the inside right position against Liverpool at Anfield in April 1930, starring in a 3-1 win. He scored his first goal soon afterwards in a 6-3 home victory over Derby. Despite netting 14 goals in 17 outings in 1931/32, he found his opportunities limited until he finally established himself in the side in 1933. He was, in fact, switched into the defence in an emergency and he succeeded Tom Leach at centre half, although he did have a few outings up front when it was necessary. An FA Cup and Charity Shield winner in 1935, he continued to play for the Owls during the Second World War, adding a further 155 appearances and 12 goals to his tally and helping Wednesday reach the 1943 League (North) Cup final. It is generally agreed that it was Millership who sent Derek Dooley to Hillsborough after facing the centre forward in a reserve game versus Lincoln. Millership's father, Bill, played for Newark.

MILLS, David John
Forward

Appearances: 19   Goals: 3
Born: Robin Hood's Bay, Whitby, 6 December 1951

CAREER
CLUBS: *Middlesbrough, West Bromwich Albion (January 1979), Newcastle United, WEDNESDAY (£34,327, February-August 1983), Newcastle United), Middlesbrough (player-coach), Darlington,*
Middlesbrough (coach), Whitby Town (player-coach), Dormans Athletic (player-coach), Newcastle United (scout and player assessment officer).
OTHER: *sales executive for a printing group in Bishop Auckland; journalist for* The People *newspaper.*

In 1979, David Mills – signed by Ron Atkinson – became Britain's costliest footballer when he joined West Bromwich Albion for £518,000. Recruited to replace Tony Brown, he was not a success, despite his record of 94 goals in 340 games for Middlesbrough, whom he helped win the Second Division (under Jack Charlton) in 1974. A hard-working player with a knack for scoring goals from all angles, he ended his career with 126 to his name in more than 500 appearances. He won eight England Under-23 caps in his first spell at Ayresome Park. The first of his 19 outings for Wednesday was against Blackburn in February 1983, his first goal following 11 days later in a 3-1 win over Cambridge. His father was killed in a car accident in 1988 and it took a while for the Mills family to get over the shock.

MILLS, Simon Ashley
Utility

Appearances: 2+4
Born: Sheffield, 16 August 1964

CAREER
CLUBS: *WEDNESDAY (August 1980-June 1985), York City, Port Vale, Boston United, Matlock Town.*
OTHER: *market trader, selling footwear.*

A skilful and adaptable player at right-back or in midfield, Simon Mills won 2 England Junior and 5 Youth caps during his early days with the Owls, for whom he made just 6 appearances in 5 years. He had 125 games for York – where he was named Clubman of the Year in 1986 – and 220 for Port Vale, being a member of the Valiants' Third Division promotion and TNT Trophy winning teams of 1989 and 1992, after undergoing a series of operations to cure a knee problem.

MIROCEVIC, Anton
Midfield

Appearances: 64+5 Goals: 7
Born: Totograd, Yugoslavia, 6 August 1952

CAREER
CLUBS: Maldost, FC Budocnost, WEDNESDAY (£250,000, September 1980-May 1983), FC Budocnost (later coach, scout).
OTHER: president of the Juvenile Football Committee of Montenegro.

Great things were expected of Anton Mirocevic, who was a record signing by Wednesday. The Yugoslav international, who spent nearly three seasons at Hillsborough, during which time he appeared in only 70 matches – the first against Orient in October, when he scored in a 2-2 draw – never really lived up to expectations, only occasionally producing his best form. An acute ball-player and a stylist in some respects, he was loved by the fans, but he had always hinted that he would end his career in Yugoslavia and this he did.

MOBLEY, Victor John
Defender

Appearances: 210   Goals: 8
Born: Oxford, 11 October 1943

CAREER
CLUBS: Oxford City, WEDNESDAY (£50, September 1961-October 1969), Queens Park Rangers, Oxford City (part-time manager), Landbase Papatoetoe (coach).

After playing in all the previous rounds, sadly Vic Mobley, a tall, solid, uncompromising blond centre-half, missed the 1966 FA Cup final with an ankle injury, suffered in a robust semi-final

Victor Mobley

encounter with Chelsea. It was a huge disappointment for the big fellow who had been a regular in Wednesday's ranks since the start of 1964/65 when he took over from Peter Swan. The recipient of 13 England Under-23 caps (the first versus Wales in 1965), he was denied full international honours (versus Holland) due to that semi-final injury but did represent the Football League. He recovered full fitness and took his appearance tally to 210 – his last 123 in succession – before transferring to QPR. He was forced to retire with an arthritic knee two years later.

MONAGHAN, James
Outside right

Appearances: 2
Born: Newburn, Co. Durham, 1890
Died: France, 15 September 1916

CAREER
CLUBS: Newburn, WEDNESDAY (£25, May 1913-August 1914), Scunthorpe & Lindsay United.

As reserve to Sam Kirkman, Jim Monaghan's two appearances for the Owls came in succession against West Brom and Tottenham in December 1913. He was killed during the First World War.

MONK, Garry Alan
Defender

Appearances: 15
Born: Bedford, 6 March 1979

CAREER
CLUBS: Torquay United, Southampton, Torquay United, Stockport County, WEDNESDAY (loan, December 2002- March 2003), Barnsley, Swansea City.

Garry Monk made his 15 League appearances in succession for the Owls when on loan from Premiership club Southampton. A strapping six-footer, he did a good job and was perhaps disappointed he couldn't make the move to Hillsborough a permanent one.

MORALEE, Martin Whitfield
Centre half

Appearances: 4   Goals: 1
Born: Newcastle, 4 March 1878
Died: Mexborough, 1936

CAREER
CLUBS: Blyth Spartans, Hebburn Argyle, WEDNESDAY (£35, May 1901-May 1904), Doncaster Rovers, Mexborough Town (player, trainer).
OTHER: miner.

A reserve with Wednesday for three seasons, Martin Moralee made his League debut in place of the injured Tommy Crawshaw against Notts County in January 1902, scoring in a 4-0 win. His son, Matthew, played for Gainsborough, Grimsby, Aston Villa, Leicester and Shrewsbury.

MORLEY, Haydn Arthur
Full-back

Appearances: 21   Goals: 1
Born: Derby, 26 November 1860
Died: Hathersage, 15 May 1953

CAREER
CLUBS: Derby Midland, Derby County, Notts County, Derby County, WEDNESDAY (free, September 1889-March 1891), Loughborough.

A well-built, strong-kicking full-back, Haydn Morley made 2 appearances for Notts County and 4 for Derby at the end of the first season of League football (1888/89). Injured in his final game for Wednesday, he helped the Owls win the Football Alliance in 1890 and had the honour of being the first player to captain Wednesday in an FA Cup final, beaten by Blackburn Rovers in that same season. He was the first player signed by Derby County after his father and uncle had founded the club. A solicitor by profession, Morley also played cricket for Derbyshire.

MORLEY, Lance A.
Goalkeeper

Appearances: 1
Born: Sheffield, 1861
Deceased by 1939

CAREER
CLUBS: WEDNESDAY (seasons 1882-84).

Brother of Haydn (above), reserve Lance Morley's only game for the Owls was in a 3-1 FA Cup defeat by Staveley in December 1883.

MORRIS, Christopher Barry
Full-back

Appearances: 73+23   Goals: 2
Born: Newquay, Cornwall, 24 December 1963

Chris Morris

CAREER
CLUBS: WEDNESDAY (July 1982-August 1987), Celtic, Middlesbrough, Bishop Auckland
OTHER: director of the family's butcher shop in Newquay.

Admired everywhere he played, Chris Morris represented England as a schoolboy and after turning professional gained 35 full caps for the Republic of Ireland. Never giving less than 100 per cent, he was a skilful, dedicated full-back whose level of concentration and will to win was outstanding. He made his League debut for the Owls on the opening day of the 1983/84 promotion-winning campaign at Swansea and became a regular in the side two years later. After leaving Hillsborough he made 210 appearances for Celtic, helping the Bhoys complete the League and Cup double in 1988 before adding a second Cup winners' medal to his collection in 1989. Following his transfer from Parkhead, he was a key member of Middlesbrough's 1995 Second Division championship side.

MORRISON, John Owen
Forward

Appearances: 40+29   Goals: 11
Born: Londonderry, Northern Ireland, 8 December 1981

CAREER
CLUBS: WEDNESDAY (April 1997-February 2003), Hull City (L), Sheffield United, Stockport County, Bradford City, Dunfermline Athletic.

Able to play as a striker or wide left, Owen Morrison, after being nursed along in the reserves, had an excellent first full season with the Owls (2001/02), scoring 8 goals in 37 outings. His performances earned him the first of his seven Northern Ireland Under-21 caps versus Bulgaria, having already represented his country at schoolboy and youth team levels. Unfortunately his performances were disappointing after that and, following a loan spell with Hull, he joined Sheffield United.

MORTON, Albert
Goalkeeper

Appearances: 42
Born: Newcastle, 27 July 1919
Died: Sheffield, July 1991

CAREER
CLUBS: WEDNESDAY (March 1938-June 1953), Rochdale.
OTHER: Army.

Competitive League football was abandoned after just three matches at the start of 1939/40 when Albert Morton was seeking to challenge for a first-team place. He did, however, take part in 118 Second World War games, including both legs of the 1943 League (North) Cup final versus Blackpool (lost 4-3 on aggregate). Morton made his League debut versus Millwall in August 1947 at the age of twenty-eight. He appeared in almost 100 games for Rochdale.

MOSFORTH, William Henry
Outside left

Appearances: 25   Goals: 6
Born: Sheffield, 2 January 1858
Died: Sheffield: 11 July 1929

CAREER
CLUBS: WEDNESDAY (August 1875-May 1888), Lockwood Brothers, Sheffield Rovers, Providence, Heeley.
OTHER: licensee.

Willie Mosforth was one of the greatest outside lefts of his era who served several clubs in the Sheffield area. Wily, fast-moving, versed in the arts of dribbling and crossing on the run, he was a great favourite with the spectators not least because of his wonderful screw-kick which he executed to perfection from all angles. An international trialist with teammate Bob Gregory for the North versus the South in 1881, he was eventually capped nine times by England between March 1877 and March 1882 and was quite outstanding on the wing when the Scots were beaten 5-4 in a thrilling encounter at The Oval in April 1879. In those days there were plenty of goals scored on the international circuit and in the 9 games he played for England, 54 were scored in total, Mosforth claiming just 3 of them. A very fit man, he often played two games in one day for different teams and, in one instance, he scored twice for Heeley and then soon afterwards hit a hat-trick for Providence against the same opposition. He was one of a number of local players who helped Lockwood Brothers reach the semi-final of the FA Cup in 1887. He was instrumental in helping form Sheffield Rovers when Wednesday refused to adopt professionalism. However, along with team-mate Tom Cawley, he put extra pressure on the club's president, John Holmes. Eventually Wednesday had a change of heart and decided to pay players a weekly wage. Once Mosforth swapped shirts with an opponent and played against Wednesday instead of for them because someone had offered him ten shillings to change sides. He also played in two FA Cup semi-final matches and two internationals in the space of ten days – such was his enjoyment of the game.

MOSS, Frank
Right half

Appearances: 23
Born: Aston, Birmingham, 16 September 1917
Died: Looe, Cornwall, 5 May 1997

CAREER
CLUBS: Worcester City, Wolverhampton Wanderers, WEDNESDAY (November 1935-May 1938), Aston Villa (player, coach).

Frank Moss

M

WARTIME GUEST APPEARANCES: Birmingham, Northampton Town, Wrexham, Stourbridge, Worcester City, Southampton, Watford.
OTHER: navy – First World War; ran a newsagent's in Kingstanding (Birmingham).

Blond-haired Frank Moss, resourceful and totally committed, was a fighter for club (football) and country (war). He joined the Owls as a professional in May 1936, making his League debut in the 2-2 draw at Liverpool in November 1936. However, with several players of similar style and ability competing to occupy the same position, Moss was transferred to Wolves, moving to Aston Villa a year later. Gaining a regular place in the side after the Second World War, he made 313 appearances for Villa. As a youngster he played in the North versus South schoolboy international trial in 1932 and was selected for the final of the English Schools Trophy that same season. He operated gunboats and destroyers during the Second World War in the Middle East. His father, Frank senior, and brother, Amos, both played for Aston Villa, and his dad also played for England.

MOSS, William
Left-back

Appearances: 1
Born: Heeley, Sheffield, 1860
Deceased by 1938

CAREER
CLUBS: Heeley, WEDNESDAY (free, August 1884-May 1885).
OTHER: licensee.

Bill Moss's only first-team appearance was against Long Eaton Rangers in the FA Cup in October 1885. He played alongside his brother for Heeley. He was employed as a file cutter.

MULLEN, James
Defender

Appearances: 254+8   Goals: 10
Born: Hedworth, Jarrow, 11 November 1952

CAREER
CLUBS: WEDNESDAY (April 1968-August 1980), Rotherham United, Preston North End, Cardiff City (player, assistant manager), Newport County (player-manager), Cardiff City (assistant manager), Aberdeen (assistant manager), Blackpool (manager), Burnley (manager), Sligo Rovers (manager), Telford United (manager), Merthyr Tydfil (manager), Little Drayton Rangers (manager), Bridgnorth Town (manager), Wales (Under-19 coach), Colwyn Bay (manager), Bromsgrove Rovers (manager).

During his playing career, Jimmy Mullen made 431 League appearances, more than half with Wednesday. Loyal, popular and dependable, he was certainly a wholehearted performer, a good reader of the game who captained Wednesday to promotion from the Third Division in 1980 after years of decline. He made his debut for the Owls as a fragile-looking eighteen year old

Jimmy Mullen

in a 4-4 draw with Hull City on Boxing Day 1970 and gained a regular place in the side in the mid-1970s, having his best seasons in 1975/76 and 1977/78. He later led Rotherham (1981) and Cardiff (1983) out of the same division to complete a rare treble. He was assistant manager to Alan Durban at Ninian Park, spent a few months in charge of struggling Newport and was Ian Porterfield's right-hand man at Aberdeen. Unfortunately he took Blackpool down from the Third to the Fourth Division but bounced back in style by guiding Burnley to the Fourth Division title in 1992.

MULLER, Adam Phillip
Striker

Appearances: 1+5
Born: Leeds, 17 April 1982

CAREER
CLUBS: Leeds United, Ossett Town, Thackley, WEDNESDAY (free, May 2000-June 2002), Worksop Town (L), Gresley Rovers, Wakefield & Emley.

A very talented youngster, Adam Muller failed to make headway at Hillsborough despite some useful performances in the reserves. His only senior start was at Burnley in October 2000.

MUMFORD, Albert Corbett
Utility

Appearances: 100   Goals: 34
Born: The Wrekin, 7 June 1865
Died: Loughborough, 30 June 1926

CAREER
CLUBS: Lockwood Brothers, WEDNESDAY (free, May 1889-September 1894), Loughborough Town.
OTHER: gas stoker.

A Football Alliance winner with the Owls in 1890, when he scored 12 goals in 19 games,

Albert Mumford had a very interesting career. His best position was right half but he also played at full-back, wing half, on the left wing and as an inside and centre forward, even taking over in goal in an emergency, when he was beaten by a penalty against Sunderland Albion in an Alliance fixture. Known as 'Clinks', he was certainly a hero at Wednesday's Olive Grove ground. A dashing sort of player with a drooping moustache, he was perhaps at his best during that 1889/90 Alliance season when the Owls also reached the final of the FA Cup – Mumford scoring against the winners Blackburn Rovers. A disappointing crowd of only 2,000 attended his benefit match in 1896. He died from cancer.

MURPHY, Daryl
Striker

Appearances: 4
Born: Waterford, Ireland, 15 March 1983

CAREER
CLUBS: Waterford, Luton Town (L), Southend United (L), Sunderland, WEDNESDAY (loan, November-December 2005).

Signed from Premiership strugglers Sunderland to inject some life back into a lacklustre attack, Daryl Murphy made only a handful of appearances for the Owls before returning to Wearside. Standing 6ft 3ins tall, Murphy cost then Black Cats manager Mick McCarthy £100,000 when he was signed from Waterford. He is a Republic of Ireland Under-21 international.

MURRAY, James Marshall
Centre forward

Appearances: 13   Goals: 4
Born: Belfast, 1886
Died: Belfast, 1950

CAREER

CLUBS: Cliftonville, Glentoran, Motherwell, WEDNESDAY (£1,250 with George Robertson, March-December 1910), Derry City.

A Northern Ireland international, capped three times versus England, Scotland and Wales in 1910 and 1911, Jimmy Murray was an all-action centre forward with pace and power. He had done well in Scottish League football before joining the Owls, scoring twice in eight games at the end of the 1909/10 season. He moved back home after nine months in Sheffield.

MUSTOE, Robin
Midfield

Appearances: 26+3 Goals: 1
Born: Witney, Oxfordshire, 28 August 1968

CAREER
CLUBS: Oxford United, Middlesbrough, Charlton Athletic, WEDNESDAY (free, August 2003-June 2004), Boston College, USA (coach).

A hard-working, skilful midfielder who covered acres of ground every time he played,

Robbie Mustoe

Robbie Mustoe was classed as a veteran when he joined the Owls, having already scored 44 goals in 560 appearances with his three previous clubs, playing in the Premiership with Middlesbrough whom he helped win the First Division title in 1995. As team captain, his class shone through at Hillsborough but injury kept him out of the team towards the end of 2003/04. He was one of several players out of contract and was duly released. His only goal for Wednesday was a last-gasp winner at home to Brighton in March 2004.

N

NAPIER, Charles Edward
Inside forward

Appearances: 56   Goals: 10
Born: Bainsford, Falkirk, 8 October 1910
Died: Falkirk, 5 September 1973

CAREER
CLUBS: Albion Rovers, Celtic, Maryhill Hibernian, Derby County, WEDNESDAY (£3,000, March 1938-September 1945), Stenhousemuir.
WARTIME GUEST APPEARANCES: Falkirk.

A two-footed, scheming inside forward, Charlie Napier was also a very useful marksman who scored over 200 goals in a long career. Capped three times by Scotland as a Celtic player (1932-35) and twice with Derby, he also represented the Scottish League on two occasions and appeared in one wartime international versus England in 1939. Positive in all he did, he scored 92 goals in 200 games for Celtic, partnering the prolific Jimmy McGrory most of the time. After gaining two Scottish Cup winners' medals (1931 and 1933) he moved into English football with Derby, for whom he netted 26 goals in 88 games before transferring to Wednesday, where he took over from George Drury. He missed only one League game in

Charles Napier

1938/39, scoring the first of his 10 goals for the Owls in a 3-2 win at West Ham in early September. He netted a hat-trick against Leeds in a Cup-tie in the April 1940 – 3 out of his 5 goals in 6 Second World War games.

NAPIER, Daniel
Half-back

Appearances: 11   Goals: 2
Born: Newcastle, 1885
Died: Newcastle, 1950

CAREER
CLUBS: WEDNESDAY (May 1906-June 1910), Northampton Town.

A Wednesday reserve for four seasons, Dan Napier made his Owls' debut on Boxing Day 1907, scoring in a 3-2 home defeat by Sunderland from the centre half position.

N'DUMBA-NSUNGU, Guylain
Striker

Appearances: 30+14   Goals: 11
Born: Kinshasha, Democratic Republic of Congo, 26 December 1982

CAREER
CLUBS: Amiens, Bolton Wanderers, WEDNESDAY (loan, September 2003, signed for £100,000, October 2003-January 2005), Preston North End (L), Colchester United, Darlington, Cardiff City, Gillingham.

Pacy 6ft 1in striker and penalty expert Guylain N'Dumba-Nsungu was leading scorer for Wednesday in his first season at Hillsborough, netting 10 goals in 32 appearances. After that his form waned and, following a loan spell with Preston, he moved 350 miles north to Darlington.

NEEDHAM, Liam Paul
Midfield

Appearances: 0+1
Born: Sheffield, 19 October 1985

CAREER
CLUBS: WEDNESDAY (May 2005), Gainsborough Trinity, Notts County.

Liam Needham, tricky and quick, developed through Wednesday's youth system and was on the fringe of first team football for quite a while before making his senior debut in the LDV Vans Trophy game versus Chester in September 2004.

NEVIN, George William
Full-back

Appearances: 2
Born: Lintz, Co. Durham, 16 December 1907
Died: Sheffield, 3 February 1973

CAREER
CLUBS: Newcastle United, Sunderland, WEDNESDAY (free, May 1930-January 1934), Manchester United, WEDNESDAY (£500, March 1934-May 1935), Burnley, Lincoln City, Rochdale.

Cool under pressure and able to challenge strongly for the ball, George Nevin, an ex-Durham miner, occupied both full-back positions during a varied career which saw him amass only 46 League appearances in 10 years. He made his senior debut for Wednesday against Blackburn in January 1933, when he deputised for Ted Catlin. His father, Ralph, three of his uncles and his nephew all played football.

NEWBOULD, Herbert
Outside left

Appearances: 8   Goals: 4
Born: Sheffield, 1858
Deceased by 1938

CAREER
CLUBS: Albion, WEDNESDAY (free, August 1880-May 1884; member of committee, director).
OTHER: president of the Hallamshire Harriers Athletic Club.

Bert Newbould served Wednesday for 4 seasons, during which time he played in 8 FA Cup games, scoring a hat-trick in a 12-2 first-round victory over Spilsby in November 1882.

NEWSOME, Jonathan
Defender

Appearances: 59+5 Goals: 4
Born: Sheffield, 6 September 1970

CAREER
CLUBS: WEDNESDAY (April 1987-June 1991), Leeds United, Norwich City, WEDNESDAY (£1.6 million, March 1996-June 2000), Bolton Wanderers (L), Gresley Rovers.

An ankle injury ended Jon Newsome's League career. Prior to that he had undergone a cartilage operation and had struggled with niggling injuries on and off for two years. He made 10 appearances in his first spell at Hillsborough and, prior to his return in 1996, played 88 games for Leeds and 76 for Norwich, helping the Elland Road club win the First Division championship and Charity Shield in 1992.

NIBLOE, Joseph
Full-back

Appearances: 129
Born: Corkerhill, Renfrewshire, 23 November 1903
Died: Doncaster, 25 October 1976

CAREER
CLUBS: Kilmarnock, Aston Villa, WEDNESDAY (£2,500 plus George Beeson, August 1934-May, 1938; part-time coach).
OTHER: worked at the Sheffield steelworks of Samuel Fox.

Joe Nibloe – a former brass moulder – began his career as a centre forward – he scored 5 times in 1 game for Shawfield – and had a few games as a wing half before settling down to become a strong, resilient full-back who cleared his lines with alacrity. He won 11 caps for Scotland between 1929 and 1932 and twice represented the Scottish League, collecting Scottish Cup winners' and runners-up medals with Kilmarnock in 1929 and 1932 respectively, before joining Aston Villa. He served the Owls splendidly for five years, making almost 130 appearances, helping the team win both the FA Cup and Charity Shield in 1935. Nibloe's son, John, who played for Sheffield United, Stoke, Doncaster Rovers and Stockport, was killed in a car crash in 1964, aged twenty-five.

NICHOLLS, Harold
Wing half

Appearances: 3
Born: Hednesford, November 1913
Died: Hednesford, circa 1985

CAREER
CLUBS: Hednesford Town, WEDNESDAY (£125, May 1934-August 1935), Wellington Town, Shrewsbury Town.

Reserve to Gavin Malloch, Harry Nicholls, an ex-miner, made his League debut against the champions Arsenal in September 1934. His father Herbert played for West Bromwich Albion.

NICHOLSON, George Henry
Inside left

Appearances: 1
Born: Sheffield, May 1863
Deceased by 1945

CAREER
CLUBS: WEDNESDAY (May 1885-April 1886), Tinsley.

George Nicholson's only game for Wednesday was against Long Eaton Rangers in an FA Cup-tie in October 1885.

NICHOLSON, Horace
Half-back

Appearances: 3
Born: Mexborough, 19 July 1895
Died: 1967

CAREER
CLUBS: WEDNESDAY (May 1913-November 1914), Bradford Park Avenue, Wath Athletic, Denaby United.
OTHER: Army – First World War.

The Owls conceded 10 goals in Horace Nicholson's 3 games, losing 6-2 to Burnley on his debut in January 1914, when he deputised for Jimmy Campbell.

NICHOLSON, Kevin John
Left wing-back

Appearances: 0+1
Born: Derby, 2 October 1980

CAREER
CLUBS: WEDNESDAY (April 1997-January 2001), Northampton Town (L), Forest Green Rovers, Notts County, Scarborough, Grimsby Town.

An England international at both Schoolboy and Youth levels, Kevin Nicholson never got a chance with the Owls, for whom he made just one substitute appearance, taking the field against Blackburn Rovers at home in August 2000. He later played over 100 games for Notts County.

NICOL, Stephen
Utility

Appearances: 43+11
Born: Irvine, Scotland, 11 December 1961

CAREER
CLUBS: Ayr United, Liverpool, Notts County, WEDNESDAY (free, November 1995-June 1998), West Bromwich Albion, Hull City, Doncaster Rovers, Boston Bulldogs (player-assistant coach), New England Revolution (assistant coach).

When experienced Scottish international Steve Nicol arrived at Hillsborough, he had already amassed a superb record at club level: 609 appearances and 48 goals. He had gained 27 full and 14 Under-21 caps and won 4 League championship, 3 FA Cup, one European Cup and one Charity Shield winners' medals with

Steve Nicol

Roland Nilsson

Liverpool, whom he served for over thirteen years. Stocky, mobile and durable, he could occupy a variety of positions, preferring a midfield role. He certainly added some composure to the Owls' side during his two and a half years at Hillsborough. He won the American League title with New England Revolution in 2003. He wore size thirteen boots.

NILSSON, Roland Nils Lennard
Full-back

Appearances: 185+1   Goals: 3
Born: Helsingborg, Sweden, 27 November 1963

CAREER
CLUBS: Helsingborg IF, IFK Gothenburg, WEDNESDAY (£375,000, December 1989-May 1994), Helsingborg IF, Coventry City, Helsingborg IF (player-coach), GAIS (manager).

At his peak, Roland Nilsson was a fine positional player, fit and strong, with superb passing ability. He was already an experienced campaigner when he moved to Hillsborough and went on to give the Owls terrific service, gaining a League Cup winners' medal in 1991. He made his debut at home to Luton Town in December

1989 and netted his first League goal in a 2-0 win over Norwich in April 1991. He fractured his ribs and punctured a lung playing for Coventry against Arsenal at Highbury in March 1999 and this effectively ended his career. Nilsson, who had three separate spells with Helsingborg, for whom he made over 200 appearances, was capped 99 times at senior level by Sweden. He was a huge favourite with the fans.

NIMMO, Ian Wallace
Forward

Appearances: 30+21   Goals: 13
Born: Boston, 23 January 1958

CAREER
CLUBS: WEDNESDAY (May 1974-June 1979), Peterborough United (L), Doncaster Rovers, Wyberton Colts (chairman).

Ian Nimmo scored 40 goals in 135 League appearances in 6 years with 3 clubs. A useful forward, he made his debut for the Owls as a substitute against Wigan in an FA Cup-tie in December 1975, netting his first goal six weeks later in a 2-0 League win over Chester.

NIXON, Eric Walter
Goalkeeper

Appearances: 0+1
Born: Manchester, 4 October 1962

CAREER
CLUBS: Manchester City, Wolverhampton Wanderers, Bradford City, Southampton, Carlisle United, Tranmere Rovers, Reading, Blackpool, Bradford City, Wigan Athletic, Tranmere Rovers (player-coach), Kidderminster Harriers, WEDNESDAY (player, coach, September 2003-May 2004), Tranmere Rovers (coach).

A real soccer journeyman, Eric Nixon, 6ft 4ins tall, agile, with a safe pair of hands, confident with his kicking and courageous, made over 650 appearances in 23 years while serving with 11 different League clubs. His final outing was for the Owls, a month before his fortieth birthday, against Grimsby in September 2003, when he was called off the subs' bench following an injury to Kevin Pressman. A great practical joker, he won the Leyland DAF Trophy with Tranmere in 1990 and collected a runners-up medal in the same competition a year later. Between August 1986 and January 1987, Nixon played in all four Divisions of the Football League – for Wolves (Fourth Division), Bradford City (Second Division), Southampton (First Division) and Carlisle (Third Division) – a record.

NOBLE, Frank
Full-back

Appearances: 2
Born: Sheffield, 26 October 1945

CAREER
CLUBS: WEDNESDAY (May 1962-July 1967), Peterborough United.

Frank Noble made his League debut against Burnley in August 1963 when he deputised for Brian Hill. His second outing came in October 1965, on the other flank, in place of the injured Don Megson. After leaving Hillsborough, he amassed 207 League appearances for Peterborough.

NOLAN, Ian Robert
Left-back

Appearances: 197+2   Goals: 4
Born: Liverpool, 9 July 1970

CAREER
CLUBS: Preston North End, Marine, Tranmere Rovers, WEDNESDAY (£1.7 million, August 1994-July 2000), Bradford City, Wigan Athletic, Southport, Halifax Town.

A Northern Ireland international, capped 18 times, Ian Nolan has an educated left foot. Versatile, with a good turn of speed, he made 114 appearances for Tranmere before joining the Owls, for whom he made his debut in a 4-3 Premiership defeat at Tottenham in August 1994. Agonisingly, he was one game short of playing in 200 competitive first-team matches for Wednesday. He suffered a stress fracture of the leg playing for Wigan at Brighton in 2001 and took time to recover.

O

OAKES, Scott John
Winger

Appearances: 7+20 Goals: 1
Born: Leicester, 5 August 1972

CAREER
CLUBS: Leicester City, Luton Town, WEDNESDAY (£450,000, August 1996-August 2000), Burnley, Crystal Palace, Cambridge United, Leyton Orient, St Albans City, Shelbourne.

An England Under-21 international, Scott Oakes made his League debut for Leicester in 1990 before going on to score 34 goals in 199 games for Luton. The son of Trevor Oakes, a member of the 1970s pop group Showaddywaddy, he came off the subs' bench no less than sixteen times in his first season at Hillsborough, but failed to establish himself in the side despite his enthusiastic commitment as an attacking midfielder. His only goal for Wednesday earned a point from a 1-1 draw at Sunderland in November 1996 – this came after he made his debut for the Owls against Aston Villa on the opening day of the 1996/97 season. His brother, Stefan, played for Leicester, Walsall, Crewe Alexandra, Notts County and Wycombe.

O'BRIEN, Burton
Midfield

Appearances: 49+20* Goals: 3*
Born: Johannesburg, South Africa, 10 June 1981

CAREER
CLUBS: St Mirren, Blackburn Rovers, Livingston, WEDNESDAY (July 2005).

After 22 games for St Mirren, but none for Blackburn, Scottish Youth and Under-21 international Burton O'Brien made almost 120 senior appearances for Livingston, with whom he won the League Cup and reached the semi-final of the Scottish Cup in 2004. An ever-present and top-scorer with eight League goals the following season, he was a strong, purposeful and creative midfielder with a splendid left foot, who had an excellent first season with the Owls.

O'BRIEN, Joseph Martin
Midfield

Appearances: 14+1 Goals: 2
Born: Dublin, 17 February 1986

CAREER
CLUBS: Stella Maris, Bolton Wanderers, WEDNESDAY (loan, December 2004-February 2005).

A Republic of Ireland Youth and Under-21 international, capped three times in the latter category, Joey O'Brien spent a very productive three months at Hillsborough, scoring on his debut against Hull. Bolton rewarded him with his first Premiership outing against Everton on the last day of 2004/05.

O'CONNELL, Patrick
Centre half

Appearances: 21
Born: Dublin, 8 March 1887
Died: London, 27 February, 1959

CAREER
CLUBS: Belfast Celtic, WEDNESDAY (£50 with Peter Warren, March 1909-May 1912), Hull City, Manchester United, Dumbarton, Ashington (player-manager), Racing Santander (manager), Atletico Madrid (manager), Betis Balompie (manager), Barcelona (manager), Real Betis (manager), Sevilla (manager), Real Santander (manager), Heulva (scout).
WARTIME GUEST APPEARANCES: Clapton Orient, Rochdale.

Pat O'Connell skippered Ireland to their first-ever home International triumph in 1914. He represented his country five times in all and also played in one victory international versus Scotland in 1919. A terrific performer at the heart of the defence, he made his League debut for the Owls against Bury on the last day of 1908/09 but was unable to command a regular place in the side after that, owing to the form of English McConnell, Jimmy Spoors and Bob McSkimming. After leaving Hillsborough, he made 73 appearances for Hull, 35 for Manchester United and, in January 1921, represented the North Eastern League against the Central League at Newcastle. He did exceptionally well in Spanish football, winning La Liga with Real Balompie in 1935.

O'DONNELL, Neil
Midfield

Appearances: 47   Goals: 2
Born: Glasgow, 21 December 1949

CAREER
CLUBS: Arsenal, Norwich City, Gillingham, WEDNESDAY (free, October 1975-May 1976), Signpost FC (manager), Sheffield Club (coach).
OTHER: now works for a Sheffield finance company.

Unfortunately, the career of Scottish Youth international Neil O'Donnell came to an abrupt end due a damaged back in 1976. Prior to that, he had appeared in well over 100 League games and made his debut for the Owls against Gillingham in October 1975.

O'DONNELL, Philip
Midfield

Appearances: 15+10   Goals: 1
Born: Bellshill, Glasgow, 25 March 1972

CAREER
CLUBS: Hamilton Colts, Motherwell, Celtic, WEDNESDAY (free, July 1999-June 2003), Coventry City, Motherwell.

Before joining the Owls, Scottish international Phil O'Donnell – winner of one full and eight Under-21 caps – made 145 appearances for Motherwell and 121 for Celtic, helping the Bhoys win the Scottish Cup in 1991 and 1995, and the Premier Division title in 1998. A hard-working left-sided player, he struggled with injuries at Hillsborough, starting only 15 matches, scoring his only goal in a 4-0 League Cup win over Watford in December 2001.

O'DONNELL, Ralph
Centre half

Appearances: 183   Goals: 3
Born: Cudworth, 17 October 1931

CAREER
CLUBS: WEDNESDAY (May 1949-May 1964), Buxton.

Fifteen years a professional at Hillsborough, Ralph O'Donnell was serving in the RAF when he made his League debut in November 1951 against Bury. He gained a regular place in the side in 1953 but after breaking a leg had to fight hard to reclaim his position, doing so two years later. He played very well when the Owls won the Second Division in 1952 and 1956, and during his last four seasons was a reliable reserve to Peter Swan. After quitting the game, he became deeply involved with schoolboy football at all levels. O'Donnell was highly regarded by those who played and worked with him.

OLIVER, Gavin Ronald
Defender

Appearances: 18+10
Born: Felling, Gateshead, 6 September 1962

CAREER
CLUBS: WEDNESDAY (April 1978-November 1985), Tranmere Rovers (L), Brighton & Hove Albion (L), Bradford City, Matlock Town.

A reserve during his seven years with Wednesday, Gavin Oliver made his debut in place of Mick Lyons at home to QPR in April 1983, having earlier appeared in his first League game when on loan with Tranmere. After leaving Hillsborough, he did very well with Bradford City, appearing in 381 competitive games.

OLSEN, Kim
Striker

Appearances: 7+5
Born: Herning, Denmark, 11 February 1979

CAREER
CLUBS: Ikast KFUM, Ikast FS, Holstebro, FC
Midtylland, Fortuna Dusseldorf, WEDNESDAY
(£15,000, February-October 2004), Silkeborg IF.

Kim Olsen, 6ft 4ins tall, struggled to get to grips
with Second Division football, and after just 12
games for the Owls – the first versus Port Vale
– he returned to Denmark.

O'NEILL, Henry
Defender

Appearances: 51
Born: Castle Ward, Newcastle, November 1894
Died: Newcastle, circa 1966

CAREER
CLUBS: WEDNESDAY (October 1919-August 1922),
Bristol Rovers, Swindon Town.
OTHER: Navy.

Harry O'Neill made his Owls' debut in a 4-2
defeat at Manchester City in October 1919. With
Jimmy Blair departing, there was big opportunity for O'Neill and he did well to a certain
extent. Able to occupy both full-back berths
and the centre half position, he made half of
his 51 appearances in 1920/21.

OWEN, Gary Alfred
Midfield

Appearances: 15+4
Born: St Helens, July 1958

CAREER
CLUBS: Manchester City, West Bromwich Albion,

Gary Owen

Panionios, WEDNESDAY (trial, July 1987, signed
for £35,000, August 1987-August 1988), Hannerdi,
Apoel Nicosia.
OTHER: art trader; now works for Manchester
radio station Centenary FM.

Early in his career, the highly skilled, round-
shouldered Gary Owen won a then record 22
England Under-21 caps and represented his
country's 'B' team and the Football League.
He left Manchester City to link up with ex-col-
league Peter Barnes and future Wednesday star
Steve Mackenzie at West Bromwich Albion. He
was well past his best – and had just recovered
from a fractured shin bone – when he joined
the Owls, for whom he made his debut as a
substitute against Oxford in August 1987. He
made 400 appearances in club football.

OWEN, Gordon
Winger

Appearances: 40   Goals: 7
Born: Barnsley, 14 June 1959

CAREER
CLUBS: Wolverhampton Wanderers, WEDNESDAY
(£50, July 1975-August 1983), Rotherham United (L),

Doncaster Rovers (L), Chesterfield (L), Cardiff City, Barnsley, Bristol City, Hull City, Mansfield Town, Blackpool, Carlisle United, Exeter City.
OTHER: worked for Yorkshire Water; a fine golfer and cricketer.

Signed by manager Len Ashurst, Gordon Owen found his progress at Hillsborough slow under his next boss, Jack Charlton, and made only 40 appearances in 8 years. Top-scorer for Cardiff in 1983/84, in a nomadic career he made over 350 senior appearances, scoring 73 goals. He played for the defeated Bristol City in the Freight Rover Trophy final in May 1986, missing a penalty in the shoot-out which secured victory for Mansfield. His father also played football.

OWEN, Niel
Midfield

Appearances: 1
Born: Bury, 14 October 1959

CAREER
CLUBS: WEDNESDAY (April 1976-May 1977), Rochdale, Stalybridge Celtic.
OTHER: worked in the printing business.

Niel Owen's only appearance for the Owls was against Oxford at home in May 1977. He came into a reshuffled team when three players were out injured.

OWUSU, Lloyd Magnus
Striker

Appearances: 30+30   Goals: 10
Born: Slough, 12 December 1976

CAREER
CLUBS: Slough Town, Brentford, WEDNESDAY (free, July 2002-March 2003), Reading (loan, signed later), Brentford.

A 6ft 1in striker, combative with an all-action style, Lloyd Owusu scored 73 goals in 195 appearances for Brentford before transferring to Wednesday, where he helped win the Third Division championship in 1999. Owls' fans thought highly of him but, unfortunately, he never quite reached the standard of play he achieved at Griffin Park. He had the pleasure of scoring on his debut in the Sheffield derby in September 2002 which the Owls won 2-0.

OXLEY, Bernard
Forward

Appearances: 14   Goals: 4
Born: Whitwell, 16 June 1907
Died: Worksop, 7 January 1975

CAREER
CLUBS: Chesterfield, Sheffield United, WEDNESDAY (£1,000, May 1934), Plymouth Argyle, Stockport County, Worksop Town, Scunthorpe & Lindsay United, Den Haag (coach), Worksop Town (manager), Leyton Orient (scout).
OTHER: served in the RAF; fireman; played cricket for Langworth.

Bernard Oxley, who preferred the right wing position, scored 14 goals in 129 outings in 6 years at Bramall Lane. He did well in his only season at Hillsborough and struck 10 times in 70 outings for Stockport. His brother Cyril played for Chesterfield, Southend and Liverpool.

P

PACKARD, Edgar John
Centre half

Appearances: 126   Goals: 1
Born: Mansfield, 7 March 1919
Died: Mansfield, 14 January 1996

CAREER

CLUBS: WEDNESDAY (December 1936-August 1952), Halifax Town, Mansfield Town (coach).
OTHER: Army; worked in the coal industry.

A strong, resolute and predominately right-footed defender, outstanding in the air, Edgar Packard's career was ruined by the Second World War. He was twenty-seven when he made his League debut, taking over from Cyril Turton for the home game with Barnsley in September 1946. He vied for the pivotal position with Turton and in 1949/50 was an ever-present in the side that won promotion from the Second Division. His only goal for the club was scored that season against West Ham when he raced eighty yards downfield, unchallenged, before firing the ball past Hammers' keeper Ernie Gregory. In November 1950 he fractured his jaw in a clash with Sunderland's Trevor Ford and, although he returned to action later that season, he was never the same player again, however he did go on to make 85 League appearances for Halifax. He served in North Africa and Italy during the Second World War, also appearing in twenty-five regional games for the Owls.

PALETHORPE, John Thomas
Centre forward

Appearances: 34   Goals: 17
Born: Leicester, 23 November 1909
Died: Slough, 6 June 1984

CAREER

CLUBS: Maidenhead United, Crystal Palace, Reading, Stoke City, Preston North End, WEDNESDAY (£3,100, December 1934-November 1935), Aston Villa, Crystal Palace, Chelmsford City, Shorts Sports, North Town (coach).
WARTIME GUEST APPEARANCES: Colchester United
OTHER: worked for The Fairley Aviation Co.

Jack 'SOS' Palethorpe was a big, bustling centre forward who won promotion from the Second

Jack Palethorpe

Division in successive seasons with Stoke and Preston (1933 and 1934) and then gained an FA Cup winners' medal with Wednesday in 1935, scoring 4 goals in 6 ties, including one inside two minutes at the start of the final against West Bromwich Albion. Although a well-liked player, it was a surprise when the Owls preferred him to Neil Dewar, but their choice proved right in the end. After leaving Hillsborough, he suffered relegation with Aston Villa (1936) and his career started to go down downhill. He did, however, play periodically during the Second World War, after effectively retiring from League football in 1939 with a record of 107 goals in 177 appearances. Initially a shoe maker, he was the life and soul of the party and was the dressing room comedian. His nephew, Chris Palethorpe, played for Reading.

PALMER, Carlton Lloyd
Utility

Appearances: 283+3   Goals: 18
Born: Rowley Regis, West Midlands, 5 December 1965

Carlton Palmer

CAREER
CLUBS: *Dudley Town, West Bromwich Albion, WEDNESDAY (£750,000, February 1989-June 1994), Leeds United, Southampton, Nottingham Forest, Coventry City, Watford, WEDNESDAY (loan, February-May 2001 and September-October 2001), Stockport County (player-manager), Darlington, Dublin City, Mansfield Town (caretaker-manager, then manager).*
OTHER: *BBC TV football pundit.*

The recipient of 18 full England caps (1982-89), the tall, long-striding Carlton Palmer also represented his country in 5 'B' and 4 Under-21 internationals, and during his career netted 40 goals in 739 appearances. He was sent off in his final game playing for Stockport against Cheltenham in February 2003, seventeen years and five months after making his League debut as a substitute for West Bromwich Albion at Newcastle. An enthusiastic footballer, he could play in any position but preferred to be in midfield, at the heart of the action. Surprisingly, the likeable Palmer never gained a winners' medal at club level. After his record £750,000 transfer to Hillsborough, he had his initial outing for the Owls in a 1-0 League defeat at Wimbledon in February 1989 and scored his first goal in a 3-0

victory over Millwall four weeks later. He took on difficult managerial jobs at Stockport and Mansfield.

PARKER, Raymond Dennis
Centre half

Appearances: 1
Born: Thurcroft, 27 January 1925

CAREER
CLUBS: *Chesterfield, WEDNESDAY (£3,250, April 1948-August 1949), Bradford City, Bolton Wanderers; scout for Doncaster Rovers, Hull City, Norwich City, West Bromwich Albion.*

Ray Parker was engaged by Wednesday as defensive cover. His only outing was against Fulham in October 1948, when he deputised for Cyril Turton in a 2-1 defeat.

PARKES, David
Centre half

Appearances: 50   Goals: 1
Born: Lye, Worcs, 18 June 1892
Died: Lye, 14 June 1975

CAREER
CLUBS: *Newcastle Town, Brighton & Hove Albion, WEDNESDAY (£1,500, March 1914-May 1920), St Luke's, Cradley Heath, WEDNESDAY (£75, December 1919-May 1920), Stoke, Llanelli, Rochdale, Macclesfield.*

The strong-tackling David Parkes made over 300 League appearances – 209 for Rochdale, for whom he starred in record wins in League and FA Cup versus Chesterfield (8-1) in 1926 and Crook (8-2) in 1927 respectively. The First World War interrupted his time with Wednesday following his record £1,500 transfer from Brighton. He had 42 outings before the hostilities, played in 7 regional games and made 8 more starts before transferring to Stoke.

PARKIN, Edward
Forward

Appearances: 1
Born: Rotherham, 1865
Deceased by 1938

CAREER
CLUBS: WEDNESDAY (1889/90)

Ted Parkin played for the Owls during their first season in the Football Alliance. He quickly went out of the game after making just one appearance.

PARTRIDGE, Richard Joseph
Midfield

Appearances: 8+12 Goals: 1
Born: Dublin, 12 September 1980

CAREER
CLUBS: Liverpool, Bristol Rovers, Coventry City, WEDNESDAY (June 2005-July 2006), Rotherham United.

Republic of Ireland Youth and Under-21 international (8 caps) Richie Partridge made 1 appearance for Liverpool, 6 for Bristol Rovers and 31 for Coventry before joining the Owls. A pacy player with good skills, he found himself on the subs' bench at the start of 2005/06.

PATERSON, Marr
Forward

Appearances: 21   Goals: 2
Born: Alloa, 1888
Died: Scotland, circa 1967

CAREER
CLUBS: Leith Athletic, WEDNESDAY (with James Campbell, February 1911-May 1912), Lochgelly United.

Hard working with good skills and a first-rate shot, Marr Paterson* made his League debut for Wednesday at Liverpool in February 1911, scoring his first goal three weeks later in a 1-0 win over Aston Villa. Two of his relatives, Peter and Robert Paterson, were also footballers.
*Some reference books list Paterson's Christian name as Mann.

PEACOCK, John
Left half

Appearances: 1
Born: Wigan, 15 March 1897
Died: Ince, Lancs, 4 March 1979

CAREER
CLUBS: Everton, Middlesbrough, WEDNESDAY (£500, August 1930-July 1931), Chelsea, Clapton Orient, Sleipnir (coach), Wrexham (trainer).

'Joe' Peacock was thirty-three when he made his only appearance for the Owls in place of Billy Smith in a 1-1 draw versus Chelsea in September 1930. A decade earlier, he had appeared in his first League game for Everton, versus Wednesday, going on to score 12 goals in 161 outings for the Merseysiders before joining Middlesbrough, with whom he won the Second Division championship in 1929. His form that season earned him a place on tour with England, playing against France, Belgium and Spain.

PEACOCK, Lee Anthony
Striker

Appearances: 42+15   Goals: 9
Born: Paisley, 9 October 1976

P

CAREER

CLUBS: Carlisle United, Mansfield Town, Manchester City, Bristol City, WEDNESDAY (free, July 2004-January 2006), Swindon Town.

Scotland Youth and Under-21 striker Lee Peacock scored 120 goals in over 400 appearances before joining the Owls. An AWS and LDV Vans Trophy winner with Carlisle and Bristol City, in 1997 and 2003 respectively, he had his off-days but, when on song, he was a very capable marksman who made his debut for the Owls versus Colchester in August 2004. At the end of that season he helped the team beat Hartlepool in the play-off final.

PEARCE, Andrew John
Defender

Appearances: 84+5 Goals: 4
Born: Bradford-on-Avon, 20 April 1966

CAREER

CLUBS: Stourbridge, Halesowen Town, Coventry City, WEDNESDAY (£500,000, June 1993-November 1995), Wimbledon, Aldershot.
OTHER: now works for a roofing company.

Andy Pearce was almost twenty-five when he made his League debut for Coventry against Leeds in March 1991. Strong in the air, he did well at Highfield Road before transferring to Hillsborough, where he partnered Des Walker at the heart of the Owls' defence. He held his place for two seasons.

PEARSON, John Stuart
Striker

Appearances: 80+48 Goals: 27
Born: Sheffield, 1 September 1963

CAREER

CLUBS: Sheffield Rangers, WEDNESDAY (free, June 1979-May 1985), Charlton Athletic, Leeds United, Rotherham United, Barnsley, Hull City, Carlisle United, Mansfield Town, Cardiff City, WEDNESDAY (n/c June-August 1995), Merthyr Tydfil, Stalybridge Celtic.
OTHER: licensee; football agent; works for Radio Sheffield.

Lanky John Pearson, who played for England at Youth and Under-21 levels, struggled to get first-team action due to the presence of McCulloch, Bannister, Cunningham and Chapman. He scored on his League debut in a 2-1 win over Bristol City in September 1980 and was on target again in each of his next three outings, later completing a rare treble by netting on his debuts in both the League Cup and FA Cup. A Second Division promotion-winner with the Owls in 1984, he quit League football in 1995 with a neck injury, having scored 66 goals in 419 appearances. He was Charlton's top marksman when they won promotion to the First Division in 1985.

PEARSON, Mark
Forward

Appearances: 42   Goals: 11
Born: Ridgeway, Derbyshire, 28 October 1939

CAREER

CLUBS: Manchester United, WEDNESDAY (£17,000, October 1963-May 1965), Fulham, Halifax Town.
OTHER: worked in engineering.

Mark Pearson played for England Schoolboys and Youth and, because of his sideburns, he was dubbed 'Pancho' at Old Trafford. An aggressive player, he was sent off twice in 1958 versus Burnley. He found it difficult to get into United's First XI but eventually made 80 appearances before transferring to Hillsborough. Unfortunately, two broken legs affected his career with Wednesday and, after recovering, he was signed for a second time by Vic Buckingham. He scored crucial goals for Fulham in April 1966 to save them from relegation.

PEARSON, Nigel Graham
Defender

Appearances: 218+6   Goals: 20
Born: Nottingham, 21 August 1963

CAREER
CLUBS: Heanor Town, Shrewsbury Town, WEDNESDAY (£250,000, October 1987-July 1994), Middlesbrough (player, coach), Carlisle United (director of coaching), Stoke City (assistant manager), West Bromwich Albion (assistant manager, coach, caretaker-manager), Newcastle (assistant manager), England Under-21 (assistant manager).

Nigel Pearson had a terrific career, making almost 550 appearances. After a fine spell with Shrewsbury, he spent almost seven years at Hillsborough, making his Owls' debut in a 3-0 defeat at Nottingham Forest in October 1987. He suffered with an injury during his first season but recovered and went on to produce some outstanding displays, starring in the 1991 League Cup final win over Manchester United. Despite two broken legs, he maintained a high degree of commitment was a superb tactician,

Nigel Pearson

cool under pressure and regularly set up counter-attacks. It was a sad occasion when he left Hillsborough, but he quickly bedded in at Middlesbrough and collected a First Division championship medal within ten months. He captained 'Boro into the Premiership in 1998, following demotion the previous season. He also lost two League Cup finals. After coaching England's Under-16 and Under-20 sides, he was reunited with Bryan Robson at West Bromwich Albion. His grandfather, Percy Mills, played for Notts County.

PEARSON, Stanley
Outside right

Appearances: 2
Born: Sheffield, March 1896
Deceased by 1975

CAREER
CLUBS: Wycliffe, WEDNESDAY (May 1917-August 1920), Main Bridge Old Boys, Huddersfield Town, Denaby United.

Stan Pearson scored 3 goals in 36 appearances for the Owls in the last two seasons of the First World War. He made his League debut at Manchester United in September 1919 and was one of five different players used on the right wing that season. He failed to make his mark with Huddersfield.

PEARSON, Trevor
Goalkeeper

Appearances: 4
Born: Sheffield, 4 April 1952

CAREER
CLUBS: WEDNESDAY (July 1970-May 1972), Heanor Town (L), Kiveton Park, Matlock Town, Norton Woodseats, Windsor BL.
OTHER: employed by British Aerospace.

Reserve to Peter Grummitt and Peter Springett, Trevor Pearson made his four League appearances for Wednesday in succession during March and April 1972, the first in a 4-0 defeat at Fulham.

PEMBRIDGE, Mark Anthony
Midfield

Appearances: 102+5   Goals: 14
Born: Merthyr Tydfil, 29 November 1970

CAREER
CLUBS: Luton Town, Derby County, WEDNESDAY (£900,000, July 1995-July 1998), Benfica, Everton, Fulham.

Mark Pembridge played for Wales Schoolboys and later added 1 Under-21, 2 'B' and 54 full caps to his collection, helping his country reach the play-offs in their qualifying group for Euro 2004. He made 70 appearances for Luton and 140 for Derby before joining Wednesday. He struggled to make an impact early on at Hillsborough but eventually asserted himself with some combative displays, despite suffering a leg injury at Arsenal which sidelined him for almost four

Mark Pembridge

months. In 2004, he reached the milestone of 500 club appearances. He made his debut for Wednesday in the InterToto Cup versus AGF Aarhus in July 1995.

PETRESCU, Daniel Vasile
Wing-back

Appearances: 30+11   Goals: 3
Born: Bucuresti, Romania, 22 December 1967

CAREER
CLUBS: Steaua Bucuresti, FC Olt, Foggia, Genoa, WEDNESDAY (£1.3m, August 1994-November 1995), Chelsea, Bradford City, Southampton, Nacional Bucuresti (player, assistant manager), Sportul Studentesc (coach).

A very talented footballer, Dan Petrescu was unsettled and, indeed, unsure of first-team football at Hillsborough after a fine first season and, as a result, was sold to Chelsea for £2.6 million – double the price Wednesday paid for him. He scored on his Premiership debut for the Owls in the 4-3 defeat to Spurs in August 1994 and later won the FA Cup, League Cup and ECWC with Chelsea. An Under-21 international, he went on to gain almost 100 full caps for Romania, whom he captained in the 1998 World Cup finals and Euro 2000. His career realised over 600 appearances.

PETRIE, Charles
Forward

Appearances: 59   Goals: 23
Born: Chorlton, summer 1895
Deceased by 1980

CAREER
CLUBS: Manchester City, Stalybridge Celtic, WEDNESDAY (£1,300, February 1922-June 1925), Swindon Town, Southampton, York City, Gorton Celtic (coach).

Charlie Petrie made his League debut for Stalybridge Celtic at the age of twenty-six and his first game for the Owls followed in February 1922 versus Nottingham Forest. A useful two-footed forward, able to occupy the three central positions, he struck his first goal for Wednesday forty-eight hours after his debut to clinch a 3-1 home win over Wolves. His League brought him 55 goals in 135 appearances.

PETRIE, Robert
Half-back

Appearances: 62   Goals: 3
Born: Dundee, 25 December 1870
Died: Arbroath, 15 March 1947

CAREER
CLUBS: Arbroath, Dundee East End, Dundee, WEDNESDAY (£50, April 1893-May 1897), Southampton, Dundee Wanderers (four spells), New Brighton Tower, Arbroath, Brechin City, Arbroath.
OTHER: moulder in a saw mill.

Brother of Jack Petrie – who scored 13 goals for Arbroath in a 36-0 Scottish Cup win over Bon Accord in 1885 – Bobby Petrie was an FA Cup winner with Wednesday in 1896. Utterly reliable, he was at his best when the chips were down and gave the Owls excellent service for four seasons, playing in all three half-back positions. He made the first of his 62 appearances versus Everton in September 1894 and played for Southampton in their 1900 FA Cup final defeat by Bury.

PICKERING, John William
Outside left

Appearances: 4
Born: Clowne, 1892
Deceased by 1978

CAREER
CLUBS: Frickley Colliery, WEDNESDAY (£50, February 1912-August 1914), Rotherham County.

Jack Pickering deputised for George Robertson in four League games in November 1913 – Wednesday losing three of them.

PICKERING, Michael John
Centre half

Appearances: 123+6   Goal: 1
Born: Mirfield, Huddersfield, 29 September 1956

CAREER
CLUBS: Barnsley, Southampton, WEDNESDAY (£50,000, October 1978-January 1984), Norwich City (L), San Diego Sockers (L), Bradford City (L), Barnsley (L), Rotherham United, York City, Stockport County.
OTHER: accounts manager for a brewery.

By the time he was twenty-two, tall, extrovert defender Mike Pickering had already appeared in all four Divisions of the Football League. He made 109 appearances for Barnsley, 51 for Southampton – helping Saints gain promotion to the First Division – and signed for Wednesday after the team had made a disappointing start to 1978/79. He immediately established himself in the side and, the following season, helped the Owls climb out of the Third Division before losing his place to Peter Shirtliff. When he quit competitive football in 1988 he had over 450 appearances under his belt.

PICKERING, William Henry
Left-back

Appearances: 9
Born: Sheffield, 10 December 1919
Died: 1983

CAREER
CLUBS: WEDNESDAY (May 1937-July 1948), Oldham

P

Athletic, Gainsborough Trinity, Worksop Town (coach, manager), Goole Town (manager).

Bill Pickering was a quick-moving, stylish defender, reserve to Ted Catlin at Hillsborough before the Second World War and to Hugh Swift after it. He made the first of his nine senior appearances against Sheffield United in October 1938 and played in 129 Second World War games.

PINNER, Michael John
Goalkeeper

Appearances: 7
Born: Boston, Lincolnshire, 16 February 1934

CAREER
CLUBS: Boston United, Notts County, Cambridge University, Hendon, Aston Villa, Arsenal, WEDNESDAY (amateur, December 1957 and March 1959), Queens Park Rangers, Manchester United, Chelsea, Arsenal, Swansea Town, Leyton Orient, Belfast Distillery.
OTHER: solicitor.

Mike Pinner was twenty-nine when he turned professional, having appeared in over 250 games as an amateur, winning 52 caps for England at that level. He starred in two Olympic Games (1956 and 1960), represented the RAF and played in four varsity matches. A fine shot-stopper, he made his first five appearances for Wednesday in succession in December 1957, when both McIntosh and Pllu were unavailable. Pinner played in thirty-two different countries.

PLATTS, Mark Anthony
Outside right

Appearances: 0+2
Born: Sheffield, 23 May 1979

CAREER
CLUBS: WEDNESDAY (May 1995-March 1999), Sheffield United, Torquay United, Worksop.
OTHER: steel erector.

An England Schoolboy and Youth international, Mark Platts made his two substitute appearances for the Owls in the Premiership, the first versus Wimbledon in February 1996 when he became the club's youngest-ever outfield player, aged sixteen years and 263 days. He joined Chris Waddle at Worksop.

PLLU, Charles Lamont
Goalkeeper

Appearances: 20
Born: Saltcoats, 28 February 1934

CAREER
CLUBS: Scarborough, WEDNESDAY (£1,050, December 1956-August 1958), Dundee, Portadown.
OTHER: worked in the building trade.

Charlie Pllu took over from the injured Dave McIntosh at the end of 1956/57 and deputised for Brian Ryalls the following season. He made his debut versus Everton in April 1957.

PORIC, Adem
Midfield

Appearances: 3+14
Born: Kensington, 22 April 1973

CAREER
CLUBS: WEDNESDAY (September 1993-January 1998), Southend United (L), Rotherham United, Notts County, Sydney Olympic, Northern Spirit, Gold Coast City.
OTHER: nightclub bouncer in Queensland.

Unable to establish himself in Wednesday's side, Adem Poric spent most of his five years at Hillsborough in the reserves or out on loan. He made his League debut versus Wimbledon in October 1993, coming on for Chris Bart-Williams. He did well in Australia.

PORTERFIELD, Ian John
Midfield

Appearances: 126+4   Goals: 5
Born: Dunfermline, 11 February 1946

CAREER
CLUBS: Leeds United, Heart of Midlothian, Glasgow Rangers, Raith Rovers, Sunderland, Reading, WEDNESDAY (£15,000, July 1977-December 1979), Rotherham United (manager), Sheffield United (manager), Aberdeen (manager), Chelsea (assistant manager), Reading (manager), Chelsea (manager), Zambia (national team manager), Ittihead (manager), Bolton Wanderers (assistant manager), Zimbabwe (coach), Oman (coach), Trinidad and Tobago (coach), Asante Kotoko (coach), Buskan Icons (manager).

Ian Porterfield will be remembered for his goal that won the FA Cup for Sunderland

Ian Porterfield

against Leeds in 1973. He made 268 appearances for the Wearsiders and recovered from a serious car crash in 1974 with determination and willpower. He made his debut for Wednesday versus Swindon in August 1977 and two seasons later starred in the Third Division promotion-winning side. He guided Rotherham to the Third Division title in 1981, lifted Sheffield United from the Fourth to the Second Division in three seasons and replaced Alex Ferguson at Aberdeen. In his last season at Pittodrie, the Dons lost 5-3 on penalties to Rangers in the Scottish League Cup final. While he was boss at Chelsea, the team were beaten by Wednesday in the 1992 League Cup semi-final. As manager of Zambia, Porterfield saw eighteen of the country's top players killed in a plane crash.

POTTS, Eric Thomas
Outside right

Appearances: 162+20   Goals: 25
Born: Liverpool, 16 March 1950

CAREER
CLUBS: Blackpool, New Brighton, Oswestry Town, WEDNESDAY (£4,000, December 1969-June 1977), Brighton & Hove Albion, Preston North End, Burnley, Bury, Witton Albion, Clitheroe.
OTHER: PFA coach.

Spotted by Wednesday scout Bill Evans, Eric Potts made his Owls' debut as a last-minute substitute against Charlton in October 1970. However, with Jackie Sinclair and John Sissons as the two main wingers, he had to wait until 1973 before gaining a regular place in the side. Once in, he stayed for three seasons, enjoying an unbeaten run of 94 appearances to February 1976. The fans' favourite, he lost his form and was replaced by Paul Bradshaw. Potts made 356 League appearances and scored 63 goals.

P

POTTS, Harry Archibald
Inside forward

Appearances: 2   Goals: 1
Born: Sheffield, circa 1865
Deceased by 1938

CAREER
CLUBS: Sheffield FC, WEDNESDAY (free, August 1897-May 1899).

Harry Potts scored on his debut for Wednesday in a 3-0 win over Bury in November 1897 when deputising for Bob Ferrier. He won the FA Amateur Cup with Sheffield in 1904

POULTER, Robert John
Goalkeeper

Appearances: 0+1
Born: Sheffield, 2 February 1986

CAREER
CLUBS: WEDNESDAY (April 2002-May 2005), Gretna.

A product of Wednesday's Academy, Bob Poulter came off the subs' bench to replace Ola Tidman for the second leg of the LDV Vans Trophy semi-final versus Blackpool in February 2004.

POWELL, Darryl Anthony
Midfield

Appearances: 8
Born: Lambeth, 15 January 1971

CAREER
CLUBS: Portsmouth, Derby County, Birmingham City, WEDNESDAY (free, January-June 2003), Colorado Rapids, Nottingham Forest.

A tall, experienced midfielder with 17 Jamaican caps under his belt, Darryl Powell joined

Wednesday on his thirty-second birthday and made his debut at Sheffield United forty-eight hours later. Prior to that, he had amassed over 400 appearances – 227 with Derby.

POWELL, Samuel
Centre forward

Appearances: 26   Goals: 9
Born: Holmes, Rotherham, 25 May 1899
Died: Sheffield, 21 June 1961

CAREER
CLUBS: Leeds United, WEDNESDAY (£1,400, March 1925-April 1930; trainer, coach).

Sam Powell scored the winning goal on his second outing, and home debut, for Wednesday versus Barnsley in March 1925 and three games later struck a hat-trick in a 3-1 victory over Fulham, ending that season with 6 goals in 8 starts. Fighting for a first-team place with Harry Hill, he helped the Owls gain promotion to the top flight, but then made only six appearances in three years, retiring after breaking his leg. Succeeding George Irwin as trainer in 1937, Powell served Wednesday for thirty-four years.

POWELL, William Methven Phillips
Left half

Appearances: 22
Born: Sutton-in-Ashfield, 21 January 1901
Died: Sutton-in-Ashfield, May 1981

CAREER
CLUBS: WEDNESDAY (August 1924-May 1927), Grimsby Town, Southend United.

A valued and reliable defender, Bill Powell made all of his senior appearances in his first season, replacing Bill Collier. He helped Grimsby gain promotion from the Second Division.

PRENDERGAST, Michael John
Forward

Appearances: 192+14   Goals: 59
Born: Denaby, 24 November 1950

CAREER
CLUBS: WEDNESDAY (October 1966-May 1978), Barnsley, Halifax Town.

A striker with an eye for goal, Mick Prendergast was injured several times during his career but always came back for more. He scored on his League debut at Newcastle in April 1969 – a match which was won 3-2 – and was a regular in the side by 1970/71, showing his mettle by netting 16 times in 41 outings. The club's Player of the Year in 1974, he ended that campaign with a broken leg and is now disabled.

PRESSMAN, Kevin Paul
Goalkeeper

Appearances: 474+4
Born: Fareham, 6 November 1967

CAREER
CLUBS: WEDNESDAY (April 1984-June 2004), Stoke City (L), West Bromwich Albion (L), Leicester City,

Kevin Pressman

Leeds United, Coventry City, Mansfield Town, Portadown, Scunthorpe United (coach).

The third highest appearance-maker in Owls' history – behind Andy Wilson and Jack Brown – Kevin Pressman served the club for twenty years. One of thirteen players released in June 2004, he represented England at Schoolboy, Youth, 'B'(3 caps) and Under-21 levels, made his League debut at Southampton in September 1987 – in place of Martin Hodge – and was in and out of the first team until establishing himself as number one in 1993/94. A fine shot-stopper with good reflexes, he tipped the scales at 15st 5lbs before leaving Hillsborough.

PRICE, Arthur
Utility

Appearances: 82   Goals: 3
Born: Sheffield, September 1892
Died: Scarborough, May 1964

CAREER
CLUBS: Sheffield United, Worksop Town, Leeds City, WEDNESDAY (£750, October 1919-November 1922), Southend United, Scunthorpe & Lindsay United, Scarborough (manager).
OTHER: licensee; steward.

Scorer of 84 goals in almost 200 appearances in all competitions for Leeds, Arthur Price joined the Owls when the Elland Road club went bust. He made his debut against Manchester City (1919) and had 13 games at inside left before switching to left half.

PRIESTLEY, R.
Forward

Appearances: 2   Goals: 1
Born: Sheffield, 1873
Deceased by 1935

P

CAREER

CLUBS: WEDNESDAY (1894/95).

Reserve Priestley scored from inside right on his League debut at Liverpool in March 1895 and was on the right wing in his second game versus West Bromwich Albion forty-eight hours later.

PRINCE, Arthur
Outside left

Appearances: 54   Goals: 7

Born: Bucknall, Staffs, 8 December 1902

Died: Nuneaton, September 1980

CAREER

CLUBS: Port Vale, WEDNESDAY (£750, May 1924-June 1928), Hull City, Chester, Walsall, Bristol Rovers.

Arthur Prince won the Second Division championship with the Owls in 1926. Blessed with a strong shot and good pace, he made his debut versus Derby in September 1924.

PRIOR, George
Utility

Appearances: 37

Born: Ashington, Co. Durham, 2 March 1898

Died: Ashington, 1 April 1977

CAREER

CLUBS: Blyth Spartans, WEDNESDAY (£350, August 1920-August 1924), Watford.

OTHER: miner.

George Prior spent four seasons with Wednesday, making his League debut at centre forward versus Birmingham in October 1920 before switching to full-back. He made 174 League appearances for Watford. His brother Jack and son Ken were both professional footballers.

PROCTOR, Mark Gerard
Midfield

Appearances: 69   Goals: 5

Born: Middlesbrough, 31 January 1961

CAREER

CLUBS: Leeds United, Middlesbrough, Nottingham Forest, Sunderland, WEDNESDAY (£275,000, September 1987-March 1989), Middlesbrough, Tranmere Rovers, South Shields, St Johnstone, Hartlepool United, Middlesbrough (coach).

England Youth international Mark Proctor made 500 appearances in League football. He was vastly experienced when he signed for Wednesday, for whom he made his debut versus Southampton in September 1987. However, he wanted more than Third Division football and returned to Middlesbrough after eighteen months, playing for them in the Zenith Data Systems Cup final versus Chelsea and in the Premiership in 1992/93.

PROPHETT, Colin George
Defender

Appearances: 120+9   Goals: 7

Born: Crewe, 8 March 1947

CAREER

CLUBS: WEDNESDAY (September 1967-June 1973), Norwich City, Swindon Town, Chesterfield, Crewe Alexandra, Cardiff City (coach).

Colin Prophett made 430 League appearances in thirteen years – 160 with Swindon. He occupied six different positions, playing best in central defence. After two seasons of second and third team football, he made his Owls debut versus Liverpool at the start of that traumatic 1969/70 relegation campaign. Prophett remained loyal to the club and had two decent years before Peter Swan returned. A Yorkshire League cricketer, he worked in insurance after retiring.

PROUD, Pattison
Left half

Appearances: 1
Born: West Auckland, 1883
Died: Newcastle, 31 March 1937

CAREER
CLUBS: Bishop Auckland, WEDNESDAY (free, August 1906-April 1907).
OTHER: miner.

Pat Proud's only game for the Owls was against Middlesbrough in January 1907, when he deputised for Bill Bartlett.

PROUDLOCK, Adam David
Striker

Appearances: 49+18   Goals: 19
Born: Telford, 9 May 1981

CAREER
CLUBS: Wolverhampton Wanderers, Clyde, Nottingham Forest, Tranmere Rovers, WEDNESDAY (loan, December 2002-January 2003; signed for £150,000, September 2003-January 2006), Ipswich Town (loan, signed later), Stockport County.

England Youth international Adam Proudlock scored 17 goals in 84 appearances for Wolves. He was a hard worker and willing competitor who scored a hat-trick in the 4-0 FA Cup win over Salisbury in November 2003. Unfortunately, Proudlock broke his leg in January 2005 and, as a result, missed the Owls' subsequent promotion success. Fit to start the new campaign, he was disciplined in September 2005 following an internal dispute and eventually moved to Ipswich.

PROUDLOVE, Andrew George
Outside left

Appearances: 12+5 Goals: 1
Born: Buxton, 15 January 1955

CAREER
CLUBS: West Ham United, WEDNESDAY (free, September 1975-February 1976), Norwich City, Hereford United, Buxton, Port Vale, Macclesfield Town, Nykopping, Bulova, Atvidabergs FF, Turku, Rio Ave.
OTHER: property developer.

Andy Proudlove made only 37 appearances in the Football League, his debut for the Owls being a substitute appearance for Prendergast in a 4-0 win over Grimsby in September 1975. He did well in Sweden and Hong Kong.

PRUDHAM, Charles Edward
Forward

Appearances: 15+6 Goals: 3
Born: Pelaw, Dateshead, 12 April 1952

CAREER
CLUBS: WEDNESDAY (August 1967-November 1974), Partick Thistle (L), Carlisle United, Hartlepool United, Workington, Stockport County, Bournemouth.
OTHER: probation officer; now works for the prison service.

Reserve Eddie Prudham made his debut for the Owls at Cardiff in January 1971 when he deputised for Jackie Sinclair on the right wing. He scored 24 goals in 95 games for Stockport.

PRYCE, John
Forward

Appearances: 59   Goals: 4
Born: Renton, 25 January 1874
Died: Scotland, December 1905

CLUBS: Renton, Hibernian, Glossop North End, WEDNESDAY (£75, February 1899-May 1901), Queens Park Rangers, Brighton & Hove Albion.

Jack Pryce was signed by Wednesday with relegation looming. An experienced forward, having scored plenty of goals north of the border, it was hoped he would inject some firepower into the front line. He failed to find the net in his eight games in the season the Owls went down. He played in 35 games the following season when the Second Division championship was won at the first attempt. He was replaced by Harry Chapman.

PUGH, John Graham
Midfield

Appearances: 149+7   Goals: 8
Born: Hoole, Chester, 12 February 1948

CAREER
CLUBS: WEDNESDAY (April 1963-May 1972), Huddersfield Town, Chester, Barnsley, Scunthorpe United.
OTHER: licensee.

Graham Pugh was capped twice by Wales at under-21 level as a Wednesday player. Quick, competent and hard working, he broke into the first team in 1966, scoring on his FA Cup debut in the semi-final clash with Chelsea. He then played in the final against Everton and had a decent 1966/67, but a series of injuries disrupted his game. Bouncing back strongly, he showed plenty of determination, but things were changing at Hillsborough and in 1972 he joined Huddersfield, retiring with over 500 senior games to his credit.

QUIGLEY, Edward
Forward

Appearances: 78   Goals: 52
Born: Bury, 13 July 1921
Died: Blackpool, 16 April 1997

CAREER
CLUBS: Bury, WEDNESDAY (£12,000, October 1947-December 1949), Preston North End, Blackburn Rovers, Bury, Mossley (player-manager), Bury (coach, scout), Stockport County (manager), Blackburn Rovers (assistant manager, manager, chief scout, youth manager), Blackpool (scout).

Big and broad, Eddie Quigley was not a picture of athleticism, but he was a very competent marksman who netted 200 goals in a fine career. He went straight into the Owls' side at inside right for the game at Plymouth in October 1947, top-scoring that season with 23 goals and again in 1948/49 with 17. He hit ten more goals to help the Owls on their way to promotion from the Second Division the following term, before becoming the most expensive footballer in Britain when he joined Preston for £26,500. After winning the Second

Edward Quigley

Division, he switched to Blackburn, for whom he netted 95 goals. He twice scored four goals in a game for Wednesday – versus West Ham in December 1947 and Chesterfield in September 1949 – and won two England 'B' caps.

QUINN, Alan
Midfield

Appearances: 169+11   Goals: 17
Born: Dublin, 13 June 1979

CAREER
CLUBS: WEDNESDAY (December 1997-July 2004), Sunderland (L), Sheffield United.

Alan Quinn's wholehearted approach made him a firm favourite with the Hillsborough faithful. An eager player, he made his Owls' debut as a substitute versus Everton in April 1998 and was a regular in the side in 1999/2000. Honoured by the Republic of Ireland at under-18 level, he won 8 Under-21 and 6 full caps and in December 2005 became the first player in 112 years of League football to score for both Wednesday and United in a Sheffield derby, when he netted the winner for the Blades at Bramall Lane. His brothers Stephen and Keith were at United with him.

QUINN, James
Left-back

Appearances: 52   Goals: 1
Born: Kilsyth, Scotland, 23 November 1947
Died: Croy, Lanark, 24 April 2002

CAREER
CLUBS: Celtic, Clyde, Maryhill Harp, WEDNESDAY (free, January-July 1976), Melbourne, Hamilton Academical.
OTHER: delivery driver.

After making 41 appearances for Celtic, Jim Quinn – whose grandfather played for Scotland

– went straight into the Owls' first team at left-back at York, partnering Peter Rodrigues. Steady and reliable, his enormous potential was never fulfilled after he was injured at Mansfield in April 1976.

QUINN, John David
Inside forward

Appearances: 184+10 Goals: 24
Born: St Helens, 30 May 1938

CAREER
CLUBS: Burnley, Everton, WEDNESDAY (£1,250, April 1959-November 1967), Rotherham United.
OTHER: owned sports shops with Peter Eustace and Gerry Young; now runs a charity team (Johnny Quinn All Stars).

It took 'Quinny' four years to establish himself in Wednesday's first team but, once in, he proved to be an outstanding asset. Essentially an inside forward, he became a utility player as time progressed and when he retired in 1976, after more than 400 appearances, he was able to look back on a job well done. National Service and the form of Tommy Craig restricted his outings early on, but he developed into a quality player. He helped the Owls win promotion to the First Division in 1961 and was a member of Wednesday's 1966 FA Cup final side. After losing his place in midfield and failing as a fullback, he became a hero at Rotherham.

QUINN, Stephen James
Forward

Appearances: 13+5 Goals: 2
Born: Coventry, 15 December 1974

CAREER
CLUBS: Birmingham City, Blackpool, Stockport County, West Bromwich Albion, Notts County, Bristol Rovers, Willem II, MK Dons, WEDNESDAY

(free, January-August 2005), Peterborough United, Bristol City.

James Quinn made his debut for Birmingham as an apprentice but failed to make an impact at St Andrew's. He scored 10 goals in 123 games for West Bromwich Albion, losing his place after ex-Wednesday star Gary Megson moved in as manager. A Northern Ireland international at youth, Under-21 and 'B' team levels, Quinn has over 40 full caps to his credit and appeared for the Owls in the 2005 play-off final versus Hartlepool.

QUIXALL, Albert
Inside forward

Appearances: 260   Goals: 65
Born: Sheffield, 9 August 1933

CAREER
CLUBS: WEDNESDAY (July 1948-September 1958), Manchester United, Oldham Athletic, Stockport County, Altrincham.
OTHER: scrap metal dealer.

Albert Quixall

An England Schoolboy international, flaxen-haired Albert Quixall was the golden boy of Hillsborough in the 1950s and was the first footballer to wear short shorts – long before they were *á la mode*. With his blond hair, dapper appearance and boyish good looks, he was adored by the girls. Out on the field of play he was brilliant at times, his creativeness, long passing and general all-round skill earning him 5 full England caps, plus 3 at Under-23 and 3 at 'B' team levels. He also represented the Football League on three occasions. He helped the Owls win the Second Division in 1952 and 1956 and, after leaving Hillsborough for a British record transfer fee of £45,000, he gained an FA Cup winners' medal with Manchester United in 1963. Some say he never quite hit the heights expected of him as a Wednesday player and it was no real surprise when manager Harry Catterick sold him – although some fans were bitterly disappointed. The first major signing made by United after the Munich air crash, Quixall scored 56 goals in 183 games for the Reds.

R

RAMSBOTTOM, Neil
Goalkeeper

Appearances: 22
Born: Blackburn, 25 February 1946

CAREER
CLUBS: Bury, Blackpool, Crewe Alexandra, Fulham, Coventry City, WEDNESDAY (£12,750, August 1975-July 1976), Plymouth Argyle, Blackburn Rovers, New Jersey Americans, Chorley, Sheffield United, Miami Americans, Bradford City, Bournemouth.
OTHER: financial consultant.

Neil Ramsbottom played over 200 times for Bury. After that he became a soccer journey-man, retiring in 1983 after amassing 450 appearances. He made his Owls debut in a 3-3 draw with Brighton in August 1975 and shared the no.1 spot with Peter Fox in his only season at Hillsborough.

RAMSBOTTOM, Thomas
Left-back

Appearances: 12
Born: Idle, Yorkshire, 13 January 1901
Died: Idle, December 1972

CAREER
CLUBS: Bradford City, Pontypridd, WEDNESDAY (£400, December 1921-March 1922).

Replacing the injured Harry O'Neill, Tom Ramsbottom did well in his 12 League games for the Owls, making his debut at Clapton Orient in December 1921.

RATCLIFFE, Milton Archie
Forward

Appearances: 12   Goals: 4
Born: Blackburn, 30 January 1893
Died: Ruislip, Middlesex, 25 January 1981

CAREER
CLUBS: Nelson, Blackpool, WEDNESDAY (£150, July 1921-January 1922), Tranmere Rovers.

Recruited as cover for Johnny McIntyre and Sam Taylor, Archie Ratcliffe scored on his Owls' debut in a 3-2 League defeat by Barnsley in August 1921.

REDDY, Michael
Striker

Appearances: 27+5 Goals: 5
Born: Kilkenny, Ireland, 24 March 1980

CAREER
CLUBS: Sunderland, Swindon Town, Hull City, Barnsley, York City, WEDNESDAY (loan, January-April 2003; again October-November 2003), Grimsby Town.

A Republic of Ireland international at both Youth and Under-21 levels – with eight caps won in the latter category – Mike Reddy had an excellent first spell at Hillsborough, but failed to recapture that form when he returned. He made his debut for the Owls at Wolves in February 2003 (lost 4-0) and was joint top-scorer for Grimsby in 2004/05.

REED, Percy
Utility

Appearances: 18
Born: Stokesley, 5 December 1890
Died: Yorkshire, September 1970

CAREER
CLUBS: Royal Navy, WEDNESDAY (May 1919-June 1921), Chesterfield, Doncaster Rovers, Denaby United, York City.

Percy Reed was among several new players signed by Wednesday after the First World War. Preferring a half-back role, he made his League debut in the 0-0 home draw with Notts County in September 1919. He failed to make an impact with any of his other clubs.

REEVES, David Edward
Forward

Appearances: 10+12   Goals: 3
Born: Birkenhead, 19 November 1967

CAREER
CLUBS: Heswall, WEDNESDAY (August 1986-August 1989), Scunthorpe United (L), Burnley (L), Bolton Wanderers, Notts County, Carlisle United,

R

Preston North End, Chesterfield, Oldham Athletic, Chesterfield, Ards, Mansfield Town, Swindon Town, Scarborough.

David Reeves made his 600th League appearance for Chesterfield versus QPR in January 2004 – having scored twice when making his debut for Scunthorpe versus Exeter in 1986. His initial outing for the Owls followed in September 1988 versus Arsenal and he scored his first League goal for the club a month later in a 2-1 win at Southampton. With a never-say-die attitude, he gave nothing less than 100 per cent. He won a Third Division medal with Carlisle in 1995 and one feels he was a player who slipped through the Hillsborough net!

REEVES, Frederick
Outside right

Appearances: 1
Born: Mexborough, 1900
Deceased by 1975

CAREER
CLUBS: Mexborough Town, WEDNESDAY (£100, July 1920-August 1921).

One of nine players used by the Owls at outside right in 1920/21, Fred Reeves' only League game was at Bury in the April when he deputised for Jack Smelt.

REGAN, William
Half-back

Appearances: 9
Born: Doncaster, 1872
Died: London, 1920

CAREER
CLUBS: WEDNESDAY (June 1894-August 1895 and August 1896-April 1898), Millwall Athletic, Brentford.

A Wednesday reserve, Bill Regan made his League debut at right half versus Liverpool in September 1895 (lost 2-1). He also played at centre half.

REILLY, John
Outside right

Appearances: 2
Born: Sheffield, 1900
Deceased by 1980

CAREER
CLUBS: Ryhope Colliery, WEDNESDAY (August 1920-May 1921), Castleford.

Another of the nine players used by the Owls at outside right in 1920/21, 'Paddy' Reilly made the first of his two appearances against Barnsley on the opening day. His second followed three months later versus West Ham. He worked and played for Sheffield Tramways.

REYNOLDS, John Bernard
Outside right

Appearances: 2
Born: Manchester, 23 September 1881
Died: Amsterdam, 8 November 1962

CAREER
CLUBS: Manchester City, Burton United, Grimsby Town, WEDNESDAY (£275, July 1905-May 1907), Watford, New Brompton, Rochdale, Switzerland (coach), Ajax Amsterdam (coach, trainer).
OTHER: Army – First World War.

Neat, compact, stocky in build, two-footed and a rare handful for defenders, Jack Reynolds had only two League outings with Wednesday – against Sunderland in April 1906 and Stoke in March 1907. After leaving the Owls, he played in the Southern League. Reynolds, who spent four years in a German concentration camp during the First World War, was rewarded with a pension by Ajax for outstanding service as a coach and trainer. His brother, Bill, also played professional football

Owls win the Charity Shield. Thereafter he worked overtime in a struggling side and was eventually replaced by Fred Walker.

RHODES, E.
Utility

Appearances: 6　　Goals: 8
Born: Sheffield: 1858
Deceased by 1938

CAREER
CLUBS: WEDNESDAY (seasons 1880-82).

Rhodes scored on his FA Cup debut for Wednesday against Turton in January 1881 and became the first player to register a four-timer for the club, doing so in a 5-1 cup win at Staveley a year later. He occupied three different positions for the Owls – outside right, centre forward and right-back. His Christian name may have been Ephraim.

RHODES, Richard Alma
Wing half

Appearances: 60
Born: Wolverhampton, 18 February 1908
Died: Wolverhampton, 21 January 1993

CAREER
CLUBS: Redditch United, Wolverhampton Wanderers, WEDNESDAY (£3,200 plus Idris Lewis, October 1935-March 1938), Swansea Town, Rochdale.
OTHER: licensee; a champion canary breeder (national champion, 1973) and a pigeon fancier.

An England Junior international versus Scotland in 1925, Dicky Rhodes was a skilful half-back who helped Wolves win the Second Division in 1932. He scored 7 goals in 159 games for the Molineux club before making his debut for the Owls in place of Wilf Sharp versus Birmingham in October 1935. Four days later he helped the

RICHARDS, Anthony D.
Outside right

Appearances: 8　　Goals: 1
Born: Dudley, 1873
Deceased by 1958

CAREER
CLUBS: Stourbridge, WEDNESDAY (1895/96).

Reserve Tony Richards deputised for Archie Brash when making his League debut versus Burnley in December 1895, scoring his only goal against Blackburn a month later.

RICHARDS, Frederick
Inside right

Appearances: 3　　Goals: 1
Born: Burton-on-Trent, 1875
Died: Burton-on-Trent, 1942

CAREER
CLUBS: Burton Wanderers, Derby County, WEDNESDAY (£100, February-August 1899), Burton Wanderers.

Fred Richards scored against Aston Villa in March 1899, when the remaining ten and a half minutes were played of a game that had been abandoned on 26 November 1898. He had made his debut in a 2-1 defeat by Everton earlier in the month.

RICHARDSON, Edward
Forward

Appearances: 11
Born: Easington, Co. Durham, 4 July 1901
Died: Fleetwood, 1972

R

CAREER

CLUBS: South Shields, Newcastle United, Huddersfield Town, WEDNESDAY (exchange for Syd Binks, November 1924-July 1925), South Shields, York City, Bradford City, Ashington.

Ted Richardson – reserve to many star players at Newcastle and Huddersfield – worked hard with the Owls, for whom he made his debut on the left wing in a 2-0 win over Wolves in November 1924.

RICHARDSON, R.
Centre forward

Appearances: 24   Goals: 10
Born: Ayr, circa 1870
Deceased by 1948

CAREER
CLUBS: Hurlford, WEDNESDAY (free, March 1891-September 1892), Ayr United.

A key member of Wednesday's Alliance side of 1891/92, Richardson scored a goal in each of his three FA Cup outings for the club in that same season, against Bolton Wanderers, Small Heath and West Bromwich Albion – the eventual winners.

RICKETT, Walter
Outside left

Appearances: 97   Goals: 11
Born: Sheffield, 20 March 1917
Died: Kettering, 25 July 1991

CAREER
CLUBS: Sheffield United, Blackpool, WEDNESDAY (£7,000, October 1949-September 1952), Rotherham United, Halifax Town, Ballymena, Dundalk (manager), Sittingbourne (manager), Ramsgate (manager), Gravesend (manager), Crystal Palace (assistant manager).

OTHER: Second World War munitions worker; worked for a cable company.

Walter Rickett was a lively, two-footed winger with a strong attacking flair, dangerous when cutting inside. He scored almost 60 goals in 200 Second World War appearances for Sheffield United and after leaving Bramall Lane played in the 1948 FA Cup final for Blackpool against Manchester United. An England 'B' international, capped with Redfern Froggatt and Hugh Swift versus Switzerland in 1950, he twice helped Wednesday gain promotion from the Second Division (1950 and 1952).

RIMMER, Ellis James
Outside left

Appearances: 419   Goals: 140
Born: Birkenhead, 2 January 1907
Died: Formby, 16 March 1965

CAREER
CLUBS: Everton, Whitchurch, Tranmere Rovers, WEDNESDAY (£1,850, February 1928-August 1938), Ipswich Town.
OTHER: licensee in Sheffield and Formby.

Ellis Rimmer, who played with Dixie Dean at Tranmere, scored two late goals to secure a 4-2 FA Cup final victory for the Owls versus West Bromwich Albion in 1935. Six months later he gained a Charity Shield winners' prize versus Arsenal, having been in the losing 'Shield' side five years earlier. Fast, tricky, a superb crosser of the ball and strong in shooting, he was well pro-portioned, took his fair share of knocks and was twice a League championship winner with the Owls in 1929 and 1930. He was a regular in the Owls' side from the day he joined until March 1938, when Irishman 'Jim' Fallon took over on the left wing, forming a great partnership with Mark Hooper. Capped 4 times by England against Scotland (scoring two goals), Germany, Austria and Spain, Rimmer also represented the Sheffield Association on 5 occasions against Glasgow. An accomplished musician, he was a pianist at a local cinema. Two of his relatives, Albert Rimmer and Jackie Woolfall Rimmer, were professional footballers.

RIPLEY, Stuart Edward
Forward

Appearances: 5+1   Goals: 1
Born: Middlesbrough, 20 November 1967

CAREER
CLUBS: Middlesbrough,   Bolton   Wanderers, Blackburn Rovers, Southampton, WEDNESDAY (loan, March-May 2001), Sheffield United.

Stuart Ripley's career was almost over when he joined the Owls. He continued to play for another season before announcing his retirement in 2002, with 622 club appearances and 51 goals under his belt. An old-fashioned winger with strength and pace, he loved to take on his full-back. He spent eight years at Middlesbrough, during which time he gained 3 Youth and 8 Under-21 caps for England and, after moving to Blackburn, won 2 full caps, also helping Rovers win the Premiership in 1995. His only goal for the Owls was scored in his second outing, in a 4-1 win over Crystal Palace in April 2001.

RITCHIE, John Henry
Striker

Appearances: 105+1   Goals: 45
Born: Kettering, 12 July 1941
Died: Stoke-on-Trent, 23 February 2007

CAREER
CLUBS: Kettering Town, Stoke City, WEDNESDAY (£80,000, November 1966-July 1969), Stoke City, Stafford Rangers.
OTHER: now works in pottery in Stoke-on-Trent.

John Ritchie

John Ritchie scored more goals for Stoke than any other player – 176. After helping the Potters win the Second Division title and establish themselves in the top flight, he surprisingly left and joined Wednesday for a record fee. He did superbly well with the Owls and in his first two seasons netted some cracking goals, top-scoring with 22 in 1967/68, reminding older supporters of Scotsman Neil Dewar, who served the club in the 1930s. However, when manager Alan Brown departed, Ritchie – who was still living in the Potteries and was struggling at times with a leg injury – became increasingly unsettled and was transferred back to Stoke. A Football League representative versus the League of Ireland in 1967, five years later he won the League Cup with Stoke. Ritchie was sent off twenty-nine seconds after coming on as a substitute during Stoke's away UEFA Cup game with FC Kaiserslautern in 1972. A complicated double fracture of the right leg ended his senior career, although he assisted Stafford Rangers for a short time. His son David played for Stoke.

ROBERTS, Sean
Goalkeeper

Appearances: 0+1
Born: Durban, South Africa, 2 January 1983

R

CAREER

CLUBS: Southern Gauteng, Manchester City, Tottenham Hotspur, Crystal Palace, WEDNESDAY (free, October 2001), St Albans City.

Signed as cover for Kevin Pressman, Sean Roberts' only outing for Wednesday came as a second-half substitute versus Burnley in January 2002. This was his only appearance in the Football League.

ROBERTSON, George
Outside left

Appearances: 173   Goals: 31
Born: Stonefield, Lanarkshire, 1884
Died: Scotland, 1962

CAREER

CLUBS: Motherwell, WEDNESDAY (£1,250 with James Murray, March 1910-May 1920), East Fife.
OTHER: Army – First World War.

Tall, lean and effective, George Robertson won four caps for Scotland – three with Wednesday. Brilliant at times, during his association with the Owls he carved many a stubborn defence apart with his teasing runs and clever wing play. He made his debut in the Football League at Bradford City in March 1910 and scored his first Wednesday goal in a 2-1 victory in the return fixture three days later. He missed only 10 games out of a possible 129 in his first three and a quarter seasons, but then missed four years due to the First World War.

ROBINS, Mark Gordon
Forward

Appearances: 17+1 Goals: 7
Born: Ashton-under-Lyme, 22 December 1969

CAREER

CLUBS: Manchester United, Norwich City, Leicester City, BK Copenhagen, Reading, Deportivo La Coruña, Panionios, Manchester City, Walsall, Rotherham United, Bristol City, WEDNESDAY (free, December 2003-June 2004), Burton Albion.

A prolific marksman throughout his career, Mark Robins moved into non-League football in 2004, having scored over 130 goals in almost 450 appearances for his twelve clubs. The recipient of FA Cup and European Cup-Winners' Cup medals with Manchester United in 1990 and 1991 respectively, he later won the League Cup with Leicester in 1997 and was capped six times at Under-21 level by England. He scored well for the Owls in his short stay at Hillsborough, including four goals in the LDV Vans Trophy tournament.

ROBINSON, Carl Philips
Midfield

Appearances: 4   Goal: 1
Born: Llandrindod Wells, 13 October 1976

CAREER

CLUBS: Shrewsbury Town, Wolverhampton Wanderers, Shrewsbury Town, Portsmouth, WEDNESDAY (loan, January-February 2003), Walsall, Rotherham United, Sheffield United, Sunderland.

When he joined the Owls on loan, Carl Robinson had over 200 appearances to his credit and was an established Welsh international with 21 full, 2 'B', 6 Under-21 and 3 Youth caps in his locker. Possessing a neat first touch, he made his debut for Wednesday in the Sheffield derby against United and scored his only goal for the club in the 2-2 draw with Norwich three weeks later. He helped Sunderland regain their Premiership status in 2005.

ROBINSON, John
Inside right

Appearances: 119   Goals: 39
Born: Shiremoor, Northumberland, 10 August 1917
Died: Shiremoor, 31 July 1972

CAREER
CLUBS: Shiremoor, WEDNESDAY (£20, August 1934-October 1946), Sunderland, Lincoln City.
WARTIME GUEST APPEARANCES: Newcastle United, Darlington, Hartlepool United, Middlesbrough.

Regarded as a young prodigy in his early Wednesday days, winning the first of four England caps at the age of nineteen – when he scored in an 8-0 win over Finland in May 1937 – Jackie Robinson's stylish play, ball control, confidence and self-belief captivated the critics until the Second World War intervened. One of the greatest inside forwards in Wednesday's history, he had a tremendous burst of speed, a cute body-swerve and a remarkable talent for scoring goals, emphasised to the full during wartime football, when he netted 90 times in 110 games for the Owls. Add those figures to his peacetime record and you can see he was a superb marksman. He was given his first taste of League action against West Bromwich Albion in April 1935 when he deputised for Ronnie Starlin g ahead of the FA Cup final, scoring in a 1-1 draw. A regular in the side from November 1936, he was joint top-scorer in 1937/38 and second behind Doug Hunt the following season. In 1942/43 Robinson was brilliant, netting 35 goals in 32 games. His career was effectively over when he fractured his right leg playing for Lincoln versus Wrexham on Christmas Eve 1949. Besides his England appearances, he also represented the Football League versus the Irish League in 1939.

Jackie Robinson

ROBSON, Thomas
Wing half

Appearances: 3
Born: Morpeth, 1909
Died: Northampton, 1975

CAREER
CLUBS: Blyth Spartans, Everton, WEDNESDAY (£3,000, October 1930-April 1932), Yeovil & Petters United, Northampton Town, Kettering Town.

A strapping defender and as hard as nails, Tommy Robson, an ex-miner, made his League debut for Wednesday in a 4-0 home win over Leicester in March 1931. His second outing was against his former club, Everton. He made 45 appearances for Northampton.

ROCASTLE, Craig Aaron
Midfield

Appearances: 27+6 Goals: 1
Born: Lewisham, London, 17 August 1981

R

CAREER

CLUBS: *Charlton Athletic, Kingstonian, Chelsea, Barnsley, Lincoln City, Hibernian, WEDNESDAY (free, February 2005-July 2006), Yeovil Town (L), Oldham Athletic.*

Craig Rocastle, cousin of the late David Rocastle, spent six years in non-League football before signing for Chelsea. He failed to make the grade at Stamford Bridge and, after loan spells with Barnsley and Lincoln, joined the Owls, whom he helped gain promotion to the First Division in 2005 via the play-offs.

RODRIGUES, Peter Joseph
Right-back

Appearances: 174   Goals: 2
Born: Cardiff, 21 April 1944

CAREER
CLUBS: *Cardiff City, Leicester City, WEDNESDAY (£45,000, October 1970-July 1975), Southampton, Romsey Town, San Diego (coach).*
OTHER: *licensee; social club steward; now living in Spain.*

Welsh Schoolboy international Peter Rodrigues turned down Newport County before joining Cardiff City. Adding Youth caps to his tally, he made his League debut in 1963 and three months later played in the first of five Under-23 internationals, following up in 1965 with the first of 40 senior appearances for his country. Possessing fine defensive qualities, he was fast over the ground and did well at Ninian Park and Leicester – for whom he played in the 1969 FA Cup final defeat to Manchester City. He made his debut for Wednesday at Charlton in October 1970 and held his place at right-back – injuries apart – until moving to Southampton. At the end of 1975/76 he celebrated in style – with another ex-Owl Jim McCalliog – by skippering Saints to a sensational FA Cup final victory over Manchester United. Rodrigues,

who suffered relegation with Leicester in 1969 and Wednesday in 1975, won the Welsh Cup in 1964 and 1965 with Cardiff.

ROGERS, Alfred
Forward

Appearances: 38   Goals: 8
Born: Ecclesfield, Sheffield, 10 April 1921
Died: Sheffield, 28 October 1992

CAREER
CLUBS: *Arsenal, WEDNESDAY (£10, March 1940-May 1950).*
OTHER: *Second World War munitions work; sports assistant at Sheffield University.*

The Second World War seriously affected Alf Rogers' career. He scored 32 goals in 96 regional games for the Owls when occupying every forward position except outside left. A clever footballer, he finally made his League debut in August 1946 in a 4-1 defeat at Luton, and scored his first senior goal twelve months later in a 5-1 reverse at Tottenham. He was playing well when he suffered a leg injury at Coventry in 1950 which forced him to retire.

ROLLINSON, Frank
Inside left

Appearances: 44   Goals: 16
Born: Eccleshall, Sheffield, 21 June 1884
Died: Sheffield, 15 September 1927

CAREER
CLUBS: *WEDNESDAY (August 1906-August 1911), Leicester Fosse, Portsmouth, Luton Town.*

Goal-hungry Frank Rollinson had his best spell in Wednesday's first team in 1909/10 when he scored 10 goals in 20 League games, including a hat-trick in a 3-0 home win over Newcastle. He lost his touch at Leicester but helped both

Portsmouth and Luton Town win promotion in Southern League football.

ROSS, Maurice
Defender

Appearances: 2
Born: Dundee, Scotland, 3 February 1981

CAREER
CLUBS: Glasgow Rangers, WEDNESDAY (loan, August-September 2005), Wolverhampton Wanderers.

Scottish international Maurice Ross (13 caps) made over 100 appearances for Rangers, with whom he gained a Premier League championship medal in 2005, playing in 13 games. A strong, forceful player, he spent only a short time with the Owls before moving to Wolves. He was charged with breach of the peace in December 2005 after an incident involving his former girlfriend.

ROSTRON, John Wilfred
Left-back

Appearances: 9
Born: Sunderland, 29 September 1956

CAREER
CLUBS: Arsenal, Sunderland, Watford, WEDNESDAY (free, January-September 1989), Sheffield United (L), Brentford, Gateshead.

Wilf Rostron's career spanned twenty years and in that time he made over 600 club appearances – 495 in the Football League. An England Schoolboy international, he made his debut for Arsenal as a winger in 1975 and was converted into a competent left-back by Watford, whom he helped gain promotion to the First Division (1982) and reach the FA Cup final two years later. He was thirty-two when he joined the Owls and the first of his nine outings for the club – before his switch over to Bramall

Lane – was against the reigning champions, Liverpool, in January 1989 (2-2).

ROWAN, Alexander
Centre forward

Appearances: 34   Goals: 12
Born: Stirlingshire, 1869
Deceased by 1948

CAREER
CLUBS: Albion Rovers, Nottingham Forest, Albion Rovers, WEDNESDAY (£75, August 1892-November 1893), Burton Swifts, Ardwick/Manchester City.
OTHER: licensee.

'Sandy' Rowan produced some excellent displays north of the border with Albion Rovers but had failed with Forest. During his eighteen-month spell with Wednesday he proved to be a class act, scoring on his debut in a 5-2 win over Accrington in September 1892. Replaced by Jock Miller, he later gave good service to Ardwick.

ROY, John Robin
Outside left

Appearances: 16   Goals: 1
Born: Woolston, Southampton, 22 March 1914
Died: Bournemouth, 24 November 1980

CAREER
CLUBS: Southampton, Norwich City, Mansfield Town, WEDNESDAY (£1,750, February 1937-March 1938), Notts County, Tranmere Rovers, Yeovil & Petters United, Southampton, Ipswich Town, Gravesend & Northfleet, Yeovil Town.
WARTIME GUEST APPEARANCES: Aberaman, Yeovil & Petters United
OTHER: engineering inspector.

Jack Roy was a fast-raiding left-winger who could cross a ball to perfection. After failing to make headway with Southampton and Norwich he did well at Mansfield, setting up plenty of goals for Ted Hartson. His transfer to Wednesday realised a record incoming fee for the Stags (£1,750), but he never really settled at Hillsborough after scoring once in a 2-0 win over Bury in December 1937. One of the few players to officially switch clubs during the war, he signed for Southampton on Christmas Day morning 1939.

RUDDLESDIN, Herrod
Wing half

Appearances: 286   Goals: 7
Born: Birdwell, Barnsley, January 1876
Died: Birdwell, 26 March 1910

CAREER
CLUBS: WEDNESDAY (May 1898-December 1906),
Northampton Town.

Strongly-built without affection or showiness, Herrod Ruddleshin was clever, adroit and fair, hardly ever committing a bad foul and doing the job simply and efficiently. Indifferent health upset his performances late on and undoubtedly cost him more honours – he won three full England caps in 1904/05 against Wales, Ireland and Scotland. Nicknamed 'Ruddy', he won the Second Division title with Wednesday in 1900 and the First Division in 1903 and 1904, after replacing Jamieson in the middle line. Struck down by illness when in his prime in 1906, Herbert Chapman tried to get him back into the game with Northampton, to no avail. His brother, Bill, played for Barnsley.

RUDI, Petter Norman
Midfield

Appearances: 81+8 Goals: 10
Born: Kristiansund, Norway, 17 September 1973

CAREER
CLUBS: Traeff, Molde FK, Piacenza, WEDNESDAY

(£800,000, October 1997-October 2000), Molde FK (L, signed later), Sporting Lokeren, Germinal Beerschot, Antwerpen, FK Austria, Molde FK.

A tall, left-sided attacking midfielder, Petter Rudi had been in excellent form for Wednesday until he suffered a leg injury in December 1999. After recovering full fitness, he was unable to recapture that early form and rarely figured again. His last outing for Wednesday was as a substitute versus Huddersfield in August 2000. Capped 27 times by Norway, Rudi also represented his country at Youth and Under-21 levels.

RUSHBURY, David Garreth
Defender

Appearances: 132+1   Goals: 8
Born: Wolverhampton, 20 February 1956

CAREER
CLUBS: West Bromwich Albion, WEDNESDAY
(£22,500, November 1976-July 1979), Swansea City,
Carlisle United, Gillingham, Doncaster Rovers,
Carlisle United, Cambridge United, Bristol Rovers,
Goole Town, Chesterfield (trainer, physio, assistant
manager, caretaker-manager, manager), Alfreton
Town (director of football).

Handed his League debut by former England right-back Don Howe at West Brom, Dave Rushbury was subsequently sold to Wednesday by Johnny Giles. Proving to be an excellent buy, his debut for the Owls came at Bury in February 1977 when he replaced John Collins at left-back. He missed only one game the following season and nine in 1978/79 before moving to Swansea. Rushbury's career, as a whole, took him all over the country and when he retired in 1987, he had 450 first-class games under his belt. He helped Swansea win promotion from the Second Division in 1981 and Carlisle from the Third Division the following year. Rushbury's son, Andy, played for Chesterfield.

RUSSELL, David Wallace
Right half

Appearances: 50
Born: Methil, Fife, 7 April 1914
Died: Birkenhead, 12 June 2000

CAREER
CLUBS: Dundee, East Fife, WEDNESDAY (£2,000, May 1938-May 1944), Walsall, Bolton Wanderers, Burnley and Aberdeen; Odense (coach), Denmark (national team coach), Bury (coach, manager), Tranmere Rovers (manager, general manager).
WARTIME GUEST APPEARANCES: Blackpool.
OTHER: RAF.

The Second World War interrupted Dave Russell's career at Hillsborough just when he had established himself in the first team. In fact, he had appeared in all 50 League and FA Cup games in 1938/39, having earlier helped East Fife win the Scottish Cup. Signed

David Russell

by Jimmy McMullan, Russell appeared in 65 regional games for the Owls, helping them reach the League War Cup final in 1943. He also represented an All British XI against a Football League XI at Hillsborough in 1941 and played in several games for the British Forces team on the Rhine. Solid rather than spectacular, after leaving Wednesday he became an excellent coach, guiding Denmark to third place in the 1948 London Olympics. He worked overtime as Bury's manager.

RYALLS, Brian
Goalkeeper

Appearances: 45
Born: Grimethorpe, Barnsley, 7 July, 1932

CAREER
CLUBS: Wath Wanderers, Wolverhampton Wanderers, Grimethorpe Athletic, WEDNESDAY (part-time November 1952, signed for £150, January 1953-July 1958), Frickley Colliery, Retford, Scarborough.

Signed as cover for Dave McIntosh, Brian Ryalls had to wait eight months before making his League debut against Sheffield United at Bramall Lane in September 1953. Upright and confident, with a safe pair of hands, he had a run of 28 outings in the First Division that season but afterwards was confined to the reserves, failing to get a game for two years.

RYALLS, Joseph
Outside right

Appearances: 2
Born: Sheffield, March 1881
Died: Sheffield, 1960

CAREER
CLUBS: WEDNESDAY (April 1902-May 1905), Barnsley, Fulham, Rotherham Town, Brentford, Nottingham Forest, Brentford, Chesterfield Town.

During his twelve years as a professional, Joe Ryalls appeared in 27 League games, his best return coming with Barnsley – 17 games. Regarded as a reserve at most clubs, his two outings for the Owls were both in place of Harry Davis – the first against Blackburn in March 1903 and the second versus Sheffield United in April 1904.

RYAN, John Bernard
Left-back

Appearances: 6+3   Goals: 1
Born: Fallsworth, 18 February 1962

CAREER
CLUBS: Oldham Athletic, Newcastle United, WEDNESDAY (£40,000 plus Pat Heard, September 1984-August 1985), Oldham Athletic, Mansfield Town, Chesterfield, Rochdale, Bury, Stalybridge Celtic, Radcliffe Borough.
OTHER: partner in a Manchester renovation company.

In his teenage days, John Ryan showed all the signs of being a future England international. He represented his country at Under-21 level but failed to go higher. Blessed with attacking flair, he possessed all the characteristics of a modern-day full-back, yet he simply couldn't perform on the big stage. After helping Newcastle win promotion to the First Division in 1984, he was injured on his debut for Wednesday against Liverpool at Anfield a few months later. He scored his only goal for the club in a 5-0 home win over Leicester shortly after. A double fracture of the leg in a friendly versus Tranmere in August 1986 virtually ended his career. He made almost 400 senior appearances and won the Notts FA County Cup with Mansfield in 1989.

SANETTI, Francesco
Striker

Appearances: 1+6   Goals: 1
Born: Rome, 11 January 1979

CAREER
CLUBS: Genoa, WEDNESDAY (free, April 1998-August 1999), Livorno, Giogionae, Lodigiani, Tewramo, Acireale.

Francesco Sanetti – 6ft 1in tall – joined Wednesday on a Bosman free transfer and made his Premiership debut as a substitute against Aston Villa in the penultimate game of 1997/98, scoring a late penalty in a 3-1 defeat. Despite having two fellow countrymen with him – Carbone and Di Canio – he never settled in England and duly returned to Italy.

SAYER, James
Centre forward

Appearances: 2   Goals: 1
Born: Mexborough, September 1862
Died: Stoke-on-Trent, 1 February 1922

CAREER
CLUBS: Mexborough, Heeley, Stoke, WEDNESDAY (free, November 1884-January 1885), Stoke, Mexborough, Stoke (secretary).
OTHER: director of Fielding Ltd, a pottery company based in Stoke-on-Trent.

Jimmy Sayer spent two months with Wednesday, scoring in the third-round FA Cup defeat by Nottingham Forest in January 1885, having made his debut in the opening round win over Long Eaton Rangers. An outside right of all-round ability, his outstanding virtue was remarkable speed over thirty to forty yards – so much so, he was referred to by supporters—especially those at Stoke—as 'the greyhound'. Sayer was capped by England in a 7-0 win over Ireland at Sheffield in February 1887 and also represented the Sheffield FA, Staffs FA and Birmingham FA. He survived a train crash at Stafford railway station in 1889.

SCOTHORN, Gary
Goalkeeper

Appearances: 2
Born: Hoyland, Barnsley, 6 June 1950

CAREER
CLUBS: WEDNESDAY (June 1965-July 1969), Barnsley (L), Johannesburg Rangers, Drumcondra, Sligo Rovers, Mansfield Town.

Reserve to Ron Springett, Gary Scothorn made his debut for the Owls in a 4-0 FA Cup win over Mansfield in February 1967. He played for the League of Ireland against a Santos team which included Pele in 1973.

SCOTT, Arthur
Defender

Appearances: 1
Born: Sheffield, 1866
Deceased by 1948

CAREER
CLUBS: WEDNESDAY (seasons 1890-92).

A reserve for two seasons, Arthur Scott made just one Football Alliance appearance for the Owls.

SCOTT, Philip Campbell
Midfield

Appearances: 3+8   Goals: 1
Born: Perth, Scotland, 14 November 1974

CAREER
CLUBS: Scone Thistle, St Johnstone, WEDNESDAY (£75,000, March 1999-May 2000).

A Scotland Under-21 international, capped four times, Phil Scott scored 35 goals in 157 appearances for St Johnstone, whom he helped win the First Division title in 1997. An attacking midfielder, he was unfortunately plagued by injury at Hillsborough and, after a bright start, managed only 11 first-team outings before his release.

SEDLOSKI, Goce
Defender

Appearances: 3+1
Born: Golemo Konjari, Macedonia, 10 April 1974

CAREER
CLUBS: Pobeda Prilip, Hadjuk Split, WEDNESDAY (£750,000, February 1998-February 1999), NK Dinamo Zagreb.

Macedonian international Goce Sedloski, nicknamed 'The Bear', had already been capped 14 times when he joined the Owls. A tall, powerful defender, he made his debut in the Premiership against Bolton soon after signing, but after three more games suffered a cartilage injury from which he never made a full recovery. He became a huge favourite with the Dinamo Zagreb fans, winning two Croatian League titles and three domestic Cup finals, while scoring over 20 goals in more than 200 appearances in 7 years.

SEED, James Marshall
Inside right

Appearances: 147   Goals: 37
Born: Blackhill, Co. Durham, 25 March 1895
Died: Farnborough, 16 July 1966

CAREER

CLUBS: Whitburn, Sunderland, Mid-Rhondda, Tottenham Hotspur, WEDNESDAY (part-exchange for Arthur Lowdell, August 1927-April 1931), Clapton Orient (secretary-manager), Charlton Athletic (secretary-manager), Bristol City (football adviser, caretaker-manager), Millwall (manager, football advisor, consultant-director).

OTHER: Army – First World War.

Jimmy Seed – a former pit worker – scored over 80 goals for Whitburn in the 1913/14 season before joining Sunderland. The First World War disrupted his stay at Roker Park and, after the hostilities had ended, his club was somewhat reluctant to retain his services, having learned he had suffered a gas attack on a French battlefield. Seemingly on the soccer scrap heap, aged twenty-four, he was invited to play for Mid-Rhondda and did well, the gas attack having had no ill effects. He then negotiated a free transfer to Tottenham and became a star performer at White Hart Lane, scoring 77 times in 254 games while helping the London club win the FA Cup in 1921 and gaining the first of five caps for England (versus Belgium).

A tireless, probing inside right, Seed was a superb strategist, possessed a terrific shot and was always alert and conscientious inside the penalty area. As captain, things didn't go too well at Hillsborough, and with games and points running out, Wednesday found themselves rock bottom of the First Division table, facing relegation. Seed's presence inspired the Owls, who avoided the drop by taking 17 points out of the last 20 – including 4 off Spurs, who were relegated! Wednesday, with Seed, Jack Allen and Mark Hooper in attack, won the League title in 1928/29 and retained the crown the following season. It had been an amazing turnaround in form for the club.

A member of the FA touring party to South Africa in 1929, Seed retired as a player in 1931 and, at the invitation of Herbert Chapman, moved into management with Clapton Orient. Chapman had plans to turn Orient into Arsenal's nursery side, but the scheme was scuppered by the Football League. Seed had to struggle through two seasons before taking charge of Charlton, steering the Valiants from the Third Division (South) to the First Division in successive seasons (1934-36) and then taking them to successive FA Cup finals in 1946 and 1947, winning the trophy on their second visit. During the Second World War he saw his team lose 7-1 to Arsenal in the 1943 Football League (South) Cup final and beat Chelsea 3-1 in the final of the same competition a year later.

Sacked by Charlton, after an 8-1 League defeat at Sunderland, Seed was ironically replaced as boss at The Valley by Jimmy Trotter, who had played for Wednesday between 1922 and 1930, starring alongside his predecessor 31 times. Seed himself received £6,000 in full settlement of all claims lodged against the club for unfair dismissal. After leaving Charlton, Seed remained in the game until 1966, spending fifty-two years in top-class football. His brother, Angus, played for Workington and managed Aldershot and Barnsley. This condensed pen-portrait is not enough to do justice to a remarkable man of football.

SEEMLEY, Ivor John
Full-back

Appearances: 23
Born: Sheffield, 30 June 1929

CAREER

CLUBS: Ellesmere Port, WEDNESDAY (£10, August 1944-June 1955), Stockport County, Chesterfield, Sutton Town.

OTHER: worked in the sales department for a steel company.

Nine years a professional at Hillsborough, Ivor Seemley made a third of his appearances in the FA Cup in 1954, playing at left-back in place of Norman Curtis. A strong tackler, he was only fifteen when he first joined the club and completed his National Service before establishing himself in the Central League side. He added 159 League appearances to his tally with Stockport and Chesterfield.

SEWELL, John
Inside forward

Appearances: 175   Goals: 92
Born: Kell, Whitehaven, 24 January 1927

CAREER
CLUBS: Notts County, WEDNESDAY (£34,500, March 1951-December 1955), Aston Villa, Hull City, Lusaka City (player-coach), Zambia (national team coach), Belgian Congo (coach).
WARTIME GUEST APPEARANCES: Workington
OTHER: car salesman for Bristol Street Motors in West Bridgford.

Jackie Sewell was a prominent inside right immediately after the Second World War. Blessed with a good turn of speed, he was astute, a fine marksman and, above all, a prescient football player who, in 1951, was the subject of a record transfer when he moved to Hillsborough,

John Sewell

topping the previous best of £30,000, paid by Aston Villa to Sunderland for Trevor Ford. A Third Division (South) championship winner with Notts County in 1950, he went on to help Wednesday twice win the Second Division title, in 1952 and 1956. In 1957, he was a member of Aston Villa's FA Cup-winning side versus Manchester United. Relegated from the top division on four occasions – with the Owls in 1951 and 1955, Villa 1959 and Hull City 1960 – he was capped six times by England, playing in those two heavy defeats at the hands of Hungary – 6-3 at Wembley in 1953 and 7-1 in Budapest the following year. Sewell also represented the Football League on four occasions – scoring a hat-trick against the League of Ireland in 1954 – and toured Canada and North America with the FA in June 1950, scoring 6 goals in 7 games, including a hat-trick in a 9-0 win over Alberta. A fine career brought Sewell almost 250 goals in 550 matches, 228 in 510 League games – and this despite suffering a baffling loss of form when least expected!

SHADBOLT, William Henry
Outside left

Appearances: 7
Born: Shrewsbury, 4 August 1932

CAREER
CLUBS: Oswestry Town, WEDNESDAY (£5,000, January 1953-March 1954), Halifax Town.

During his fourteen-month stay at Hillsborough, Bill Shadbolt played in seven League games, all on the left wing in place of Dennis Woodhead.

SHAKESPEARE, Craig Robert
Midfield

Appearances: 18+3 Goals: 1
Born: Great Barr, Birmingham, 26 October 1963

S

CAREER

CLUBS: Walsall, WEDNESDAY (£300,000, June 1989-February 1990), West Bromwich Albion, Grimsby Town, Scunthorpe United, Telford United, Blakenhall, Aberystwyth Town, West Bromwich Albion (scout, youth team coach).

Creative midfielder Craig Shakespeare scored 59 goals in 355 games for Walsall before joining the Owls in readiness for the 1989/90 season. In the side from the outset, he made his First Division debut against Norwich and claimed his only goal for the club in an 8-0 League Cup win at Aldershot. Injured in the return game with the Canaries, he was sidelined for a while, returning for one game before signing for West Brom, for whom he netted 16 times in 128 outings. He found himself on the subs' bench for most of his time with Scunthorpe.

SHARP, Wilfred
Defender

Appearances: 58   Goals: 2
Born: Bathgate, Scotland, 8 April 1907
Died: Sefton South, June 1981

CAREER

CLUBS: Clydebank, Airdrieonians, Tunbridge Wells Rangers, Airdrieonians, WEDNESDAY (£750, November 1934-May 1936), Bradford Park Avenue, Burton Town.

A well-built, strong-tackling defender, Wilf Sharp practised for hours in his back garden as a youngster. He made over 100 appearances in Scotland before joining Wednesday following an injury to Gavin Malloch. Horace Burrows switched over to the left to accommodate him in the half-back line. He did well for the remainder of that season, scored once in 30 starts and held his position for the first half of 1935/36 before fading from the scene. Sharp was a reserve for the Scotland v. England international in 1934.

SHAW, Bernard
Full-back

Appearances: 109+4   Goals: 4
Born: Sheffield, 14 March 1945

CAREER
CLUBS: Sheffield United, Wolverhampton Wanderers, WEDNESDAY (£34,200, June 1973-May 1976), Worksop Town.
OTHER: licensee.

A stern tackler, keen and competitive, Bernard Shaw won England Youth and Under-23 caps as a Sheffield United player and appeared for Wolves in the 1972 UEFA Cup final defeat by Spurs. He joined Wednesday with over 300 appearances under his belt and made his debut for the Owls against Swindon in August 1973, missing only four games that season. In and out of the side the following year, he was back to his best in 1975/76 before his release by manager Len Ashurst after the team had finished twentieth in the Third Division.

SHAW, Bernard L.
Forward

Appearances: 1
Born: Sheffield, June 1864
Died: Sheffield, 1925

CAREER
CLUBS: Hallam, WEDNESDAY (seasons 1885-87), Sheffield FC, Arsenal, Sheffield FC.

Bernie Shaw spent two seasons as a reserve with the Owls, making his only senior appearance on the left wing against Long Eaton Rangers in an FA Cup-tie in October 1855 which Wednesday lost 2-1. He helped the team win the annual Wharncliffe Charity Cup the following year. His father, John, was a founder member of Hallam FC and later became a Tory MP and president of the Sheffield FA.

SHAW, John Stephen
Centre forward

Appearances: 65   Goals: 27
Born: Doncaster, 10 April 1924

CAREER
CLUBS: Rotherham United, WEDNESDAY (£7,800, June 1953-June 1959), Denaby United, Doncaster Rovers (scout).
OTHER: fitter's mate at British Ropes, Balby, playing for and running the works' football team.

A local League championship winner with Yorkshire Main Colliery in 1944, ex-miner Jack Shaw turned down the opportunity to join Wolves before scoring 122 goals in 262 League games for Rotherham, netting more than anyone else in the country in 1950/51 – 46. One of several centre forwards signed by Wednesday in an attempt to fill the gap left by Derek Dooley, he netted 17 times in 1953/54, helping the Owls reach the semi-final of the FA Cup. A modest fellow, Shaw played in the Second XI as a wing half in his last season at Hillsborough.

SHAW, Jonathan
Striker

Appearances: 9+15 Goals: 2
Born: Sheffield, 10 November 1983

CAREER
CLUBS: WEDNESDAY (April 2000-November 2004), York City (L), Oldham Athletic, Burton Albion, Cheltenham Town.

A striker with strength and good control, Jon Shaw had a handful of outings in his first season as a professional with Wednesday but never really established himself in the side. He was impressive during his loan spell at York.

SHELLEY, Albert
Forward

Appearances: 3   Goals: 2
Born: Birmingham, 1915
Deceased

CAREER
CLUBS: Birmingham, Oakengates, Gloucester City, WEDNESDAY (£300, January-August 1937), Torquay United (two spells), Gloucester City.

Bert Shelley, who could play in all five forward positions, scored on his League debut for Wednesday against Wolves in January 1937, when deputising for Mark Hooper. His second goal followed in his third match, clinching a 3-2 win at West Brom. He netted 15 times in 41 games for Torquay.

SHELTON, Gary
Midfield

Appearances: 237+4   Goals: 24
Born: Carlton, Nottingham, 21 March 1958

CAREER
CLUBS: Nottingham Forest, Walsall, Aston Villa, Barry Town, Notts County, WEDNESDAY (£50,000, March 1982-July 1987), Oxford United, Bristol City, Rochdale, Chester City (player, assistant manager, coach), West Bromwich Albion (coach).

Capped once for England Under-21s – versus Finland in 1985 – the creative and hard-working Gary Shelton, who started out as a striker, amassed 553 appearances and scored 62 goals during his career. After useful spells with Walsall and Aston Villa, he helped Wednesday gain promotion to the First Division in 1984. Outstanding that season, he was voted the Owls' Player of the Year. He was coach under ex-Wednesday star Gary Megson when West Bromwich Albion reached the Premiership in 2002 and 2004.

Gary Shelton

SHELTON, George
Winger

Appearances: 18
Born: Attercliffe, Sheffield, 25 September 1899
Died: Exeter, 24 February 1934

CAREER
CLUBS: Attercliffe, WEDNESDAY (free, January 1920-May 1922), Exeter City, New Brighton.
OTHER: Army – First World War; licensee.

One of forty-two players used by Wednesday in 1919/20, George Shelton, who could play on both wings, made his League debut against Preston North End at Deepdale in February 1920. He made the 100th League appearance of his career for New Brighton versus Wigan Borough seven years after his first. He was only thirty-four when he died.

SHEPHERD, James
Right half

Appearances: 2
Born: Scotland, 1867
Died: Sheffield, December 1925

CAREER
CLUBS: Dundee, WEDNESDAY (August 1892-April 1894), Chesterfield.

A reserve defender, the first of Jim Shepherd's senior appearances was against Sunderland in September 1893, when he deputised for Harry Brandon.

SHERIDAN, John Joseph
Midfield

Appearances: 233+11   Goals: 33
Born: Stretford, Manchester, 1 October 1964

CAREER
CLUBS: Manchester City, Leeds United, Nottingham Forest, WEDNESDAY (£500,000, November 1989-November 1996), Birmingham City (L), Bolton Wanderers, Doncaster Rovers, Oldham Athletic (player, coach, joint caretaker-manager, manager).

John Sheridan was almost forty when he retired, having made 763 appearances at club and international level, scoring 109 goals. A brilliant passer of the ball, he won 34 caps for

John Sheridan

the Republic of Ireland and also represented his country in 2 Youth, 1 'B', 2 Under-21 and 2 Under-23 internationals. His superb goal won the 1991 League Cup final for Wednesday versus Manchester United. He made his debut against Nottingham Forest in November 1989 and netted his first two goals for the Owls in successive League matches against Derby and Coventry in March 1990. He won the First Division title with Bolton in 1997 as Latics' manager.

SHINER, Roy Albert James
Centre forward

Appearances: 106   Goals: 96
Born: Ryde, Isle of Wight, 15 November 1924
Died: Isle of Wight, 28 October 1988

CAREER
CLUBS: Ryde Sports, Portsmouth, Wolverhampton Wanderers, Cheltenham Town, Huddersfield Town, WEDNESDAY (player exchange, July 1955-November 1959), Hull City, Cheltenham Town.

Roy Shiner was a rumbustious centre forward whose wholehearted play responded to the promptings of Froggatt, Fantham and Quixall during his four years at Hillsborough. One of manager Eric Taylor's finest captures, he was an ever-present in 1955/56, banging home 33 goals to help the Owls clinch the Second Division title. Three years later his haul of 28 went a long way towards helping Wednesday win the same division again. After losing his place to Keith Ellis, Shiner joined relegation-threatened Hull. Three other players were involved in his transfer from Huddersfield.

SHIRTLIFF, Paul Robert
Midfield, defender

Appearances: 8+2
Born: Hoyland, Barnsley, 3 October 1962

CAREER
CLUBS: WEDNESDAY (June 1978-July 1984), Northampton Town, Frickley Town, Boston, Dagenham & Redbridge, Gateshead, Barnsley (coach).
OTHER: worked in the aerospace industry.

Paul Shirtliff played in the same Wednesday side as his brother Peter (below) when making the first of his eight appearances for the club as a substitute versus Grimsby Town in April 1981. An England semi-professional, he made 30 appearances for Northampton after leaving Hillsborough. A broken leg ended his career.

SHIRTLIFF, Peter Andrew
Defender

Appearances: 357+2   Goals: 12
Born: Chapeltown, Barnsley, 6 April 1961

CAREER
CLUBS: WEDNESDAY (June 1977-June 1986), Charlton Athletic, WEDNESDAY (£500,000, July 1989-August 1993), Wolverhampton Wanderers, Barnsley, Carlisle United, Barnsley (assistant manager, player-coach), Leicester City (reserve coach), Mansfield Town (assistant manager, caretaker-manager, manager).

Except for a period in 1985 when he played second fiddle to Lawrie Madden, Paul Hart and Colin Morris, Peter Shirtliff served Wednesday well in both his spells at Hillsborough. In between times he scored two dramatic late goals in the 1987 play-off final replay at Birmingham, keeping recently promoted Charlton in the top flight at Leeds' expense. The London club made a big profit in hard cash when they transferred Shirtliff back to Wednesday. One of the Owls' finest post-war servants, Shirtliff starred in the 1991 League Cup final win over Manchester United and captained the side on several occasions. He made his League debut at Peterborough in

S

August 1978 and the following season played just three times when promotion was gained from the Third Division. He won a regular place in the side in 1980/81 and over the next five years produced some brilliant displays, helping the Owls clinch promotion to the First Division in 1984. He continued to perform well when he returned to Hillsborough and retired in 1997 with 625 senior appearances to his name.

SHORT, James William
Inside right

Appearances: 2
Born: Bedlington, 9 December 1911
Died: South Shields, December 1995

CAREER Jarrow, WEDNESDAY (£200, November 1931-August 1933), Brighton & Hove Albion, Barrow.

A reserve-team player at Hillsborough, both of Jim Short's League outings came at the end of the 1932/33 season – against Manchester City and Grimsby – when Mark Hooper was injured. Short was also a fine crown green bowler.

SHUTT, Carl Steven
Striker

Appearances: 43+5 Goals: 21
Born: Sheffield, 10 October 1961

CAREER
CLUBS: WEDNESDAY (April 1976), Spalding United, WEDNESDAY (free, May 1985-October 1987), Bristol City, Leeds United, Birmingham City, Manchester City, Bradford City, Darlington, Kettering Town (player, manager), Bradford Park Avenue (player, manager).

Carl Shutt made his League debut for the Owls as a substitute at Oxford in August 1985,

Carl Shutt

scoring his first goal in the 2-2 home draw with Coventry two months later. In a lengthy career, he netted over 100 goals in more than 400 games, having his best spells with Leeds and Bradford, gaining both Second and First Division championship winners' medals with the Elland Road club in 1990 and 1992 respectively. He could also play in goal and in midfield.

SIBON, Gerald
Striker

Appearances: 116+34   Goals: 43
Born: Delan, Holland, 19 April 1974

CAREER
CLUBS: VV Dalen, FC Groningen, FC Twente, VVV Venlo, Roda JC, Ajax Amsterdam, WEDNESDAY (£1.5 million, July 1999-January 2003), SC Heerenveen, PSV Eindhoven.

Standing 6ft 5ins tall, Gerald Sibon had a very disappointing first season with Wednesday, failing to make an impact in a struggling side. After starting off as first choice, he was replaced by Andy Booth but returned later. As time progressed, however, he improved considerably, producing excellent displays and making himself a firm favourite with the fans. He was the Owls' leading scorer in 2001/02 – with 13 goals – and again in 2002/03 – with 9. He gained winners' medals for victories in both the Dutch League and cup.

SIMEK, Franklin Michael
Defender

Appearances: 88+1 *   Goals: 1 *
Born: St Louis, Missouri, USA, 13 October 1984

CAREER
CLUBS: Arsenal, QPR (L), Bournemouth (L), WEDNESDAY (free, June 2005).

Capped by his country at Youth level, Frankie Simek made one senior appearance for the Gunners versus Wolves in a League Cup-tie at Highbury in 2003 which was won 5-1. His debut for the Owls came at Stoke on the opening day of the 2005/06 League programme, performing well in a 0-0 draw. He went on to have an outstanding first season with the Owls.

SIMMONITE, Gordon
Right-back

Appearances: 1
Born: Sheffield, 25 August 1957

CAREER
CLUBS: Rotherham United, WEDNESDAY (free, August 1975-August 1978), Boston United, Blackpool, Lincoln City, Grimsby Town (youth coach), Stockport County (assistant manager), Lincoln City (assistant manager), Gainsborough Trinity, Lincoln City, Matlock Town, Buxton.
OTHER: served in the police force.

A solid defender, Gordon Simmonite made just one appearance for Wednesday at Chesterfield

in February 1977, when they lost 2-0. In 1978/79 he gained England semi-professional honours with Boston, but suffered a fractured ankle in 1985 which almost ended his career. He helped Lincoln regain their Football League status as Vauxhall Conference champions in 1988.

SIMMONS, Antony John
Forward

Appearances: 2+3
Born: Stocksbridge, 9 February 1965

CAREER
CLUBS: WEDNESDAY (April 1981-November 1983), Queens Park Rangers, Rotherham United, Lincoln City, Cardiff City, Gainsborough Trinity, Spalding United, Holbeach United, Lincoln United.
OTHER: employed by European Gas Turbines.

An England Youth international, capped in 1983, Tony Simmons found it tough at Hillsborough and made only five appearances for the Owls, the first in August 1982 against Middlesbrough, coming on as a substitute for Anton Mirocevic in a 3-1 win. He later played in almost 100 League games for Rotherham.

SIMMONS, William
Outside right

Appearances: 1
Born: Sheffield, 1879
Died: 1911

CAREER
CLUBS: Parkgate, WEDNESDAY (July 1899-July 1902), Barnsley (L), Doncaster Rovers.

As a replacement for Archie Brash, Bill Simmons' only League game for Wednesday came in their 5-0 home win over Loughborough in January 1900.

S

SIMPSON, George
Outside left

Appearances: 164   Goals: 39
Born: Jarrow, August 1883
Died: circa 1958

CAREER
CLUBS: Jarrow, WEDNESDAY (£10, March 1902-March 1909), West Bromwich Albion, North Shields.

The attributes of George Simpson* were speed and clever dribbling. He succeeded Spiksley in the Owls' forward line and scored the winning goal – a header – in the 1907 FA Cup final, having helped Wednesday clinch the Football League title in 1904. Simpson, who made his League debut in March 1903 and represented Sheffield against Glasgow in the annual challenge match, failed to settle down after leaving the Owls.
*This player has sometimes been confused with Vivien Simpson (below).

SIMPSON, Vivien Sandell
Forward

Appearances: 38   Goals: 11
Born: Sheffield, 1883
Died: Outtersteene, France, 13 April 1918

CAREER
CLUBS: Sheffield FC, WEDNESDAY (December 1900-November 1907), Norwich City, Northern Nomads.

An amateur throughout his career, Vivien Simpson assisted Wednesday, when required, over a period of seven years, appearing in 38 games. He scored some important goals – the first two coming in a 4-0 home League win over Wolves in January 1904. He appeared for the North versus the South in an England international trial. He lost his life during the First World War.

SINCLAIR, John Evens Wright
Outside right

Appearances: 105+4   Goals: 16
Born: Culross, Fife, 21 July 1943

CAREER
CLUBS: Dunfermline Athletic, Leicester City, Newcastle United, WEDNESDAY (£30,000, player exchange with David Ford, December 1969-August 1973), Chesterfield (L), Durban City (L), Dunfermline Athletic, Stenhousemuir.
OTHER: National Coal Board employee.

Jackie Sinclair cost Newcastle a near-record fee of £67,500 when he was signed from Leicester, having scored 53 goals for the Foxes. A sprightly and positive footballer, he was a cute winger, small and slight, endowed with beguiling ball trickery and control. He was also an expert penalty-taker, always hitting the ball hard and low. He made his debut for Wednesday against Arsenal in December 1969 and scored his first goal for the club against Ipswich the following month.

Capped by Scotland against Portugal in 1966, Sinclair gained an Inter Cities Fairs Cup winners' medal with Newcastle that same year, having been a Scottish Cup finalist with Dunfermline twelve months earlier. His uncle, Scottish international Tommy Wright, played for Sunderland, his brother, Willie, for Falkirk and Huddersfield and his cousin, also named Tommy Wright, for Leicester. Sinclair's own son, Chris, appeared in the 1991 Scottish Cup final for Dunfermline.

SINTON, Andrew
Forward

Appearances: 74+7 Goals: 3
Born: Cramlington, 19 March 1966

CAREER
CLUBS: Cambridge United, Brentford, Queens Park

Andy Sinton

Rangers, WEDNESDAY (£2.75 million, August 1993-January 1996), Tottenham Hotspur, Wolverhampton Wanderers, Burton Albion, Bromsgrove Rovers, Fleet Town (player-manager).

An England international, with 12 full, 3 'B' and 3 Schoolboy caps to his credit, Andy Sinton made 104 appearances for Cambridge, 182 for Brentford and 190 for QPR before joining the Owls for a record fee. An enterprising player who preferred to occupy the left-wing position, Sinclair did well with Wednesday before transferring to Spurs, with whom he gained a League Cup winners' medal in 1999. When he pulled out of top-class football in 2002 to join Nigel Clough's Burton Albion, Sinton had amassed 749 appearances and netted 84 goals.

SISSONS, John Leslie
Outside left

Appearances: 125+1   Goals: 15
Born: Hayes, 30 September 1945

CAREER
CLUBS: West Ham United, WEDNESDAY (£65,000, August 1970-December 1973), Norwich City, Chelsea, Tampa Bay Rowdies, Cape Town City.
OTHER: director of a motor company in South Africa.

Scorer of four goals on his Schoolboy debut for England, John Sissons went on to win Youth and Under-23 caps for his country. Initially an inside left, he became the youngest player ever to score in an FA Cup final when hitting the target for the winners West Ham against Preston in 1964. He was also the second youngest to appear in such a final, behind Howard Kendall, his opponent in that same contest. Twelve months later, he was again a star performer as the Hammers lifted the European Cup Winners' Cup after beating 1860 Munich. At that juncture – having been converted into a winger by Ron Greenwood – his career looked certain to take off, but alas that never quite happened. He made his debut for the Owls on the left wing against Blackburn in August 1970, taking over from Tony Coleman. After leaving Hillsborough, he huffed and puffed along with Norwich and Chelsea before emigrating in 1975. He struck 53 goals in 264 games for West Ham.

SLATER, John Brian
Forward

Appearances: 3
Born: Sheffield, 20 October 1932
Died: Sheffield, 13 September 1999.

CAREER
CLUBS: Wednesday Amateurs, WEDNESDAY (free, June 1951-July 1954), Grimsby Town, Rotherham United, Chesterfield, Burton Albion, Denaby United.
OTHER: played cricket; worked for British Steel; kitchen fitter.

John Slater played as an inside forward and on the left wing during his career. Reserve to Redfern Froggatt and Jackie Sewell at Hillsborough, he made his League debut for the Owls in a 1-0 win at West Bromwich Albion in December 1954 – revenge for a 5-4 defeat twenty-four hours earlier. He died from cancer.

SLAVIN, Hugh
Full-back

Appearances: 55
Born: Kirkdale, Liverpool, 1883
Deceased by 1960

CAREER
CLUBS: Birkenhead, WEDNESDAY (£120 with Chris Dodds, May 1904-April 1909), Sheffield Boys (trainer). OTHER: coach for Sheffield Schools Athletics Association; chairman of the Yorkshire County Schools Association; member of the English Schools FA.

Signed as cover for Billy Layton and Harry Burton, Hugh Slavin had 18 outings in his first season with Wednesday, making his debut in a 2-0 win over Manchester City in November 1904. Never a first-team regular, he was always cool and confident in whatever he did – never letting a winger tantalise him for long periods.

SLYNN, Frank
Outside left

Appearances: 46   Goals: 5
Born: Moseley, Birmingham, 10 February 1924

CAREER
CLUBS: Birmingham City, WEDNESDAY (free, September 1946-December 1950), Bury, Walsall. OTHER: employed by a steel firm.

Frank Slynn was a strong and mobile footballer who served Wednesday for over four years.

He made his League debut on the left wing at Birmingham in November 1946 and scored the first of his five goals in a 4-3 defeat at Newport the following month. He made over 50 League appearances for Bury and Walsall.

SMAILES, Andrew
Forward

Appearances: 40   Goals: 15
Born: Radcliffe, Northumberland, 21 May 1895
Died: Shepton Mallet, 6 October 1978

CAREER
CLUBS: Blyth Spartans, Newcastle United, WEDNESDAY (£1,500, October 1922-October 1923), Bristol City, Rotherham United (player, trainer, manager), Middlesbrough (scout), Scarborough (manager).
OTHER: Army – First World War.

Well built, strong and quick, Andy Smailes scored goals on a regular basis throughout his career. He packed a strong right-foot shot and was first choice at Newcastle for two seasons, scoring 30 times. He continued to do well with Wednesday, for whom he made his debut at Fulham in October 1922, netting his first goal a week later at Clapton Orient in a match that ended 2-2. He appeared in 162 games for Bristol City and as Rotherham manager guided them to their highest ever League position in 1955. He was related to the Charlton brothers (Bobby and Jack) and Jackie Milburn through marriage.

SMALL, Wade
Striker

Appearances: 13+9*   Goals: 2*
Born: Croydon, Surrey, 23 February 1984

CAREER
CLUBS: MK Dons, WEDNESDAY (exchange deal

involving Diallo and Jon-Paul McGovern, July 2006).

Small was signed from Milton Keynes Dons in an exchange deal involving Drissa Dillo and Jon-Paul McGovern in July 2006. He was an apprentice with Wimbledon before turning professional in 2003. A skilful, pacy striker, he eted 15 goals in 115 games for the Dons.

SMELT, John William
Forward

Appearances: 16   Goals: 2
Born: Rotherham, December 1895
Died: Carlisle, September 1968

CAREER
CLUBS: Rotherham County, Portsmouth, WEDNESDAY (free, February 1921-October 1922), Bangor City, Barrow.
OTHER: Army – First World War.

Jack Smelt occupied all five forward positions during his career but always preferred the right wing. He made his debut for the Owls versus Blackpool in February 1921, when he deputised for Alf Capper in a 1-1 draw. His first goals for the club came in a 6-0 drubbing of Wolves later that season. His brother, Len, was also a professional footballer.

SMITH, Dean
Defender

Appearances: 61+1 Goals: 1
Born: West Bromwich, 19 March 1971

CAREER
CLUBS: West Bromwich Albion, Walsall, Hereford United, Leyton Orient, WEDNESDAY (free, February 2003-August 2004), Port Vale, Leyton Orient (youth team coach).

Dean Smith made 166 appearances for Walsall and 146 for Hereford before taking his tally past the 600-mark with Orient. An aggressive defender, he captained the Owls in 2003/04 when a near ever-present. An inspiration to his teammates, Smith was one of a number of out-of-contract players who were released at the end of that season. He made his debut for Wednesday against Crystal Palace soon after joining.

SMITH, Ian Paul
Midfield

Appearances: 22+8 Goals: 2
Born: Easington, Co. Durham, 22 January 1976

CAREER
CLUBS: Burnley, Oldham Athletic, Torquay United, Hartlepool United, WEDNESDAY (free, July 2003-July 2005), Kidderminster Harriers.

Left-sided midfielder Paul Smith followed his manager Chris Turner to Wednesday from Hartlepool and made an excellent start to his career at Hillsborough, scoring a couple of goals when the team was flying. However, a stress fracture of the foot set him back and, during his absence, performances on the field slumped. A knee injury sidelined him later on.

SMITH, James
Goalkeeper

Appearances: 79
Born: Sheffield, 11 April 1863
Died: Sheffield, December 1937

CAREER
CLUBS: Nether Club, WEDNESDAY (free, December 1883-May 1893), Rotherham County.

Jim Smith's real name was James Clarke – he preferred to use Smith as a pseudonym when playing football! The recipient of a Football Alliance championship winners' medal with the Owls in 1890, Smith was big and brave and gave the club excellent service for a decade, appearing in almost 200 first-team matches, 79 in serious competition. He made his debut in the FA Cup-tie against Long Eaton Rangers in November 1884 and helped Wednesday win the Sheffield Challenge Cup in 1887 and 1888, and the Wharncliffe Charity Shield in 1886 and 1888. Replaced between the posts by Billy Allan, he made just one League appearance for Rotherham. Initially a steel melter – and later melting shop manager – at the Atlas Works of John Brown & Co, Smith was the founder of the famous Atlas & Norfolk Sports Club.

SMITH, John
Forward

Appearances: 18   Goals: 1
Born: Ayrshire, Scotland, 1866
Died: Byker, Newcastle, 3 February 1911

CAREER
CLUBS: Kilmarnock, Newcastle East End, Kilmarnock, Sunderland, Liverpool, WEDNESDAY (£50, August 1893-August 1894), Newcastle United. OTHER: licensee.

Despite being a forward, Jack Smith scored only one goal for Wednesday – in a 4-1 League win over Stoke in December 1893. Very popular in the north-east, he was tricky and hard working and helped Sunderland win the League title in 1892. He was only forty-four when he died after a short illness.

SMITH, John Thomas
Centre forward

Appearances: 1
Born: Chester Moor, 8 April 1905
Deceased by 1992

CAREER
CLUBS: Annfield Plain, Blackpool, Blyth Spartans, West Stanley, WEDNESDAY (£10, August 1934-June 1937), Gateshead.

Strong and well built, Tom Smith – nicknamed 'Gunboat' – could also play on the right wing. He was twenty-nine when he joined Wednesday, having not previously played League football. He made his debut in the First Division versus Blackburn in January 1935, deputising for Jack Palethorpe. After leaving Hillsborough he scored 33 goals in 49 games for Gateshead.

SMITH, Mark Craig
Defender

Appearances: 351+1   Goals: 20
Born: Shirecliffe, Sheffield, 21 March 1960

CAREER
CLUBS: Sheffield Boys, WEDNESDAY (April 1976-July 1987), Plymouth Argyle, Barnsley, Notts County, Port Vale, Huddersfield Town, Chesterfield, Lincoln City (player, coach), Notts County (coach), Barnsley (coach), WEDNESDAY (Under-19 Academy coach, July 2003).

A very capable defender, Mark Smith gained five England Under-21 caps during his time at Hillsborough. A great organiser, he proved a steady influence as he matured over the years. He made his League debut against Colchester in April 1978 and helped the Owls climb out of the Third Division and into the First between 1980 and 1984, missing very few games in the first three seasons. He had a long spell as captain and his dedicated service and loyalty to Wednesday earned him a testimonial before he left for Plymouth after losing his place in the team. A useful penalty-taker, he netted 11 times from the spot for the Owls. Smith played for five different clubs in 1992/93 and his lengthy career realised 620 appearances – 510 in the Football League of which 282 were with the

Owls. He also represented the Football League Second Division versus Italy's Serie 'B'.

SMITH, Norman
Wing half

Appearances: 23
Born: Newburn, 12 December 1897
Died: Newcastle, 18 May 1978

CAREER
CLUBS: Mickley Athletic, Newburn, Huddersfield Town, WEDNESDAY (£1,600, December 1927-August 1930), Queens Park Rangers, Kreuzlingen FC (player-coach), St Gallen (coach), Newcastle United (trainer, caretaker manager), England (trainer), Football League (trainer).

Norman Smith was thirty when he signed for Wednesday. A rugged competitor, able to occupy both wing half berths, he had helped Huddersfield win the League Championship in 1925 before having his first outing with the Owls against Sunderland in December 1927. He made all his appearances for the club that season and was a regular in the reserves after that. Smith was Newcastle's trainer for twenty-three years.

SMITH, Royston Leonard
Goalkeeper

Appearances: 97
Born: Shirebrook, Sheffield, 22 September 1916
Deceased by 2000

CAREER
CLUBS: Selby Town, WEDNESDAY (£10, February 1936-December 1948), Notts County.

Roy Smith's career at Hillsborough was seriously disrupted by the Second World War. Prior to the conflict he made 45 appearances between the posts and during the hostilities played in 24 regional games before having a further 52 outings between 1946 and 1948. Tall and competent, with good anticipation, he made his debut for the Owls against Bolton in March 1937 in place of Jack Brown and had his best pre-war run in the first team from January to April 1939. He made 110 League appearances for Notts County, helping the Magpies win the Third Division (North) title in 1950.

SMITH, Wilfred Samuel
Defender

Appearances: 233   Goals: 5
Born: Neumünster, West Germany, 3 September 1946

CAREER
CLUBS: WEDNESDAY (April 1961-August 1970), Coventry City, Brighton & Hove Albion, Millwall, Bristol Rovers, Chesterfield, Atherstone.
OTHER: now runs two retails businesses in Leicestershire.

Wilf Smith, who captained both Sheffield Boys and England Youth, gave Wednesday excellent service for eight years, during which time he won six Under-23 caps and thrice represented the Football League. A member of the Owls' 1966 FA Cup final team, he was eighteen when he made his debut in a 4-1 League win over Blackpool in December 1964, deputising for the injured Gerry Young. The following season he occupied the right half and both full-back positions, playing at right-back in the Wembley Cup final. After a decent spell in the no.2 shirt, he switched to the left to accommodate Harold Wilcockson halfway through the 1969/70 season. He played in 135 League games for Coventry – who signed him for a record fee of £100,000 – and, on retirement, had chalked up almost 500 appearances at club level. Smith's first game at Hillsborough was as a fifteen year old for Sheffield Schools versus Nottingham Schools. When he was born, his father was a soldier in Germany.

S

SMITH, William Shiel
Left half

Appearances: 29   Goals: 1
Born: South Shields, 22 October 1903
Died: London, circa 1985

CAREER
CLUBS: Jarrow, WEDNESDAY (£50, August 1927-May 1933), Brentford, Crystal Palace, Burnley, Accrington Stanley.

Bill Smith made his League debut for Wednesday in place of the injured Billy Marsden in the 1-1 home draw with Sheffield United in February 1930 before 54,400 fans. He had his best spell in the first team in 1931/32 when he scored his only goal in a 3-2 win at Chelsea. He did reasonably well with Palace and Burnley.

SNODIN, Glynn
Utility

Appearances: 65+9 Goals: 1
Born: Rotherham, 14 February 1960

CAREER
CLUBS: Doncaster Rovers, WEDNESDAY (£135,000, June 1985), Leeds United, Oldham Athletic, Rotherham United, Heart of Midlothian, Barnsley, Carlisle United (player-coach), Gainsborough Trinity, Scarborough (coach), Doncaster Rovers (assistant manager), Charlton Athletic (coach).

Glyn Snodin scored over 90 goals in almost 600 appearances in eighteen years – 350 for Doncaster. Able to occupy a variety of positions, he spent two seasons at Hillsborough, making his Wednesday debut at left-back in a 5-1 League defeat at Tottenham, netting his only goal two months later in a 1-1 draw at QPR. Snodin played with his brother, Ian, at Doncaster and was later appointed as his assistant at Belle Vue in 1998.

Glynn Snodin

SOLTVELDT, Trond Egil
Midfield

Appearances: 81   Goals: 4
Born: Voss, Norway, 15 February 1967

CAREER
CLUBS: Dale IF, Ny-Krohnborg, Viking Stavanger, Brann Bergen, Stoke City, Rosenborg, Coventry City, Southampton, WEDNESDAY (loan, January 2001, signed for £200,000, March 2001-June 2003), Brann Bergen, Hovding.

A Norwegian international midfielder with four caps, Trond Soltveldt made 69 appearances for Coventry and 39 for Saints before joining the Owls. Quiet and respected, 6ft 1in tall, with a true professional attitude, he had been plagued by injuries prior to his move to Hillsborough and was out of action for six weeks. He settled in immediately with the Owls and became the driving force in midfield. Strong in the tackle, hard working, with an eye for an opening, he made his debut against

Tranmere shortly after signing and scored his first goal in the 2-1 win at West Bromwich Albion in mid-March 2001. Prior to entering the English game, Soltveldt had hit 62 goals in 189 League games in Norway.

SONNER, Daniel James
Midfield

Appearances: 49+14   Goals: 4
Born: Wigan, 9 January 1972

CAREER
CLUBS: Wigan Athletic, Burnley, Bury, Preussen Koln, FC Erzgebirge, Ipswich Town, WEDNESDAY (£75,000, October 1998-August 2000), Birmingham City, Wolverhampton Wanderers, Walsall, Nottingham Forest, Kidderminster Harriers, Peterborough United, Port Vale, Southend United, Port Vale.

The recipient of 4 'B' and 13 full caps for Northern Ireland, Danny Sonner was a League Cup runner-up in 2001 and gained promotion to the Premiership the following year with Birmingham. A competent midfielder, strong in style and full of energy, he made his debut for Wednesday in a 1-0 defeat at Coventry forty-eight hours after joining and scored his first goal in a 4-1 win at Blackburn in February 1999. He made almost 300 appearances with English League clubs.

SPIKSLEY, Frederick
Outside left

Appearances: 337   Goals: 126
Born: Gainsborough, 25 January 1870
Died: Goodwood, Suffolk, 28 July 1948

CAREER
CLUBS: Gainsborough Trinity, WEDNESDAY (free, January 1891-October 1904), Glossop, Leeds City, Southend United, Watford, AIK (coach), Sweden national team (coach), Bayern Munich (coach), Nuremburg (coach), Barcelona (coach), Real Club España OD (player-coach), Reforma Club (coach), Fulham (coach), Nuremburg (coach), Lausanne Sports (coach).
OTHER: Army (interned in August 1914); a fine ice-skater, rower, swimmer and sprinter who also enjoyed horse racing.

One of the celebrities of the 1890s, 'Flying' Fred Spiksley – 5ft 6ins tall and of slight build – was a tremendously effective outside left. He was extremely quick and a fine dribbler who scored some stunning and crucial goals, many of them from well outside the penalty area. He required a partner as fast as himself in order to shine and produce his best form. An FA Cup winner with Wednesday in 1896, he helped the Owls to win the Second Division title in 1900 and carry off the First Division prize three years later.

He joined Wednesday by accident. Held up in Sheffield after agreeing to sign for Accrington, he met up with Owls' star Fred Thompson and, following a few words with club secretary John Holmes, he quickly changed his mind and signed for Wednesday. He scored twice from the inside left position in his first competitive outing for the club against Bolton in an FA Cup-tie in January 1892 (won 4-1) and lined up on the right wing for Wednesday's first League game at Notts County the following September.

Certainly one of the best footballers ever to represent the Owls, he is credited with the first hat-trick at Owlerton. He netted twice in the 1896 FA Cup final win over Wolves and also scored twice on his international debut, helping England thrash Wales 6-0 in March 1893. He played six times more for his country – scoring three extra goals – and twice represented the Football League – against the League of Ireland in 1894 and the Scottish League in 1903. A respected coach in Sweden, Germany, Mexico, Spain and Switzerland, he collapsed and died at a Goodwood race meeting in 1948.

SPOORS, James
Defender

Appearances: 272   Goals: 5
Born: Jarrow, July 1888
Died: Aston, Sheffield, 3 February 1960

CAREER
CLUBS: Jarrow, WEDNESDAY (£10, April 1908-May 1920), Barnsley.
OTHER: licensee.

Jimmy Spoors could occupy any defensive position and did so with authority during his twelve years with Wednesday. Signed by manager Bob Brown, he made his League debut against Middlesbrough in November 1908 and when Willie Layton retired he bedded himself in at right-back, later switching to the left. A consistent performer through to the end of 1914/15, he made 15 appearances for the Owls during the First World War. Spoors married the daughter of ex-Wednesday star Jack Hudson.

SPRINGETT, Peter John
Goalkeeper

Appearances: 207
Born: Fulham, 8 May 1946
Died: Sheffield, 28 September 1997

CAREER
CLUBS: Queens Park Rangers, WEDNESDAY (£40,000 exchange with brother Ron, June 1967-July 1975), Barnsley, Scarborough.
OTHER: policeman (South Yorkshire).

Peter Springett made 160 appearances for QPR before joining the Owls, his experienced brother Ron switching to Loftus Road. An England Youth international, he also gained six Under-23 caps and was a League Cup and Third Division championship winner with Rangers in 1967. A fine, agile, courageous 'keeper with a solid frame, his first outing for the Owls was at West Ham in August 1967. Ousted by Peter Grummitt, he bounced back in 1973 and held his place until Peter Fox took over. He made over 200 appearances in five years with Barnsley before becoming PC Springett, working at both Hillsborough and Bramall Lane on match days.

SPRINGETT, Ronald Derrick
Goalkeeper

Appearances: 384
Born: Fulham, 22 July 1935

CAREER
CLUBS: Victoria United, Queens Park Rangers, WEDNESDAY (March 1958-June 1967), Queens Park Rangers, Valley United;
OTHER: Army – based in Egypt; ran a sports shop and decorating and gardening business in London.

Until Nigel Worthington took over the crown, Ron Springett was Wednesday's most-capped player, starring in 33 internationals for England – his first versus Northern Ireland in 1959. He also represented the Football League on nine occasions. A

Ronald Springett

brave, dependable custodian, with cat-like agility and phenomenal anticipation, he was superb in the latter stages of 1957/58 – his first season. Had manager Eric Taylor signed him earlier, it is possible that Wednesday would not have been relegated. The following season he was again outstanding as the Owls won the Second Division title, and in 1960/61 he helped Wednesday finish runners-up behind double-winners Tottenham. The last line of defence in the 1966 FA Cup final defeat by Everton, he made his debut for Wednesday against Bolton in March 1958 and played his last game versus Leeds in May 1967. He was named in Alf Ramsey's forty-strong 1966 World Cup squad as cover for Gordon Banks. Peter Bonetti was the other 'keeper. Springett retired with 507 appearances under his belt.

The Springett brothers played against each other twice – Wednesday winning both games. There was a Springett on the books at Hillsborough from March 1958 to December 1974, and between them Peter and Ron amassed 571 appearances for the Owls. For Wednesday and QPR, their combined total was 874 and during their respective careers they played 1,120 top-level matches. Ron turned down Sunderland to sign for Wednesday in 1958. His daughter, Terry, is an England women's international footballer.

SPURR, Thomas
Defender

Appearances: 35+5*
Born: Leeds, 13 September 1987

CAREER
CLUBS: WEDNESDAY (apprentice, February 2004, professional June 2006).

Left-sided defender Tom Spurr is energetic, athletic, strong and competitive and played superbly well for the Owls' second string before making his senior debut towards the end of the 2005/06 campaign.

SRNICEK, Pavel
Goalkeeper

Appearances: 52
Born: Bohumin, Czechoslovakia, 10 March 1968

CAREER
CLUBS: Victoria Bohumin Juniors, ZD Bohumin, Dukla Tabor, Banik Ostava, Leicester City, Newcastle United, Olympique Marseille, Banik Ostrava, WEDNESDAY (free, November 1998-June 2000), Brescia, Cosena, Wolverhampton Wanderers, Portsmouth, West Ham United, Beira Mar, Newcastle United.

Czech international Pavel Srnicek, who won 49 caps, made 188 appearances for Newcastle, gaining a Division One championship winners' medal in 1993. He gave the Owls excellent service until switching his allegiance to Italy. He was third choice at Portsmouth.

STACEY, William Heaton
Utility

Appearances: 5
Born: Sheffield, March 1848
Died: Sheffield, 5 November 1903

CAREER
CLUBS: Hallam, WEDNESDAY (free, August 1876-May 1883).

Bill Stacey was a versatile footballer, quick but not always reliable. The first 2 of his 5 FA Cup appearances for the Owls were in goal, against Blackburn Rovers in December 1880 and Darwen in February 1881. His other appearances were as a full-back. A strong player, he made almost 100 appearances in all games for the Owls and helped the team win the Sheffield Challenge Cup in 1877, 1878 and 1881, and the Wharncliffe Charity Cup in 1879. He was named as reserve for England in 1874 and captained Wednesday on several occasions. His brother, Frank, also kept for Wednesday.

STAINROD, Simon Allan
Forward

Appearances: 8+7   Goals: 2
Born: Sheffield, 1 February 1959

CAREER
CLUBS: Hillsborough Celtic, Sheffield United, Oldham Athletic, Queens Park Rangers, WEDNESDAY (£250,000, February-September 1985), Aston Villa, Stoke City, Racing Club Strasbourg, FFC Rouen, Falkirk (player, caretaker-manager), Dundee (player-caretaker, manager), Ayr United (manager)
OTHER: football agent.

Simon Stainrod was an aggressive striker who had a knack for being in the right spot at the right time. He also had a fiery temper and was often in trouble with referees. An England Youth international, he scored 97 goals in 336 appearances in twenty-five years in Britain and France. He helped QPR win the Second Division title in 1983, netted a four-timer for Aston Villa on his debut in the League Cup versus Exeter City in 1985, and was Wednesday's joint record signing at £250,000 (with Mirocevic). He spent just seven months at Hillsborough, netting his first goal against his former club, QPR, in April 1985. His father was an amateur with the Owls and Sheffield United.

STANIFORTH, Ronald
Full-back

Appearances: 107   Goals: 2
Born: Newton Heath, Manchester, 13 April 1924
Died: 1988

CAREER
CLUBS: Manchester Boys, Newton Albion, Stockport County, Huddersfield Town, WEDNESDAY (player exchange deal, July 1955-October 1959), Barrow (player-manager), Hull University (coach), WEDNESDAY (assistant coach, chief coach, youth coach, July 1970-January 1976).
OTHER: worked in a Barrow shipyard.

Ronald Staniforth

Signed in 1955 as part of the Roy Shiner, Tony Conwell and Jackie Marriott four-player exchange deal, Ron Staniforth was both stylish and polished, a right-back perfectionist who was unruffled in deportment, possessing a clean strong kick and exceptional positional sense. A competent all-round defender, he made 223 appearances for Stockport and 118 for Huddersfield before joining the Owls. He made his debut in a 5-2 win over Plymouth in August 1955 and scored the first of his two goals against the same team in the return fixture at Home Park four months later. Capped eight times by England in 1954, playing in that 7-1 defeat by Hungary in Budapest, he also starred for the 'B' team and helped Huddersfield gain promotion to the First Division in 1953. He won two Second Division championship medals with Wednesday in 1956 and 1959, and it was a pity the club didn't spot him sooner! As manager, he twice had to seek re-election to the Football League with Barrow.

STAPLETON, William
Right-back

Appearances: 19
Born: Sheffield, January 1895
Died: Sheffield, 15 June 1929

CAREER

CLUBS: *Mexborough Town, WEDNESDAY (free, September 1915-October 1920), Swansea Town.*
OTHER: *Army – First World War.*

For most of 1919/20, Bill Stapleton shared the right-back berth with Tom Brittleton and Jimmy Spoors, with other players slotting in from time to time. In fact, six different players occupied that position all told. The strong-kicking Stapleton appeared in 73 First World War games before finally making his League debut against Middlesbrough in August 1919. He left Hillsborough following the arrival of Jack Bellas.

Ronnie Starling (right) before the 1935 FA Cup final

STARLING, Ronald William
Inside forward

Appearances: 194   Goals: 31
Born: *Pelaw-on-Tyne, 11 October 1909*
Died: *Sheffield, 17 December 1991*

CAREER

CLUBS: *Newcastle United, Usworth Colliery, Washington Colliery, Hull City, Newcastle United, WEDNESDAY (£3,250, June 1932-January 1937), Aston Villa; Nottingham Forest (player-coach), Beighton MW.*
WARTIME GUEST APPEARANCES: *Northampton Town, Hereford United, Nottingham Forest, Walsall, WEDNESDAY (April 1941).*
OTHER: *ran a newsagent's shop near Hillsborough.*

Wednesday's skipper in their 1935 FA Cup final victory over West Bromwich Albion, Ronnie Starling also helped the Owls win the Charity Shield that same year. A terrific footballing strategist whose tactics could turn the course of a game in a matter of minutes, he possessed all the tricks of the trade and often produced them out on the field of play. At his peak, Starling was rated better than the great Scottish international Alex James and one biography noted that he was 'a ball playing genius'. Nicknamed 'Flutterfoot', he once netted 8 goals in a junior game and 45 in a season. He gave Wednesday tremendous service for almost five years, making his debut in August 1932 versus Blackpool, scoring his first goal four days later at Everton.

After leaving Hillsborough for a record fee of £6,900, he helped Aston Villa win the Second Division title in 1938 and retired with a record of 65 goals in 431 competitive games. He made over 200 appearances during the Second World War, including 136 for Villa, and was sixty when he played in his last charity match. After a successful trial, Starling won two caps for England versus Scotland in April 1933 and April 1937 – the latter in front of 149,547 fans at Hampden Park. He also played for an International XI against a District XI in September 1940 and appeared in four FA Cup semi-finals with different clubs in nine years: Hull in 1930, Newcastle in 1932, Wednesday in 1935 and Villa in 1938 – and he could preach a sermon as well as any vicar!

STEFANOVIC, Dejan
Defender

Appearances: *65+7 Goals: 5*
Born: *Vranje, Yugoslavia, 20 October 1974*

CAREER

CLUBS: *Yumco Vranje, Red Star Belgrade, Vradnicki Belgrade, WEDNESDAY (£2 million with Darko Kovacevic, December 1995-November 1999), Perugia, OFK Belgrade, Vitesse Arnhem, Portsmouth.*

Capped 23 times by Serbia and Montenegro – four with Wednesday – Dejan Stefanovic, 6ft 2ins tall, joined the Owls with his fellow countryman Kovacevic in a joint record transfer. He spent three and a half years at Hillsborough, during which time he produced some fine perform-ances at the heart of the defence. Undoubtedly a class player and comfortable on the ball, at times he gets caught out of position, but his overall displays have always been solid. He made his debut for the Owls as a substitute against Nottingham Forest in December 1995 and scored his first goal for the club in the ninetieth minute to earn a point at Chelsea in December 1996. When he returned to England after four years away, Stefanovic became Portsmouth's most expensive player at £1.85 million.

STEPHENSON, George Ternent
Forward

Appearances: 45   Goals: 20
Born: Seaton Delaval, 3 September 1900
Died: Derby, 18 August 1971

CAREER

CLUBS: *New Delaval Juniors, New Delaval Villa, Leeds City, Aston Villa, Stourbridge (L), Derby County, WEDNESDAY (£4,850 with Teddy Davison, February 1931-July 1933), Preston North End, Charlton Athletic (coaching staff, assistant man-ager, scout), Huddersfield Town (assistant manager, manager), Derby County (coach).*
OTHER: *licensee; worked in the Rolls Royce factory, Derby.*

A former grocer, smithy and pit worker, George Stephenson, like his brother Clem, was an

England international, capped against France and Belgium in 1928 and France in 1931, having earlier played in a junior match versus Scotland in 1920. An intelligent, cultured footballer, Stephenson scored 120 goals in 319 League games in his career, netting four-timers in two First Division matches for Derby. Small in stature, with a big heart, he made his debut for the Owls versus Bolton in February 1931 and struck his first goal in his next match, a 5-3 defeat at Liverpool. After leaving Hillsborough, he was a key performer at Preston, helped Charlton win the Third Division (South) title in 1935 and scored 22 goals in almost 100 outings for Villa. A respected manager, he found it hard going at times with Huddersfield, who battled continuously against relegation. He eventually quit with Second Division football looming. His son, Bob, also played football for Derby and, as a cricketer, kept wicket for Derbyshire and Hampshire.

STERLAND, Melvyn
Right-back

Appearances: 338+9   Goals: 49
Born: Sheffield, 1 October 1961

CAREER

CLUBS: *Middlewood Rovers, WEDNESDAY (June 1978-March 1989), Glasgow Rangers, Leeds United, Boston United (manager), Denaby United, Hallam.*
OTHER: *football agent.*

An England international who was capped once at senior level, seven times by the Under-21s and also for the 'B' team, Mel Sterland also represented the Football League. An aggres-sive, tireless, all-action footballer with a heart of gold, and known to everyone as 'Zico', he made his debut for Wednesday as a second-half substitute against Blackpool in the penultimate League game of 1978/79. He gained a regular place in the side in 1981, going on to appear in

Mel Sterland

almost 350 matches, helping the team win promotion to the top flight in 1984. He netted several cracking goals for Wednesday, claiming 11 in 1985/86. Voted supporters' Player of the Year in 1983, he battled against injury before his transfer to Rangers. He never settled at Ibrox Park and was back in Yorkshire within four months. A First Division championship winner with Leeds in 1992, he added 144 appearances and 20 goals to his tally before quitting top-class football in 1994.

He underwent a life-saving operation to remove a blood clot in 2003.

STEVENS, J.
Left half

Appearances: 5
Born: Sheffield, circa 1857
Deceased by 1938

CAREER
CLUBS: WEDNESDAY (1881/82).

The tough-tackling Stevens played in five FA Cup games for Wednesday in 1881/82 – the first against Staveley, the last versus Blackburn in the semi-final.

STEVENSON, Thomas
Wing half

Appearances: 2
Born: Clyde, circa 1873
Died: Glasgow, circa 1951

CAREER
CLUBS: Clyde, WEDNESDAY (free, August 1897-June 1898), Clyde.

Tom Stevenson spent one season with Wednesday, playing in two League games – the first against Sunderland in September 1897 and the second at Nottingham Forest in February 1898. He made over 100 appearances in his two spells with Clyde.

STEWART, James
Inside forward

Appearances: 142   Goals: 59
Born: Gateshead, 7 June 1883
Died: Gateshead, 23 May 1957

CAREER
CLUBS: Todds Nook, Gateshead NER, WEDNESDAY (May 1902-August 1908), Newcastle United, Glasgow Rangers, North Shields (player-manager), Derby County (scout).
OTHER: worked as a commercial traveller.

'Tadger' Stewart had a repertoire of fine skills that delighted spectators and was a regular goalscorer throughout his career, finding the net in Wednesday's 1907 FA Cup final victory over Everton, having notched a vital goal in the semi-final victory over Arsenal. Capped three times by England versus Wales and Scotland, and after his record £1,000 transfer to St James' Park, he struck 53 goals in 138 games for Newcastle, gaining a League championship medal in 1909 and an FA Cup runners-up medal two years later. Unfortunately Stewart had a reputation for swearing and was once suspended indefinitely by the directors at Newcastle for using bad language towards a member of staff. Besides football, he also enjoyed a game of billiards.

STEWART, Reginald Percy
Centre half

Appearances: 8
Born: Sheffield, 15 October 1925

CAREER
CLUBS: Sheffield YMCA, WEDNESDAY (September 1944-July 1950), Colchester United, Hastings United, Clacton Town.
OTHER: ran a sport and leisure club.

An England Schoolboy international, Reg Stewart played in 8 senior and 3 Second World War matches for the Owls. He made his senior debut in the FA Cup versus Mansfield Town in January 1946 and followed up with his League baptism at Manchester City nine months later when he deputised for Cyril Turton. After leaving the Owls, Stewart played for Colchester in their first season of League football (1950/51) and made almost 300 appearances for the Layer Road club in seven years. His father was a professional with Derby County.

STEWART, Simon Andrew
Defender

Appearances: 7+1
Born: Leeds, 1 November 1973

CAREER
CLUBS: WEDNESDAY (May 1990-June 1993), Shrewsbury Town (L), Fulham, Woking, Kingstonian,
Spalding United (manager).
OTHER: teacher at Bedford college.

Commanding centre-back and former Lincolnshire Boys player Simon Stewart was handed his debut for the Owls by manager Trevor Francis during a fixture pile-up at the end of the 1992/93 season against Ipswich Town. Failing to establish himself at Hillsborough, he later won the FA Trophy with Kingstonian in 1999 and 2000.

STOCKDALE, Robert Keith
Left-back

Appearances: 6
Born: Redcar, 30 November 1979

CAREER
CLUBS: Middlesbrough, WEDNESDAY (loan, September-October 2000), West Ham United, Rotherham United, Hull City.

A Scottish international, capped four times at senior level and twice by the 'B' team, Robbie Stockdale had earlier played in one Under-21 game for England. A good tackler, he appeared in 91 games for Middlesbrough and had loan spells with three other clubs before joining Hull City in 2005. He made his debut for Wednesday against Nottingham Forest in September 2000, taking the place of Andy Hinchcliffe who was injured.

STORRAR, David McKinnon
Outside left

Appearances: 4
Born: Lochgelly, 16 October 1933

CAREER
CLUBS: Wath Wanderers, WEDNESDAY (April 1948-May 1954), Grimsby Town, Scunthorpe United, Frickley Colliery.

OTHER: *employed on the railways and twice won the Yorkshire senior golf title.*

David Storrar deputised for Dennis Woodhead in each of his four League games for Wednesday, making his debut at West Bromwich Albion in December 1952 in a match that was won 1-0.

STRANGE, Alfred Henry
Inside forward, wing half

Appearances: 273
Born: Ripley, Derbyshire, 2 April 1900
Died: Ripley, 7 October 1978

CAREER
CLUBS: Ripley Town, WEDNESDAY (trial, August 1918), Portsmouth, Port Vale, WEDNESDAY (£1,230 plus Harry Antiss, February 1927-May 1935), Bradford Park Avenue, Ripley Town, Raleigh Athletic, Corsham United.
OTHER: worked down the pit and ran a poultry farm in Ripley.

After spending the first third of his career as an inside forward, Alf Strange turned into

Alf Strange

a brilliant right half who gained 20 caps for England and twice represented the Football League. Swift in the tackle and a purveyor of fine passes and long-range shooting, he helped Wednesday win two League titles (1929 and 1930) but was in the reserves when the FA Cup was won in 1935. Making the breakthrough with Portsmouth – for whom he netted five goals versus Gillingham in January 1923 – he did well with Port Vale before making his debut for the Owls at inside left in a 4-1 League win over Sunderland in February 1927. His first outing as a wing half was against Spurs in April 1928 and he remained a permanent fixture in the side at right-half until losing his place to Leach in 1934. After that he covered for Leach, Burrows and Sharp.

STRATFORD, Charles Laughton
Half-back

Appearances: 11
Born: Sheffield, 1858
Died: 1927

CAREER
CLUBS: WEDNESDAY (August 1877-April 1885).
OTHER: worked as an electroplater.

An efficient and versatile defender, Charlie Stratford occupied all three half-back positions for Wednesday. He made his senior debut in an FA Cup-tie versus Darwen in February 1881 and played his last game in the same competition against Nottingham Forest in January 1885. He was a Sheffield Cup and thrice Wharncliffe Charity Cup winner.

STREETS, George Henry
Goalkeeper

Appearances: 2
Born: Nottingham, 5 April 1893
Died: Nottingham, 25 July 1958

CAREER
CLUBS: Nottingham St Margaret's, Raleigh Athletic, Mansfield Mechanics, WEDNESDAY (£50, April 1913-March 1915), Grantham Town, Notts County, Boston Town, Newark Town.
OTHER: Army – First World War.

George Streets' first game for Wednesday was at Bolton in September 1913 as stand-in for Teddy Davison. Later in the season he conceded six goals at home to Burnley. Streets, who was a very confident 'keeper, had the great Albert Iremonger as his ally at Meadow Lane, yet still managed 133 League appearances for Notts County.

STRINGER, Christopher
Goalkeeper

Appearances: 8+4
Born: Sheffield, 19 June 1983

CAREER
CLUBS: WEDNESDAY (September 1999-June 2004).

Third choice at Hillsborough, Chris Stringer, 6ft 6ins tall, looked very promising when playing at first-team level but never quite made the required breakthrough – a spate of injuries certainly didn't help his cause. He made his debut for Wednesday as a first-minute substitute versus Wolves in August 2000, after Kevin Pressman had been sent off.

STRINGFELLOW, James Francis
Inside right

Appearances: 21   Goals: 5
Born: Sutton-in-Ashfield, March 1888
Died: Lincoln, 1966

CAREER
CLUBS: Ilkeston United, WEDNESDAY (£85, December 1908-April 1911), Mansfield Town, Portsmouth,

Heart of Midlothian, Weymouth, Bournemouth, Scunthorpe & Lindsay United.

Frank Stringfellow scored over 140 goals in more than 400 appearances either side of the First World War, including 91 in 213 League outings for Portsmouth. A shade on the small side, but of stocky build, he was quick and elusive and certainly gave defenders plenty to think about with his all-action style. He made his debut to Wednesday against Preston in February 1909 and netted his first goal for the club in a 3-1 defeat at Newcastle a year later.

STRUTT, Brian John
Right-back

Appearances: 2
Born: Malta, 21 September 1959

CAREER
CLUBS: WEDNESDAY (April 1975-May 1981), Matlock Town, Worksop Town, Gisborne City, Mount Manganui.
OTHER: worked for an electrical and household firm in New Zealand.

A reliable reserve, Brian Strutt's two appearances for the Owls came at Blackpool in November 1979 and at home to Rotherham in February 1980, filling in for Ray Blackhall both times.

STUBBS, Francis Lloyd
Goalkeeper

Appearances: 18
Born: Woodhouse Eaves, Leicestershire, 13 April 1878
Died: Loughborough, 11 May 1944

CAREER
CLUBS: Loughborough Town, WEDNESDAY (£50, May 1900-April 1903), Loughborough Wednesday.
OTHER: butcher; mayor of Loughborough (1942).

Frank Stubbs' career with Wednesday effectively ended in September 1901. He took a bang on the head while conceding six goals in a League game against Notts County. His place went to Jack Lyall.

SUNLEY, David
Centre forward

Appearances: 135+13   Goals: 26
Born: Skelton, Saltburn, 6 February 1952

CAREER
CLUBS: Preston North End, Middlesbrough, WEDNESDAY (June 1968-January 1976), Nottingham Forest (L), Hull City, Lincoln City, Stockport County, Tsuen Wan, Stafford Rangers, Burton Albion, Matlock Town.
OTHER: builder's labourer.

Neat and progressive in style, David Sunley's career produced 45 goals in 324 League appearances. He had his best years at Hillsborough, making his debut for the Owls versus Birmingham City in December 1970, netting the first in a 3-1 win over Portsmouth three months later.

SURTEES, John
Forward

Appearances: 50   Goals: 8
Born: Percy Main, Co. Durham, 1 July 1911
Died: Percy Main, 16 July 1992

CAREER
CLUBS: Willington Juniors, Percy Main Amateurs, Middlesbrough, Portsmouth, Bournemouth Athletic, Northampton Town, WEDNESDAY (free, December 1934-March 1936), Nottingham Forest, Darlington (manager), WEDNESDAY (scout, November 1948-1960).
WARTIME GUEST APPEARANCES: York City.

An FA Cup winner with Wednesday in 1935, John Surtees had struggled to get first-team football at Middlesbrough, Portsmouth and Northampton and played in just 20 League games for Bournemouth. He made his debut for the Owls in place of Starling versus Birmingham soon after joining the club, doing well enough to retain his place – Starling was switched to inside left. He notched his first goal in a 2-1 home win over West Bromwich Albion in January 1935.

SUTHERLAND, George
Right-back

Appearances: 3
Born: New Scone, Perth, Scotland, 1876
Deceased by 1948

CAREER
CLUBS: Perthshire, WEDNESDAY (November 1894-May 1897).
OTHER: baker.

Reserve to Jack Earp, George Sutherland's League debut was against Wolves in November 1894. His brother, Donald, played for Grimsby and Burton Swifts.

SWAN, Peter
Centre half

Appearances: 289+2
Born: South Elmsall, 8 October 1936

CAREER
CLUBS: Doncaster Schools, WEDNESDAY (May 1952, banned May 1965; re-signed, June 1972-August 1973), Bury, Matlock Town, Worksop Town.
OTHER: licensee.

Regarded as one of the best 'stopper' centre halves of his day, Peter Swan, tall, long-legged, strong, dominating and hard to beat on the ground and in the air, was playing some of the best football of his career when, in 1964, following an article published in a Sunday newspaper, he and two of his teammates, Tony Kay and David Layne, plus others, were found guilty of being involved in a betting coup to fix the result of a League game between Wednesday and Ipswich Town. They were sent to prison and banned from professional football. It was a crushing blow to Swan and, indeed, to Wednesday. Swan duly served his sentence and returned to Hillsborough in 1972. Capped three times by England at Under-23 level, Swan appeared in 19 full internationals (1960-62), taking over from the great Billy Wright. He also represented the Football League on five occasions and helped the Owls win the Second Division title in 1959 and finish runners-up in the First Division two years later. Replacing Don McEvoy at the heart of the Owls' defence, he made his League debut at Barnsley in November 1955 and gained a regular place in the side in 1958. Twice an ever-present – in 1959/60 and 1962/63 – he lost eight years of football for being stupid! Swan's son, Peter, scored on his League debut for Doncaster in 1980. Swan's autobiography was published in 2006.

SWIFT, Humphrey Mills
Outside left, full-back

Appearances: 195
Born: Sheffield, 22 January 1921
Died: Sheffield, 24 January 1970

CAREER
CLUBS: Lopham Street Methodists, WEDNESDAY (August 1942-August 1951, remained on groud staff).
WARTIME GUEST APPEARANCES: Sheffield United.

Hugh Swift – a Second World War discovery by Wednesday – developed into a classy defender, a model professional who possessed a terrific sliding tackle. He loved to play on wet, muddy grounds and, besides his wonderful full-back play, he was quick, kicked long and true and, above all, tackled strongly but fairly, often judging his challenges to perfection. He started out on the left wing and actually made his debut for the Owls in that position in a regional game against Doncaster in August 1942. He played in 136 matches – scoring 6 goals – during the war, playing in the first leg of the 1943 League (North) Cup final. He made his League bow at Luton in August 1946, having played at right-back in six FA Cup games earlier in the year. Swift seemed set for honours but sadly his career was cut short on medical grounds at the age of thirty. He had suffered a double fracture of the jaw at Coventry in February 1950 which, at the time, ended a run of 140 consecutive first team appearances. An England 'B' international, capped against Switzerland in 1950, Swift was one of the Wednesday's finest players between 1946 and 1955.

SYKES, Joseph
Half-back

Appearances: 31   Goals: 1
Born: Sheffield, 8 January 1896
Died: Swansea, 4 September 1974

CAREER
CLUBS: WEDNESDAY (August 1919-July 1924), Swansea Town (player, trainer, assistant manager).
OTHER: Army – First World War.

Joe Sykes occupied all three half-back positions for Wednesday. Well built, he had his best spell in the first team between September and November 1920. He made his Owls' debut versus Liverpool in March 1920 and his last game was against Stockport four years later. He made 345 appearances for Swansea, the majority at centre half, skippering the Swans to promotion from Division Three (South).

SYMM, Colin
Midfield

Appearances: 19+4 Goals: 1
Born: Dunston-on-Tyne, 26 November 1946

CAREER
CLUBS: Redheugh Boys Club, Gateshead, WEDNESDAY (May 1965-June 1969), Sunderland, Lincoln City, Boston United, Consett, scout for several clubs.
OTHER: worked for the Derwent District Council.

A neat and tidy footballer, Colin Symm made his debut for the Owls at Everton in October 1966, when he deputised for John Fantham, and scored his only goal in a 5-0 win over his future employers, Sunderland, in March 1967.

T

TALBOT, Andrew
Striker

Appearances: 4+21 Goals: 5
Born: Barnsley, 19 July 1986

CAREER
CLUBS: Barnsley, Dodworth MW, WEDNESDAY (apprentice, February 2004; professional, November 2004-May 2006), Scunthorpe United, Luton Town (L, January 2007).

A pacy, wiry forward with an eye for goal, 'Drew' Talbot made his debut for the Owls as a substitute against Peterborough in October 2004. He scored five goals that season, including vital ones against Hull in the League and Hartlepool in the play-off final.

TAYLOR, Charles Stanley
Forward

Appearances: 7
Born: Sheffield, September 1897
Died: Sheffield, December 1963

CAREER
CLUBS: Norfolk Amateurs, WEDNESDAY (free, August 1919-May 1921), Norton Woodseats, Sheffield United, Denaby United, Mexborough Town, Worksop Town.
OTHER: Army – First World War.

Able to play in the three central forward positions, Stan Taylor was one of several recruits who played for the Owls in 1919/20. He made his League debut against Preston in February 1920 when he deputised for the injured Charlie Binney.

TAYLOR, Ian Kenneth
Midfield

Appearances: 11+7 Goals: 2
Born: Birmingham, 4 June 1968

CAREER
CLUBS: Moor Green, Port Vale, WEDNESDAY (£1m, July-December 1994), Aston Villa, Derby County, Northampton Town.

A workaholic in midfield, Ian Taylor was the main driving force at Port Vale – he netted 35 goals and won the AGT Trophy in 1993. Unfortunately he was played out of position at Hillsborough and never settled, moving to his boyhood heroes, Aston Villa, for whom he rattled in another 43 goals, one coming in their 1996 League Cup final win over Leeds. He reached the milestone of 500 club appearances and 100 goals in 2006.

T

TAYLOR, James
Left half

Appearances: 20
Born: Newcastle, circa 1885
Died: circa 1917

CAREER
CLUBS: Wallsend Park Villa, WEDNESDAY (May 1907-August 1910), Leicester City, Doncaster Rovers.
OTHER: Army – First World War.

A Wednesday reserve, Jim Taylor made his League debut on New Year's Eve 1907 against Woolwich Arsenal, deputising for Bill Bartlett in a 6-0 win. He made 13 of his 20 appearances for the Owls in 1909/10 – one on the left wing at Sunderland. It is believed that Taylor was killed during the First World War.

TAYLOR, Kevin
Midfield

Appearances: 136+9   Goals: 28
Born: Wakefield, 22 January 1961

CAREER
CLUBS: WEDNESDAY (April 1977-July 1984), Derby County, Crystal Palace, Scunthorpe United, Frickley Athletic, Farsley Celtic, Bradford Park Avenue, Leeds United (scout).

Kevin 'Ticker' Taylor did a steady job at Hillsborough. A hard worker, he made his League debut at Plymouth in January 1979 and gained a regular place in the First XI a year later, helping the Owls clinch promotion from the Third Division. He played very well at times, especially in the early 1980s, before slipping out of favour. The first player for whom Derby manager Arthur Cox paid a transfer fee, Taylor did moderately well with the Rams, appeared in almost 100 games for Palace – scoring 15 goals – and scored 30 times in 195 appearances for Scunthorpe.

TAYLOR, Paul Anthony
Midfield

Appearances: 5+1
Born: Sheffield, 3 December 1949

CAREER
CLUBS: Loughborough College, WEDNESDAY (free, June 1971-July 1973), York City, Hereford United, Colchester United, Southport, San José, Los Angeles Skyhawks, Team Hawaii, Gillingham (assistant manager, manager), Walsall (coach, caretaker-manager, general manager).
OTHER: now runs his own soccer consultancy business.

Mark Taylor made only 20 League appearances for his first four clubs, but after joining Southport added a further 95 to his tally in three seasons. Given his senior debut by the Owls, as a twenty year old, at QPR in August 1971, his last appearance followed thirteen months later versus Carlisle. He had a tough time as manager of Gillingham.

TAYLOR, Robert Mark
Midfield

Appearances: 10+1
Born: Birmingham, 22 February 1966

CAREER
CLUBS: Walsall, WEDNESDAY (£50,000, June 1989-September 1991), Shrewsbury Town (l, signed later), Hereford United, Nuneaton Borough, Redditch United (player-coach).

Influential midfielder Mark Taylor made almost 400 senior appearances in 16 years but only 11 for Wednesday. Able to create and defend, he played a few games as a full-back and helped Shrewsbury win the Division Three title in 1994 and reach the Auto Windscreen Shield final in 1996. He made his debut for the Owls at Luton in August 1989.

TAYLOR, Samuel James
Forward

Appearances: 128   Goals: 39
Born: Sheffield, 17 September 1893
Died: Sheffield, 12 March 1973

CAREER
CLUBS: Silverwood Colliery, Huddersfield Town, WEDNESDAY (£3,500, January 1921-May 1925), Mansfield Town, Southampton, Halifax Town, Grantham (two spells), Chesterfield, Lanelli, Loughborough Corinthians.
WARTIME GUEST APPEARANCES: Bradford Park Avenue, Rotherham County.
OTHER: Army – First World War.

A brilliant forward, Sammy Taylor led the Huddersfield attack in the 1920 FA Cup final defeat by Aston Villa. He scored 45 goals in 67 games for the Terriers before joining the Owls – one of manager Bob Brown's first major signings. He made his debut at Port Vale in January 1921 and went on to form fine partnerships with Jimmy McIntyre, Charlie Petrie, Andy Smailes and Sid Binks before transferring to Mansfield after rejecting terms at Hillsborough. Taylor's career realised 200 goals at various levels – 105 in the Football League.

TAYLOR, William
Inside left

Appearances: 17   Goals: 4
Born: Crook, Co. Durham, June 1896
Died: Lincoln, 1977

CAREER
CLUBS: Crook Town, Norfolk Amateurs, WEDNESDAY (free, July 1919-August 1922), Doncaster Rovers (two spells), Mansfield Town (two spells), Mexborough (two spells), Worksop Town.

The hard-working Bill Taylor never really made his mark with Wednesday, despite some enterprising displays. He made his League debut against Aston Villa in April 1920 and scored his first goal forty-eight hours later to earn a 1-0 win over Oldham Athletic. After leaving Hillsborough, he provided much of the guile in the Mansfield attack as they won two Midland League titles in the mid-1920s. Taylor was also a fine billiards player and an accomplished classical and jazz pianist.

THACKERAY 'Fred'
Defender

Appearances: 10
Born: Sheffield, 1878
Deceased by 1948

CAREER
CLUBS: Montrose Works, WEDNESDAY (free, August 1898-May 1904), Gainsborough Trinity, Rotherham Town.

Thackeray was an adaptable defender, strong but a shade overweight at times. He spent six seasons with the Owls, mainly as a reserve, and made his debut against Aston Villa in March 1901 when he replaced Tom Crawshaw who was away on England duty. It is uncertain as to what Thackeray's real Christian name was; it could have been Charles or Harold, but everyone called him 'Fred'.

THOMAS, Walter Keith
Inside left

Appearances: 10   Goals: 1
Born: Oswestry, 28 July 1929

CAREER
CLUBS: Oswestry Town, WEDNESDAY (£3,000, September 1950-July 1952), Cardiff City, Plymouth Argyle, Exeter City, Oswestry Town.
OTHER: served in the RAF and army; teacher to blind children.

T

Keith Thomas found the competition for first team football far too great at Hillsborough and, after spending two seasons with Wednesday, he moved to Cardiff. His first appearance for Wednesday was in a 4-0 defeat at Wolves in March 1951. He then played in the first eight games of 1951/52 which ended with the club winning the Second Division championship trophy. As Flying Officer Thomas, he appeared in representative matches for the RAF.

THOME, Emerson Augusto
Defender

Appearances: 69+2 Goals: 2
Born: Portro Alegre, Brazil, 30 March 1972

CAREER
CLUBS: Internacional, SC Coimbra, Farense, Benfica, WEDNESDAY (free, March 1998-December 1999), Chelsea, Sunderland, Glasgow Rangers, Bolton Wanderers, Wigan Athletic, Derby County.

Thome, 6ft 1in tall and physically strong, takes no prisoners. He spent eighteen months at Hillsborough, during which time he produced some excellent performances, playing alongside Des Walker. He made his debut for the Owls at Barnsley in April 1998 and scored the first of his two goals in a 2-0 FA Cup win over Stockport in January 1999. He never settled at Chelsea, struggled with injuries at Sunderland, played in the 2004 League Cup final for Bolton and helped Wigan reach the Premiership in 2005.

THOMPSON, Emil Guy
Utility

Appearances: 25
Born: Bradford, 1 January 1892
Died: Cleethorpes, circa 1952

CAREER
CLUBS: South Shields, Rotherham Town, Portsmouth, WEDNESDAY (£100, May 1921-August 1922), Bradford Park Avenue, Grimsby Town, Castleford Town, Denaby United, Scunthorpe & Lindsay United.

'Ernie' Thompson won a Southern League championship medal with Portsmouth in 1920 before joining the Owls. A player with great adaptability, he appeared at left half, outside right, inside right and centre forward in a fifteen-year career which was severely dented by the First World War. The first of his 25 outings for the Owls was on the right wing away to Notts County in September 1921.

THOMPSON, Frederick
Full-back, half-back

Appearances: 45   Goals: 3
Born: Sheffield, 1870
Died: Sheffield, May 1898

CAREER
CLUBS: Sheffield Hastings, WEDNESDAY (free, July 1887-October 1890), Lincoln City, WEDNESDAY (November 1890-August 1891), Nottingham Forest.

A member of the Owls' Football Alliance championship-winning side of 1890 – making 15 appearances– Fred Thompson occupied every defensive outfield position during his career. A fine footballer, confident and durable, he made his debut for Wednesday at left-back in an FA Cup-tie against Belper in October 1887 and the following year helped the team win both the Sheffield Challenge and the Wharncliffe Charity Cups. He added a second Alliance winners' medal to his collection with Forest in 1892. Dogged by poor health, he was only twenty-eight when he died.

THOMPSON, Garry Lindsay
Striker

Appearances: 42+2 Goals: 8
Born: Kings Heath, Birmingham, 7 October 1959

CAREER
CLUBS: Coventry City, West Bromwich Albion, WEDNESDAY (£450,000, October 1985-July 1986), Aston Villa, Watford, Crystal Palace, Queens Park Rangers, Cardiff City, Northampton Town (player, reserve-team manager, coach), Brentford, Bristol Rovers (coach, caretaker-manager), Brentford (assistant manager, coach, manager).

Rugged, determined, efficient, strong in the air and on the ground, and afraid of no-one, striker Garry Thompson's career spanned twenty years, during which time he played in all four divisions. After netting 49 goals in 158 games for Coventry and winning 6 England Under-21 caps, he spent two and a half years with West Bromwich Albion – scoring 45 goals in 105 outings – before joining the Owls for a record £450,000 to replace Imre Varadi who went to The Hawthorns. He didn't quite hit top form with Wednesday but still gave a good account of himself before switching to Villa Park in 1986. He struck 19 times in 73 matches for Villa, helping them win promotion from the Second Division in 1988. He retired with 164 goals to his credit in 614 appearances. Unfortunately, he didn't do too well as a manager.

THOMPSON, GAVIN
Outside left

Appearances: 23 Goals: 2
Born: Winchburgh, West Lothian, Scotland, 1869
Died: Dundee, 1933

CAREER
CLUBS: Heart of Midlothian, Cambuslang, Third Lanark, WEDNESDAY (free, May 1891-June 1892), Stockton, Dundee Fairfield.

Gavin Thompson spent just the one season with Wednesday. Sharp and penetrative, he played in all three FA Cup-ties in 1891/92 – the first against Bolton Wanderers. His other 20 senior appearances were made in the Football Alliance.

THOMPSON, John
Forward

Appearances: 40 Goals: 12
Born: Cramlington, 21 March 1915
Died: Sheffield, November 1996

CAREER
CLUBS: Cramlington Juniors, Hartford Celtic, Blyth Spartans, WEDNESDAY (free, June 1933-May 1946), Doncaster Rovers (two spells), Chesterfield (two spells), Southport, Halifax Town.
OTHER: Army – Second World War; worked in the steel industry.

Jack Thompson's thirteen-year association with Wednesday was seriously interrupted by the Second World War and, to a certain extent, by injury. A talented inside forward, prior to 1939 he had done well when covering for Hooper, Starling, Robinson and Matthews and scored 6 goals in 15 outings in 1936/37 – his best season – having made his League debut against Sunderland in November 1933. He also notched 52 goals in 112 Second World War games for Wednesday, appearing in the 1943 League (North) Cup final versus Blackpool.

THOMPSON, Ronald
Outside right

Appearances: 1
Born: Sheffield, 24 December 1921
Died: Sheffield, 10 February 1988

CAREER
CLUBS: Wadsley Church, WEDNESDAY (£10,

September 1940-May 1947), York City, Gainsborough
Trinity.
WARTIME GUEST APPEARANCES: Rotherham United,
Leicester City
OTHER: RAF

Taking over from Oscar Fox for his only appearance for the Owls versus Everton in an FA
Cup-tie in January 1947, Ron Thompson also
netted six times in 28 wartime appearances.

THOMPSON, William Alan
Defender

Appearances: 167+6   Goals: 4
Born: Liverpool, 20 January 1952

CAREER
CLUBS: WEDNESDAY (July 1967-August 1976),
Stockport County, Portland Timbers, Bradford City,
Scunthorpe United.

A dependable central defender, strong in the
tackle and in the air, Alan Thompson spent
nine years at Hillsborough. His first three were
spent as a third and then second team player,
before he finally made his League debut against
QPR in September 1970. He starred in 34 games
that season but had to wait until 1973 before
establishing himself in the side. Unfortunately,
injuries affected his last term at with the club. He
made over 100 appearances for Stockport.

TIDMAN, Ola
Goalkeeper

Appearances: 15+1
Born: Malmö, Sweden, 11 May 1979

CAREER
CLUBS: UC Kick, Malmö FF, AA Gent, La Louviere,
Bolton (trial), Wolves (trial), Tranmere (trial),
Bradford City, Stockport County, WEDNESDAY (free,
July 2003-December 2004), FC Midtjylland.

Capped by Sweden at both Youth and Under-
21 levels, Ola Tidman started 2003/04 as
Wednesday's first choice 'keeper. However, a
broken hand and subsequent loss of form saw
him replaced by Pressman, and after that the
Swede struggled to regain his confidence.

TODD, Samuel John
Defender

Appearances: 24+2 Goals: 1
Born: Belfast, 22 September 1945

CAREER
CLUBS: Glentoran, Burnley, WEDNESDAY (£44,444,
May 1970-May 1974), Mansfield Town (L), Great
Harwood, Padiham.
OTHER: worked in a West Belfast power station.

Capped four times by Northern Ireland at
Under-23 level, Sammy Todd went on to play
in 11 full internationals – 3 with Wednesday. A
positive defender who could also perform in
midfield, he was able to withstand the heftiest
of challenges and made 128 appearances for
Burnley before joining the Owls for whom he
made his debut in a 1-0 win over Charlton in
August 1970.

TOMLINSON, Charles Conway
Outside left

Appearances: 77   Goals: 12
Born: Sheffield, 2 December 1919
Died: Yorkshire, 11 February 1971

CAREER
CLUBS: Woodburn Alliance, WEDNESDAY (ama-
teur, April 1935-April 1939), Bradford Park Avenue;
WEDNESDAY (£1,500, August 1944-March 1951),
Rotherham United, Worksop Town.
WARTIME GUEST APPEARANCES: Rotherham United,
Chesterfield

Charlie Tomlinson was released in 1939 by Owls' manager Jimmy McMullan who thought he was too fragile to become a professional footballer! He proved the boss wrong and came back in 1944. He scored 21 goals in 85 games at the end of the Second World War and made his senior debut against Mansfield in the FA Cup in January 1946. He became the scorer of the quickest goal in Wednesday's history – just twelve seconds into the League game at Preston in October 1949. He was given the nickname 'Shadows' by his first boss, Billy Walker, due to his slight build.

TOMLINSON, David Ian
Outside right

Appearances: 0+1
Born: Rotherham, 13 December 1968

CAREER
CLUBS: WEDNESDAY (April 1985-August 1987), Rotherham United, Gainsborough Trinity, Boston United, Barnet, Peterborough United, Kettering Town, Matlock Town, Dagenham & Redbridge, Witton Albion, Stalybridge Celtic and others.

Dave Tomlinson's six-year League career realised just 13 appearances – 7 as a substitute. His only game for Wednesday came in a 6-1 defeat at Leicester in January 1987 when he replaced Brannigan.

TOONE, George
Half-back

Appearances: 21
Born: Nottingham, 6 September 1893
Died: Nottingham, 21 July 1950

CAREER
CLUBS: Northvale, Sherwood, Sneinton Institute, Notts County, Watford, WEDNESDAY (£240 plus George Prior, August 1924-September 1925),

Ilkeston Town, Scarborough Penguins.
OTHER: Army – First World War.

A reserve with Notts County, for whom he made just one League appearance, George Toone played in the Southern League with Watford before being engaged by Wednesday. He stayed at Hillsborough for one season, making his debut in a 4-1 defeat by Leicester in October 1924 and later had a run of 20 consecutive first-team outings up to 10 April 1925. His father, George senior, played for England in the 1880s.

TOPHAM, John H.
Outside left

Appearances: 16   Goals: 2
Born: Chesterfield, 1872
Deceased by 1948

CAREER
CLUBS: Staveley, WEDNESDAY (free, May 1896-May 1902).

Basically a reserve, Jack Topham made the first of his 15 appearances for the Owls at Sunderland in October 1899 when he deputised for Fred Spiksley. His only goal came in a 6-0 home win over Burton Swifts in March 1900, when the Second Division championship was in sight.

TOSELAND, Ernest
Outside left

Appearances: 12   Goals: 2
Born: Northampton, 17 March 1905
Died: Northampton, 19 October 1987

CAREER
CLUBS: Higham Ferrers Town, Queens Park Rangers, Coventry City, Manchester City, WEDNESDAY (£1,575, March 1939-May 1940).

Ernie Toseland scored 75 goals in 409 appearances for Manchester City, gaining FA Cup and League Championship winners' medals in 1934 and 1937 respectively, as well as winning the Lancashire Cup. He hardly missed a game between 1929 and 1938 and was unlucky not to win a full England cap; his only representative honour was an appearance for the Football League against the Irish League in September 1929. Fast and tricky, he made his debut for the Owls in a 2-1 home win over West Brom in March 1939 and netted in successive matches against Norwich and Luton soon afterwards. He played Cheshire League football until he was forty-one.

TROTTER, James William
Inside, centre forward

Appearances: 160   Goals: 114
Born: Easington, Co. Durham, 25 November 1899
Died: St Albans, 17 April 1984

CAREER
CLUBS: Bury, WEDNESDAY (£1,900, February 1922-July 1930), Torquay United, Watford, Charlton Athletic (trainer, assistant manager, manager), England (trainer).
OTHER: worked on munitions during the First World War.

A prolific scorer throughout his career, Jimmy Trotter netted two five-timers for Wednesday, against Portsmouth in December 1924 and Stockport County in September 1925. He partnered Jimmy Seed in the Owls' attack for many years and had his best season at Hillsborough in terms of goal-grabbing in 1925/26, when his haul of 38 set a new club record and helped the team win the Second Division championship. When the same division was won again in 1929/30, Trotter's contribution was only 1 goal in 6 starts, Jack Allen replacing him at centre forward. After leaving Hillsborough, Trotter scored 26 times for Torquay in 1930/31, but struggled with injuries after that, eventually retiring with a cartilage problem. After an initial breaking-in period as trainer and right-hand man to his former teammate Seed at The Valley, he then embarked on a difficult managerial career with Charlton. A dour, determined, forthright character, Trotter was a man of few words and struggled during his five years in office – Charlton being relegated from the First Division in 1957 with only 22 points. He was trainer to the England team under manager Walter Winterbottom.

TRUSTFULL, Orlando
Utility

Appearances: 11+11   Goals: 3
Born: Amsterdam, Holland, 4 August 1970

CAREER
CLUBS: Rivalen, Blauw Wit, Haarlem, SVV Dordrecht, FC Twente, Feyenoord, WEDNESDAY (£750,000, August 1996-May 1997), Vitesse Arnhem (player, coach).

A Dutch international, capped twice as a Feyenoord player, Orlando Thrustfull spent one season at Hillsborough, during which time he certainly played some smart football. He gained a regular place in the Owls' side in November 1996 and opened his goal account in the 2-0 win over Nottingham Forest. After that, however, he struggled with his form and fitness, and was released at the end of the campaign.

TUDGAY, Marcus
Striker

*Appearances: 54+7 *   Goals: 16 **
Born: Shoreham, 3 February 1983

CAREER

CLUBS: Derby County, WEDNESDAY (free, January 2006).

A 6ft 3ins tall striker, Marcus Tudgay suffered a shoulder injury with the Rams which certainly affected his performances at Pride Park, yet he still scored 18 goals in 99 appearances before moving to Hillsborough. Able to play as a wide man, he holds the ball up well and made an impressive start to his Owls' career, netting on his debut in a 3-0 win over Crewe.

TUMMON, Oliver
Winger

Appearances: 47   Goals: 12
Born: Sheffield, 3 March 1884
Died: Sheffield, 8 October 1955

CAREER

CLUBS: South Street New Connexion, Gainsborough Trinity, WEDNESDAY (free, March 1902-June 1910), Gainsborough Trinity, Oldham Athletic, Sheffield United, Barnsley.
OTHER: was a crown green bowls champion.

Olly Tummon was a forceful player, direct with a powerful shot and able to occupy both flanks. He was unlucky not to win a full England cap in 1907, Newcastle's Jock Rutherford being preferred instead. He found it tough at times with Wednesday, especially early on, making less than 50 appearances in 8 years. Twice an ever-present for Gainsborough, he was absent only 6 times in 3 years with Oldham, helping the Latics reach the semi-final of the FA Cup and finish runners-up in the First Division in 1915. Tummon scored 49 goals in 248 League games for his 6 major clubs.

TURLEY, Michael Douglas
Wing half

Appearances: 4
Born: Rotherham, 14 February 1936

CAREER

CLUBS: WEDNESDAY (April 1951-October 1956), Burnley.

A reserve at Hillsborough, Mike Turley's League debut came in a 0-0 draw at Aston Villa on New Year's Day 1955. A week later he played in the FA Cup-tie against Hastings United.

TURNER, Christopher Robert
Goalkeeper

Appearances: 205
Born: Sheffield, 15 September 1958

CAREER

CLUBS: WEDNESDAY (March 1975-July 1979), Lincoln City (L), Sunderland, Manchester United, WEDNESDAY (£175,000, September 1988-November 1991), Leeds United (L), Leyton Orient (player,

Chris Turner

joint manager), Hartlepool United (manager), WEDNESDAY (manager, November 2002-September 2004), Stockport County (manager).

An England Youth international, Chris Turner had an excellent career in goalkeeping, making 588 appearances while serving with 6 different clubs. He made his League debut for the Owls against Walsall in August 1976 – taking over from Peter Fox – and in 1991 was a League Cup winner at Wembley – against his former club Manchester United. As joint manager of Orient with John Sitton, Turner gained promotion from the Third Division in 1994. He did a useful job in charge at Hartlepool but had the misfortune to see Wednesday relegated to the Second Division when he was in office at Hillsborough in 2003. He was subsequently replaced in the hot seat by Paul Sturrock and followed ex-Wednesday stars Eddie Quigley, Andy Wilson, Gary Megson and Carlton Palmer as boss of Stockport.

TURNER, Lian
Goalkeeper

Appearances: 11
Born: 26 January 1984

CAREER
CLUBS: Stirling Albion, Chester City, Crystal Palace, Wycombe Wanderers, Doncaster Rovers, Everton, WEDNESDAY (loan, February-April 2007).

Turner, a Scotsman, was on loan at Hillsborough from Everton during February to April 2007.

TURTON, Cyril
Defender

Appearances: 151
Born: South Kirkby, 20 September 1921
Died: South Kirkby 31 December 1999

CAREER
CLUBS: Frickley Colliery, Rotherham United, WEDNESDAY (£200, December 1943-May 1954), Goole Town, South Emshall (trainer, manager). OTHER: Army – Second World War.

It was said that Cyril Turton could run backwards faster than he could run forwards! Whatever the case, he was a splendid defender, cool under pressure and enjoyed a fine ten-year career. He made his first appearance for the Owls in a regional game against Mansfield in October 1944 and less than two years later starred in his first League game at Luton (August 1946). A regular in the side in 1947/48 and 1949/50, Turton lost his place through injury to Edgar Packard but came back and helped the Owls win the Second Division title in 1952.

TYNAN, Thomas Edward
Striker

Appearances: 105+2   Goals: 37
Born: Liverpool, 17 November 1955

CAREER
CLUBS: Liverpool, Swansea City, Dallas Tornadoes, WEDNESDAY (£8,000, September 1976-October 1978), Lincoln City, Newport County (£25,000,

Thomas Tynan

February 1979), Plymouth Argyle (two spells), Rotherham United, Torquay United, Doncaster Rovers, Goole Town (player-manager).
OTHER: pub landlord; taxi driver.

Tommy Tynan had a great career. A brilliant marksman, he netted 320 goals in 792 games while serving with 9 different clubs in 20 years. Top marksman in the country in 1982/83 with 31 goals for Newport, he certainly had his best goalscoring years with Plymouth, for he netted 138 in 302 outings, playing in the 1984 FA Cup semi-final. He also did well with Newport, with whom he won the Welsh Cup in 1980 and played in Europe. He and Rodger Wylde netted 75 goals between them as Wednesday's main strikers (1976-78) and it is certainly possible, that had Tynan been with a more fashionable club, he may well have gained international honours. Annoyingly, he also appeared for Liverpool.

U

ULYETT, George
Goalkeeper

Appearances: 1
Born: Sheffield, 21 October 1851
Died: Sheffield, 18 June 1898

CAREER
CLUBS: Ecclesfield, WEDNESDAY (free, August 1882-May 1883).

Injury forced George Ulyett into early retirement. His only appearance for the Owls was as Harry Ledger deputy in a 4-1 FA Cup defeat by Notts County in February 1883. Later in the season he helped Wednesday win the Wharncliffe Charity Cup. Stricken down with pneumonia after watching the Yorkshire-Kent cricket match at Bramall Lane, he died shortly afterwards.

USHER, Brian
Outside right

Appearances: 66+2 Goals: 3
Born: Belmont, Co. Durham, 11 March 1944

CAREER
CLUBS: Sunderland, WEDNESDAY (£20,000, June 1965-June 1968), Doncaster Rovers, Yeovil Town.
OTHER: now works in insurance.

A competent, fast-moving winger with a positive attitude, Brian Usher made 71 appearances for Sunderland before making his Owls debut against the League Champions Manchester United in August 1965. With the odd exception, he held his place until the following March, when he suffered a serious leg injury in the Sheffield derby. Out of action for quite a while, he missed the FA Cup final, and, in fact, made only nine appearances in 1966/67 before reclaiming his place the following season. After leaving Hillsborough, Usher made over 175 appearances for Doncaster.

V

VARADI, Imre
Striker

Appearances: 108+13   Goals: 46
Born: Paddington, London, 8 July 1959

CAREER
CLUBS: Letchworth Garden City, Tottenham Hotspur (trial), Cambridge United (trial), Sheffield United, Everton, Benfica, Newcastle United, WEDNESDAY (£170,000 plus David Mills, August 1983-July 1985), West Bromwich Albion, Manchester City, WEDNESDAY (£100,000, exchange for Carl Bradshaw, September 1988-February 1990), Leeds United, Luton Town, Oxford United, Rotherham United, Mansfield Town, Boston United (two spells), Scunthorpe United, Matlock Town (player-manager), Guiseley (player-

V

coach), Denaby United (player-coach), Stalybridge Celtic (assistant manager, coach), Sheffield FC. OTHER: football agent; worked for the PFA; pundit on local radio and Sky Sports.

'Ray' Varadi was a consistent scorer throughout his career. A favourite at most ports, he was fast, alert and keen-eyed and had over 50 goals under his belt before joining Wednesday in 1983. He made a tremendous impact during his two-year spell, notching several classic goals in a haul of 40 in less than 100 outings. His 17 goals in 1983/84 went a long way towards helping the Owls clinch promotion. Voted the club's Player of the Year the following season, he failed to agree terms with the Owls and moved to West Brom for a then record fee of £285,000, set at tribunal. After slipping into the Second Division with Manchester City, he had a less successful second spell with Wednesday before regaining top-flight status with Leeds in 1990. Varadi scored a total of 178 goals in 502 competitive appearances for his major clubs. His brother, Fernando, played for Fulham.

Imre Varadi

W

WADDLE, Christopher Roland
Forward

Appearances: 130+17   *Goals: 15*
Born: Heworth, Gateshead, 14 December 1960

CAREER
CLUBS: trials for Sheffield United, Sunderland and Coventry City; Tow Law Town, Newcastle United, Tottenham Hotspur, Olympique Marseille, WEDNESDAY (£1m, July 1992-September 1996), Falkirk, Bradford City, Sunderland, Burnley, Hollinsend, Brunsmeer, Torquay United, Staveley Town (three spells), Worksop Town, South Normanton Athletic, WEDNESDAY (coach, December 1998-June 2000).
OTHER: football pundit for Sky Sports and local radio.

Chris Waddle – a former seasoner in a sausage and pie factory – had a wonderful career. He netted almost 150 goals in 715 club matches, won 62 caps for England, played in one Under-21 international and represented the Football League. Excellent with Newcastle (52 goals in 190 games), he helped the Magpies gain promotion to the First Division in 1984 before starring for Spurs – scoring 42 goals in 177 outings. He then became a star in Provence after his record £4.25 million transfer to Marseille. Nicknamed 'Le Dribbleur Fou' he gained three French League winners' medals in succession (1990-92) and collected runners-up prizes in both the 1991 French and European Cup finals before contributing greatly to Wednesday's cause in the 1990s. A quality footballer, and the club's first £1 million signing, he made his Owls' debut against Everton in August 1992 but, unfortunately, was plagued by injury during his time at Hillsborough. When fit, he produced some exquisite performances and netted some stunning goals that thrilled the fans. He was voted the FWA Footballer of the

Chris Waddle

Year in 1993, aged thirty-two. Often choosing to play wide on either flank, he possessed a superb body swerve, was quick over twenty to thirty yards, had neat dribbling skills, could cross a ball with precision and could also unleash a thundering shot. He represented England in the 1986 and 1990 World Cup finals but had the misfortune to miss from the spot in the penalty shoot-out with Germany in the semi-final in the latter tournament in Italy. Waddle once cut a record with Glenn Hoddle entitled 'Diamond Lights' which entered the top ten in 1987. His cousin, Alan Waddle, played for Liverpool among others.

WALDEN, Richard Francis
Full-back

Appearances: 115   Goals: 1
Born: Hereford, 4 May 1948

CAREER
CLUBS: Aldershot, WEDNESDAY (free, January 1976-August 1978), Newport County, Farnborough Town, Basingstoke Town.

OTHER: manager of Midas Leisure Ltd, Hampshire.

Richard Walden made 406 League appearances in 11 years for Aldershot before joining the Owls. Professional in his methods, he was solid, compact and resilient and during a splendid career amassed well over 700 club appearances – 657 in the Football League. He was twenty-five when he moved to Hillsborough, being signed as cover for Bernard Shaw, and when Shaw left, Walden took over at right-back. He formed excellent partnerships with Dave Rushbury and David Grant in front of goalkeepers Chris Turner and Bob Bolder. Walden, who made his debut for the Owls was against Hereford in January 1976, won the Welsh Cup with Newport in 1980 and reached the quarter-finals of the European Cup Winners' Cup the following season.

WALKER, Colin
Forward

Appearances: 2+1   Goals: 3
Born: Rotherham, 1 May 1958

CAREER
CLUBS: York City, Barnsley (two spells), Matlock Town (two spells), Gisborne City (two spells), Sutton Town, Doncaster Rovers (two spells), Cambridge United, Haworth CI, WEDNESDAY (free, August 1986-December 1987), Darlington (L), Torquay United (L), Gisborne City (player-manager), Doncaster Rovers, Barnsley (coach), York City (assistant manager).

New Zealand international Colin Walker – 40 caps gained, 20 goals scored – made far more appearances for Gisborne City than he did with any other major clubs. He made a sensational start to his Owls' career, being the first substitute to score a hat-trick – doing so in just sixteen minutes – in a 7-0 League Cup win over Stockport at Maine Road in October 1986.

WALKER, Cyril John
Inside forward

Appearances: 4
Born: Pirton, Herts, 24 February 1914
Died: Chatham, 7 July 2002

CAREER
CLUBS: Hitchen Town, Watford (two spells), Gillingham, WEDNESDAY (£1,150 with Fred Lester, October 1937-September 1938), Chelmsford City, Short Sports; Norwich City, Dartford (two spells), Chatham.
WARTIME GUEST APPEARANCES: Raith Rovers, Crystal Palace, Brighton & Hove Albion, WEDNESDAY (October-December 1941), Norwich City, Watford.
OTHER: RAF – Second World War; school caretaker.

An intelligent footballer with good skills, Cyril Walker made only 17 League appearances during his professional career – 10 with Gillingham. A reserve with all of his major clubs, the first of his four outings for Wednesday was away to Manchester United in October 1937, when he appeared in a reorganised forward line. He played for the RAF against Norwich during the Second World War.

WALKER, Desmond Sinclair
Defender

Appearances: 362
Born: Hackney, London, 26 November 1965

CAREER
CLUBS: Nottingham Forest, Sampdoria, WEDNESDAY (£2.75 million, July 1993-June 2001), Burton Albion, Nottingham Forest (caretaker-manager), Mansfield Town (retired 2006).

In 2005, at the age of forty, the ever-reliable and dependable Des Walker had made over 870 appearances for his 4 major clubs. He was rewarded with a testimonial by Nottingham Forest four months after leaving The City

Desmond Walker

Ground, where he had been employed (in two spells) for fourteen and a half years. One of the fastest recovering centre-backs of his era, Walker was strong in all aspects of defensive play and his noble efforts earned him 59 England caps plus 7 at Under-21 level. He won the League Cup in 1989 and 1990 and the Simod and Zenith Data Systems Cups in 1989 and 1992 respectively – all with Forest. Penned as being the ultimate footballing centre half, Walker was cool, undemonstrative, skilful and utterly unflappable, and could be relied upon to give a thoroughly professional performance out on the pitch. 'Mr Consistency', he was terrific with Wednesday, making the first of 362 appearances for the Owls against Liverpool at Anfield in August 1993 and his last against Barnsley in April 2001.

WALKER, Frederick
Wing half

Appearances: 10   Goals: 1
Born: Wednesbury, 3 July 1913
Died: Walsall, March 1978

CAREER
CLUBS: *Walsall, WEDNESDAY (free, May 1937-May 1938), Chelmsford City.*
OTHER: *Army – Second World War.*

A reserve with Walsall and the Owls, Fred Walker spent two years at Hillsborough. Able to occupy both wing half positions, he made his debut against Spurs in September 1937 and scored his only goal in a 1-1 home with Blackburn in April 1938.

WALKER, Thomas
Right-back

Appearances: 287   Goals: 3
Born: *Cross Crols, Stirlingshire, 4 March 1902*
Died: *Sheffield, 7 March 1973*

CAREER
CLUBS: *Cross Crols, Haverbridge, Sternburn Thistle, Bo'ness, Vale of Grange, Bradford City, WEDNESDAY (£1,900, February 1926-April 1936; trainer; coach until May 1967).*

Signed by manager Bob Brown for just £1,900, Tom Walker helped the Owls clinch promotion from the Second Division at the end of his first part-season at Hillsborough. He later formed a wonderful partnership with Ernie Blenkinsop and collected successive League Championship-winning medals in 1929 and 1930, missing only one game in the former campaign. During his time with Wednesday, Walker suffered his fair share of set-backs and there's no doubt that his biggest disappointment was to miss the 1935 FA Cup final win over West Bromwich Albion. He was surprisingly dropped in favour of Joe Nibloe early in the year, having missed only one of the club's previous 30 cup matches. Walker did, however, receive a winners' medal despite only sitting on the bench! He represented the Sheffield FA and served Wednesday as a player, trainer and coach for over forty years.

WALKER, William Baird
Forward

Appearances: 19   Goals: 5
Born: *New Cummock, Ayrshire, 5 May 1893*
Deceased by 1978

CAREER
CLUBS: *New Cummock, Lugar Boswell, Bradford City, Lanemark, Birmingham, Coventry City, Merthyr Town, Bristol City, WEDNESDAY (exchange for Andrew Smailes, October 1923-August 1924), Weymouth (player-manager), Redditch Town, Leamington Town (2 spells, the second as player-manager).*
WARTIME GUEST APPEARANCES: *Leicester Fosse*
OTHER: *Army – First World War.*

The hard-shooting Billy Walker scored six hat-tricks for Birmingham's Second XI in 1914/15. After the war he did well with Coventry, also netting 24 goals in 80 League games for Merthyr and 7 in 37 for Bristol City. He made his debut for the Owls in a 1-1 draw at Nelson in October 1923, taking over from Sid Binks at centre forward. He lasted only one season before moving to Weymouth.

WALL, Andrew Arthur
Outside right

Appearances: 3
Born: *Cresswell, Derbyshire, 25 November 1949*

CAREER
CLUBS: *WEDNESDAY (April 1965-August 1969), Workington, Boston United, Goole Town, Worksop Town.*
OTHER: *chauffeur.*

The first of Adrian Wall's three League outings for Wednesday was against Chelsea at Hillsborough in April 1968 when he deputised for the injured Brian Usher. He scored twice in 24 games for Workington.

WALLER, George
Utility

Appearances: 32   Goals: 5
Born: Sheffield, 3 December 1863
Died: Sheffield, 11 December 1937

CAREER
CLUBS: Park Grange, WEDNESDAY (free, 1886-August 1890), Middlesbrough Ironopolis, Sheffield United (player-coach).
OTHER: played cricket for Yorkshire (1893-96); ran a sports shop in Sheffield.

A Football Alliance winner with the Owls in 1890, George Waller could play equally well at half-back or on the left wing. Fast and clever, he could deliver the perfect cross and scored on his FA Cup debut for Wednesday in a 3-2 win over Belper in October 1887, later appearing in the final against Blackburn Rovers in March 1890.

WANDS, Alexander Mitchell Doig
Left half

Appearances: 18   Goals: 1
Born: Cowdenbeath, 5 December 1922

CAREER
CLUBS: Wallsend Boys, Gateshead, WEDNESDAY (free, 1945-May 1947), Doncaster Rovers, Boston United, Peterborough United, Corby Town, Kettering Town, Loughborough United, Rothwell Town (manager).
OTHER: employed by a steel company.

Alex Wands made the first of 17 Second World War appearances for Wednesday in December 1945 and later that season played in 6 FA Cup matches. He made his League debut at Leicester in September 1946 and eventually lost his place to Joe Cockroft.

WARBOYS, Alan
Forward

Appearances: 76+6 Goals: 13
Born: Goldthorpe, Yorkshire, 18 April 1949

CAREER
CLUBS: Doncaster Rovers, WEDNESDAY (£20,000, May 1968-December 1970), Cardiff City, Sheffield United, Bristol Rovers, Fulham, Hull City, Doncaster Rovers.
OTHER: licensee; HGV driver.

Alan Warboys scored 137 goals in 483 League games with 4 different clubs in all four divisions over a period of seventeen years. A gutsy performer, strong and consistent, always catching the eye with his excellent work-rate and willpower, he formed an excellent strike partnership (known as 'Smash and Grab') with Bruce Bannister at Bristol Rovers, helping the Pirates win promotion to the Second Division in 1974. In that same season he netted four times in an 8-2 televised win over Brighton. Former Wednesday full-back Don Megson signed him for the Eastville club. Warboys made his debut for Wednesday against Spurs in August 1968 – taking over from John Ritchie – but had to wait until his fourteenth outing before netting his first goal, which earned a point from a 1-1 draw with West Ham. He retired with a back injury in 1982.

Alan Warboys

WARD, Thomas Alfred
Centre forward

Appearances: 39   Goals: 20
Born: Tow Law, 6 August 1917
Died: Scunthorpe, November 1992

CAREER
CLUBS: Crook Town, WEDNESDAY (£50, March 1937-September 1948), Darlington.
WARTIME GUEST APPEARANCES: Portsmouth, Darlington, Mansfield Town.
OTHER: Army – Second World War.

A prolific scorer with the amateur club Crook Town, Tom Ward's career in the Football League was seriously affected by the Second World War, although he managed 25 goals in 78 regional games for the Owls, making his senior debut in the FA Cup against Mansfield in January 1946 – almost nine years after joining the club. His League debut followed against Luton that August and he registered his first goal on his home ground forty-eight hours later against Barnsley. After leaving Hillsborough, Ward gave Darlington excellent service for 6 seasons, scoring 32 goals in 119 Division Three (North) matches.

WARE, Harry
Forward

Appearances: 12   Goals: 1
Born: Birmingham, 22 October 1911
Died; Stoke-on-Trent, 28 October 1970

CAREER
CLUBS: Hanley St Luke's, Cobridge Celtic, Stoke St Peter's, Stoke City, Newcastle United, WEDNESDAY (£1,700, May-November 1937), Norwich City, Northwich Victoria (two spells as manager), EDO Haarlem (trainer), Port Vale (trainer), Crewe Alexandra (manager), Stoke City (assistant trainer, scout).
WARTIME GUEST APPEARANCES: Northampton

Town, Nottingham Forest, Stoke City, Crystal Palace, Watford.

The son of a famous boxer, Harry Ware played with Stanley Matthews when Stoke won the Second Division in 1933. A former potter, he scored 16 goals in 53 games for the Staffordshire club before transferring to Newcastle in 1935. He never fitted in at St James' Park nor, indeed, at Hillsborough, making his debut for Wednesday at centre forward against Chesterfield in August 1937. His only goal earned a point against Swansea. He did much better with Norwich, scoring 14 goals, but due to a chest wound received in the Normandy landings, he retired, aged thirty-four. After two years as trainer with EDO Haarlem (Holland), six seasons in charge of Northwich Victoria and a spell as trainer with Port Vale, he managed Crewe Alexandra from June 1958 to May 1960 and, for the last ten years of his life, served as assistant trainer and then scout for Stoke City.

WARHURST, Paul
Utility

Appearances: 81+7 Goals: 18
Born: Stockport, 26 September 1969

CAREER
CLUBS: Manchester City, Oldham Athletic, WEDNESDAY (£750,000, July 1991-August 1993), Blackburn Rovers, Crystal Palace, Bolton Wanderers, Stoke City, Chesterfield, Barnsley, Queens Park Rangers, Carlisle United, Notts County, Grimsby Town, Chester City, Preston North End, Blackpool, Forest Green Rovers, Wrexham, Barnet.

The versatile Paul Warhurst has, at various stages during his adventurous career, occupied six different positions while amassing 400 senior appearances and scoring 30 goals. Sold by Manchester City without ever appearing in their first team, he spent almost

Paul Warhurst

three seasons with Oldham before joining Wednesday, making his debut for the Owls against Aston Villa in August 1991 when he partnered Nigel Pearson in defence. He remained a regular in the side, injury and suspension apart, until he left Hillsborough for Blackburn. After that he became something of a soccer nomad, and between March 2003 and March 2004, he served six different clubs. Capped eight times by England at Under-21 level, Warhurst gained a League Cup winners' medal with Blackburn in 1995 and played alongside Jon Beswetherick for Forest Green Rovers in 2005.

WARREN, Peter
Left-back

Appearances: 7
Born: Dublin, 1885
Died: Dublin, circa 1961

CAREER
CLUBS: Belfast Celtic, WEDNESDAY (£50 with Paddy O'Connell, December 1909-May 1912), Shelbourne, Millwall.

The strong-kicking Peter Warren never really adapted to life in the Football League and made

only six appearances for the Owls, his debut coming against Woolwich Arsenal in November 1913 when he replaced Walter Holbem at left-back. He was capped twice by Northern Ireland against England and Scotland in 1913.

WATLING, Barry John
Goalkeeper

Appearances: 1
Born: Walthamstow, London, 16 July 1946

CAREER
CLUBS: Leyton Orient, Bristol City, Notts County, Hartlepool United, Seattle Sounders, Chester, Crewe Alexandra, Rotherham United, WEDNESDAY (free, January-March 1976), Barea Park (player-coach), Charlton Athletic, Maidstone United, Chatham, Bromley, Sittingbourne.

Barry Watling made 218 League appearances during his career – 139 for Hartlepool. His only game for Wednesday came in a 2-0 defeat by Swindon in January 1976, when he deputised for Peter Fox.

WATSON, Donald
Forward

Appearances: 10   Goals: 4
Born: Barnsley, 27 August 1932

CAREER
CLUBS: Worsborough Bridge, WEDNESDAY (£25, September 1954-November 1956), Lincoln City, Bury, Barnsley, Rochdale, Barrow, Buxton.
OTHER: driver for a double-glazing firm.

A useful player with good skills and an eye for the goal, Don Watson played under the shadow of Jack Shaw and Arthur Hukin with Wednesday and, as a result, his first-team appearances were limited to just 10 in 2 seasons. His first appearance was in a 7-2 League defeat at Tottenham in January 1955, where he helped to ease the disappointment by scoring one goal. An ever-present in Bury's 1960/61 Third Division championship-winning side, his League career realised 85 goals in 278 appearances.

WATSON, Gordon William George
Forward

Appearances: 42+46   Goals: 21
Born: Sidcup, Kent, 20 March 1971

CAREER
CLUBS: Kingfisher, Charlton Athletic, WEDNESDAY (£250,000, February 1991-March 1995), Southampton, Bradford City, Bournemouth, Portsmouth, Hartlepool United, WEDNESDAY (trial, July-August 2003).
OTHER: director of Kickers Indoor Sports Ltd.

An FA Youth Cup runner-up with Charlton in 1987, Gordon Watson gained the first of two England Under-21 caps against Wales three years later – after being named Barclays Young Eagle of the Month for October 1990. A prolific marksman at intermediate level with Charlton – he hit 45 goals in 1988/89 – Watson never got a look-in with the seniors, especially after the London club had been relegated in 1990. He improved with Wednesday, although appearing as a sub more often than in the starting line-up. He made his debut for the Owls against Notts County in March 1991 and scored the first of his 21 goals at Oldham in April 1993, having suffered career-threatening injuries in between. In February 1997, the unfortunate Watson was again in the wars, sidelined with a fractured leg; after that he was in and out of the treatment room with niggling injuries. He attempted a comeback with Wednesday in 2003 – to no avail – and retired with 48 goals to his name in 227 appearances.

WATSON, James
Inside right

Appearances: 1
Born: Sheffield, 1862
Deceased by 1938

CAREER
CLUBS: WEDNESDAY (seasons 1884-86).

An unknown Wednesday reserve, Jim Watson's only outing for the club was in the FA Cup against Long Eaton Rangers in October 1885 (lost 2-0).

WATSON, Stephen Craig
Defender

Appearances: 11
Born: North Shields, 1 April 1974

CAREER
CLUBS: Newcastle United, Aston Villa, Everton, West Bromwich Albion, WEDNESDAY (loan, February 2007).

Watson, the former Newcastle United, Aston Villa and Everton defender, was signed from West Bromwich Albion on loan in February 2007. He played for England at Youth level before going on to gain one B and 21 Under 21 caps. He was troubled by injury during his time at Hillsborough.

WATTS, Julian David
Defender

Appearances: 16+4 Goals: 1
Born: Sheffield, 17 March 1971

CAREER
CLUBS: Frecheville CA, WEDNESDAY (trial, 1986), Sheffield United, Rotherham United, WEDNESDAY (£130,000, March 1992-March 1996), Shrewsbury

Town (L), Leicester City, Crewe Alexandra, Huddersfield Town, Bristol City, Lincoln City, Blackpool, Luton Town, Northern Spirit.
OTHER: now runs his own business in Worksop.

Julian Watts had an interesting eleven-year career in professional football. He made 240 appearances, gained a League Cup winners' medal with Leicester in 1997, had his best spell with Luton – making 87 appearances – and spent three seasons in Australia. He was never a regular in the Owls' side, making his debut as a substitute in the Premiership game at Coventry in March 1993.

WEAVER, Alexander Edward
Centre forward

Appearances: 6   Goals: 1
Born: Weymouth, 22 June 1902
Died: Weymouth, 18 April 1976

CAREER
CLUBS: Wycombe Wanderers, WEDNESDAY (free, June 1924-May 1926), Worcester City.
OTHER: RAF.

Reserve to Jimmy Trotter, Alec Weaver made his League debut against Oldham in January 1925 and scored his only goal for the club in his fourth game to earn a point from a 1-1 draw at home to Manchester United.

WEAVER, Nicholas James
Goalkeeper

Appearances: 14
Born: Sheffield, 2 March 1979

CAREER
CLUBS: Mansfield Town, Manchester City, WEDNESDAY (loan, November 2005-January 2006).

Capped by England on ten occasions at under-21 level, Nicky Weaver had made over 170 appearances for Manchester City, gaining a Second Division championship winners' medal in 2002, before joining the Owls on loan. He lost concentration at times and, as a result, conceded vital goals.

WEBSTER, Arnold
Centre forward

Appearances: 1
Born: Birchover, 3 March 1913
Died: Matlock, 26 February 1982

CAREER
CLUBS: Birchover, WEDNESDAY (April 1936- May 1937), Frickley Colliery, Darley End United.
OTHER: Army – Second World War.

Arnold Webster's only League appearance for Wednesday was at Stoke in April 1937, being the tenth player used at centre forward that season.

WEBSTER, Frederick Joseph
Centre forward

Appearances: 1
Born: Sheffield, 1864
Deceased by 1938

CAREER
CLUBS: WEDNESDAY (May 1886-April 1888).

Joe Webster's only appearance for the Owls was at Belper in an FA Cup-tie in October 1887.

WEBSTER, John
Outside right

Appearances: 29   Goals: 5
Born: Sheffield, 1869
Died: Sheffield, circa 1940

CAREER
CLUBS: Attercliffe, WEDNESDAY (May 1890-October 1895), Rotherham Town, Gainsborough Trinity.
OTHER: licensee.

John Webster scored 15 goals in 95 League appearances, producing his best form with Gainsborough. He made his debut for Wednesday in the Football Alliance in 1890 and had his first outing in the Football League at Newton Heath in September 1893. A sprightly player who loved to hug the touchline, he retained the right-wing position until Archie Brash replaced him in 1894.

WEIR, William Findlay
Half-back

Appearances: 72   Goals: 1
Born: Glasgow, 18 April 1889
Died: France, 9 July 1918

CAREER
CLUBS: Maryhill, WEDNESDAY (£20 with James Miller, February 1910-September 1912), Tottenham Hotspur.

Scottish junior international Findlay Weir, who appeared regularly for the Owls, was a constructive half-back who made his debut for the Owls in February 1910 against Notts County, taking the place of Bill Bartlett. He made 119 first-team appearances for Spurs before losing his life with the Royal Engineers in the First World War.

WELSH, Fletcher
Centre forward

Appearances: 12   Goals: 4
Born: Galashiels, Scotland, 16 August 1893
Died: Glasgow, 1963

CAREER
CLUBS: Raith Rovers, Heart of Midlothian, Raith Rovers, WEDNESDAY (£1,800, January 1920-October 1920), Third Lanark.
OTHER: employed in Leith shipyards.

A very competent, hard-working and aggressive player, Fletcher Welsh did well north of the border before joining the Owls. He scored some superb goals, including the winner on his debut for Wednesday against Everton in January 1920. He lost his place to Jim McIntyre.

WEST, Colin
Striker

Appearances: 55+5 Goals: 13
Born: Wallsend, 13 November 1962

CAREER
CLUBS: Sunderland, Watford, Glasgow Rangers, WEDNESDAY (£150,000, September 1987-February 1989), West Bromwich Albion, Port Vale, Swansea City, Leyton Orient, Northampton Town, Rushden & Diamonds, Northwich Victoria, Hartlepool United (coach, assistant manager), WEDNESDAY (assistant manager, coach, November 2003-September 2004), Stockport County (assistant manager).

Colin West

Colin West struggled at times to find the net, especially as an Owls' player – some fans wore T-shirts bearing the slogan 'I saw Colin West score'. Nevertheless, he proved his critics wrong by netting 157 goals in 550 appearances for his ten major clubs. He was on target on his debut for the Owls against his former club Watford in September 1987. Six years later he helped Swansea reach the Division Two play-offs but was sent off in the semi-final against another of his old clubs, West Brom.

WEST, Frederick
Utility

Appearances: 7
Born: Sheffield, 1859
Deceased by 1914

CAREER
CLUBS: Heeley, Exchange, WEDNESDAY (free, August 1881-April 1882), Lockwood Brothers.

Fred West played in eight FA Cup matches in 1881/82, collecting a runners-up medal after the Owls had lost in the final to Blackburn Rovers. Able to play at right half, as a forward or on the wing, he made his debut against Staveley in the second round.

WESTLAKE, Francis Arthur
Full-back

Appearances: 117
Born: Bolton-on-Dearne, 11 August 1915
Died: Doncaster, 13 February 1999

CAREER
CLUBS: Thurnscoe Victoria, WEDNESDAY (£100 with reserves George Tepper and Arthur Bloomfield, May 1937-July 1950), Halifax Town, Denaby United.
WARTIME GUEST APPEARANCES: Bournemouth, Bradford City, Leeds United.
OTHER: Army – Second World War; grocer.

One of hundreds of players whose career was disrupted by the Second World War, Frank Westlake nevertheless gave Wednesday excellent service before, during and after the hostilities. Besides his 117 senior appearances for the club, he also starred in 35 regional matches between 1939 and 1946. He made his League debut against Luton in March 1938 and after the war formed a successful full-back partnership with Hugh Swift, the pair making over 100 consecutive appearances together. Westlake eventually gave way to Vin Kenny and in 1950 joined Halifax.

WESTWOOD, Ashley Michael
Defender

Appearances: 91+5 Goals: 9
Born: Bridgnorth, Shropshire, 31 August 1976

CAREER
CLUBS: Manchester United, Crewe Alexandra, Bradford City, WEDNESDAY (£150,000, August 2000-July 2003), Northampton Town.

Ashley Westwood, an England Youth international, won the FA Youth Cup with Terry Cooke as a Manchester United player before developing into a very solid and reliable centre half at Crewe, for whom he made 125 appearances. Despite having several defensive partners, he had three excellent seasons with the Owls, making his debut against the team he supported as a lad, Wolves, in August 2000. He became Northampton's captain.

WHALLEY, John William
Inside right

Appearances: 5
Born: Bradford, 17 February 1897
Died: Morecambe, 3 August 1972

CAREER
CLUBS: Crystal Palace, WEDNESDAY (£100, August

1919-June 1920), Halifax Town.
WARTIME GUEST APPEARANCES: Portsmouth
OTHER: Army – First World War.

All of John Whalley's five appearances came in April 1920 when he partnered Bill Harvey on the right wing, making his debut against Newcastle. He had 141 League outings with Halifax.

WHELAN, Glenn David
Midfield

Appearances: 123+6   Goals: 13
Born: Dublin, 13 January 1984

CAREER
CLUBS: Manchester City, Bury, Wycombe Wanderers, WEDNESDAY (free, July 2004).

Republic of Ireland Youth and Under-21 international midfielder Glenn Whelan had a fine first season with the Owls, scoring in the play-off final against Hartlepool. He was voted his country's Young Player of the Year in 2005.

WHITAKER, Colin
Outside left

Appearances: 1
Born: Leeds, 14 June 1932

CAREER
CLUBS: Farsley Celtic, WEDNESDAY (free, November 1951-June 1953), Bradford Park Avenue, RAF, Shrewsbury Town, Queens Park Rangers, Rochdale, Oldham Athletic, Barrow, Ashton United, Stalybridge Celtic (player-manager), Buxton Town (manager).
OTHER: played cricket and golf; now owns property in Spain.

Never given a realistic chance at Hillsborough, Colin Whitaker went on to score 109 goals – including 8 hat-tricks – in almost 350 League

appearances, having by far his best spell at Shrewsbury, where he scored 59 goals. His only outing for Wednesday was against QPR in March 1952 when he deputised for Dennis Woodhead. A speedy winger, skilful and confident, he played in the losing Rochdale side in the 1962 League Cup final. An RAF posting to Germany meant he missed an England Under-23 cap as a Bradford player.

WHITE, Arthur Henry
Forward

Appearances: 2   Goals: 1
Born: Handsworth, Sheffield, 1869
Deceased by 1948

CAREER
CLUBS: WEDNESDAY (August 1889-April 1891), Heanor Town, Loughborough Town.

Bill White was a reliable reserve during Wednesday's first season of Alliance football. Some reference books have an Arthur White playing for Sheffield United.

WHITEHOUSE, John Charles
Forward

Appearances: 10   Goals: 1
Born: Smethwick, 4 March 1897
Died: Halesowen, 3 January 1948

CAREER
CLUBS: Smethwick Hall, Blackheath Town, Redditch, Birmingham, Derby County, WEDNESDAY (£2,000, February 1929-August 1930), Bournemouth, Folkestone Town, Worcester City (player-manager), Derby County (scout).
WARTIME GUEST APPEARANCES: Derby County, Chelsea.

A Second Division championship winner with Birmingham in 1921, Jackie Whitehouse was a pugnacious forward with a reputation for being one of the game's hard men. Never averse to 'mixing it', he was sent off three times during his career. He scored 35 goals in 115 games for the Blues and 86 in 200 appearances for Derby, helping the Rams win promotion to the top flight in 1926. He scored four goals for the Rams when they beat Wednesday 8-0 in March 1927 and then netted in his first game for the Owls in a 3-2 win over Bury in March 1929.

WHITHAM, John
Forward

Appearances: 62+9 Goals: 31
Born: Burnley, 8 December 1946

CAREER
CLUBS: Burnley, WEDNESDAY (free, October 1964-May 1970), Liverpool, Cardiff City, Reading, Worksop Town, Hallam.
OTHER: licensee; police social club steward.

Jack Whitham made 111 League appearances in a twelve-year career – 63 with Wednesday. An England Under-23 international, capped against Wales in 1968, his goalscoring exploits made him a popular figure at Hillsborough. His moderate appearance tally in five and a half years was due to the many hours he spent in the treatment room – his courageous style taking its toll. He made a terrific start with the Owls, scoring twice on his debut as a substitute in a 7-0 win over Burnley in May 1967. After his surprise transfer to Anfield, he found competition fierce. He won the Welsh Cup with Cardiff in 1974 and finished with a flourish at Reading. He played in over 400 games for Johnny Quinn's All Stars charity team. His grandfather, Private Thomas Whitham of the Coldstream Guards, was awarded the VC for war efforts in Belgium in 1917.

WHITHAM, Terence
Defender

Appearances: 4
Born: Sheffield, 14 August 1935

CAREER
CLUBS: WEDNESDAY (August 1950-June 1961), Chesterfield, Worksop Town, Matlock Town and others.

Terry Whitham was an Owl for eleven years, playing mainly in the reserves. He had to wait until October 1956 before making his League debut against Luton, when he deputised for Tom McAnearney in a 2-0 defeat. He made 66 League appearances for Chesterfield.

WHITTINGHAM, Guy
Forward

Appearances: 104+26 Goals: 25
Born: Evesham, 10 November 1964

CAREER
CLUBS: Oxford City, Waterlooville, Yeovil Town, Portsmouth, Aston Villa, Wolverhampton Wanderers, WEDNESDAY (£700,000, December 1994-November 1998), Wolverhampton Wanderers (L), Portsmouth (loan, signed later, coach, assistant manager), Watford, Peterborough United, Oxford United, Portsmouth, Wycombe Wanderers, Newport Isle of Wight, AFC Newbury.
OTHER: Army, PFA regional coach.

Guy Whittingham was a strong, willing forward, bought out of the army by Portsmouth in 1989. Nicknamed 'Corporal Punishment' at Fratton Park, Whittingham scored 127 goals in 357 appearances for Pompey, whom he helped, as he did Wycombe, reach the FA Cup semi-final in 1992 and 2001 respectively. He was thirty when he joined the Owls, but still gave great service, averaging 1 goal every 5 matches before returning to Portsmouth. He netted twice on his debut for the Owls in a 4-1 win at Everton on Boxing Day 1994 and ended that season as second top-scorer behind Mark Bright.

WHITTON, Stephen Paul
Forward

Appearances: 25+12   Goals: 8
Born: East Ham, London, 4 December 1960

CAREER
CLUBS: Coventry City, Seiko, West Ham United, Birmingham City, WEDNESDAY (£275,000, March 1989-January 1991), Halmstad BK (L), Ipswich Town, Colchester United (player-coach, caretaker manager, manager).
OTHER: partner in a Colchester-based ink cartridge business.

A West Ham supporter as a lad, Steve Whitton started his career 100 miles away in Coventry before signing for the Hammers in 1983, having made 82 appearances for the Sky Blues. Strong and mobile, he never really established himself at Upton Park and, after thriving at Birmingham (35 goals in 119 games), he joined Wednesday, for whom he made his debut in a 3-1 win over Charlton in March 1989. After leaving Hillsborough, he won a Second Division medal with Ipswich in 1992 before playing, coaching and managing Colchester.

WICKS, Peter
Goalkeeper

Appearances: 14
Born: Hemsworth, 14 May 1948

CAREER
CLUBS: WEDNESDAY (June 1965-April 1970), Barnsley (L), Cape Town Spurs.
OTHER: builder's labourer.

Reserve to Ron Springett at Hillsborough for five years, England Youth international Peter Wicks made the first of his 14 appearances for Wednesday in a 4-2 defeat at Liverpool in January 1964 at the age of sixteen years and 257 days. Disappointed not to get more first-team football, he later did well in South Africa.

WILCOCKSON, Harold
Full-back

Appearances: 43   Goals: 1
Born: Sheffield, 23 July 1943

CAREER
CLUBS: Hillsborough Boys Club, Rotherham United, Doncaster Rovers, WEDNESDAY (exchange for Ian Branfoot and Archie Irvine, December 1969-May 1971), Doncaster Rovers, Goole Town.
OTHER: HGV driver.

Harry Wilcockson made 109 League appearances for Rotherham and 111 in two spells with Doncaster. Strong with good pace, he occupied both full-back berths and made his debut for the Owls against Arsenal in December 1969, scoring his only goal (the winner) against QPR in September 1970. He returned to Belle Vue when Peter Rodrigues and Ken Burton became Wednesday's recognised full-back pairing.

WILKINSON, Derek
Outside right

Appearances: 231   Goals: 57
Born: Stalybridge, 4 June 1935

CAREER
CLUBS: Stalybridge Celtic, Dukinfield, WEDNESDAY (£100, November 1953-March 1965).
OTHER: played golf and snooker; drove a fork-lift truck; worked as a French polisher.

Derek Wilkinson

Derek Wilkinson, an England Youth international who also represented the Football League on two occasions (1959), gave Wednesday supreme service for over eleven years before injury forced him to retire, aged twenty-nine. Essentially a winger with good pace and a strong shot, he could also play inside or centre forward and made his League debut in a 5-3 defeat at Cardiff in November 1954, but he had to wait until 1957 before gaining a regular place in the side. A vital member of the Owls' 1958/59 promotion-winning attack when he scored 12 goals in 39 games, he then helped the team reach the FA Cup semi-final in 1960 by netting twice in the sixth round win over Sheffield United. The following year he was Wednesday's star when top-flight status was reclaimed after a season in the Second Division. He and his twin brother, Eric, played together against Sunderland in September 1958.

WILKINSON, Eric
Outside left

Appearances: 1
Born: Stalybridge, 4 June 1935

CAREER
CLUBS: Dukinfield, WEDNESDAY (free, March 1958-May 1960).
OTHER: engineer.

Eric Wilkinson's only game for Wednesday was on the left wing with his twin brother Derek on the right, in a thrilling 3-3 draw at Sunderland in September 1958.

WILKINSON, Harry
Utility

Appearances: 11
Born: Sheffield, 1857
Deceased by 1938

CAREER
CLUBS: Spital Chesterfield, WEDNESDAY (free, August 1881-April 1883).

Primarily a defender, Harry Wilkinson made his only start for the Owls at left-back in an FA Cup-tie against Staveley in December 1881. After that he lined up at centre forward, centre half and right-back, but missed the 1882 FA Cup final through injury.

WILKINSON, Howard
Outside right

Appearances: 22   Goals: 3
Born: Netherthorpe, Sheffield, 13 November 1943

CAREER
CLUBS: Sheffield United, Hallam, WEDNESDAY (free, June 1962-July 1966), Brighton & Hove Albion, Boston United (player-manager, coach), Notts County (coach, assistant manager, manager), WEDNESDAY (manager, June 1983-October 1988), Leeds United (manager), England semi-professional team (manager), England Under-21s (coach, assistant manager, manager), England (manager), Sunderland (manager), Shanghai

Howard Wilkinson

Shenshua (coach), Leicester City (assistant coach), Notts County (non-executive director), coached in China.
OTHER: FA director of coaching; League Managers' Association chairman.

An England Youth international with five caps, Howard Wilkinson had an unspectacular playing career, despite scoring 19 goals in 129 League games for Brighton. Standing in for Alan Finney, he made his League debut for the Owls in a 5-1 win over Burnley in September 1964 and scored his first two goals in a 4-2 defeat at West Ham in October 1965. He tasted management for the first time with Boston and gained a degree in physical education at Sheffield University. A teacher for a while, he was an FA regional coach in Sheffield before leading the England semi-professional team to victory in the Four Nations championship in 1979. Later in charge of England's Under-21 and senior sides, he had no money

to spend on new players at Notts County, but was pretty successful during his first three years in charge at Hillsborough, guiding the Owls back into the First Division in 1984 and into the semi-finals of the FA Cup. After leaving Wednesday (replaced by Peter Eustace) he took Leeds to the Second Division championship in 1990 and to the League Championship in 1992, pipping Manchester United in a thrilling run-in. Six months after taking Leeds to the 1996 League Cup final he was sacked. He was the quiet man of football.

WILKINSON, James
Left-back

Appearances: 1
Born: Sheffield, 1860
Deceased by 1938

CAREER
CLUBS: WEDNESDAY (1881/82).

Jim Wilkinson's only senior game for the Owls was in the 1882 FA Cup semi-final replay defeat by Blackburn Rovers when the defence was reshuffled following an injury to his namesake Harry. He helped the Owls win the Wharncliffe Charity Cup that same year.

WILKINSON, Jack
Outside left

Appearances: 79   Goals: 7
Born: Wath-upon-Dearne, Yorkshire, 13 June 1902
Died: Mexborough, April 1979

CAREER
CLUBS: Wath Athletic, WEDNESDAY (£450, October 1925-May 1930), Newcastle United, Lincoln City, Sunderland, Hull City, Scunthorpe United, Burton Town, Ransomes & Markes (manager).
OTHER: ran a greengrocer's shop.

Jack 'Ginger' Wilkinson scored over 100 goals in five seasons as a youngster before joining Wednesday. A small and crafty winger, he netted on his League debut in a 2-0 win over Hull in April 1926 and helped the Owls clinch promotion that same season. A regular in the side in 1926/27, he eventually lost his place to Ellis Rimmer. He did well with Newcastle, helped Lincoln win the Midland League and during his career notched 53 goals in 227 competitive matches.

WILLIAMS, Andrew
Midfield

Appearances: 1
Born: Dudley: 29 July 1962

CAREER
CLUBS: Dudley Town, Solihull Borough, Coventry City, Rotherham United, Leeds United, Port Vale, Notts County, Huddersfield Town, Rotherham United, WEDNESDAY (n/c June-July 1995), Hull City, Scarborough, Gainsborough Trinity, Matlock Town, Guiseley.
OTHER: employed by Rotherham Borough Council.

One of five non-contract players recruited for the InterToto Cup competition, Andy Williams' only game for the Owls was against FC Basel in that competition in June 1995. He won the Second Division title with Leeds in 1990 and made over 300 League and cup appearances during his career (1985-96).

WILLIAMS, David Rees
Forward

Appearances: 173   Goals: 8
Born: Abercanaid, Merthyr, February 1900
Died: Abercanaid, 30 December 1963

CAREER
CLUBS: Abercanaid, Pentrebach, Merthyr Town,

WEDNESDAY (£1,500, June 1922-October 1927), Manchester United, Thames Association, Aldershot, Merthyr Town, Glenavon.
OTHER: worked for the Hoover company, Merthyr and coached the works' football team.

Honoured by Wales as a schoolboy, Rees Williams made his mark with Merthyr, for whom he made 65 Third Division (South) appearances in 3 seasons. A dashing outside right, full of tricks, he had the unenviable task of succeeding the legendary Billy Meredith on the international front and won 4 of his 8 full caps as a Wednesday player. He quickly established himself in the Owls' side, made his debut at Rotherham in August 1922 and four years later won a Second Division championship medal. Recognised as one of the game's fastest wingers in the 1920s, his career realised 259 League appearances and 16 goals. He committed suicide, aged sixty-three.

WILLIAMS, Leonard Horace
Full-back

Appearances: 9
Born: Dalton Brook, Rotherham, 17 May 1898
Deceased by 1968

CAREER
CLUBS: Wath Athletic, WEDNESDAY (free, July 1923-May 1926), Stockport County, Wolverhampton Wanderers, Swansea Town, Oswestry Town, Wellington Town.

An efficient footballer, good on the ball and totally committed, Len Williams played in 150 League and FA Cup games in his career – only 9 with Wednesday. He made his debut in place of Felton against Leeds in January 1924 and afterwards understudied Blenkinsop and Inglis.

WILLIAMS, Leslie
Goalkeeper

Appearances: 11
Born: Thurcroft, 27 March 1935

CAREER
CLUBS: Rotherham United, WEDNESDAY (free, July 1952-January 1957) Swindon Town, Rotherham United, Boston United (two spells), Corby Town. OTHER: licensee.

Les Williams made only 11 League appearances – all with the Owls – during his entire career. Reserve to McIntosh, Capewell and Ryalls at Hillsborough, he made his debut against Liverpool in August 1955. His brother Ted played for Nottingham Forest and Northampton.

WILLIAMS, Michael Anthony
Midfield

Appearances: 20+9 Goals: 1
Born: Bradford, 21 November 1969

CAREER
CLUBS: Ossett Town, Leeds United, WEDNESDAY (free, February 1991-July 1997), Halifax Town (L), Huddersfield Town (L), Peterborough United (L), Burnley, Oxford United, Halifax Town, Worksop Town, Ossett Town.

The strong-running Michael Williams was an Owl for six years, during which time he made only 29 appearances, the first as a substitute in a 5-2 win over Southampton in April 1993. He made his League debut on loan to Halifax five months earlier.

WILLIAMS, Paul Anthony
Forward

Appearances: 94+20   Goals: 28
Born: Stratford, London, 16 August 1965

CAREER
CLUBS: Aveley, Clapton, Woodford Town, Charlton Athletic, Brentford, WEDNESDAY (£600,000, August 1990-September 1992), Crystal Palace, Sunderland, Birmingham City, Charlton Athletic, Torquay United, Southend United, Canvey Island and others.

Fast and tricky, Paul Williams appeared in almost 100 games for Charlton, against whom he made his Wednesday debut in August 1990. A League Cup winner that season, he had three good years at Hillsborough before helping Crystal Palace reach the Premiership as First Division champions. Capped by England 4 times at Under-21 level and on 3 occasions by the 'B' team, Williams scored 82 goals 346 appearances over a period of 11 years.

WILLIAMSON, Charles Harold
Left-back

Appearances: 66+1 Goals: 1
Born: Sheffield, 16 March 1962

CAREER
CLUBS: WEDNESDAY (May 1978), Lincoln City (L), Southend United (L), Chesterfield, Stafford Rangers, Goole Town, Gainsborough Trinity, Matlock Town, Eastwood Town and others.

A regular for Wednesday in 1981/82, Charlie Williamson, well built and resolute, made his League debut in a 2-0 win at Reading in December 1979 as deputy for David Grant. He helped the Owls win promotion to the First Division in 1984 and made almost 150 appearances in his career.

WILSON, Andrew
Forward

Appearances: 547   Goals: 218
Born: Irvine, Ayrshire, 10 December 1880
Died: 13 March 1945

Charlie Wilson

CAREER

CLUBS: *Irvine Royal Academy, Irvine, Irvine Meadow, Clyde, WEDNESDAY (£200, May 1900-May 1919), Bristol Rovers (manager), Oldham Athletic (manager), Stockport County (manager).*
OTHER: *a founder member of the Hillsborough golf club.*

Andy Wilson, Wednesday's all-time record appearance-maker and goalscorer, also won 6 caps for Scotland – 4 against England between 1907 and 1913 – and represented the Anglo-Scots against a Scottish XI in 1903. A weighty but fast opportunist, difficult to contain and dispossess, he could shoot with both feet, head the ball hard and direct, and was without doubt a great sportsman, despite the close attention of the robust defenders who tried to mark him. A record signing from Clyde for £200, he was twice a League Championship winner with Wednesday – 1903 and 1904 – and collected an FA Cup winners' medal in 1907. Top-scorer in eight of his sixteen seasons with the Owls, he was a great hero of the fans. As a manager, he was a quiet, deep-thinking man whose team talks were always concise and to the point, and he came close to guiding Oldham into the First Division in 1930 – the Latics lost their last match at Barnsley and finished third. Two of his brothers, David and James, were also professional footballers. David played for Scotland and also managed Nelson and Exeter City.

WILSON, Charles
Utility

Appearances: 61
Born: Heeley, Sheffield, 20 July 1905
Died: Kidderminster, April 1985

CAREER

CLUBS: *Stonehouse, Hallam, Sheffield United, Chesterfield, West Bromwich Albion, WEDNESDAY (£3,000, February 1928-March 1932), Grimsby Town, Aston Villa, Coventry City, Kidderminster Harriers (two spells), Peterborough & Fletton United, Worcester City, Brierley Hill Alliance.*
WARTIME GUEST APPEARANCES: *Charlton Athletic, Aldershot.*
OTHER: *Kidderminster police; licensee; wholesale tobacconist rep.*

The youngest player ever to appear in a League game for West Brom, Charlie 'Tug' Wilson was only sixteen years and seventy-three days old when made his debut against Oldham in October 1921. An opportunist striker at The Hawthorns, he scored 45 goals in 133 games for the Baggies and won three successive Central League championship medals in the 1920s before joining the Owls. He and Ellis Rimmer made their first starts for Wednesday against Newcastle in February 1928, and in 1930/31 Wilson replaced the unfortunate Billy Marsden. The Owls used him in the forward line, at left-back and also at left half.

WILSON, Daniel Joseph
Midfield

Appearances: 127+10   Goals: 14
Born: Wigan, 1 January 1960

CAREER
CLUBS: Wigan Athletic, Bury, Chesterfield, Nottingham Forest, Scunthorpe United, Brighton & Hove Albion, Luton Town, WEDNESDAY (£200,000, August 1990-June 1993), Barnsley (player, manager), WEDNESDAY (manager, July 1998-May 2000), Bristol City (manager), Milton Keynes Dons (manager), Hartlepool United (manager).

A Northern Ireland international, capped 24 times (six as an Owl), Danny Wilson had a wonderful career. After being rejected by Wigan, he made 105 senior appearances for Bury, 117 for Chesterfield, 155 for Brighton, 142 for Luton, 137 for Wednesday and 89 for Barnsley, plus a few more with Forest and Scunthorpe, to finish with 786 under his belt for clubs and country – he also netted 116 goals. Twice a League Cup winner with Luton in 1988 and 1989, he helped the Owls win the same competition in 1991 when, along with goalscorer John Sheridan, John Harkes and Nigel Worthington,

Danny Wilson

Wednesday out-witted and out-played Alex Ferguson's Manchester United in centre-field. A genuine craftsman, with adept control and stratagems which were a delight to witness, Wilson made his debut for the Owls in a 2-0 League win at Ipswich in August 1990 and netted his first goal for the club in a 4-0 victory over Brighton two months later. As a manager, he gallantly, and perhaps surprisingly, led Barnsley into the Premiership in 1997 but was unable to keep the Owls in the top flight in 2000. He twice took Bristol City into the Second Division play-offs and performed a miracle by keeping the MK Dons in League One in 2005. Wilson's son, Laurie, an Irish Youth international, was a reserve at Wednesday (2003-05).

WILSON, George
Centre half

Appearances: 197   Goals: 5
Born: Kirkham, Preston, 14 January 1892
Died: Blackpool, 25 November 1961

CAREER
CLUBS: Fleetwood, Morecambe, Blackpool, WEDNESDAY (£2,500, March 1920-July 1925), Nelson.
OTHER: licensee.

An England international, with 12 caps won between 1921 and 1924, George Wilson also represented the Football League on 4 occasions during the same period. He started out as a centre forward with Blackpool before the First World War and after the hostilities developed into the best centre half in Great Britain. He worked prodigiously during every game, was fast over the ground, wonderful at heading and a stylist in his overall play. Never a dirty player, he timed his tackles to perfection and during a splendid career amassed over 450 club appearances, scoring almost 40 goals. He joined Wednesday for a substantial fee in March 1920 and made his debut against

W

Liverpool forty-eight hours later, but was unable to save the club from relegation that season. He played superbly at the heart of the Owls' defence for five years, captaining the side several times while also leading his country on three occasions, twice against Scotland. The Hillsborough faithful loved Wilson and praised him greatly for his enthusiasm, work-rate and consistency. He was one of a number of players who rejected the new terms offered in 1925 and subsequently moved to Nelson for a record fee of £2,500. He continued playing for another five years.

WILSON, James
Forward

Appearances: 1
Born: Sheffield, 1860
Died: Blackburn, 1929

CAREER
CLUBS: WEDNESDAY (August 1891-May 1893), Darwen.

A reserve with the Owls, Jim Wilson's only appearance for the club was in the Football Alliance in 1891/92. He scored 8 goals in 32 League games for Darwen.

WILSON, Joseph
Outside left

Appearances: 3
Born: Southwick, Sunderland, June 1901
Died: Durham, 1973

CAREER
CLUBS: Manchester United, Durham City, WEDNESDAY (£110, June 1923-June 1924), Norwich City.

A useful player with good pace, Joe Wilson learned his trade in the Wearside Leagues. A regular in Wednesday's Second XI, he made

the first of his three senior appearances against Bradford City in August 1923 in place of Joe Harron. He made 41 appearances for Norwich.

WILSON, Laurie
Midfield

Appearances: 1+2
Born: Brighton, 5 December 1984

CAREER
CLUBS: WEDNESDAY (June 2001-July 2004), Luton Town, Burton Albion, Gresley Rovers, Grantham, Belper Town, Kidderminster Harriers.

Gritty and hard working, Laurie Wilson made his first and last appearances for the Owls in FA Cup games against Scunthorpe in December 2003, playing against Carlisle in the LDV Vans Trophy in between. Nigel Clough signed him for Burton.

WILSON, Mark Antony
Midfield

Appearances: 3
Born: Scunthorpe, 9 February 1979

CAREER
CLUBS: Bottesford Town, Manchester United, Wrexham, Middlesbrough, Stoke City, Swansea City, WEDNESDAY (loan, January-February 2004), Doncaster Rovers, Livingston, Dallas Burn.

A former England Schoolboy, Youth and Under-21 international, Mark Wilson made ten appearances for Manchester United but was never in contention as a first-team regular at Old Trafford. He started off well at Middlesbrough but then fell from favour and afterwards struggled to make an impact, having loan spells with several clubs. The first of his three outings for the Owls was against Peterborough in February 2004.

WILSON, S.
Right-back

Appearances: 2
Born: Sheffield, 1861
Deceased by 1938

CAREER
CLUBS: WEDNESDAY (seasons 1884-86).

Registered with Wednesday for two seasons, Wilson's two appearances were against Long Eaton Rangers and Nottingham Forest in the FA Cup in 1884/85. He also played in several non-competitive games.

WINDASS, Dean
Forward

Appearances: 2
Born: Hull, 1 April 1969

CAREER
CLUBS: North Ferriby United, Hull City, Aberdeen, Oxford United, Bradford City, Middlesbrough, WEDNESDAY (loan, December 2001), Sheffield United, Bradford City.

Dean Windass has had a wonderful career. He was twenty-two when he made his League debut for Hull and, although frequently in trouble with referees, he's a good, honest, down-to-earth battler, a great professional who, in 2006, reached the milestone of 200 goals and 600 club appearances. His two appearances for the Owls, in place of Simon Donnelly, were against Millwall and Gillingham.

WINTERBOTTOM, Harry
Forward

Appearances: 50   Goals: 11
Born: Sheffield, 19 December 1861
Died: Sheffield, 1932

CAREER
CLUBS: Suffolk, Heeley, WEDNESDAY (April 1879-April 1892), Providence, Attercliffe, Exchange, Lockwood Brothers, West Bromwich Albion.

When Wednesday gave up their amateur status in 1887, not all their players turned professional – Harry Winterbottom was one who did not. Working at the time as a bone haft and scale cutter, he was a skilled craftsman on the field as well as off, giving opposing defenders plenty to think about. He was direct, had two good feet and was said to be one of the fastest wing forwards of his day, on a par with West Brom's England international Billy Bassett. In fact, Albion signed Winterbottom as cover in 1888. A Football Alliance championship winner with the Owls in 1890, Winterbottom's debut came in Wednesday's first-ever FA Cup-tie against Blackburn Rovers in December 1880, but he had to battle against injury quite a lot during his career, missing several games in the mid-1880s.

WISE, Franklin
Right-back

Appearances: 1
Born: Sheffield, 1865

CAREER
CLUBS: WEDNESDAY (1887/88).

Frank Wise played in Wednesday's FA Cup-tie against Belper in October 1887 when Teddy Brayshaw was injured, Fred Thompson switching to left-back.

WITCOMB, Douglas Frederick
Wing half

Appearances: 230   Goals: 12
Born: Cwm, Ebbw Vale, 18 April 1918
Died: Redditch, July 1997

Douglas Witcomb

CAREER
CLUBS: Cwm Villa, Tottenham Hotspur, Northfleet, Enfield, West Bromwich Albion, WEDNESDAY (£6,500, February 1947-November 1953), Newport County, Llandudno Town, Redditch United.
WARTIME GUEST APPEARANCES: Grimsby Town, Swansea Town, Leicester City, Newport County, Lovells Athletic.
OTHER: employed by and played for IHD Alloys & Alkamatic Works.

Duggie Witcomb played alongside Ron Burgess (the future Spurs and Wales left half) for Ebbw Vale Schools before working down the pit and playing for Cwm Villa at weekends. Informed by his doctor that he was not strong enough to play competitive football, the resilient Witcomb was determined to succeed. He trained long and hard and, after a few games with Enfield, became a professional with West Brom, disproving the doctor's prognosis. He developed into a fine player. Quick, cunning and an excellent passer of the ball, possessing a strong, right-foot shot, he spent ten years at The Hawthorns, making over 120 appearances for the Baggies while representing Wales in 10 full internationals and starring for an All British side against the Football League in 1939. Signed by Wednesday to solve a huge problem at half-back, he made his debut against Spurs in March 1947, setting up two goals in a 5-1 win. He helped the Owls gain promotion to the First Division in 1950 and two years later, after relegation, won a Second Division championship medal. Sadly, Witcomb lost his life in an accidental drowning in 1997.

WOOD, Darren Terence
Utility

Appearances: 10+1
Born: Scarborough, 9 June 1964

CAREER
CLUBS: Middlesbrough, Chelsea, WEDNESDAY (£400,000, January 1989-May 1990).
OTHER: ran a delicatessen.

Darren Wood had appeared in almost 250 League games with his 2 previous clubs when he joined the Owls. An England Schoolboy international, he teamed up with his former manager John Neal at Chelsea and won the FMC in 1986. A competent full-back who could also play effectively in midfield, the first of Wood's outings for Wednesday was against Liverpool in January 1989. At the end of that season he was presented with a championship winners' medal following Chelsea's triumph in the Second Division. Wood's career ended prematurely due to a back injury.

WOOD, Richard Mark
Defender

Appearances: 93+11   Goals: 4
Born: Ossett, 5 July 1985

CLUBS: Ossett Trinitarians, WEDNESDAY (free, July 2001-May 2007).

Giant 6ft 3ins defender Richard Wood had an excellent early period at Hillsborough, but in 2003/04 his form was only described as 'moderate'. He bounced back the following season, taking his appearance tally past the 50 mark while establishing himself in the side. An honest performer with plenty to offer, he made his League debut as a substitute at Brighton in April 2003 and scored on his full debut in a 7-2 win at Burnley five days later. He was in the Owls' play-off final-winning team against Hartlepool in 2005.

WOODALL, Brian Harold
Outside left

Appearances: 22+3 Goals: 6
Born: Chester, 6 June 1948

CAREER
CLUBS: WEDNESDAY (August 1963-October 1970), Oldham Athletic (L), Chester, Crewe Alexandra, Oswestry Town, Rhyl, Colwyn Bay.

Able to play on both wings, Brian Woodall made his League debut for Wednesday as a substitute against Coventry in February 1968 and started his first game at home to Newcastle the following month. A useful reserve, unable to hold down a regular place in the side, he scored in his first game for Oldham in a 5-0 win over Notts County in 1970.

WOODHEAD, Dennis
Outside left

Appearances: 226   Goals: 75
Born: Sheffield, 12 June 1925
Died: Sheffield, 26 July 1996

CAREER
CLUBS: Hillsborough Boys Club, WEDNESDAY (May 1941-September 1955), Chesterfield, Derby County (two spells), Southport, Frickley Colliery, Worksop Town, Retford Town (manager), Chesterfield (office staff), WEDNESDAY (development officer, commercial manager, May 1971-June 1987).
OTHER: RAF – Second World War.

Dennis Woodhead was a dashing outside left with pace, smart footwork and a fierce shot. He also occupied the centre forward berth in an emergency and still produced some enterprising displays. Born with football in his blood – his grandfather was former Wednesday star Billy Betts – Woodhead made just one wartime appearance for the Owls, when on leave from his duties as a flight engineer with the RAF. He added three more appearances to his tally in League football in 1946/47 before gaining a regular place in the side the following season after his release from the forces. He scored twice in eight starts in 1949/50, when promotion was gained to the First Division and, following relegation, he played his part in a second promotion-winning campaign in 1951/52, when the Owls won the title. Two years later he helped Wednesday reach the 1954 FA Cup semi-final, scoring 3 goals in 7 ties. When relegation was suffered in 1955, Woodhead left Hillsborough for Chesterfield. He later had a decent spell with Derby, netting 24 goals in 94 League games and helping the Rams win the Third Division (North) championship in 1955. He spent one month with Southport, being ordered to return to Derby because of a knee injury. Woodhead was employed at Hillsborough for some thirty years.

WOODS, Christopher Charles Eric
Goalkeeper

Appearances: 137+1
Born: Boston, Lincolnshire, 14 November 1959

Chris Woods

CAREER
CLUBS: Priory Celtic, Nottingham Forest, Queens Park Rangers, Norwich City, Glasgow Rangers, WEDNESDAY (£1.2 million, August 1991-May 1996), Reading (L), Colorado Rapids, Southampton, Sunderland, Kansas City Wizards, Burnley, Everton (coach).

Chris Woods never played in a League game for Nottingham Forest, making seven appearances for Brian Clough's club in the League Cup and gaining a winners' medal in 1978. Earning a second winners' medal in the same competition in 1985 with Norwich, he also helped the Canaries twice win promotion from the Second Division, in 1982 and 1986, as champions. With Rangers he won 4 Scottish Premier titles (1987, 1989, 1990 and 1991), 3 Scottish League Cup finals (1987, 1989 and 1991) and set a British record for playing 1,196 minutes without conceding a goal. Capped by England at Youth level, he later played in 2 'B', 6 Under-21 and 43 full internationals while amassing a total of 739 club appearances – 230 with Rangers. Standing 6ft 2ins tall and weighing almost 15st (in his prime), Wood was a first-class 'keeper – daring, with good reflexes and a safe pair of hands enabling him to deal comfortably with high crosses. He took over from Chris Turner for Wednesday at the start of 1991/92, making his debut in a 3-2 home defeat by Aston Villa on the opening Saturday. He missed only one League game in his first season at Hillsborough. His great uncle was Eric Houghton, who played for Aston Villa, Notts County and England between the two world wars.

WOOLHOUSE, Henry
Forward

Appearances: 80   Goals: 36
Born: Ecclesfield, Sheffield, 1868
Died: Sheffield, December 1911

CAREER
CLUBS: Sheffield FC, WEDNESDAY (free, August 1888-May 1895).

A Football Alliance championship winner with the Owls in 1890, Harry Woolhouse enjoyed a lot of success with Wednesday. He made his debut at centre forward in an FA Cup-tie against Notts County in February 1889 and went on to score 5 goals (all against Halliwell) in 10 outings in that competition. Brother Frank played for Wednesday's Second XI and also for Walsall in the 1890s.

WORRALL, John Edwin
Right-back

Appearances: 116
Born: Buxton, Derbyshire, 2 October 1891
Died: Chesterfield, 24 July 1980.

CAREER
CLUBS: The Comrades, Buxton, WEDNESDAY (£35, May 1910-June 1919), Fulham, Aberdare Athletic, Watford, New Brighton, Southport, Shirebrook, Ripley Town, Derbyshire Schools (coach), Tottenham Hotspur (coach).
WARTIME GUEST APPEARANCES: Chelsea, Tottenham Hotspur, Buxton
OTHER: worked for the Borough of Wandsworth Council.

Ted Worrall was a thoughtful and stylish player who possessed a remarkable sense of anticipation. He kicked long and accurate but was perhaps far too one-footed to become a world-class defender. Nevertheless, he gave Wednesday excellent service until the outbreak of the First World War. He made his debut against Preston in January 1911 when he deputised for Jimmy Spoors, and thereafter remained first choice. He played twice in war-time football for the Owls and after leaving the club he made 96 appearances for Fulham, 84 for New Brighton and 75 for Southport. He was the nephew of the famous England goalkeeper Sam Hardy.

WORTHINGTON, Nigel
Utility

Appearances: 413+4   Goals: 14
Born: Ballymena, Ireland, 4 November 1961

CAREER
CLUBS: Ballymena, Notts County, WEDNESDAY (£100,000, February 1984-July 1994), Leeds United, Stoke City, Blackpool (player-manager, manager), England Under-21s (coach), Norwich City (assistant manager, caretaker-manager, manager), Leicester City, Northern Ireland (manager).

Nigel Worthington

After breaking the ice with Ballymena, Nigel Worthington made 85 appearances for Notts County before joining the Owls. An excellent left-sided player, able to perform at left-back, in midfield or out wide, he was a vital member of the side that won promotion to the First Division in 1984. Nicknamed 'Irish' by the fans, he then played a big part as Wednesday established themselves in the top flight and in 1991 celebrated with a League Cup winners' medal at Wembley. He left Hillsborough three years later with his career appearance record standing at an impressive 555, and he'd also collected the first 50 (a Wednesday record) of what was to become a final tally of 66 full caps for Northern Ireland, having previously played for his country's youth team. As a manager he guided Norwich in and out of the Premiership (2004 and 2005).

WORTLEY, George
Left-back

Appearances: 1
Born: Sheffield, 1861
Deceased by 1938

CAREER
CLUBS: WEDNESDAY (seasons 1883-85).

George Wortley's only game for the club was against Nottingham Forest in the FA Cup in January 1885.

WRIGHT, Ernest Victor
Forward

Appearances: 2
Born: Bloxwich, Walsall, 24 January 1909
Died: Wednesbury, March, 1964

CAREER
CLUBS: Bloxwich Strollers, Bristol City, Rotherham United, WEDNESDAY (£1,900, October 1930-

February 1933), Rotherham United, Liverpool, Plymouth Argyle, Chelmsford City.
WARTIME GUEST APPEARANCES: Crystal Palace, Millwall, Walsall.

Vic Wright was a lively player who established a fine reputation during his two spells with Rotherham. He packed a powerful right-foot shot and during his career scored over 75 goals in League and cup football. He made his Wednesday debut against Aston Villa in October 1931 when he deputised for George Stephenson in a re-jigged front line. Wright was the nephew of the former Aston Villa, Small Heath and England winger Charlie Athersmith.

WRIGHT, James
Full-back

Appearances: 4
Born: Okehampton, North Devon, 11 September 1910
Died: Grimsby, December 1978

CAREER
CLUBS: Okehampton, Exeter City, Torquay United, Grimsby Town, WEDNESDAY (£600, March 1935-March 1936), Guildford City, Swansea Town, Hartlepool United.

A stocky defender with a powerful kick, Jim Wright made 28 League appearances for Torquay and 27 for Grimsby before moving to Hillsborough as cover for Ted Catlin. He made the first of his three appearances for the Owls in a 4-0 defeat at Derby in March 1935.

WRIGHT, John
Inside left

Appearances: 110   Goals: 42
Born: Hamilton, 4 February 1873
Died: Southend, 1946

CAREER
CLUBS: Hamilton Academical, Clyde, Bolton Wanderers, WEDNESDAY (£200, November 1898-March 1902), Hamilton Academical, Bolton Wanderers, Plymouth Argyle, Watford, Southend United.

Initially a left-winger, John Wright was converted into an inside forward after leaving Clyde and was an ever-present in his first season with Bolton. He went on to score 22 goals in 128 appearances for the Trotters in three seasons before making his debut for Wednesday in the famous match against Aston Villa which was abandoned through bad light after seventy-nine and a half minutes in November 1898. He netted the first of his 43 goals soon afterwards in a 2-2 draw at Newcastle but couldn't save the team from relegation. The following season he netted 26 goals in 33 League games as the Owls won the Second Division championship at the first attempt. Wright also suffered relegation after his return to Bolton in 1903. His two sons were both footballers – Billy had a trial with Wednesday in 1919 and played for Bolton and Reading, while Doug assisted Newcastle United and Lincoln and was capped by England in 1938.

WRIGHT, Percy Lionel
Outside left

Appearances: 22   Goals: 6
Born: Darley Dale, Derbyshire, 1890
Died: Matlock, 10 July 1971

CAREER
CLUBS: Heanor Town, WEDNESDAY (£55, May 1910-March 1914), West Ham United, Chesterfield.

A reserve during his four seasons with Wednesday, Percy Wright covered for George Robertson whom he replaced when making a scoring debut in a 1-1 draw with Everton in April 1911.

WYLDE, Rodger James
Forward

Appearances: 182+12   Goals: 66
Born: Sheffield, 8 March 1954

CAREER
CLUBS: WEDNESDAY (July 1970-February 1980), Burnley (L), Oldham Athletic, Sporting Lisbon, Sunderland, Barnsley, Rotherham United, Stockport County (player, physio).

A tall, polished yet sometimes controversial striker, Rodger Wylde had a very successful career, scoring over 150 goals in more than 400 appearances, having his best spell at Hillsborough. He made his debut for the Owls against Middlesbrough in November 1972 and netted the first of his 66 goals in his third outing at home to Millwall. He netted 8 times in 15 League games when promotion was gained from the Third Division in 1980. He was at Stockport when ex-Wednesday star, Carlton Palmer, was manager there.

YOUNG, Gerald Morton
Utility

Appearances: 335   Goals: 16
Born: Jarrow, 1 October 1936

CAREER
CLUBS: Newcastle United, Hawthorn Leslie, WEDNESDAY (May 1955-May 1971, coach, care-taker-manager), Barnsley (coach).
OTHER: ran a sports shop in Sheffield with John Quinn.

No Wednesday supporter could ever forget Gerry Young's error in the 1966 FA Cup final

Gerald Young

which presented Everton's Derek Temple with the winning goal after the Owls had initially led 2-0. A model professional, he was a regular in the first team for seven years from 1963 after taking over from Tony Kay. Prior to that, and following his debut against Blackpool in March 1957, he had made less than 40 appearances in 6 years, having completed his apprenticeship as an electrician before turning professional at the age of eighteen. Capped by England against Wales in November 1964 (deputising for Bobby Moore), he was all set for a second international outing versus Holland a few weeks later but ruptured a thigh muscle four days before the match and was forced to withdraw. He had a testimonial match at the end of his last season at Hillsborough (1971) before joining the coaching staff. When Derek Dooley was dismissed, Young took over as caretaker-manager.

Academy players with Wednesday in 2006/07 (not listed elsewhere)

Josh Aston (striker, midfield); Andy Broadbent (right-back, midfield, ex-Sheffield Rangers); Aaron Jameson (goalkeeper); Kyle Jordan (striker); James Kay (left-back); David Kee (striker); Leon Lekaj (defender), brother of Rocky, born in Kosovo – joined the Owls from Norwegian club SF Grei in July 2006; Sam Liversidge (full-back, winger); David McClements (midfield – played for the Irish Football Institute before joining the Owls in November 2005, capped at Under-17 level); Liam McMenimin (defender – Northern Ireland Youth international); Richard O'Donnell (goalkeeper); Craig Tawton (defender, midfield) and Todd Wood (striker).

Other players and personnel associated with Sheffield Wednesday

George Beadles

An Owls reserve who won two caps for Wales, appeared in the 1925 FA Cup final for Cardiff against Sheffield United and was awarded the Serbian Gold Medal for gallantry during the First World War.

Tom Bishop, brothers Fred and Thomas Butler, Samuel Charles and Daniel Davy

All 1870s and '80s players who starred in Sheffield Charity Cup and Wharncliffe Charity Cup competitions.

Sir Charles Clegg

Capped by England against Scotland in the first international played in Glasgow in 1872; helped Wednesday win the Sheffield Challenge Cup (1878) and the Wharncliffe Charity Cup (1879); refereed 1882 and 1892 FA Cup finals; member of the FA Council Committee; FA chairman and vice-president; chairman and president of the Football League's Appeal Committee; president of the Sheffield & Hallamshire FA and chairman of Wednesday from June 1899; knighted in 1927 for services to the Board of Trade and football; played in the first ever floodlit match at Bramall Lane in October 1878.

Sir William Clegg, OBE

Wednesday player from 1868-80; an England international, capped versus Scotland in 1873 and Wales in 1879; also played for Sheffield FA; became a Wednesday director; practised as a solicitor with brother Charles in the family firm, Clegg & Sons; was Lord Mayor of Sheffield (1893-99); knighted in 1906 for services to football and awarded the OBE in 1891 for his work on Sheffield Munitions Tribunal (First World War).

Eric England

Owls' secretary who served the club for thirty-seven years.

Bruce Grobbelaar

The former Liverpool star who signed on free transfer in July 1997 as goalkeeping cover.

Jimmy Harrop

A half-back reserve with Wednesday in 1903/04 who later won the FA Cup with Aston Villa.

Roy Hattersley

Former deputy leader of the Labour Party and Owls fanatic.

Iain Hesford

Goalkeeper Iain Hesford joined Wednesday from Blackpool in August 1983 and left for Sunderland three years later without making the first team, but he appeared in almost 500 senior games during his career.

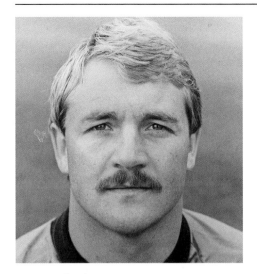

Iain Hesford

Jim Holton

The ex-Manchester United and Scotland defender, who had a brief spell at Hillsborough at the end of his career but did not make the first team.

Idris Hopkins

An outside right who went on to win 12 full caps for Wales, having been a reserve with Wednesday in 1930/31.

Stuart Jones

Reserve goalkeeper Stuart Jones cost Wednesday £20,000 when he was signed from Weston Super Mare FC in 1998, but failed to make the first team and moved to Torquay United in February 2000.

Andrew Kiwomya

A forward who was registered with Wednesday in 1986/87 but was released to Dundee without playing in the first team. He also played for Leeds United, Doncaster Rovers and Fulham.

Jack Lambert

Jack Lambert had an unsuccessful trial with Wednesday in 1921. He went on to score 98 goals in 143 League games for Arsenal.

John McMillan

A Wednesday reserve whose career ended tragically when he had a leg amputated at the age of eighteen.

Frank Melling

An England amateur international trialist who failed to make the grade as a player with Wednesday. He later became Sheffield United director.

David Mobley

Vic's brother and a reserve defender, he never got into the first team but made 29 League appearances for Grimsby Town in 1969/70.

David Storf

David Storf was an Owls' youth and reserve-team winger for five years before moving to Rochdale in 1963 and then switching to Barrow in 1967. He made over 300 League and cup appearances after leaving Hillsborough.

David Wetherall

A Defender who never got a chance in the first team at Hillsborough. He went on to make over 250 appearances for Leeds United (1991-1999) and almost 250 for Bradford City.

Some of the many guest players (not listed elsewhere) who appeared for Wednesday in wartime

First World War: J. Harrop (Aston Villa), S. Hatton (WBA), W. Hibbert (Newcastle United), E. Islip (Huddersfield Town), J. Roulson (Birmingham), F. Womack (Birmingham).

Second World War: W. Ardron (Rotherham United), L. Armeson (Coventry), H. Barton (Sheffield United), M. Burgin (WBA), S. Burton (West Ham), A. Calverley (Huddersfield), E. Collett (Arsenal), J. Curnow (Hull), H. Donaldson (Notts Co.), S. Fisher (Barnsley),

K. Gadsby (Leeds), C. Hanks (Bolton), J. Hawkswell (Chesterfield), G. Hinsley (Bradford City), T. Johnson (Sheffield United), G. Jones (Tranmere), G. Laking (Middlesbrough), H. Medhurst (West Ham), F. Melling (Corinthians), W. Reynolds (Rochdale), J. Smith (Sheffield United), F. White (Sheffield Utd), N. Wilkinson (Stoke), F. Wright (Crystal Palace), H. Wright (Wolves), J. Wynn (Rochdale).

Wednesday Managers

From the outset in 1876, Wednesday's team affairs were organised by secretary Arthur Joshua Dickinson – a former amateur – with assistance from committee members, the trainer, captain and senior players. The club appointed its first full-time manager in 1920 – Robert Brown – and since then there have been twenty-five managerial changes at the club, some men having two spells in charge.

Manager	From	To
Arthur Dickinson	August 1876	May 1920
Rob Brown	June 1920	September 1933
Joe McClelland	September 1933	December 1933
Billy Walker	December 1933	November 1937
Jimmy McMullan	January 1938	April 1942
Eric Taylor	April 1942	August 1958
Harry Catterick	August 1958	April 1961
Vic Buckingham	May 1961	April 1964
Allan Brown	August 1964	February 1968
Jack Marshall	February 1968	March 1969
Tom McAnearney*	March 1969	June 1969
Danny Williams	July 1969	January 1971
Derek Dooley	January 1971	December 1973
Jim McAnearney*	December 1973	January 1974
Steve Burtenshaw	January 1974	October 1975
Len Ashurst	October 1975	October 1977
Jack Charlton, OBE	October 1977	May 1983
Howard Wilkinson	June 1983	October 1988
Peter Eustace	October 1988	February 1989
Ron Atkinson	February 1989	June 1991
Trevor Francis	June 1991	May 1995
David Pleat	June 1995	November 1997
Ron Atkinson	November 1997	May 1998
Danny Wilson	July 1998	March 2000
Peter Shreeves*	March 2000	June 2000
Paul Jewell	June 2000	February 2001
Peter Shreeves	February 2001	October 2001
Terry Yorath	October 2001	October 2002
David Burrows*	October 2002	November 2002
Chris Turner	November 2002	September 2004
Paul Sturrock	September 2004	October 2006
Sean McAuley*	October 2006	November 2006
Brian Laws	November 2006	

* Caretaker-manager

NB: The McAnearney brothers, Dooley, Wilkinson, Eustace, Francis, Wilson, Burrows and Turner all played for the Owls (see individual write-ups).

Arthur Dickinson

Arthur Dickinson was also the club's financial secretary and the first shareholder (purchasing ticket no.1 for £5). He served on the FA Council, the international selection committee and was associated with the Sheffield & Hallamshire FA for forty years and the Owls for almost forty-four – celebrating two League Championship triumphs, Second Division glory, two FA Cup final wins, the Football Alliance title, plus many local cup victories. He died aged seventy-nine.

Rob Brown

In office for thirteen years, Rob Brown won the First Division twice and the Second Division once. He died in March 1935, aged sixty-two.

Joe McClelland

Joe McClelland was former secretary-manager of Halifax Town and Brown's assistant – he reverted back to that role under Walker. Also honorary secretary of the Midland Combination, he was awarded a long service medal by the West Riding FA.

Billy Walker

Billy Walker's 531 appearances for Aston Villa produced 244 goals, including a hat-trick of penalties against Bradford City in 1921. An FA Cup winner in 1920, he won 22 England caps and as manager led Wednesday and Nottingham Forest to FA Cup victories in 1935 and 1959 respectively. He died in 1964, aged sixty-six.

Jimmy McMullan

Jimmy McMullan, a Scottish international with 16 caps, made 242 appearances for Manchester City (1925-33), gained two FA Cup runners-up medals and helped Partick win the Scottish Cup. He was manager of Maidstone United, Oldham, Aston Villa and Notts County. He died in Sheffield in 1964, aged sixty-nine.

Eric Taylor

Eric Taylor oversaw the Owls' yo-yo act between the First and Second Divisions in the 1950s. He started as an office boy, was assistant-secretary, general manager (1958-73) and served Wednesday for forty-four years. Presented with the Football League's Long Service Medal, he died in 1974, aged sixty-two.

Harry Catterick

Harry Catterick elevated the Owls into the First Division in 1959. As Everton's manager he won two League titles and the FA Cup (versus Wednesday) in 1966. He played for Stockport, Everton and Manchester United (guest) and also managed Crewe, Rochdale and Preston. He died at Goodison Park in 1985, aged sixty-five.

Vic Buckingham

Vic Buckingham played for Spurs either side of the Second World War and also managed Bradford Park Avenue, West Bromwich Albion (1954 FA Cup winners), Ajax (Dutch League and Cup winners, 1961 and 1962), Fulham, Ethnikos, Barcelona (Spanish Cup winners 1971, signed Johan Cryuff) and Sevilla.He also coached in Norway, Oxford University and Pegasus. He died in 1996, aged seventy-nine.

Vic Buckingham (right)

Allan Brown

Allan Brown played for Huddersfield, Burnley and Notts County (1933-54), was manager at Turf Moor and Sunderland and coached in Norway and Plymouth Argyle. An FA Cup runner-up in 1947 (Burnley) and 1966 (Wednesday) he died in 1996, aged eighty-two.

Jack Marshall

Jack Marshall's playing career with Burnley was cut short through injury. He was coach with Bury, Stoke City, England and the Owls and boss of Rochdale and Blackburn (where he was also a physiotherapist). Assistant to Brown, he died in 1998.

Danny Williams

Between 1946 and 1960, Danny Williams made 461 League appearances for Rotherham, whom he later coached and managed, and managed both Swindon (two spells) and Mansfield.

Steve Burtenshaw

Steve Burtenshaw played for Brighton (1952-66) and was coach at Arsenal and QPR before

Wednesday. He was also caretaker-manager of Everton and Arsenal and boss of QPR.

Len Ashurst

Len Ashurst won England Youth and Under-23 honours and played for Sunderland (1957-71). Manager of Hartlepool and Gillingham before Wednesday, he was later in charge of Newport Co, Cardiff (two spells) and Sunderland, coached the Kuwait national team and was assistant at Blackpool. He won the Welsh Cup with Newport in 1980.

Jack Charlton

England World Cup winner Jack Charlton OBE scored 95 goals in 770 games for Leeds between 1953 and 1973. He gained 35 caps, played in 1 'B' international, represented the Football League 6 times and was Footballer of the Year in 1967. A Second Division and League Championship winner with Leeds in 1964 and 1969, he won the League Cup and Inter Cities Fairs Cup in 1968 and the FA Cup in 1972 and, as manager, guided Middlesbrough to the Second Division title in 1974. Later boss of Newcastle and the Republic of Ireland (the first non-Irishman to take that job), he led the Irish to the World Cup finals in 1990 and 1994 and also to the 1988 European Championships.

Ron Atkinson

The first of Ron Atkinson's two spells as Wednesday boss lasted twenty-seven months, during which time the Owls won the League Cup and gained promotion from the Second Division in 1991. Liverpool-born, he helped Oxford United gain a place in the Football League (1962) and win the Fourth Division in 1964. As a manager he led Cambridge United to the Third Division title (1977), Manchester United to two FA Cup final triumphs (1983 and 1986) and Aston Villa to League Cup glory (1994). He also managed West Bromwich Albion, Atletico Madrid, Coventry and Nottingham Forest and has acted as technical advisor at Swindon and Peterborough.

Ron Atkinson

David Pleat

David Pleat also managed Luton Town, Spurs (two spells) and Leicester, having played for Nottingham Forest, Luton, Shrewsbury, Exeter and Peterborough, retiring early through injury. He guided Luton to the Second Division title in 1972 and Spurs to the FA Cup final in 1987.

Peter Shreeves

Peter Shreeves was acting manager at Hillsborough before Paul Jewell. He played for Reading and Wimbledon (among others), was manager of Spurs in 1991/92 and was coach at Charlton, QPR, Spurs and Watford and assistant manager to the Welsh national team. He was manager at Barnet from 2002 to 2004.

Paul Jewell

As manager, Paul Jewell took both Bradford City (1999) and Wigan (2005) into the Premiership. A Liverpool reserve, he made 137 League appearances for Wigan, 269 for Bradford City and 5 for Grimsby.

David Pleat

Terry Yorath

Terry Yorath played with Charlton at Leeds between 1967 and 1973, making almost 200 appearances. A Welsh Schoolboy and Under-23 international, he won 59 caps and also played for Coventry, Spurs, Vancouver Whitecaps, Bradford City and Swansea, managing the latter two clubs. He also managed the Welsh national team.

Paul Sturrock

Paul Sturrock, capped 20 times by Scotland between 1981 and 1987, twice won the League Cup with Dundee United and was voted SFW Player of the Year in 1982. Appointed manager at Hillsborough a month into the 2004/05 season, he had previously lifted Plymouth out the Second Division but struggled with Premiership side Southampton. He also managed Dundee United and St Johnstone. He was sacked by Wednesday after a run of poor results. Later became manager of Swindon Town.

Sean McAuley

Caretaker-boss Sean McAuley, a Scotland Youth and Under-21 international defender, played for Manchester United (reserves), St Johnstone, Chesterfield, Hartlepools United, Scunthorpe United, Scarborough, Rochdale and Halifax Town between 1990 and 2005, making well over 275 senior appearances.

Brian Laws

Brian Laws was manager of Scunthorpe United for nine years before taking over at Hillsborough. He guided the Iron to promotion to Division One in 2005. As a player, Laws served as a right-back with Burnley, Huddersfield Town, Middlesbrough, Nottingham Forest, Grimsby Town, Darlington and Scuthorpe. He amassed well over 600 senior appearances – 209 with Forest, with whom he twice won the League Cup (1989 and 1990). He also won the Third Division title with Burnley (1982) and gained one England 'B' cap. He was born in Wallsend on Tyne on 14 October 1961.

Assistant managers, coaches, trainers and physiotherapists

Some of the men who have been assistant-manager, coach, trainer, scout and physio at the club: Bill Asprey (ex-Stoke City); Clive Baker (ex-Norwich, Barnsley & Ipswich goalkeeper); Richie Barker (ex-Derby County, Notts County and Peterborough); Frank Barlow (ex-Sheffield Utd and Chesterfield); Danny Begara (ex-manager of Stockport); Frank Blunstone (ex-Chelsea and England); Neville Briggs (chief scout); Bill Bromley; Gordon Clark (ex-Manchester City player and WBA manager); Teddy Craig; Malcolm Crosby (ex-Aldershot, Wrexham and York player, Sunderland manager); Joe Davis (ex-Burton Utd and Coventry); John Dickens; Willie Donachie (ex-Manchester City, Oldham and Scotland); Tom Eggleston (ex-Derby County, Leicester and Watford); Dave Ewing (ex-Manchester City); Percy Frith; David Galley; John Harris (ex-Chelsea, Sheffield Utd and Chester manager);

George Irwin (ex-WBA and Crystal Palace); Ernie Jackson (ex-Grimsby Town); Rob Johnson; Bill Muscroft; Jim O'Neill (ex-Gillingham, Notts Co. and Mansfield); Jack Paramore; Albert Phelan (youth team); Maurice Setters (ex-Exeter City, WBA, Manchester United, Stoke, Coventry, Charlton and England Under-23 international; 1963 FA Cup winner and assistant to Jack Charlton with the Republic of Ireland; also Doncaster manager); Alan Smith (ex-York City); Bobby Smith; David Smith (ex-Burnley, Brighton and Bristol City, also manager of Mansfield, Southend, Plymouth, Dundee and Torquay); Kevin Summerfield (ex-WBA, Walsall, Shrewsbury and Birmingham, Paul Sturrock's assistant at Plymouth, Southampton and Hillsborough); and Tony Toms.

BIBLIOGRAPHY

Books and reference works

Dickinson, J. and J. Brodie, *The Wednesday Boys* (Pickard Communication)
Farnsworth, Keith, *Sheffield Wednesday: A Complete Record 1867-1987* (Breedon)
Goldsworthy, M., *We Are The Champions* (Pelham Books)
Horsnell, B. and Lamming, D., *Forgotten Caps* (Yore Publications)
Hugman, B.J. (ed.), *PFA Footballers' Factfile 1996-2001* (Queen Anne Press)
Hugman, B.J. (ed.), *PFA Footballers' Factfile 2002-06* (Queen Anne Press)
Hugman, B.J. (ed.), *PFA Footballers' Factfile* (AFS)
Hugman, B.J. (ed.), *PFA Premier & Football League Players' Records 1946-1998* (Queen Anne Press)
Joyce, M., *Football League players' Records: 1888-1939* (Tony Brown/Soccer Data)
    Lamming, D., *Who's Who of Scottish Internationalists: 1872-1982* (AFS)
Spiller, R. (ed.), *AFS Football Who's Who: 1902-03, 1903-04, 1907-08, 1909-10* (AFS)

Other Publications

Sheffield Wednesday official programmes: 1919-2005
Sheffield Wednesday handbooks, reviews, magazines, supporters guides, 1954-2005
Rothmans Yearbook, vols 1-36, (1970-2005).

I have also referred to several newspapers, various club histories and Who's Who guides, autobiographies and biographies of players and managers, general football books and magazines and hundreds of club programmes.